All I
to Know About
Filmmaking I
Learned from

the Toxic Avenger

For information on booking Lloyd Kaufman to speak at your College , Festival or Convention please contact
Troma Attn: Booking Lloyd Kaufman 36-40 11th Street Long Island City, NY 11106
or email lloyd@troma.com.

For details on bulk purchases, educational use, promotions , and book excerpts please contact Troma c/o Promotions 36-40 11th Street Long Island city, NY 11106
or email PR@troma.com or call 718-391-0110

All I Need
to Know About
Filmmaking I
Learned from
the Toxic Avenger

Lloyd Kaufman and James Gunn
Introduction by Roger Corman

Troma Entertainment, Inc.
Published by Troma Entertainment, Inc.
36-40 11th Street
Long Island City, NY 11106

Copyright 1998 by Troma Entertainment, Inc.

ISBN: 1456399365

Visit our website at www.troma.com
PRINTED IN THE UNITED STATES OF AMERICA

9781456399368

STEP #1

If you want to make your own independent movies like
we do here at Troma Studios,
first you must marry a person named Pat.
Then follow the 653,000 steps detailed in the following pages.

—L.K.

To Michael Herz—genius, gentleman, and most sensitive lifetime partner

contents

x Contents

acknowledgments

Special Acknowledgments:

Jerome Rudes, whose idea it was to write this shit
Fifi Oscard, who represented this shit
Elizabeth Beier, who had the courage to green-light this shit
Barry Neville, who made this shit shine
Richard Sillett, who cleaned up all this shit

Extra Special Acknowledgments:

James Gunn, who gave me a lot of shit
Fiona Apple

People who helped with this book:

Fifi Oscard
R. L. Kaufman, aka Moo
Sigrun Kaufman
Charles Kaufman
Susan Kaufman
Roger Kirby
Jennifer Kennedy
John G. Avildsen
Jeff Sass
Phil Rivo
Richard Lewin
Milton Gould
Julie Stepanek
Patrick Cassidy
Maris Herz

Roger Corman
Jane Jensen
Stan Lee
Sam and Christa Fuller
Gabe Friedman
Jane Kober
Ken Moltner
Vivian Polak
Eric Sherman
Rick Gianasi
Jesus Perez
Derek Solomon
Alan Quasha
Jon Foster

Introduction
by Roger Corman

Over the course of his career, Lloyd Kaufman has cited me as an early influence. He claims that my films convinced him of the possibility of creating compelling, well-acted stories about provocative subjects on modest budgets. I suppose I should be honored. However, having spent countless hours in Lloyd's company over the years and having been exposed to his oeuvre, I am not sure I should be held culpable for any part of the Dali-esque mutation of modern cinema that Lloyd has birthed.

Although I may be blameless in the siring of the Troma brand of movies, I must say that I admire the way that Lloyd and Troma have become something of idols themselves for many of today's major young film directors and certainly for those of tomorrow. His satirical, iconoclastic directing style reminds me of Duchamp's painting of the Mona Lisa with a mustache. It is at this point—where the anarchic meets the ridiculous—that Lloyd has taken up permanent residence and people have taken notice across the globe.

I got my first real inkling of Lloyd's unique grasp on the world's imagination when we were both honored at the Tokyo International Film Festival in 1986. During the trip, he was swarmed constantly by mobs of teenage Japanese *Toxic Avenger* fans. During this trip, I first began to appreciate the scope of his vision. The Troma Team, as he and longtime partner Michael Herz refer to themselves, takes the tra-

Kaufman is seen here being dwarfed by two friends and mentors, Roger Corman (l.) and Samuel Z. Arkoff (r.). Kaufman has often referred to these two men as the Mozart and Beethoven of independent cinema, while boastfully claiming the mantel of Zamfir the Pan Pipe Player of independent cinema as his own.

ditional genres of horror and science fiction and adds their own irrepressible, sometimes inexplicable, sense of humor to create a bouillabaisse of unforgettable yet likable characters and films—indeed, a sort of cosmos. A Troma Universe . . . subversive yet demented, extreme yet idealistic, violent yet romantic. A universe embraced by psychotic aberrants and the Cinematheque Français at the same time.

Over the years, this Troma worldview has won them a rabid worldwide following and has attracted many talented people looking for a break. Troma's willingness to take risks and its scorn for mere imitation makes its twenty-five-years-and-counting history all the more improbable and amazing. At the core of the company is the friendship and mutual respect of Lloyd and Michael Herz, two of the smartest and fairest men in this business. In a world often characterized by instability and infighting, these two have forged a bond that has lasted many movies and business cycles. As this book proves, their story and the story of the company itself is at least as compelling as anything in the *Class of Nuke 'Em High* series.

More than a history, this book is valuable as a primer for young filmmakers on both the spiritual and practical sides of independent filmmaking. This book provides a "how-to" for a young filmmaker who wants to make his/her/its first film outside of Hollywood. Even as the book takes you through the steps from pre- to post-production, one will begin to appreciate the true impetus behind Troma's success. Lloyd is one of the great true believers in independent cinema. His fervor has drawn acolytes to the shrine of independence like rabid moths to a toxic flame. It is the do-it-yourself, anything-for-the-shot, shoot-on-a-shoestring spirit that makes the impossible entirely possible and has kept Troma alive and thriving for this past quarter century.

It is this spirit, and the resultant entertainment, that ensures Troma's continued life—not only as a studio, but as a byword for intelligent, hard-edged movies that have staked out a place happily outside the mainstream. By buying this book, I know you have acknowledged as much and perhaps have similar ideals. If so, you have bought the right book. I know you will join me in thanking Lloyd for setting down as much of himself—the revolutionary humor, technical expertise, and plain old moral purpose—as a book can capture. As much as I cherish Troma's and Lloyd's past achievements, I look forward to their future and to seeing how much farther they can go with a few dollars, some toxic goo, and a dream.

Greetings from Tromaville: Land of Green Fluids

one

We're ready, Lloyd," said Moira.

I couldn't speak with my mouth full of Bromo Seltzer and green food dye. So I squealed and pointed and stomped one foot instead.

"He wants a napkin," said Troma employee Mike Shapiro. Mike was well-versed in the language of Kaufmanology.

Moira took a rag from the camera crew, and wiped away a green rivulet twisting down my chin. I smiled in thanks.

Moira was a CNN reporter. She and her crew were doing a piece on the upcoming twenty-fifth anniversary of Troma Studios, the world's oldest independent film studio. The crew, Shapiro, and I had trudged up to the musty third floor of the Troma Building to get away from the neurotic pace of the Troma marketing team downstairs. CNN wanted to film me doing "The Toxic Meltdown." Now that the rivulet was gone, and my mouth was about to burst from the pressure, I was ready. I gave Moira thumbs up. The DP* aimed his BetaCam.

"Action!" Moira shouted. "Vomit!"

I widened my eyes. I bobbed my head back and forth like a dime-store figurine with a spring for a neck. I opened my mouth: the bright

---

*Director of photography.

green foam gushed forth. It dripped down my face, a bubbling, frothing, seemingly endless mass, drenching my shirt and bow tie.

In case YOU want to try it at home, *here's how*:

1 Mix 1 Dixie cup full of water with 1/2 tablespoon of green food dye. The water should be dark green. If it's not, dump in more dye. This isn't an exact science.

2 Depending upon the size of the effect you're after, place 1 to 3 tablespoons of Bromo Seltzer *inside your mouth* (CAUTION: Do not swallow*).

3 Drink the green food dye and water combination from the Dixie cup. Again, do not swallow. Just let it set there in your mouth.

4 Let the Bromo Seltzer and liquid foam inside your mouth. Wait until it is a huge, healthy froth before you open your mouth and release its emerald beauty into the post-orificial world.

5 Bask in the glory.

The CNN crew squealed with laughter. They applauded. I lifted my chin high, proudly, majestically, regally.† The last of the green crap spilled from my mouth. I threw my arms triumphantly into the air.

Then I saw my partner Michael Herz walking in with three men in Armani suits. They were the film investors Michael had been preparing for all week. The investors were neither laughing nor applauding. Instead, they stared numbly at me, seemingly wondering how a retarded man had become the president of a movie studio.

Well, that's a long story.

If you want to hear it, you've come to the right place.

---

*Unless you have a hangover.

†You might find me repeating myself a lot like this. By contract, this book has to be 75,000 words. I think I can knock off a large chunk of that just by really making use of my modifiers.

A SHORT BREAK TO EXPLAIN TROMA

To understand Troma, you must first know a bit about Taoism:

Taoism is a Chinese philosophy and system of religion based on the classic tome *Tao-te-ching*. Most believe it was founded on the teachings of Lao-Tzu of the 6th century B.C.E., although it was most likely written in the 3rd century B.C.E. Taoism prescribes an ideal human condition of simplicity and freedom from desire achieved from following the Tao. The Tao is the spontaneous, creative, effortless path dictated by natural events in the universe. That is, if three Aryan skinheads are holding you down and cornholing you with a leg of lamb, you say, well, I can't do anything about it so I might as well lie here and enjoy myself. In Tromaville, the Tao helps creativity; you never shut yourself off to ideas no matter how ludicrous they seem, and you keep this creative flow going during production. Taoism spouts sayings like, "The great organization is not organized," which is a boost to the Troma Team's morale for obvious reasons. Taoism employs the symbol of the dual principles of life, the yin (the passive, female cosmic principle) and the yang (the active masculine principle). The two forces are intertwined and interdependent. Since no force is completely masculine or feminine, each has a spot of the other. The yin and the yang also symbolize two one-eyed tadpoles playing. For those of you reading aloud on the subway, "Taoism" is pronounced "dou'iz'em," NOT "tā'ô iz em." We don't want the crackhead next to you thinking you're illiterate.

Troma Entertainment is my progeny.* For almost 25 years, Troma has made and distributed low-budget films of, shall we say, an unusual nature—films that our well-known slogan proudly proclaims as "MOVIES OF THE FUTURE." These films deal with what the media calls sex and violence, but which I call "A typical day in my brain." Troma first rose to prominence (I'll concur that this word is of a suspicious nature when regarding Troma) in the late seventies with raunchy comedies like *Squeeze Play* and *The First Turn-On*. In the eighties, we made our mark with gory-sexy-horror-comedies like *The Toxic Avenger* films, *Surf Nazis Must Die*, and *Class of Nuke 'Em High*. We have recently reentered the limelight with *Tromeo & Juliet* and *Sgt. Kabukiman NYPD*. We have been honored in tributes by the Cinematheque Français, the American Film Institute, and the British Film Institute. Quentin Tarantino, Sam Raimi, Peter Jackson, and others have cited Troma

---

*Being that human beings are not autogenous, I had a partner in this procreation: Michael Herz.

as an inspiration. As I mentioned earlier, we are perhaps the world's oldest independent film studio.

This is all a fluke.

What you're holding is supposed to be a How to Succeed in Low Budget Films book. That's what Penguin Putnam, the publishers, have hired me to write. Unfortunately, in addition to that sounding a tad bland, I don't think I'm the correct choice of author for that particular topic. So if you want to discover how to prosper in the film industry while creating films that lie outside the norm, RETURN THIS BOOK NOW. Get your money back before it's too late. This book may be able to help you make movies a bit more cheaply, but it's not going to help anyone make money off their movies. Why? Because Troma *does everything exactly the opposite of how it should be done.* The paradox of the yin and the yang applies to us: We fly where there is no sky, float where there is no water, walk a perfect chalk line when we are drunk off our asses. Especially that last one.

So, my friend, I can't teach you much of anything. Troma movies do exactly what low-budget films *shouldn't* do. Our films defy genre. There are few Troma "romance" films, or "action" films, or "comedies." Instead Troma movies mix all these things together, use bits here, pieces there, a Jackson-Pollockian canvas of everything that has come before them. We are the Cuisinart of cinema. And that is a definite no-no. Video stores, in particular, are hesitant to place films on their shelves that don't fit under the restrictive headings that hang above the aisles.*

Also, we don't follow conventional wisdom when it comes to "plot." A few years ago a pamphlet was going around Hollywood on exactly how, point-by-point, to construct a plot; it was fascinating, based upon Joseph Campbell's archetypes of myth. But how in the hell could I ever construct something like that when I'm more worried about the weather changing from one shot to the next?† Or a priest throwing us off location when we've only finished shooting half the drug scene footage we need on the altar of his church? When making a Troma

---

*That's why God created "Troma Sections" in many video stores.
†See chapter 11 for the horrifying facts.

movie, we often film not what *we want* but what *we can get*. Not to mention the fact that I have an extremely short attention span. I have an easy time concentrating on the "effect." It's the "cause" I have difficulty with. When watching a Troma movie, you must not only suspend your disbelief: you must lock it up in a small iron crate and torture it.

Another thing every young filmmaker should focus on is getting the proper training. I, however, never attended film school. I am not what most people would call "a Master of the Form"—I never even sat in the bleachers at the Academy Awards, and I'm still not sure what someone means when they say you're "crossing the line."* Young filmmakers should also make good movies. Now, although I feel as if I've been lucky on a few occasions, many of the movies in the Troma library are, to use a technical term, goat shit.

So it isn't because of talent or style that Troma has survived.

Now, I have read in newspaper articles and seen on TV that Troma has been successful because of our business savvy. Like explaining away the numerous reportings throughout history of frogs raining from the sky as "mass hysteria," this strikes me as giving an easy answer to an unexplained phenomenon. In business, we also do none of the things that a movie studio is supposed to do. Unlike other low-budget film studios, we seldom presell our movies, so they don't make a profit before they're released.† Troma doesn't do this because: A) We're unorganized, B) It's not easy selling Troma movies, which results from C) We don't quickly make a movie out of a current trend that's popular in the media so that we can cash in. We also don't piggyback on larger films, as the great Roger Corman did in releasing *Carnosaur* on the heels of *Jurassic Park* or *Lords of the Deep* after *The Abyss*. I wish we

---

*EDITOR'S NOTE: Lloyd: Crossing the line, in filmmaking, is when someone cuts together a shot of a subject, and then cuts to a second shot of the subject 180 degrees opposite—that is, directly on the other side. It is said to disorient the audience's sense of place, but has been used successfully by certain great directors (of which you are one, I assure you) to catch the viewers off guard.

†Many low-budget companies sell films before they've begun shooting. Often they will have nothing more than a title and a poster, not even a script, and they will have already netted a profit.

were smart enough to do this. We aren't. Plus, our research and marketing department is one guy stuffing press releases in envelopes and licking them shut.

Finally, we definitely have the wrong attitude. At least by Hollywood standards. Our attitude is that we love and care about our films. "That's madness!" you must be saying. "Anyone who knows anything knows that the way to make a successful picture is to take a cold and cynical approach! Every moment should be geared toward bringing in additional dollars, and not spent on any sort of personal regard for your work!" I concur a hundred percent. That is how a movie *should* be made. But we screw it up because we do what we do with heart. Our films may be goat shit. But they're goat shit for which we have lots of affection.

If there's any reason at all we exist, it's because the world needed to have one Troma, and we just happened to be there.

So there is absolutely no way that this book is going to help you make money in the movie industry . . . *Unless* . . . Wait a second!

If you follow everything that this book tells you, and then *do exactly the opposite*, you will, without any doubt in my mind, make truckloads of cash! There's no way it can fail! Heck, I guarantee it. And, if it fails, Penguin Putnam will pay you a million dollars.*

BACK TO THE DRIPPING GREEN CHIN
(A TYPICAL DAY IN TROMAVILLE) . . .

"Nice to meet you," I said, as I shook an investor's hand. The green foam dripped down my neck, clumping around my chest hairs, rolling down my stomach, into my pants . . . I'll stop there. I don't want this to get too hot. Not yet. Not until we get to the chapter on my passionate, kinky love affair with Mariah Carey.†

"Nice . . . to meet . . . you . . . too," the investor said, his hand a dead salmon in my palm. Michael Herz glared at me as if I'd just dropped twelve grams of cocaine in the toilet. He ushered the investors away.

---

*EDITOR'S NOTE: This is a lie.
†EDITOR'S NOTE: This is another lie. Cut it out.

Jennifer, our receptionist, ran into the room. She grabbed my arm. She whispered in my ear:

"David wants to ask you some questions."

"Who's David?" I asked, somewhat timidly. I was afraid he was someone whose name I should have known. Perhaps the new guy with the cracked glasses downstairs. I have a difficulty with names. I often call new employees by names other than their own for weeks. (And I'm not including "asshole" or "dimwit"—I mean "Frank" or "Klement" instead of "Hector." I called my wife "Bridget" the first five years of our marriage until she reminded me that she was "Pat." I have three beautiful daughters, and, if you hold on for a minute while I check my pocket organizer, I'll tell you their names.)

"David's the guy with the Japanese television crew," Jennifer informed me. "He wants to interview you."

There had been a second television crew, composed completely of Asians, running around the Troma Building. I had wondered what they had been doing there. No one tells me anything: we're in the communications industry but we seldom make a point of doing it.

Konnichiwa," I said into the TV camera, trying to remember my Japanese, which is difficult, since I really only know the few phrases I picked up while filming *The Toxic Avenger II* in Japan. I still had the green shit all over my chin. You need cold cream to clean it off. There hadn't been enough time.

"Welcome to 'Mondo TV,' Lloyd," David said. He thrust the microphone further into my face. I backed into the desk behind me, where the Director of Acquisitions watched a possible pick-up* featuring a naked girl rubbing a tortoise over her breasts. Over David's shoulder, I saw Moira and the CNN crew interviewing an intern whose first day was today and who smelled like pot.

"Um, *konnichiwa,*" I muttered again.

"Lloyd, tell me, where do you get your strange ideas for your wacky Troma movies?"

---

*Though our most popular films were produced in-house, most of the films in the Troma library are pick-ups. A pick-up is a film that was produced outside of Troma. We buy the rights to distribute it. We "pick it up." Clever, huh?

Troma cofounder Michael Herz rehearses his show-stopping "Thumbie the Puppet" routine to the delight of all his friends.

I thought, then replied: "Ummm . . . *shiri* . . . *kara* . . . Troma . . . *ito de.*"

The Asian crew laughed. David called "Cut."

"What?" I said.

"You just said you pull Troma by a string out of your ass," David told me.

"Oh. Can we do that again?"

"LLOYD!!" Tony Rosen was standing on the other side of the room, beyond a precariously stacked pile of ¾-inch dubbing machines. He waved his arms over his head. Tony was twenty-three years old, an excitable Yale grad who had started out as an intern a year before and was now the head of Troma Team Video. If it was as easy to work your way up at Chrysler as it is at Troma, you could go from the assembly line to CEO in two years.

"Lloyd!" Tony screamed again. "The box art for *Cannibal: The Musical* has got to be OUT to the printer's in FIFTEEN MINUTES or else we won't be able to make the street release DATE!"

"I guess that pulling ideas out of my ass line will have to stay," I told David.

Tony and I trampled down the steps to the first floor.

HERZ AND KAUFMAN, BUTT BUDDIES

Michael Herz and Lloyd Kaufman are the Odd Couple of low-budget films. Herz is quietly charming, neat, and composed. He seems to have no desire to bring attention to himself. Kaufman's the opposite: decked out in bright green pants, Day-Glo orange socks, and a red bow tie, he swivels nervously in his chair as he speaks, constantly taking calls in mid-conversation.

These two men would seemingly not be able to suffer the tics of the other for 25 minutes. However, they have been friends and business partners for 25 years. To add to the Tromaville family feeling, Michael's wife, Maris, has been an integral part of Troma since its inception; Lloyd's wife, Pat, also worked for Troma until she became the New York State Film Commissioner in 1995.

"Michael and I have never even signed a contract between us," says Kaufman. "We've never needed to co-sign checks. Any minute one of us wanted, we could abscond with the entire Troma savings account and never return. Our entire relationship, business and personal, is based on trust."

Kaufman and Herz are also the longest running co-directing team around, having directed eight films together: *Waitress!*, *Stuck on You*, *The First Turn-On*, *The Toxic Avenger I, II*, and *III*, *Troma's War*, and *Sgt. Kabukiman NYPD*. In addition, they've coproduced *Squeeze Play*, *Tromeo & Juliet*, *Class of Nuke 'Em High I, II*, and *III*, and more, and executive produced other features by young filmmakers around the world. They are known throughout the industry for their grassroots marketing success, their thrift, and their run-down building in Manhattan's Hell's Kitchen, which acts as a sort of boot camp for young people who want to try their hands at filmmaking.

On a movie set, Kaufman, an experienced cinematographer, focuses primarily on the setting up of shots; Herz deals with the direction of the actors. In the business place, Herz focuses more on the brass tacks, whereas Kaufman deals with the creative and marketing facets of the company. Still, their positions overlap greatly in every endeavor. Because their long-lasting relationship is unheard of in an industry where executives normally move from company to company every six months, there can be little doubt but that Herz and Kaufman are secret ass pirates.

The first floor is the museum and nerve center of the Troma Building. Lining the walls are the crumbling latex masks and miniatures from our films: among them, the insect from *Bugged*, three of its six legs sprawling smashed-up by its side; Brett Piper's beautiful foot-high miniatures from *Class of Nuke 'Em High Part II*; and Pericles Lewnes' giant larva from *Sgt. Kabukiman NYPD*. Beneath these archaeological wonders is the cluster of desks that forms the Troma Team nerve center: the writer, marketing director, art director, and interns. Tony and I wove our way through all this. As I am not athletically inclined, I almost tripped over a carton of *Tromeo & Juliet* promotional air fresheners (coconut scented—the whole building smelled like tropical fruit for weeks). Eventually, we arrived at Gadi's desk.

Gadi was the art director. His name was pronounced "God-ee" but I pronounced it "Gad-ee," being that he was new and I have this problem with pronouncing names. He designed the Troma movie posters, video boxes, catalogs, and warnings on the bathroom walls not to throw paper towels in the toilet. He designed these things on a computer. I wish I could tell you what type of computer it is, but I know nothing about them. But it's big, and it cost more to buy than *Invasion of the Space Preachers* did to make.

The computer screen displayed the video box art for *Cannibal: The Musical*. I didn't like what I saw.

"I can't read the words '*The Musical*,' " I said. "I can read '*Cannibal*,' but I can't read 'The Musical.' The farnt is messy."

"The what?" said Gadi.

"The farnt. The type."

"The font."

"Right. Make it clearer."

"We're trying to hide that it's a musical," Tony said.

"Hide it?"

"In video, horror titles sell best, Lloyd. So here's what we're gonna do. We're gonna make the box art look like a horror movie. Then you know what's gonna happen?"

"What?"

"The retailers will buy it."

"A unique concept for a Troma movie."

"We're moving in a new direction."

"But it doesn't make any sense."

"It does make sense, Lloyd. It does. Trust me on this one."

"Just the fact that the word 'Musical' is in the title, doesn't that show that, in addition to being a horror film, it's also a comedy and a musical?"

"That's why we're trying to hide it! Increase the blurriness factor."

Let's talk about ethics for a moment: If we were selling the Troma movie *Croaked: Frog Monster from Hell*, I would promote it as a heavy melodrama if that would ship more units. Why? Because *Croaked: Frog Monster from Hell* is one of the films in the "goat shit" genre I mentioned earlier. It is, in fact, one of the worst films in the Troma library of 150 films and that, my friends, is very bad.* It doesn't matter what

---

*See chapter 12, "The Five Worst Troma Movies."

you sell *Croaked* as, people are going to take it home and either A) have a good laugh at the wretchedness of the whole thing, or B) be horribly disappointed, in which case they probably had no business bringing home a movie called *Croaked: Frog Monster from Hell* in the first place. But *Cannibal: The Musical* is one of the best movies in the Troma library. It's extremely funny, and the tunes are catchy and impossible to get out of your head.* Therefore, it seems to me that people who want a horror movie are going to be disappointed when they bring it home and people who want an unusual musical-comedy are going to miss out. Tony's point was well taken: Perhaps we'd make more money up front if we sold the film as horror. More people want a horror film than want a weird musical-comedy. But, still, I got into this business first and foremost to entertain people and make movies. If you have something good, you want to get it to the right people.

I was about to relate this to Tony when the new kid with the glasses whose name I couldn't remember yelled from across the room:

"Lloyd, line three! Barry Neville!"

"Ooo! I have to get that," I said.

"Lloyd, we HAVE to get the box art OUT," Tony said, panic in his eyes.

"Barry's the editor for Penguin Putnam. He's doing my book."

"*You're* writing a book?" Tony asked. The three Tromites within hearing distance momentarily stopped and stared at me, dumbfounded.

"Well, yeah, er . . ."

"What about . . . grammar?" one of the office assistants said.

"Um . . ."

"Lloyd, as one who has been conferred a bachelor's degree in English, let me give you a little literary advice," Patrick Cassidy, the writer, exclaimed. "First: there are other forms of punctuation besides exclamation points. There's a little dot—it's called a *period.* Two dots on top of one another is called a *colon.*" The Tromites around Patrick were cracking up. "Second: there are adjectives that

---

***Cannibal: The Musical*—featuring eight great songs!—is now available at video stores (not quite) everywhere.

don't begin with the prefix 'Tro'—words besides 'Tromatic,' 'Tromen-dous,' and 'Tromalicious.' Words like, say, 'pretty,' or 'funny'—"

They were laughing hysterically. I started to back away.

"LLOYD, DON'T GO!" Tony said.

"Uh . . ."

I darted before Tony could grab me. I hurtled over a box of *Def by Temptation* videos, and into the bathroom. I had to go to the bathroom before I got on the phone with Barry, otherwise I'd be preoccupied and would make piss jokes the whole time, and I didn't want Penguin Putnam to get the wrong idea about my sense of humor. I mean, the book was going to be a classy affair, sort of like Dominick Dunne. While I urinated, I thought of the great action movie *Bullitt* with Steve McQueen, where the hero is taking a piss in the last scene. After a huge glorious action sequence, McQueen is just another human re-strained by his bodily functions, taking a piss. Maybe someday I'll make a film where the action hero is farting in somebody's face in the last scene. I ran out of the bathroom, slid across the floor beneath Tony's clutch, and into my office.

My office, I am certain, is different from those at major studios. First of all, it is dusty. There are parts of the Troma Building that have never, not once, in twenty years, been cleaned. For the first seven or eight years in the Troma Building we said we'd get around to doing some handiwork, but somehow that never occurred. Eventually, it be-came a point of honor not to clean it.

The second unusual aspect of my office is that I share the space with Troma cofounder Michael Herz. His desk is directly across from mine. We must face each other for eight or nine hours a day. This is a much better deal for me than for Michael, since he is much better-looking than I am. On Michael's desk everything is perfectly in place. My desk is covered with stacks of papers and old food and promo videos and other items. Just this year—and this is no lie—I found a letter from former Troma employee Jeff Sass written to me more than eight years ago at the bottom of a pile. He was surprised to hear back from me. But I always answer my letters, even if it's in the subsequent de-cade.

Now Michael had his head tilted back. He was asleep. All that smil-ing around the investors must have worn him out. This was a good thing. I needed some privacy while talking to Barry about creative matters.

"Barry! Hello! How do you do? Greetings! How are you?"

"Uh, great. How are you, Lloyd?"

"Fantastic! Terrific! Excellent! Great! Absolutely great!"

"Why all the synonyms?"

"No reason." I didn't tell him I knew I would possibly use this conversation in the book, and this would chip away at that 75 thou real fast.

"Lloyd, I've been thinking about how you should approach the first chapter."

"I've been thinking too," I said. "But not about the book. Mostly about Alicia Silverstone giving me a hot mustard rubdown."

Barry laughed politely. He coughed.

"Yes, well. Lloyd, you know, a good way to start the book might be to have you receiving some sort of award and, as you stood there on stage, holding the award, the audience's wild applause is overcoming you, and you think back over the twenty-five years of Troma Studios: what you had to do to get there. And that's when we start in on the details of how to make low-budget films."

"Mm."

"Pretty good, huh?"

"Oh yeah," I said. "Yeah."

"You don't like it."

"No! I think it's one of the ten best ideas I've ever heard!"

"Fantastic! Let's do it!"

"But there's, I think, a couple problems."

"What's that?"

"That's how the movie *All About Eve* began. Anne Baxter was at that award ceremony receiving that award thing. And you saw what happened to her!"

"I didn't catch that one."

"Eve clawed her way to the top and at the end of the film she gets clawed by another just like her. I don't want to get clawed, Barry."

"No. I understand that."

"Of course you do."

"But this is a totally different work, Lloyd."

"But I'm very superstitious. And another thing."

"Yes?"

Recalling something, I reined in my enthusiasm.

"Barry, could you hold on for a second?"

"Sure."

I put Barry on hold. I buzzed the intercom up to Jonathan Taub, the business affairs guy. I didn't want to start tossing my innermost being out in front of Barry for his approval or disapproval before I was sure I was getting paid.

"Jonathan!"

"Hey, oh dark master of the cinematic realm," Jonathan said. The radio spouted loud rock music in the background. The French interns giggled.

"Get serious," I said. "It's not playtime. Has Penguin Putnam sent in the signed K?!"*

"Um, yeah, this is it right here. I set my coffee on it. Does that matter?"

"All right, good." I picked up Barry's line again. "Sorry, Barry."

"No problem."

"Now here's another thing: What kind of crowd would I be speaking in front of? I've never won an Academy Award, or a Golden Globe, or a Tony. I've never even gotten a People's Choice Award. Almost everyone I know has one of those. But not me. Not one. Now, we could put me in a place where I would actually have a likelihood of being—like signing autographs at a comic book convention with thirteen pimply, 800-pound teenage boys waiting in line . . . but, you'd have to admit, Barry, that would be sort of pathetic."

"The Cinematheque Français honored you a couple years back, didn't they?"

"Yes, but, well, that would be in French. None of the Americans would understand it."

"Then we can trans—"

"After the first French word they'd be in the 'Returns' line at Barnes and Noble quicker than you could have Maurice Chevalier sing a love song to a Nazi."

"You're losing me."

"See, I was sort of thinking about something else."

---

*K = contract

"I'm open."

"One possibility would be to begin with a chapter that takes place in the Troma Building, on a typical day, or maybe a day a little more typical than usual. Everything will be going crazy. On the third floor, there will be a crew from a big TV station filming, and on another floor there will be another crew also filming. And then we can go through some of the other things I have to do: making business deals, choosing poster art, and so on. I'll keep getting interrupted and dragged from one member of the Troma Team to the next. I'll put in some of the funny little things we say to each other. It'll be great. What do you think?"

Long pause.

"I'll have to get back to you on that one, Lloyd."

"Oh. Okay. Well. You know, whatever you want."

"We'll think of something."

"Yeah, sure."

I hung up. The new guy with the cracked glasses set two enormous suitcases down in front of me. They were covered with Kabukiman stickers, "I Love Toxie" stickers, and Troma logo stickers. Among them was an "I Love Satan" sticker.

"Who put that Satan sticker there?" I asked.

The guy with the glasses started laughing. I heard the Troma Team snickering outside my door.

"Shoot," the guy with the glasses said. "We hoped you wouldn't notice."

"I like it. What are these bags, anyway?"

"I got them ready. For your trip to L.A."

"Oh. Thanks, Cliff." I thought for a moment. "I'm going to L.A.?"

"My name's Roger. Your plane leaves at two."

"I know your name. Montgomery Clift was my neighbor when I was a kid. You remind me of him. That's why I accidentally called you that. My plane leaves at two *tomorrow*, Roger."

"No. Gabe fucked up when he was ordering your tickets."

"WHAT!?"

"No one told you?"

"NO ONE TELLS ME ANYTHING! THIS IS WHY WE SUCK! THIS IS WHY I'M GOING TO BLOW MY FUCKING BRAINS OUT!"

[*The next few moments are deleted. They involve cursing loudly and tossing airplane tickets at the wall and generally venting spleen. It was childish, and I'm eliminating it as I'd rather you continue to hold your positive image of me.*]

"I just—all I want to know is if I have everything packed that you want packed," the new guy said. Sweating. Deer-in-the-headlights gaze.

I calmed down. It was important that I get to Los Angeles: I was up for reelection on the AFMA* board and I had a meeting with Matthew Duda from Showtime. I'm not a big fan of Hollywood or L.A. But I do sometimes look forward to going, for no other reason than I know that Dave Schultz, the head of our incredibly tiny L.A. office, will have a warm and cuddly bottle of vodka waiting for me. I don't look forward to the *trip*, however, as carrying the huge suitcases often detaches my humerus† bones from my shoulder sockets. But we're too cheap and too disorganized to send them ahead (the suitcases, not my humerus bones.)

"What's in the bag?" I asked.

"Twenty Kabukiman for President buttons. A Troma Video Ten pack. Fifty *Tromeo & Juliet* slicks. Four Toxie videos. The new press release."

"Okay. Thanks, William."

"Roger."

"I know your name. See, I had a friend named William at Yale. You remind me of him. He was an intelligent, good-looking young man."

The speed of Tromaville always increases threefold when I'm on my way out the door carrying two suitcases packed with Troma crap. If you can, try reading all of the following sentences *at one time*—that will give you an idea of how I felt:

Michael Herz is flapping a p.o. (purchase order) for advertising in front of me. He's saying I allowed us to go $12,000 over-budget on the *Tromeo & Juliet* theatrical release in Los Angeles. I tell him

---

*The American Film Marketing Association, a group of independent filmmakers, producers, and studios. For the past few years, I've been elected to the board.
†Unlike my sense of humor, which was detached a long time ago (see—just like Dominick Dunne).

400 bucks just wasn't enough. • Patrick is shoving some papers into my back, telling me that I have to sign off on some new text for the Tromaville World Wide Web site. • Tony is running in circles around me like a hyena drooling for my dead flesh. "Lloyd, the *Cannibal* box ART has GOT to go OUT toDAY!" • The Director of Acquisitions tells me that *Killer Condom* is the best movie he's seen come through in years, and that we should acquire it. It's only an $80,000 advance. "Offer him 800!" I say. • My doctor calls with the results from the test last week, and says I have skin cancer, and that I must have it removed before it spreads. • The marketing dude is sticking a pencil in my side, telling me we need to spend more money on the theatrical release of *Tromeo & Juliet.* • Maria Fridmanovich, our bookkeeper, hands me a check to sign, which I do, even though I have no idea to whom it is going or for how much. • Jennifer tells me I have a call from Andrew Cozine, the *Schlock & Schlockability* screenwriter. I tell her to tell him I'm in the editing room and can't come to the phone. • CNN films me telling Jennifer to tell a lie. • David and his Japanese crew are following me around and I'm mutilating every Japanese word I've ever known, and they think this is just hilarious, and if I was strong enough to lift one of these enormous bags over my head, I just might break David's fucking neck. Although I like him. He's a nice guy. He just happens to be here at the wrong moment.

And then I went out the door. The cacophony continued behind me. The Troma Team grappled for the back of my shirt, like the zombies in *Chopper Chicks from Zombietown*. I escaped onto the New York City streets.

It was raining.

Hard.

There were no taxis.

I was sitting on the plane, staring out at the clouds, when I remembered what my doctor had said 1,500 miles behind me:

"Lloyd, we have the results of the skin samples we took last week."

"Uh-huh," I answered, simultaneously trying to read the text for Troma's web site Patrick had handed me. It was an article entitled "The Five Reasons the NRA Is a Big Pile of Fuck."

"It seems that you have skin cancer," my doctor said.

"Uh-huh." I held my hand over the receiver. I looked at Patrick. "You can't put this on the Troma web site!"

"Was that a sob?" my doctor said.

"What?"

"Are you crying?"

"No, I was just . . . saying something to someone . . . Skin cancer, huh?"

"Yes. But there's no need for worry. We'll set up an appointment for you next week, some extremely minor surgery, and we'll have it out of there. How's Thursday?"

"Thursday. Okay, sure."

"Lloyd, we have this amazing platform, to make a difference," Patrick said. "We have to take advantage of our position."

"We can't do that!" I told Patrick.

"Hey, we put up all those opinion pieces about the MPAA."*

"Two o'clock good?" the doctor said.

"Sure, sure," I said.

"I'll see you then."

"Bye." I hung up. I looked at Patrick. "But the NRA has nothing to do with movies! Also, we didn't call the MPAA 'a big pile of fuck'! I don't even know what a big pile of fuck is!"

Now, as I took another bite of chicken *a la United Airlines*, everything fell into perspective. I lived in a world where I spent days talking about the creation of the Penis Monster in *Tromeo & Juliet*, and less than two minutes talking to the doctor about how I had come down with a case of the Big C. Everything in my life had to do with MOVIES. I spent 95 percent of my waking moments talking about them, watching them, dreaming about them, making them, or trying to acquire the cash to make them. I was just a spoke on the much larger wheel of Troma. As I gazed out the airplane window and into the blue sky, I felt strengthened by this knowledge. My world went outside the boundaries of my own life, onto something that had a greater meaning. That's what Troma was for me. Although it wasn't the same as holding an award in front of a wildly applauding crowd, the *feeling* was awful close.

A flight attendant gazed at me as she bent to take away my empty tray. She smiled, sadly, sweetly. She didn't look away. *This* is a moment, I thought. This dear, wonderful woman must have seen the light of revelation in my eyes. She must feel about something in her life the way I do about movies; she must be aware of a larger significance to the world. She is obviously a flight attendant of amazing empathy. On some deeper level, she and I are one in that sad joy that connects all

---

*For years I've railed against the Motion Picture Arts Association, the group responsible for giving films ratings (PG, PG-13, R, etc.); they're unfair and too expensive, and well-known for screwing the indies and new filmmakers.

Kaufman calmly receives the news that *Tromeo & Juliet* received a good review in *The New York Times*.

humanity. I smiled back at her. I nodded: Yes, yes, I know exactly how you feel.

Then she said:

"Sir, there's something . . . green . . . all over your chin."

"Ooo!"

Below the Basement two
of the Film Industry

That next Thursday the doctor removed the skin cancer from my left cheek. There's no trace left now. So if you were afraid for a moment that this book was going to be TV-movie-like, sermonizing about a dying man reflecting on his life and his work shortly before he kicks off, forget it. The skin cancer subplot, though true, was just a literary device to get to that thing about the flight attendant noticing my green chin, which is more important and definitely has more comedic appeal. Hell, many people get skin cancer. Very few are able to vomit green foam on a biweekly basis. And that's exactly the type of nonlinear logic I'd like to focus on in this chapter, which is all about the first "movies" I ever made.

On to the sex and violence . . .

HOW I BECAME A CELLULOID-HUGGING NANCY BOY

If not for entering Yale University in 1964, I would have done something useful with my life. At first things were all right: I had a fulfilling major in Chinese Studies. I had a fondness for languages and other cultures. I thought I'd be a social worker and teach people with hooks for hands how to finger paint (or something like that). This was the sixties and we all wanted to make the world a better place. As did

I, until God placed me in a dormitory with two cinephiles and fucked my life.

Let me explain.

Robert Edelstein and Eric Sherman were movie fanatics who happened to be placed in my dorm. Robert, from New York, was my roommate; our beds were foot-to-head and every night I smelled the aroma of his Godard-loving feet. Eric lived next door; his old man was the Hollywood director Vincent Sherman.*

Until then my love had been Broadway musicals, not film. The pomp and extremity that would later be such an important part of Troma movies has its roots on the New York stage. Celluloid was crass, *but the theater!* Dancing girls in skimpy glittering costumes! Curtains, pulleys, and mechanical lifts! Live animals on stage! I adored Rodgers and Hart. I knew all the words to *Candide*. I took pride in being one of the eight people who had seen Broadway flops like *WildCat*, *Dough Re Me,* and *Subways Are for Sleeping*. But I had no idea who John Ford was. Preston Sturges? Doesn't ring a bell. Charlie Chaplin? He's a goofy actor, right?

Then came Eric and Robert, the twin avatars of my destruction. They were the cochairs of the Yale Film Society. The Film Society exhibited the works of Ford and Sturges, of Hawks, Keaton, Ulmer, and Sirk, of Warhol, Welles, Renoir, and Leisen. Corman. Lang. Fuller. Kurosawa. I could literally fill pages with the names of the great men† with whose works Robert and Eric barraged me (and I *would* fill pages, if Barry Neville wasn't beginning to get wise to my overuse of lists and modifiers).

Imagine me as Patty Hearst, a brainwashed victim of Eric and Robert's *Clockwork Orange*-like manipulations. They punctured my world with the Cahiers de Cinema, Andrew Sarris, and dialectics on the Freudian use of milk jugs in Tashlin's *The Girl Can't Help It*. Eventually I too became a celluloid-hugging nancy boy. Raccoon-eyed and weathered, a man obsessed. I needed to see every movie ever made.

---

*My favorites of his are *The Adventures of Don Juan* (1948) and *The Hard Way* (1942).

†And Leni Reifenstahl and Ida Lupino. I'd like to say "great men and women but," sadly, in our sexist cinema history, this is not the case.

I wanted to eat them, dream them, put them in an eyedropper and let them seep into my optic nerve. I always had a competitive nature. Now I needed to catch up to Robert and Eric. They were so far ahead of me. Every week I'd get the TV guide. I'd circle the films I was going to watch, and plan my schedule of dating (seldom), parties (occasionally), and masturbation (constantly) around the movies.

Still, it was always a hobby. I was going to become a social worker, perhaps teach hobos how to paint smiley faces on beads and then put the beads on strings (or something like that). But then I saw *To Be or Not to Be*.

Directed by Ernst Lubitsch, *To Be or Not to Be* (1942) starred Carole Lombard, Jack Benny, and Robert Stack. It contained Lombard's last film appearance and what is considered Benny's grandest performance. I had seen Lubitsch's *Ninotchka* earlier in the year, and had enjoyed it immensely. But *To Be or Not to Be* blew me away. Now, I had been blown away numerous times that year: I had just seen and been blown away by *The Magnificent Ambersons*, *Sullivan's Travels*, and *The Searchers*, not to mention Stan Brakhage's overwhelming *Art of Vision* and Russ Meyer's *The Immoral Mr. Teas*. But, for some reason, it was during *this* moment of being blown away that I decided that there was nothing more in life I needed to do than make movies. I didn't want to *help* the hobos and the people with hooks for hands; *I wanted to film them*. As I watched Benny and Lombard use their thespian skills to thwart invading Nazi troops, my decision was absolutely conclusive. However, it was not an overwhelming spiritual revelation. Rather, it was as simple as making a decision to get up from the Lay-Z-Boy and walk into the other room. It just was.

So—considering that Lubitsch, Lombard, and Benny are all dead—if you want to blame someone for bringing Troma into the world, find Robert Stack and throw an apple at his head.*

Shortly after watching *To Be or Not to Be*, I went to Chad.

There I made a pig movie. Wait till you hear about it.

---

*EDITOR'S NOTE: Once again, he's not serious here.

BEYOND EVERETT: THE REAL CHAD

One of the best things about being sent to Chad, Africa, as a guinea pig for the Peace Corps was that I got laid much more than I did in the States. Of course, I had to pay for it—but only five bucks a pop (or a bar of soap).

In 1966, I took off my second year at Yale to live abroad (and on broads) in the north-central African country Chad. Chad was formerly part of French Equatorial Africa but became independent in 1960. The Peace Corps was considering shuffling in their usual band of merry elitist idealists but decided first to induct a few "pathfinders"* such as myself for an extended tour. This was presumably to see if the natives of Chad would kill us. If they did kill us, the Peace Corps would probably have found another backwards country to "civilize."† When I arrived, Chad was, to be politically correct, "Technologically Special" (i.e., sticks = guns, rocks = the Chad space program).

Now, you may think I'm getting offtrack here. "Where's the Toxic Avenger?" you might be saying. "Did you make *Sgt. Kabukiman NYPD* in Chad?" Barry, the editor of this book, wants me to make sure I relate everything to Troma movies. But, believe it or not, living in Chad *does* relate to Troma.

FIRST OF ALL, many of these African women with whom I melded had large breasts and ran around topless. Women in Troma movies also often have large breasts and run around topless.

SECOND, the living conditions in Chad were sub-slum. I had to sleep in the bush with no plumbing or electricity, bombarded by mosquitoes and hundred-degree temperatures, awakened by barking baboons running past my shed in the middle of the night. During my year there I contracted dengue fever, equatorial pneumonia, twenty (yes) varieties of diarrhea, and a litany of disgusting venereal diseases,‡ including once when I truly believed there were *eyes growing on my*

---

*Speaking of, *Pathfinder* (1987), the Laplander classic, is one of my favorite (and one of the most disturbing) films of all time.
†Incidentally, the Peace Corps did enter directly after I left. They were booted out a few weeks afterwards.
‡Roger Corman merely directed *Invasion of the Crab Monsters*. My little guy and I actually experienced said invasion in the bush of Chad.

penis (the fever had dazed me a bit). Likewise, the living conditions on a Troma set are less than exemplary. We often have to sleep on the floor, crap in paper bags, go for days without sleep, and are overrun by barking baboons.* And we've been known to make plastic creatures that don't just *appear* to be penises with eyes growing out of them but *are*, in fact, such.†

"There is no more difficult job than working on a Troma movie," I often tell someone when they come to work for us. And fortunately I had Chad to teach me how to put up with any sort of humiliation or adverse living condition.

THIRD, I learned that if you want to keep people's attention, chop up a living being. While in Chad, I filmed the slaughter of a pig by Chadvillians with my 16-millimeter Bolex movie camera. (Or, rather, they didn't slaughter the pig with my Bolex—I filmed, with the Bolex, the slaughter. This grammar thing isn't the cakewalk it first appeared to be.) As the pig screamed, they slit its throat with a king-size machete, then chopped the animal up into small pieces. Upon returning home, I screened the film for family and friends. They were outraged. Pissing people off, I discovered, is one of the few satisfying things on this forsaken planet.

LAST, AND MOST IMPORTANT, my experience in Chad taught me that the mainstream's value system was not necessarily the most valid. The people of Chad assessed the universe in a very different way than I had, with a certain sophistication and beauty that opened me up to the fact that my own upper-class Manhattan-made worldview was extremely narrow. I think, in many ways, I would prefer to live life as the people of Chad did. I mean, assuming, of course, they had Hostess Snow Balls and Game Boys and microwave ovens.

So, that's the connection, Barry.

Now: there was one African girl that I recall most of all. Her name was Dimanche Dieu Donnee, which means "God-given on Sunday." And God gave her to me on Sundays many times. She had the pen-

---

*Though, again, I guess I should call the crew by the more politically correct term, "Stupid Retards."

†See next chapter for the origin of the huggable, lovable Penis Monster—he's *everybody's* type of guy!

dulous breasts of which I spoke earlier. She wore a dress fashioned of African cotton adorned with the face of John F. Kennedy. She had no idea who JFK was, but she found it pleasing aesthetically. With her warm body beneath me, the face of the youngest American President flipping and flopping against my pleasure zones, I knew this was the most magnificent time in all my life. The only drawback to this now is that every time I see the Zapruder film I get an erection. I admit, this has little or nothing to do with Troma, but, dammit, Barry, how can I leave something like that out?

GASOLINE AND *RAPPACCINI*

And then I helped Robert Edelstein make a 16-millimeter film entitled *Rappaccini*. Eighty minutes long. His second directorial effort. He allowed me to be the producer. This meant I got Robert coffee and cleaned out the toilets and put up half the money for the film (3,000 smackers). I had acquired the money that I invested on this film, and other films later, by living at home and saving money I made from the stock market and from pumping gas.

A TRUE MOMENT IN THE GAS STATION

I was about to stick the gas nozzle in the tank, when another station employee, Brett (who later went to prison for stabbing his wife in the eye), hollered my name. I turned. Brett was holding up a *Playboy* centerfold and laughing. He was making fun of me; Brett, for some reason, had decided I was gay, probably because I was short, Jewish, and went to Yale. Lamentably, while turning, I pressed down on the gas handle without realizing it. Gasoline splashed all over the customer sitting in the driver's seat. He was wearing a suit. The man began to scream: "WHAT IF I HAD BEEN SMOKING A CIGARETTE? GOD ALMIGHTY! WHAT IF I HAD BEEN SMOKING?" He screamed this repeatedly. It was interesting to me because he didn't seem to care about his suit being ruined. All that mattered was that in some parallel existence he could be bursting into flames. I handed the man some of those blue napkins, the ones you use to clean off the windshield. This only made him angrier.* Back to *Rappaccini*—

---

*EDITOR'S NOTE: I'm becoming increasingly aware that digressing is a real serious problem here, Lloyd.

Rappaccini was based on a Nathaniel Hawthorne short story, which set the stage for future Troma movies based on classical works, such as *The Good, the Bad, and the Subhumanoid* based upon *Comedy of Errors*, *Tromeo & Juliet* based upon *Romeo & Juliet*, and *Chopper Chicks in Zombietown* based upon *The Old Man and the Sea*.* It concerns the story of Dr. Rappaccini, who raises his daughter in a garden of poisonous plants, and she in turn becomes poisonous. Pretty cool, huh?

Well, not really. Although accomplished for a student film, *Rappaccini* was slow. The acting was proficient (it starred Perry King, a fellow student of ours at Yale, who later went on to *The Lords of Flatbush, Andy Warhol's Bad*, and the TV show *Riptide*). I was 100 percent dedicated to Robert's vision as director. This is an attitude I'd take with every director I would ever work with. However, I did have a few *secret* ideas about how to improve Hawthorne's story. For instance, I thought there could have been many, many nasty thornbushes in the garden, which tore off the heroine's clothes every time she crossed the room: "Darn! I'm naked again!" But I kept this and other thoughts to myself.

The film played at a few colleges and was fairly well reviewed by the college newspapers and audiences.

"Good God, man!" many of you are probably saying. "How on earth could you have possibly made a film for six thousand DOLLARS?! That's ridiculous!" I completely concur. Therefore, when I was ready to shoot my own feature-length film I did it for two thousand.

THE GIRL WHO RETURNED (AND WAS EVEN MORE BORING THAN WHEN SHE LEFT)

> IMAGINE: Opening Shot: College girls on a football field doing calisthenics.
> CUT TO: A dark-haired girl stretching her legs out and touching her toes.
> CUT TO: Another girl, bending to touch the ground.
> CUT TO: Another girl doing jumping jacks.

Now, imagine this same sequence of events, repeated again and again and again—for more than ten minutes. In grainy black and white.

---

*All right, so I made this last one up. But I didn't think two movies were enough to account for a trend.

BEFORE YOU FALL IN LOVE
THINK OF... 𝕽appaccini
(coming soon)

There is no quickening of the motion. No narrative force from one shot to the next. It seems it won't ever stop. Oh, yeah, and it's mostly silent, with just a bit of narration tagged on. And though it's outdoors it's still poorly lit.

Now, in the same film, later on, imagine: A girl jogging. We probably see her jog forty or fifty laps in this one film alone. Lots of jogging.

If you can truly imagine all this, then you have a pretty good idea of what my first film, *The Girl Who Returned*, is like. I was trying to use repetition in the same way Warhol did, and failed horribly. In the name of research for this book, I had the privilege of watching *The Girl Who Returned* for the first time in almost thirty years.

Ow.

I made the film during my sophomore year at Yale.* I had deter-

---

*And I was crushed later on when the critic from the *Yale Daily News* referred to the film as "sophomoric."

mined that the best way to learn about filmmaking was to make a film of my own. But I didn't really know what to make. Short, psychedelic films, the celluloid versions of lava lamps, were popular at the time. Film school students were churning out these things by the dozens. So, being that I always seem to go against the grain,* I decided to make a feature-length comedy.

The Girl Who Returned told the story of an alternate existence, where the world is divided into two lands: Luxembourg, which is composed completely of women, and Mongolia, which is composed completely of men. Every four years these two lands come together to compete in a series of Olympic events to determine the supremacy of the world.

A FEW THINGS OF NOTE ABOUT *THE GIRL WHO RETURNED*:

1 It features a young Michael Herz and his future wife, Maris, in a goofy shot-putting competition. Maris wins. I had directed the normally dignified Michael to act like Ralph Cramden. Just this year, when we got *The Girl Who Returned* transferred to video for the first time, the Troma Team enjoyed playing it endlessly when Michael and Maris were in the room, for nothing more than the sheer pleasure we derived from their degradation.

2 I edited one scene of the film while tripping on acid. There is no discernible difference between this scene and the rest of the film. (Of course, I could have let a chimpanzee edit a scene, and there probably wouldn't be any discernible difference there either. They say if you put five thousand monkeys in a room typing they will write the complete works of Shakespeare within a million years. Likewise, if you put two monkeys in a room with movie cameras they will make *The Girl Who Returned* in about twelve days.)

3 Despite my amateurishness, this film taught me a lot about shooting and editing. I shot it with my Bolex, which you need to wind and which only runs for about forty seconds. Since you can't have any shots longer than that, I was required to intercut a lot.

---

*Except my cinematography, where for thirty years grain has been a hallmark.

Also, because a Bolex has no sync sound (you need a motor-driven camera for sound synchronization), I had to get meaning across in picture only. Film is a primarily visual medium, and I had no choice but to deal with this. Using hundreds and hundreds of shots, I experimented with actions, reactions, etc., without being tied down by sound. I was influenced by the composer John Cage (who used silences to enhance his music) and the experimental work of Stan Brakhage, and I put long strips of black leader between scenes. However, the audience didn't understand; they kept looking back at the projector, thinking the bulb had burnt out. I learned that when technique fails or distracts it can seriously harm your film.

4 *The Girl Who Returned* actually returned a profit. This was basically unheard of for a student film. We charged a one dollar admission at the Yale Film Society and other colleges, which was considered rather ballsy. People seemed to be interested in seeing a film by a student that was feature length and wasn't the visual equivalent of Doors lyrics. Here I learned another important lesson: ONCE THEY PAY TO GET INTO THE ROOM, THEY'RE BASICALLY TRAPPED, also known as EVEN IF THEY WANT THEIR MONEY BACK, MOST PEOPLE WON'T ASK. This wasn't exactly the flower-power thinking of my generation, but, you know, most of the "idealists" from Yale in those years are today spending most of their time figuring out ways to exploit the talents of little brown people at factories in Third World countries.

5 Posters are important (this is also called marketing, but you can only call it that if your budget is over four figures). We played on the Yale campus at the same time as Frank Borzage's film noir masterpiece, *Strange Cargo*. The poster for Borzage's film, unfortunately, didn't have a picture of a young woman on her back, her incredibly perky mounds pointed straight up at the sky, with a semi-orgasmic expression on her face. Our film did. Nine people went to his movie. 377 went to ours.

6 *The Girl Who Returned* starred Gretchen Herman, an attractive girl with nice breasts who didn't wear a bra. It had a small amount of slapstick. These were the only things in the movie audiences seemed at all interested in. This would affect me later when choosing subject matter for Troma films.

Here's an anecdote about filming *The Girl Who Returned*:

Roger Kirby, a friend of mine from childhood, was attending Stanford, where I shot part of the movie. It was *his idea* to get the jogging footage of Gretchen, due to her pert breasts and proclivity for bralessness.

Roger revved up his LandRover. I sat on the roof, aiming the Bolex as Roger drove. We zipped after the girl, following her down the street as she jogged. "Boy, I love women exercising," I thought at the time. "I just can't get enough of this." We bumped along. I *just knew* that this was the best footage in the film! My heart pounded in unison with Gretchen's perky bosom! Since Roger had a hilarious sense of humor, he suddenly veered off the road, drove up into the woods, and slammed my head into an overhanging tree limb.

SLAM!

Ha. Ha. Ha.

I flipped down onto the back of the Rover. I gripped onto the rear bumper, the tips of my shoes bouncing along on the grass behind me, clutching on to my Bolex, more valuable to me than my mother with its sleek black casing and its Vario-Switar 200mm lens, as the echoing, maniacal laughter of "my good buddy" Roger wafted back from the driver's seat.

I was truly a filmmaker!

Last week Roger and I had lunch, and I brought this up. Roger said, "Yeah, maybe that wasn't so nice after all." This was suddenly occurring to him for the first time.

For those of you who like "The Kevin Bacon Game," where every actor can be connected to Kevin Bacon through movies, here's how to attach Roger to Kevin Bacon in three steps.*

0 Roger was in *Metropolitan*,† by Whit Stillman. He played the aging socialite in the bar at the end of the film. Christopher Eigeman was also in this film.

---

*EDITOR'S NOTE: Lloyd, now you're getting WAY off the point here.
†For Kaufman's own reputed role in *Metropolitan*, see "The Case of Patient X: 'Thespian' " in chapter 14.

BEFORE YOU TRY TO FALL IN LOVE, THINK OF **THE GIRL WHO RETURNED**

THE GIRL WHO RETURNED TRIED TO FALL IN LOVE: THE GIRL WHO RETURNED GOT BURNED,

★ ★ ★

A Lloyd Kaufman Production

THE GIRL WHO RETURNED

Man vs. Woman . . . OLYMPICS as you've never seen 'em.

●

WORLD PREMIERE OCTOBER 30th

1 Christopher Eigeman was in *Kicking and Screaming* with Eric Stoltz.

2 Eric Stoltz was in *Naked in New York* with Jill Clayburgh.

3 Jill Clayburgh was in *Starting Over* with Kevin Bacon.

UNDER THE BOTTOM RUNG

After I graduated from Yale, I was faced with two job opportunities: A) I could be a PA* on *The Owl and the Pussycat*, Herbert Ross' high-profile Hollywood movie starring Barbra Streisand and George Segal, or B) I could take the important role of *shit boy* at the sub-basement, low-budget Cannon Films. A guy called me:

"Lloyd, this is Allen Schwartz. We've got a position in the editing room down here at Cannon."

"Ooo. What's the position?"

"Shit boy."

"*Shit* boy?"

"Uh-huh."

"Oh. Well, as a shit boy, what would I, you know, do, exactly?"

"Horrible shit. Bringing the editors coffee and sucking their asses will be the best of it. After a few days, you'll *pray* for a day of sucking ass. You'll have to lug reels around to all the different boroughs. In the rain. You'll have to clean out the goddamn toilets. Aging starlets will bring in their poodles, and you'll have to clean up their piss when they piss on a strip of film. And when the film is fucked-up from having piss all over it, it will be your fault. You know why?"

"No."

"Because the disgusting pissing, shitting, farting, vomiting, syphilitic poodle will be one rung up the ladder from you. And we hate that fucking dog. We torture it when the aging starlet's not looking. But you, YOU . . . anyway, what do you say, Lloyd? You want the job?"

"Well, I was offered this big deal 'establishment' job," I said. "But, you know, I don't think that's my bag, dig? So, yeah, man. Shit boy. Sounds good. I just dig movies."

It was the sixties, after all, and I didn't want to sell out. Or maybe I had a precognition that Babs Streisand was going to become the whiniest, most boring "major" film director ever. Maybe I knew that twenty-six years later, on a plane returning from the Brussels International Film Festival, I'd have to sit through *The Mirror Has Two Faces* in which Babs is magically transformed from an ugly duckling

---

*Production Assistant.

into . . . a hawk-nosed cow with legs like two sausage skins filled with cottage cheese. I didn't want that to wear off on me. Thus I became a shit boy.

The job did suck, Schwartz didn't lie about that. But there were some side benefits. For instance, Cannon would often acquire cheap, dreadful films and then add footage of soft-core sex to make them suitable fare for the grind houses on 42nd Street. They'd acquire, say, a sub-typical cowboy movie called *Blazing Guns on the High Sierra* or some such nonsense, add footage of cowpokes who actually *did* poke cows, and change the title to *The Wicked Western.* I bet you've often wondered who shot that sexy footage that looks so out-of-place in those films?

Have you guessed yet? Give up?

ME!

I'd assist people like Billy Sachs* and editor George Norris.† I'd load the camera. Hold up bounce boards. Watch actresses pretend to moan in ecstasy when it was obvious they'd rather be at home watching *The Guiding Light.* Clean the toilets after Billy Sachs took a particularly large shit. Be the continuity clerk (Ha! Just kidding!‡) Wipe the sweat from the actors' testicles.

I thought: Now THIS, my friends! THIS is FILMMAKING!

AVILDSEN, JOE, AND A DRUNK UNNAMED ACTOR

John Avildsen, future director of *Rocky* and *The Karate Kid*, had just finished making a film entitled *Guess What We Learned in School Today?* for Cannon. I first met him in the editing room, where my career of rewinding infinite numbers of 1,000-foot reels of 35mm

---

*Who later went on to do more respectable fare like *Galaxina* (1980) and *The Incredible Melting Man* (1977), for which he won the Academy Award for Best Director.**

** Just checking to make sure you're actually paying attention when you read these things.

†Who would later on cut *Joe, Squeeze Play*, and *Troma's War.*

‡A continuity clerk makes sure that A) in any given scene, you get all the necessary coverage and angles, and B) that everything matches from one shot to the next. The great director John Cassavetes once said, "Matching is for sissies." Likewise, on a Troma set we have the adage, "Continuity is for pussies."

film and cleaning the shit stains off the bottom of the toilet was in full swing. Since I had done such a fine job of rewinding 1,000-foot reels and cleaning up *his* shit, I guess, Avildsen asked me to come and work for him as a production assistant on his new film, *Joe*.

I was delighted. Since Cannon was backing *Joe*, they lent me to him. The script to *Joe* was originally entitled *The Gap*. Avildsen hired Norman Wexler for a rewrite. Wexler got the idea for *Joe* from *Speed Is of the Essence*, which is about a rich girl from Connecticut who gets involved with a speed freak drug dealer. Norman changed the focus to hard hats who hated the hippies. By emphasizing the working class in the story, Norman added a lot of grit and heart and made the movie unique. He received an Oscar nomination for best screenplay for *Joe*. . . . Pretty good for a movie costing less than $500,000.

CRY UNCLE

After Kaufman's exemplary job on *Joe*, Avildsen hired him as production manager on his next feature, *Cry Uncle*. *Cry Uncle* was the brainchild of Lee Hessel, who was most famous for importing "art" films like *Anita, the Swedish Nymphet* and *Ilsa, She-Wolf of the SS* into the States. The script was based upon a straightforward pulp novel called *Lie a Little, Die a Little*, the serious story of a suave, handsome private investigator. By the time Avildsen and screenwriter David Odell were through with it, however, the P.I. was fat and perverted, and the story was semi-surreal and extremely raunchy.

"The way Odell dealt with the clichéd original script was inspiring," Kaufman now says. "Out of this low-budget piece of schlock he was able to eke something both unique and commercial."

Cry Uncle opened in 1972. The film had an X rating. If you look closely, it actually includes one scene of graphic oral sex and some delightful simulated necrophilia. (Kaufman likes to believe that the actress giving the blowjob later went on to fame under the name Meryl Streep. Upon investigation, this is revealed to be a fallacy). Despite the X rating, the film played in over 1,000 theaters around the country, and was at one point number one in the nation. Being that Kaufman had actually invested some of his own money into the film, it was a financial high point in his early career. Today Troma studios owns the rights to *Cry Uncle*; it remains one of the best films in the Troma library.

Steve Tisch was a production assistant on *Cry Uncle*; he was later demoted to producer of *Forrest Gump*.

We had a fairly well-known actor* slated to play the character of Joe. On my first day of working for the production, I was sent to bring

---

*I'll tell you his name if you send in 1,000,000 *Toxic Avenger* proofs-of-purchase seals.

him to wardrobe. I entered his room. The big lug of a man was leaning back in his chair, staring at the wall. I called to him. He didn't turn. I said his name a few more times. Nothing. I stomped loudly around the apartment. Nope. I made some hooting noises. Still he didn't turn. I stood there quietly, literally wringing my hands. Here he was, the star, completely unwilling to look or listen to the peon that was myself. My first day on the job, and already I was a failure. I was about to depart when he turned and gazed at me. He smiled. The tough exterior fell away to reveal a warm, friendly nature. Then he tried to speak. His tongue seemed to have been cyber-genetically replaced with a half-dead fish that slapped, slushed, and rolled around inside his mouth.

He was drunk off his ass.

I tried to lift him out of the seat and push him out of the apartment. He collapsed to the floor. I splashed water on his face, tried to pull him up. There was no going. I surrendered. Turned around. Left.

A few days later we *were* able to get the guy out of his room. He and Frank Vitale,* the unit manager, and I were on the escalator at Alexander's for wardrobe. There, the thespian did a very interesting thing: he whipped out his schlong and began to urinate on my leg. At this point, he was fired. My knee was grateful to the producers. Peter Boyle, who later went on to do *Young Frankenstein*, replaced him.† When Peter Boyle auditioned for Avildsen, he clinched the part by improvising to the line ". . . you show me a welfare worker who's not a nigger-lover and I'll massage your asshole." Boyle added the line ". . . and I ain't queer." There is a lesson here.

Joe costarred, in her first film role, Susan Sarandon, who had an incredible tripping-on-acid-and-painting-her-face-with-lipstick scene (almost as good as her standing-in-the-open-window-and-putting-lemon-on-her-nipples-as-Burt-Lancaster-watches-from-the-street scene in Louis Malle's *Atlantic City*).

My first day on the set of *Joe* was a high point of my career. The crew buzzed around me. The lights heated up the room. Avildsen acted as the foreman, keeping everything in place. The scene took place

---

*Later to produce our *The Battle of Love's Return* and *East End Hustle*.
†Boyle was actually Avildsen's original choice, but the producers had thought he was too young.

around a furnace. We used the enormous blimped Mitchell camera that took two people to lift. After Avildsen had set the shot, I sneaked a peek through the viewfinder. Now, as you may or may not know, looking through a camera's viewfinder without asking the D.P. is considered taboo. But no one was watching and I couldn't restrain myself. The shot was wonderfully composed: the fire raging in the furnace, a pinpoint of light flickering on the icy metal surface, which was, in turn, a sharp line against the warm backdrop of red bricks. It was so beautiful, I knew beyond a doubt that this was going to be a great film. I had done everything I could to stay out of the Vietnam War, but for this movie I'd give my life.

My tactic was simple: SMOTHER THE ASSIGNMENT. I arrived two hours early every day and left two hours after everyone else had gone home. I may not know too much about the art of filmmaking, but I do know that it takes a large amount of sacrifice. Sometimes I believe I had a choice between film and life—and I chose film. I gave my life to *Joe*, not only in time, but in concentration. Nothing is more disappointing to filmmakers and performers than when the crew doesn't focus on the production at hand, when they don't press their minds into it. When I'm directing a film, I often yell out, "EVERY-BODY FOCUS!" Call it a religious belief of mine, but this communal concentration adds some intangible "it" to a production. Even if the members of the crew aren't doing anything hands on, their quiet zeal adds a certain magic. Another thing: THE CELLULOID PICKS UP EVERYTHING—pre- and postproduction, love and contempt, concern and carelessness, honesty and hypocrisy. I stayed focused on *Joe*. I was always on standby, so I could be there with anything that was needed before someone asked. And because of this, not only do I believe I helped the film, but Avildsen noticed and appreciated me.

A LITTLE FUN AT CANNON

It was blazing hot, and I was on the subway lugging an enormous reel-to-reel tape recorder to Staten Island. Staten Island is reputed to be one of the boroughs of New York City, but anyone that lives here knows that it is, in fact, another country—a large island like England or Ireland, only with more ceramic lawn animals.

The reel-to-reel had stuck into my side, torn away some skin, and I was bleeding. I got off the subway. I carried this huge machine nine more blocks to the location, where I was greeted by a man with a cigar. He screamed at me for bringing him a reel-to-reel with blood on it.

I apologized.

On the subway back to Cannon, my anger and humiliation rose, flaming, overtaking me. I prepared a speech.

I threw the door open and marched straight into Allen Schwartz's office. I slapped my hand on his desk.

"Listen!" I cried. "I'm a Yale graduate! I directed *The Girl Who Returned*, a movie that netted over 350 dollars—that's probably more than *The Wicked Western*! I've broken my ass for you! I've picked up poodle shit with my bare hands! And I think I am, to be blunt, Mr. Schwartz, a little *overqualified* for messengering gigantic reel-to-reels that look as if they're props from *The Incredible Shrinking Man*!"

Schwartz set down his pen. He leaned back in his seat, just a bit. Looked at me.

"All right," he said. "Then leave."

"Uh . . . what?"

"Go ahead. Don't demean yourself any further. Go."

"Well, you know, I was just tossing out some ideas."

"Good ideas too. Don't stand for the indignity of it all, Lloyd. Walk out now."

"Uh, the toilets were looking a little dirty."

"They were?"

"Yeah."

"Hm."

"So I better get back out there and clean them up."

"Right."

"You need anything else delivered?"

"I don't—"

"This. Do you need this delivered?"

"That's my desk."

"Uh, well, you know, I have a strong back, so it wouldn't be much of a problem."

I stepped backwards until I was out the door.

Shortly after that I was let go.

* * *

Time to make another movie. Although *The Girl Who Returned* had been a financial success, the experience of watching it was akin to having your arm eaten to the bone by a cageful of starving rats. So I made a firm resolution: My next film would be a *good* one.

Instead, however, I made *The Battle of Love's Return*.

THE MAKING OF *STAR WARS* (well, actually, it's the making of *THE BATTLE OF LOVE'S RETURN*. But that's no reason I shouldn't cash in on the hype.)

"All of this is quite interesting, Lloyd," you might be saying. "But we want to learn something of practical use to up-and-coming young filmmakers like me."

To that I'd say:

Well, first of all, the plural "filmmakers" doesn't agree with the singular pronoun "me" (I'm really getting into this grammar stuff).

Then I'd say: Well, later on there *will* be a discussion of what-to-do and what-not-to-do when picking up Malaysian streetwalkers while shooting in that special land.

But until then, we have:

THE UPSIDE-DOWN AND BACKWARDS EFFECT

Perhaps there's a technical film school term for this, but we on the Troma Team know it by the above name or as THAT THING, YOU KNOW, WHERE YOU TURN THE CAMERA UPSIDE DOWN? YOU KNOW WHAT I'M TALKING ABOUT, RIGHT? The *purpose* of the effect is to give the illusion of heavy impact.

Let me give you an example of a successful execution.

On *Tromeo & Juliet* we needed a shot of a fist shoving a tattoo needle into the camera lens. This would be a POV* of Troma action star Steven Loniewski† as his eyeball is poked out. Now, obviously, no actor, no matter how athletically inclined, has the muscle control to

---

*Point-of-view.
†Star of Troma TV's *Tromaville Café* and Mirella Krespi's *I Put a Spell on You* (1997).

shove a tattoo needle full speed ahead at a $500,000 camera and then stop a hair's breadth from the $30,000 lens. So, what you do is this:

You turn the camera upside down.

You put the tattoo needle so it's almost touching the lens, turn on the camera, and pull the needle away as quickly as possible.

Then, when you cut the film, you flip the film strip around so that the first frame is last and the last frame is first (i.e., the film runs backwards), which means you are also turning the film upside down from the way it was shot (which was upside down to begin with, get it?).

What you are left with is a shot of a tattoo needle rushing for the lens. In the same scene in *Tromeo & Juliet*, we also placed the needle against Steven's eye, turned the camera upside down, and pulled the needle away.* We were able to cut these two shots with a third shot of the needle actually entering the eye socket of a fake head to create something shocking and real.

That was the successful attempt. Now, let me give you an example of a not-so-successful attempt. It happened during my first sound feature as director, *The Battle of Love's Return* (teaching us all that the primary purpose of first sound features is "fuck-up and learn").

I wanted to have a man (me) get hit by a car (which I'm sure was the fervent hope of anyone who saw *The Girl Who Returned*). So, with the camera upside down, I filmed myself lying down, rolling toward the car, standing up with my knees touching the car, and then having the car back away. When I flipped the film to play forward it was supposed to look as if the car hit me and caused me to roll across the street. Instead it looked ludicrous. However, when I intercut it with other shots: the front of the car, a look of surprise on my face, a streetlight, it looked . . . well, ludicrous. I had simply used the technique over too long of a shot instead of in short, simple strokes.

That was only one of the many difficulties on *The Battle of Love's Return.*† The movie, the story of one man's journey to find himself, was originally set to star my childhood friend Richard Lewin, who

---

*For many years we did most of our tattoo-needle-in-the-eye scenes right side up, but we changed as the vogue for one-eyed actors became passé.

†These long Troma titles really help me in rushing toward the 75,000 word mark. I think I'll write two or three chapters on *Class of Nuke 'Em High Part III: The Good, the Bad, and the Subhumanoid*, and use the title a whole, whole lot.

was a fat guy. Not only do I think fat people are more interesting than thin people, you also save money on props since they fill up so much of the screen. But Richard backed out at the last minute.

So in the lead role we cast an atrocious actor with no screen charisma. I don't know if you've ever seen the old Japanese "animated" cartoons where it's simply a still image of a cartoon with a human mouth talking in place of the cartoon's mouth. This actor was about as good an actor as one of those guys.

You could say it was a mistake for me to cast myself in the lead. I was so bad that I didn't act in another one of my movies for twenty-five years, when the crew forced a cameo on me in *Tromeo & Juliet.**

The Girl Who Returned taught me a lot about filmmaking, but I had done it while still a student. There had been a lot less at stake. *The Battle of Love's Return* was my initiation into the Hell of filmmaking. First of all, there was a lot riding on it: *Battle* had a HUGE budget—over $8,000 was invested by myself, Frank Vitale, and a Yale classmate of mine named Garrard Glenn. Here are some pictures of them:

FRANK

GARRARD

Well, I'm not all that much of a drawer.

---

*EDITOR'S NOTE: However, see sidebar in chapter 14, "Patient X: Thespian," where Kaufman guilted his friends into giving him roles in films.

Secondly, I had more to concentrate on than in *The Girl Who Returned*. I had realized films with large crowd scenes could be a lot more impressive, so we had a lot of extras (whom we today call "actor persons"). That meant crowd control. I had more locations and more indoor scenes, which meant more lighting and more time setting up. The addition of sound—a whole other sense!—was enormous. Finally, I had to concentrate on acting in addition to directing. Directors and actors often have an adversarial relationship, and as a performer I was very difficult to deal with. Not a day went by where I didn't want to punch myself in the face. Smug bastard.

The film costarred Lynn Lowry, the exquisite ingenue who would later star in Cronenberg's *They Came from Within* and Romero's *The Crazies* (and many of my self-pleasuring fantasies).

One of the great movie myths is that when actors are involved in a heavily sexual situation they are, in no way, "turned-on." I often read articles with big movie stars, occasionally married, who claim that when they are doing a bedroom scene "they are just doing a job." They'll spout off sentences like, "Yeah, me and [insert name of utterly ravishing movie babe or hunk here] had to take off our clothes and rub up against each other and shove our tongues in each other's mouths. But, you know, we just giggled about it. We just felt so SILLY. People think that it's sexy, but the average person on the street doesn't know what it's like, with all the crew and the lights and everything."

BULLSHIT!

I've choreographed my fair share of sex scenes. The actors have one of two reactions: either an impossible-to-escape lust or, in the case of performers who have grown to hate each other, utter disgust. It's funny that these same actors who claim to feel nothing sexually talk about some climactic, melodramatic scene in a totally different manner: "You know, I was so into the character, that when I said those lines, I felt it, man, like to my inner bone. And I don't know where it came from, but I started to sob, sob profusely, and then I looked up and I saw that the director was sobbing, and I looked over at my costar, and he was sobbing. The entire crew was sobbing. And there was a dog in the scene, and I looked over at the dog, and the dog was sobbing."

What's the point, Lloyd?

The point of all this is to give me another chance to talk about sex. But ANOTHER POINT is that IT IS IMPOSSIBLE TO ESCAPE

On the set of *Battle of Love's Return*, Kaufman performs his now famous "pull my finger" routine, provoking paroxysms of laughter from the crew. *Battle of Love's Return* cameo actor Oliver Stone stole this routine for use in his own stinker, *Heaven and Earth*.

YOUR EMOTIONS ON SET. Making a film, as an actor, director, camera person, or even art designer, means you must invest your emotions in it for it to be successful. Yet you need to simultaneously control your actions. And, as Hitchcock supposedly fell in love with his leading ladies, I fell in love with Lynn Lowry.

Hard.

But, because I was so dedicated to the film, I didn't want to do anything to jeopardize it, so I said, "Listen, Melvin"—for some reason I was calling myself Melvin at the time; I think it was sort of a put-down considering the whole director/actor rivalry thing that was going on—"Listen, Melvin. The things you're feeling are fine. But put them into the movie instead of into your life. Put your love for Lynn Lowry into the way you film her. But don't get tangled up with her. If you do, your loyalties are going to be in question and you won't be able to act objectively."

So I waited until after the movie was finished before I put the moves on her. It was at a dinner party celebrating Tricia Nixon's en-

An ecstatic Lynn Lowry expresses her tremendous admiration for Kaufman's directorial style, as Kaufman subtly incorporates the use of cue cards into their conversation.

gagement, of all things. I yawned and put my arm around her. Being the master of interpreting subtle body language that I am, I knew by how the left side of Lynn's lip curled up and a bit of vomit dribbled down her chin that she probably wasn't interested.

On *The Battle of Love's Return* I also set my mother's country home on fire.

There was a war scene in *Battle*. Frank Vitale and I decided to film it in the place where I spent much of the Vietnam War: my mother's meadow. We did everything we could do to make the setting look natural. We set smoke bombs off in the grass. We took the red things out of the gun muzzles. We raped the locals (or at least yawned and put our arms around them).

The camera was rolling. I crawled on my belly through the long grass. Smoke billowed behind me. I tried to find the right expression: a cross between bloodlust and terror. "Your face looks stupid!" the director told me. "Shut up, shadow of a man!" I screamed back.

I noticed my ass was getting hot. I turned.

Mammoth flames were blazing behind me. The smoke bombs had ignited the grass.

I screamed like a little girl.

"Shit," Vitale said.

The crew grabbed anything we could to beat out the flames. Sound blankets. Tripods. I tried to grab Allan Moyle,* the first A.D., but he wasn't too hip on that, so I used my plastic rifle, which melted, and my army helmet after that, which also melted. We threw dirt on the fire, most of which flew back into our faces. The flames grew. They spread quickly across the lawn. My mother was having breakfast in bed. The maid drew the curtains open on her picture window just as the fire consumed her ping-pong table. Luckily, the flames weren't traveling in the direction of her home. They were heading for the neighbors'. Mr. McKendrick's white moon-face was staring at us aghast from his window.

Eventually, we called the fire department. They took care of it in a couple of minutes. Shortly thereafter, Mr. McKendrick developed "pains in his chest," which he claimed were brought on by a fear of being burnt alive. The funny thing was, when he discovered my old man was a high-powered attorney, the pains instantly vanished.

My mother was not pleased. She gave me Hell in front of all the other guys. I showed off to my friends by kicking the living shit out of her right there on the spot.

ADDITIONAL THINGS I LEARNED ON THE SET OF
THE BATTLE OF LOVE'S RETURN

· That my two acting techniques are the expressionistic style of Buster Keaton and Charlie Chaplin and the supra-expressionistic style of the Tasmanian Devil, Daffy Duck, Larry, and Curly.

· When you aren't paying actors, make sure you can trust them. In *Battle*, both my father and good friend Oliver Stone† were in primary roles. Use relatives and friends as much as possible. Otherwise an actor "Standing by" will become an actor "Walking home and eating a bologna sandwich."

· Use relatives' homes as well: because we shot at the home of my wonderful

---

*Who later went on to direct *Pump Up the Volume* (1990) and *Empire Records* (1995).

†For more info on Stone, see chapter 4.

Battle of Love's Return was a tour de force for Kaufman—not only did he distinguish himself with his lousy writer/director/producer skills, but also proved himself a lousy actor. In this scene from the film, Kaufman recreates one of his more successful encounters with the opposite sex.

mum, we didn't have to pay a hefty location fee, and, because she loves me, she never kicked us out.

· There was a fourth point here, but I can't presently remember.

The Battle of Love's Return played in New York at the old Thalia Theater on the Upper West Side. We didn't want to pay for a critics' screening. Howard Thompson of *The New York Times* actually came over to my mother's house to review it. He watched it projected onto a stand-up screen in my bedroom. The *New York* magazine critic Judith Crist, like most women, refused to come to my bedroom, so we relented and rented a theater. Crist threw her feet up on the seat in front of her, scowled through the entire film, and didn't glance at me on the way out the door. "That ugly cow!" I thought to myself, knowing with

all my heart that she was going to skewer my movie. But when I read the review Ms. Crist wrote a few days later, comparing me to Woody Allen and Mel Brooks, I realized she was quite beautiful indeed. The most negative review probably came from my father. When asked by a newsman what he liked best about the film, my old man replied, "The part where Lloyd dies."

In promoting the movie, I learned about guerrilla marketing. We made a stencil of the film's logo and spray-painted it all over the city: streets, sidewalks, brick walls, dead bums. Once we were stopped by the NYPD. The officer took the stencil, cracked it over his leg, and threw it in a trash can. Frank Vitale and I simply waited for him to leave, removed the stencil from the trash can, and went on our merry spray-painting way. We also glued our posters all over the city. This pissed off more than a couple Chinese restaurants whose plate glass windows we covered.

Battle of Love's Return today shows occasionally on television. Initially, though, it didn't make much of a profit. At the time we sent out letters to 20,000 colleges in the country announcing the film's availability. We received a total of ONE response, from Leas McCrae Junior College in Banner Elk, North Carolina. The school's primary claim to fame was that it was the second highest college east of the Mississippi. They flew me in. I had a good time, although I was extremely disappointed to find out that by "highest" they were talking about altitude.

Incidentally, did you know that North Carolina has the tenth-largest population of any state in America? I was very surprised to find this out. I thought it was much smaller.

Is That a Crushed Watermelon You Have for a Head, or Are You Just Unhappy to See Me?

(OR, SPECIAL EFFECTS IN RIND-SIGHT)

Throughout the years, Troma has discovered numerous ways to create special effects without creating large budgets. The easiest way to save money on special effects is, of course, to hire a special effects artist with little experience looking to break into the movie business. If he has any talent, and a few of them do, you won't be able to hold on to him for more than two movies before he's off creating blood and dismemberment for a Cronenberg, Spielberg, or Carpenter.

Special effects have been an important part of the evolution of Troma. By adding gore and toxic magic to sex comedies we created our own universe. Some have described these effects as chintzy, flimsy, tacky, or some other adjective ending in "y." But by letting the audience see the seams on our makeshift latex-and-syrup, we are, in fact, allowing them to become a part of the imaginative process it takes in creating the film. I have long said that Troma movies were one of the first interactive mediums. Our intention is not to dazzle, but to create a true spiritual connection between the audience and the film. As the *New York Times* film critic Stephen Holden has said, "You can't be a stupid person and enjoy Troma movies. It's only intelligent people that 'get' Troma films." That is why our special effects are "differently abled" than those of Hollywood Studios—we have faith in the imagination and humanity of our audience.

Well, okay, that's mostly bullshit.

But I *do* think that Troma movies have done well, even amazingly well, in the area of special effects, considering our limited resources. At times, we have even come close to realism. And I also think that it is true that there's something refreshing about our grassroots style of sex and violence. It's nice to go see a movie that doesn't pretend it's any better than you.

That said, I have concocted this list in case you're considering starting a low-budget movie studio of your own. This is the first of five sections that will pertain directly to the process of making movies. Many of the situations in these chapters refer to *Tromeo & Juliet*. The reasons for this are twofold: 1) Because of today's technology, this more current information will be more helpful to the young filmmaker, and 2) I just got finished with *Tromeo*, so I don't have to slam my vodka-pickled memory against the reef trying to remember what happened, like I do on most of this book.

8 SUPER-DUPER TIPS ON CREATING AND DEALING WITH SPECIAL EFFECTS

1. EVERYDAY EATS MAKE GOOD GORE FODDER*

Let's start with the most important special effect first: head crushing. No classic Troma film is complete without a head crushing or two. You may think we here at Troma love smashing skulls because, well, it looks cool and we enjoy seeing people's brains being pummeled like rotten grapes. But this is far from true. The Troma Team and I abhor seeing the ghastly sight of smashed craniums.

However, it *is* very cheap, and when we choose between thrift and moral fortitude, you can guess which will always win out.

When the child's head was crushed in *The Toxic Avenger* the sight was so realistic that you may think we actually destroyed a real child's head. That *would* be one way of saving money, but you'd probably blow

---

*Not to be confused with good gore Muddah in Charles Kaufman's *Mother's Day*.

the excess cash on cigarettes as presents for your "bitch" during your prison term. I assure you, any squashing of children's heads on Troma sets was done distinctly *off-camera*. What few people know is that anyone can squash a head without actually killing someone. All you need are one of two food items you can get at any local supermarket.

Cantaloupe. In *The Toxic Avenger*, the child's head was nothing more than a simple cantaloupe. There was no face mold or latex skin. We merely rigged a child's body and put a cantaloupe loaded with cranberry sauce at the top of it. When the tire crosses over it, it created a splatterific sight. As with all special effects, editing is an important part of the magic—you can't let the camera linger for too long lest the audience sees it is not a squashed head but common produce. (In a later skit on *Troma's Edge TV*, our short-lived cable television channel, we parodied this situation. Two Tromettes get into a catfight. One of them throws the other to the ground, and swings an aluminum baseball bat above her head. We cut from a high-angle shot of the first Tromette on the ground screaming in terror, to a low-angle shot of the second Tromette ready to swing the bat, to a shot of an enormous watermelon on the ground, painted Caucasian color with a huge, screaming oval for a mouth, two black dots for eyes, and a bad wig. Then the bat comes down upon the watermelon, smashing it apart. The effect is surprisingly violent, which teaches something about the power of editing, as well as the innate human fear of head injuries.)

Ground Beef. In *Tromeo & Juliet*, we decided to add a head-crushing at the last minute—we wanted the heroic, pedophilic priest to use his special blend of papal martial arts to step on and squash the skull of the goon, Vic. Because it was added to the script so late, the special effects artist, Louie Zakarian, wasn't prepared. The job was left to our harried prop artist, Samara Smith.

"But, Lloyd, I don't know how to make a fake head!" she said.

"Well, learn, dammit! All you need is some ground hamburger meat," I told her. Louie Zakarian, standing close by, shook his head in disdain.

"You can't do that. It's against everything I stand for," he muttered.

"Then make a new fake head!"

"I don't have the time, Lloyd. I have to finish *Sammy's* fake head by Tuesday."

"Fake heads!" I cried. "Everybody's making such a big deal about fake heads! All you need is a tan balloon with a smiley face on it! It's the magic of cinema! These days everyone has to go around molding heads, applying real hair to the eyebrows. When I was a kid, we couldn't afford all that stuff."

Andrew Weiner, the Associate Producer, was standing by.

"When I was a kid, we were so poor we couldn't even afford *real* heads," he said. "We had to put big blocks of cheese on our shoulders. We couldn't see a damn thing. We'd be walking into walls. We also had to walk to school through the snow in our bare feet. These kids, they don't understand anything, do they, Lloyd?"

"That's hilarious, Andrew," I said. "You're fired.* Samara, just get the hamburger meat, some Kayro syrup, and red food dye, and everything will be all right."

"It's not gonna work," Louie said. "You got to have a brain, a cerebellum, an abscess behind the nose—"

But it did work, just fine. Samara took a head mold that had been discarded from Louie's workshop because it was covered with unintentional bubbles (it was a mold of the actor Patrick Connor's head, as opposed to that of John Fiske, the actor who was about to be killed— but what the Hell, nobody would notice that). Samara filled it up with a mix of ground beef, Kayro syrup, and red food coloring. We put the head on the floor, atop a pillow wearing the clothes John Fiske had been wearing in the first part of the scene (we made him wear a red bandana around his neck, to hide the split). We filmed the priest's foot squashing the head from two angles. The meat and goo spilled out from under the sides.

Due to the cutting from one angle to the other in editing, people actually make a noise of discomfort when they watch this in the theater. No one has ever come up to me and said that they noticed it was Patrick Connor's head and not John Fiske's. The shots are never held long enough that you can see that the sleeves of the jacket are flat, without flesh. And it took even the editor Frank Reynolds months on the job before he noticed that the body doesn't have any hands.

---

*Weiner actually went on to finish *T & J*, but shortly thereafter went to work for Orion Pictures, where, coincidentally, cantaloupes run the company.

Troma may let you down when it comes to many things, but never, ever, will we fuck you over when it comes to a crushed skull.

2. RECYCLE FAKE LIMBS AND RUBBER CREATURES

The Troma basement is a testament to the fact that we *never throw away anything.* We have stacks of signs, monsters, and limbs used in Troma movies.

There was a fake leg made for *Class of Nuke 'Em High Part III: The Good, the Bad, and the Subhumanoid.* The leg is pretty simple: It has a shoe, a blue pant leg, and a bloody stump with some white bone protruding. Since its original appearance, that dismembered limb has appeared in two additional films and four episodes of *The Tromaville Café.* By reusing this fake leg, it is estimated we have saved over 400,000 dollars (well, okay, maybe that's pushing it). Sure, sometimes it's ripped off the body of someone wearing *brown* pants, but what kind of detail freak notices a little thing like that?

Likewise, the great larva creature created by Pericles Lewnes for *Sgt. Kabukiman NYPD.* As the Evil One begins to mutate at the end of the film, he goes through the stage of being a large, expanding and contracting larva. The creature is green. Later, in the script for *Tromeo & Juliet,* a meat factory worker was supposed to bring a "dead, deformed, dog-looking thing" to the head of the factory, London Arbuckle, and say that he found it dead in the basement. To that, London says, "Looks mighty tasty! We'll make hot dogs out of it. Why don't you throw it in with the pig snouts, tails, and ears?" This, coscreenwriter James Gunn and I thought, was a fairly funny joke. But was it funny enough to spend money on creating a "dead, deformed, dog-looking thing"? The answer was, sadly, no. However, we were able to salvage the joke by simply *painting the green larva red.* Unlike the Patrick Connor–John Fiske head situation, a few people actually *have* noticed this subtle sign of continuity between pictures. Since then, the larva has appeared in numerous TV shows, interviews, and congressional subcommittees.

A few other things which, if you look closely, you will see popping up in numerous Troma movies and television shows:

1 The burnt female corpse from *Troma's War* (currently on raggedy display in the Troma U.K. offices).

2 The monster in *Def by Temptation* (previously the Evil One in *Sgt. Kabukiman NYPD*).

3 Sean Gunn's mutilated hand from *Tromeo & Juliet* (used in 52 different Troma movies; well, all right . . . 51).

3. TO THE UNTRAINED EYE, ULTRASLIME IS ALL FOUR HUMOURS

Although this book is not in the business of promoting products, there is on the market one marvelous substance that would be impossible not to mention. That product is *Ultraslime*. Ultraslime is a clear, odorless substance that comes in a large jar. It at first seems the consistency of the Slime you would buy as a kid (or Gak for the Nickelodeon generation), until you realize it has one remarkable attribute all its own: It sticks to fucking everything, like Dr. Seuss' Oobleck.

I tell you, when making a violent film, you cannot have enough. You can use it in its clear form as a sort of slimy drool dripping from the reusable larva's fangs. You can also use it clear to cover the body of any latex creature you have molded. This instantly changes the creature from looking lifeless and rubbery to being slimy and very much alive. Or you can dye the Ultraslime green and use it as radioactive waste dripping from the Toxic Avenger's mop. Or, if you mix a dollop of Ultraslime with brown, green, or yellow, and rub it between your fingers so that the resins give it a harder consistency, it makes a great booger.

But Ultraslime works best when you color it red and apply it to limbs being dismembered. To tear off an arm in a ground-shakingly real manner:

1 Dye a cup of Ultraslime red.

2 Stuff one of your arms down the side of your shirt, pretending to have one arm.

3 Apply gobs of red Ultraslime to the stump end of a fake arm.

4 Stick the arm against your shoulder.

5 Tear that sucker off!

6 Pretend to scream in agony.

As you'll see, long strings of goop will stay attached to your shoulder as the arm is yanked away. Are the strings of goop supposed to be veins? Tendons? Muscle? Who knows, but it all looks horrifyingly gory.* You can use Ultraslime in all sorts of nasty ways: to tear open a person's chest, rip off ears, fingers, legs, asses, pull back the scalp from the skull, etc. Since few people have actually seen these things happen in reality, they will assume that there is some sort of substance inside of all of us that is incredibly sticky.

One word of warning: Because Ultraslime *is* so sticky, you must use extreme care while handling it. It does not come off easily. If you carry around a creature with the stuff on it, it will attach a long string of slime to everything it touches. You must always carry scissors with you to cut the snot-like strings of slime, lest you find you and your surroundings permanently engaged. Ever see the end of the original *The Fly*? The "Help me, help me!" part? That will give you an idea of one horrific possibility.

4. NO MATTER HOW STUPID IT LOOKS, PRETEND IT'S REAL

There are moments when the special effects don't come out exactly as we planned, but we have to live with them anyway. At this point, it is up to the actors to save the day.

In *Class of Nuke 'Em High*, the monster at the end of the film looks sort of like a child's art project made from old trash. It is, however, supposed to be a horrifying demon attacking our young heroes, played by Janelle Brady and Gilbert Brenton. Thankfully, Janelle and Gilbert did not roll their eyes and say, "What the Hell, I'm supposed to be afraid of this big wad of gunk?" If they did this instead of gaping in wide-eyed terror, the critics and audiences probably wouldn't have called this movie, "Delightfully cheesy" or "An A-1 slice of camp!" It's the seriousness that makes it funny.

---

*If you can't afford the three bucks for the Ultraslime, use pieces of string soaked in spaghetti sauce and attach to the stump. We used to do this before Ultraslime came onto the scene.

"Friends, Tromans, Countrymen, Lend me your ears . . ." This special effect from *Tromeo & Juliet* looks impressive, until you realize that, due to a minor error on the part of the special effects team, this actor's actual ear was torn off. On the bright side, it provided Kaufman with another take of the scene, which was eventually cut from the movie.

You can also distract the viewer from poor special effects by cutting to the reactions of an unruly and overacting crowd: See the crowd being disgusted at Melvin's less-than-inspired original contact with toxic waste in *The Toxic Avenger*, or the crowd watching the bugs skittering from the Devil's stomach in *Toxic Avenger III*. Even better: The unrestrained glee with which Will Keenan approaches the popcorn pouring from Jane Jensen's pregnant belly in *Tromeo & Juliet*, as well as the true panic and agony Sean Gunn unleashes as he attempts to stuff his brains back in his head in the same film.

Best of all is Valentine Miele in *Tromeo & Juliet*. Val plays Murray Martini, who gets a club imbedded in the side of his head, then dies in the arms of Tromeo. The evil Tyrone Capulet has been carrying the club around throughout the film—it has the face of Hitler on one side and a huge spike on the other. Roshelle Berliner, the production designer, created the original club, which could swing into the fake replica of Val's head. It was up to the special effects artist Louie to make a second club, which would be jutting from the side of Val's head while he was on his deathbed.

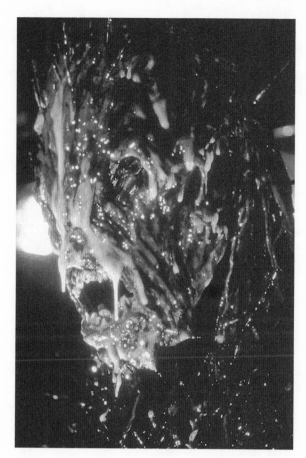

To make up for the low pay on the set of *Class of Nuke 'Em High*, all male members in the crew were treated to free oral sex during down time, courtesy of this Tromatic monster.

When Val entered the set in his makeup, I was furious. The "club" in the side of his head was more like a stub—it was at least eight inches shorter than the real club. Even worse, it wasn't made of a stiff material—it seemed to be composed of foam rubber, so that it wobbled around every time Val moved. I was pissed that it looked so ludicrous, but had no other choice. We *had* to film it. We had already been on the set—an actual body-piercing parlor—long past the time we had promised the owners we'd go.

In the end it was Val who redeemed the whole thing. It was as if he was actually dying. He wept as he said good-bye to his friends and he actually sobbed through the stupid joke we had him say as well. His performance was so powerful that the actors with him, Will Keenan and Stevie Blackehart, were also crying. After we had finished shooting, I turned and saw tears streaming down James Gunn's face. I turned again and saw that the DP, Brendan Flynt, was also weeping. In a way, this made me even angrier—here we have this kid turning in this powerhouse performance, and it has to be decimated by this stupid rubber club.

Little did I know that the reviews would find something exciting in even this:

The scene of Murray Martini dying in the arms of Tromeo and Benny Que (Stephen Blackehart) is deep, raw, and affecting. The magic of the scene and Valentine Miele's performance doesn't come despite the bizarre club sticking out of the side of his head, but because of it. In the contrast of cheesy effect to the heavy drama, we as an audience see a combination unique to the screen. The effect is eerie, disturbingly humorous, and absolute genius.*

Go figure.

5. A PUPPET CAN MAKE YOU FAMOUS

Puppets can be much maligned. Like the wonderful mimes, many people don't like them. They say the same things: "Punch and Judy suck." "Fuck the Muppets." "You can cornhole Howdy Doody for all I care." I, however, am not among their number. I am not an anti-puppet guy. I loved *Mr. Rogers'* King Friday. I was attracted to His Queen, Sarah Saturday, as well—was attracted to the idea of fucking her and getting a hand job from a greasy puppeteer at the same time. I will spend the rest of my life trying to spread the good word of puppetry.

See, a puppet has helped to make me famous.

The scene in *Tromeo & Juliet* called for a penis monster. It was a dream sequence, where Juliet is wading in a child's pool in an other-worldly room. A character credited as Fabio Lookalike approaches her. They begin to kiss, tenderly. Slowly, Juliet reaches down his pants . . . something begins to stir . . . suddenly, from between the Fabio Look-alike's legs comes a huge creature . . . it springs up out of his pants, speeding toward Juliet, its enormous jaws ready to . . .

"It's got to be really big," I said to Louie, thinking back to the towering erection we created in *Class of Nuke 'Em High*.

"Sure, we can do that," he said.

"Is there some way—mechanically perhaps—that it can shoot out of the guy's drawers, nine or ten feet?" James Gunn said. "Going toward Juliet's face, as if . . . as if . . ."

---

*© 1997 *FilmTopics*, from "The Art of *Tromeo & Juliet*," by Mark Cummings.

Jane Jensen (r.) and Joseph Anthony (l.) were not surprised later to find that the three-foot penis monster, Harry Bahls (c.), was made from a cast of Kaufman's member.

"As if she's going to give it a blowjob?" Louie said.

"No! As if it's going to crush her fucking skull!" James said.

"Calm down, dude."

"It needs to be really big," I said. "The audience needs to *care*. It needs to be big."

So, you can imagine our surprise when Louie showed up with a rubber sheath that he puts over his arm, up to his elbow.

"What the fuck is that?" James said.

"It's the Penis Monster," Louie said.

"Where's the full-size one?"

"This is it."

"No! It's supposed to be . . . springing. . . . It's supposed to be a . . . huge . . . an animated, mechanical . . . you know, like a pillar . . . that . . . *that* . . . that . . ."

"That's a puppet," I said sadly. "A Penis Kermit."

Louie covered the creature in Ultraslime and shoved his arm up the leg of the Fabio Lookalike Joseph Anthony's shorts. The Penis Monster emerged from the waistband as if it was an exceedingly large, though far from springing and mechanical, member. As Louie made the creature move and talk, his elbow rubbed against Joe's crotch. I don't think the combination of Ultraslime and Joe's pubic hair was exactly what the actor would describe as "sexy."

When we were finished, I had few hopes for the pitiful scene.

But then came the first market screening. The crowd saw the Penis Monster appear and went crazy. The same thing happened at every festival and theater where it was shown. They loved the little guy. Louie's arm was imbued with magic. People were calling it "Cute," "Charming," "Brilliant," "Dashingly handsome." There wasn't a review or article on the movie that didn't mention him. We began to get requests for interviews and appearances. HBO wanted *me* to appear on their "It's a Very Troma Christmas" TV special, as long as I brought the Penis Monster along. I reminded myself: Basically, *E.T.* was a puppet. I can see it now: Sequel after sequel of Penis Monster films. I see action figures! Bedsheets! Jammies!

So don't knock puppets.

6. OTHER USES FOR SHIT CLOTH

If you are at your home as you read this, here's a hilarious trick to play upon your wife, husband, girlfriend, boyfriend, or parents. All you need is toilet paper, some red food dye, and a loaded .44 revolver.

1 Close the door to a room that no one will enter for a while. You'll need a few minutes.

2 Write a suicide letter. Make it something that blames your "suicide" upon whoever is present in the home with you. "Dear Mom and Dad: I would have never done this if you had given me the love and concern you had given Peter. Mom, I'll always remember that time you forgot my birthday. Dad, guess you should have come to more of my Little League games. It's obvious that I'm 'second best' in your book. Good-bye. I'm sure you won't miss me much." Got it?

3 Mix the red food coloring with water. Or better yet, with Kayro syrup if you have any handy.

4 Tear off tiny swathes of toilet paper and soak them in the colored liquid.

5 Stick the soaked toilet paper to the back of your head as if it's gore spilling from your skull. Throw some swatches onto the wall behind you as if some bits and pieces of your brain have been blasted there.

6 Fill your mouth with the remaining liquid, and let it run down your face.

7 Fire the .44 (uh . . . no, *not* into you—into the ceiling or wall).

8 Lie on the floor as if you're dead and wait for the fun to begin!

You may think this toilet paper thing is too cheap and good to be true, but we use it in almost every Troma movie when we're in a pinch. You can create bullet holes, bloody gashes, flesh splattered onto furniture, all with this simple recipe.

7. NEVER TRUST A PYRO

Pyrotechnics are the guys who create fires and blow things up in movies. Obviously, they're all a little fucked up. They elected to create fires and blow things up for a living. Therefore, you should never trust one. Herewith:

On *Tromeo & Juliet* there was a sequence at the end of the film where Tromeo and his one love commit suicide.* Tromeo sticks a rifle in his mouth and pulls the trigger. It was the last minute idea of the stunt coordinator, Marcos Miranda; the pyrotechnic, Neil Ruddy; and Will Keenan, the actor who played Tromeo, that they would apply a small squib†—that is, a minor explosive with a blood packet—to the back of Tromeo's head. This would blow up and splatter the wall.

"No way," I said. Here was a pyrotechnic, Neil Ruddy, with very little experience who wanted to risk Will's skull. A minor debate occurred—mostly from Will—but in the end I prevailed. There was no way I was going to risk Will's health in even the slightest. Perhaps if

---

*This scene was cut from the final film, though it's available as an added bonus on the unrated consumer tape.
†See chapter 11—on *Troma's War*—for thousands of them.

it was one of the earlier, less talented Troma actors—but not Will, no way. Instead, Louie Zakarian rigged up a squirt-tube and crouched behind Will. We shot Will dead-on from the front: he jammed the gun in his mouth. He pulled the trigger. Louie squirted the blood onto the wall behind him. The effect ends up eerily real. After that shot, we stuck bloodied toilet paper to the wall.

The following day, we needed to shoot part of the film's finale, where Juliet's evil father Cappy gets locked in the "Time Out Box"—a large Plexiglas box where he had formerly put his daughter when she had been "naughty." Because of an unfortunate set of earlier plot occurrences, Cappy also has a smashed computer monitor on his head. He looks out of the smashed glass. A long electric cord dangles from the back of the monitor. In the story, Juliet grabs the plug and stuffs it into a socket. As anyone who has studied Troma electronics knows, this will cause the head inside the monitor to explode.

And that's all that was supposed to happen. The face was supposed to explode and splatter onto the glass box. We put a fake head inside the monitor. Inside the latex face Neil Ruddy set up a few minor explosives—four to be exact.

It was the DP, Brendan Flynt, who thought four bombs were too much. He repeatedly told Neil that he thought so. "You only need one," he said. Louie Zakarian also questioned this action. But no one listened to them.

Luckily, we had cleared the studio warehouse where we were filming. The ceiling was about a hundred feet up. A thick black material called Duvotene surrounded the glass box. It was draped like nebulous walls around it.

"But just the face is supposed to explode," I said. "Why do we need to clear the room?"

"Just in case," said the stunt coordinator.

We set three cameras running, then darted away from them. I crouched behind a plastic shield with Neil and Marcos. Everyone else ran out behind a steel door.

Neil set the charge. It did the trick. The face exploded.

As did the whole head. And the computer monitor around it. And the fake body beneath it. And the glass box itself, which went flying into thousands of shards. The fluorescent bulbs hanging from the ceiling were destroyed, as was the Duvotene. And about half the warehouse. It caused several thousand dollars worth of damage.

All I could do was remember the day before, when the same pyrotechnic wanted to rig up Tromeo's skull with similar explosives. Thank God the damage wasn't done to Will's head, I thought.

After all, we still had more scenes with him to shoot.

8. WHEN IN DOUBT, VOMIT GREEN FOAM

See chapter 1.

Lloyd Kaufman   Barry Neville
Michael Herz   Oliver Stone
starring in

Are You There, God?*
It's Me, Lloyd.

four

THE RENAISSANCE DINER. FEBRUARY 1997.

I've been eating here a lot lately. It's close, two blocks north of the Troma Building. The food's delicious. And best of all (considering I might end up footing the bill), it's cheap.

Barry and I are in a booth in the corner, below the wall TV. I glance up at the well-worn tube occasionally, checking out the bodies of the soap opera starlets when they're in wide-shot.

Barry has the first three chapters on the table in front of him.

My first book.

So I'm a bit nervous. Then again, I'm *often* nervous. Almost everyone I know in the film industry is nervous. It's this anxiety that propels all of us. If it wasn't there, would I have worked so hard and so obsessively for John Avildsen in the early days? And, were it not for my innate and organic wired-ness, would I have wrapped myself in the demented cocoon of my own making, the Troma Universe? Probably not. My greatest bane is also my salvation.

And now here's Barry, a nice young man with an attractive profes-

---

*Because if you are, and you read this chapter, then you know you can go screw yourself.

sorial sport jacket and tie, a pair of specs, and 61 pages of my life in his well-manicured paws. I shift in my seat uncomfortably. This vulnerability I'm feeling is one of the most difficult aspects of choosing a life in the creative professions. Most people living in the actual universe don't understand it. If you put your all into something—a movie, book, painting, piss-animal drawn in the snow, whatever—it's as if your guts are on display in a glass case for everyone to see, and often to judge—especially in our fucked-up, all-or-nothing, thumbs-up/thumbs-down culture. Everything can be reduced to good or bad or number of stars, one through four. We artists and entertainers work our entire lives to have our work viewed by others. But the truth is, when people finally see it, it's somewhat humiliating.

In short, I hope that the worst Barry has found in the first three chapters is that I have a tendency to confuse "it's" and "its." I don't want to write the whole thing again. Even worse, I don't want Putnam to fire me. If so, Troma will have to give back the advance; Michael Herz and Pat would murder me.

Barry and I look at each other. We bob our heads. We smile. I'm trying to keep this stupid smile on my face, but it's difficult. The smile's like a caterpillar with a life of its own. It wants to do its own thing. I feel as if I may sob.

"So, um, what do you think of the chapters?" I utter.

"They're great!" Barry says. But he has the same sorry smile on his face, forcing it into place.

"You didn't like it, did you?"

"Well, I didn't NOT like it. I liked some of it, Lloyd."

"Which parts?"

"Um, I liked where you save Tromeo's life. That's good."

"The section about *Joe* is bad, I know that. I just couldn't seem to get into it like I got into the rest of them."

"You got into the rest of them?"

"Yeah. Doesn't it seem like—?"

"Oh, yes. Definitely."

Our waitress, Dominique, leans against the side of our table. All the waitresses here wear the same basic outfit (white shirt, black skirt), but Dominique wears her skirt a bit shorter than the others. Which I like. I suggest the broccoli soup to Barry (it's only two bucks). He gets an omelet instead ($5.35). I order two poached eggs, very well done. I repeat this—poached eggs, well done, but in New York waitresses don't listen. So I follow it up with "I don't like mucus on my eggs." That gets Dominique's attention.

"Lloyd," Barry says.

"Yes?"

"The part about the hookers in Chad."

"Mm-hm."

"I mean, you know, we were sort of hiring you to write a How-To book on *filmmaking*."

"All filmmakers have sex with prostitutes."

"They do?"

"Yes."

"Really?"

"It's rampant."

"Oh."

"Was that part less well-written?"

"*Less* well-written? No, not especially."

"Because my wife Pat proofread the chapters. But I temporarily took those pages out. That and the thing about masturbating to Lynn Lowry."

"Oh. Well, you know, Lloyd, there's another part that seems a little strange. Sometimes you seem to blur—now, correct me if I'm wrong—the line between fiction and nonfiction a little bit."

"I do?"

"The sex scene with you and Whitney Houston."

"That's something I just sort of threw in there. By the seat of my underpants, so to speak." I smile meekly, hoping to encourage Barry to at least smile at my *jeu de mots*.

"A twenty-seven-page pornographic interlude between you and Whitney?"

"You think I should take it out."

"Maybe."

"Done. I'll submit it to *The New Yorker* as a short story. Anything else?"

Dominique sets our plates down in front of us.

"I guess I'd just like to talk about what's going to be in the next chapter," Barry says.

"Well, I've written most of it, and it's going pretty well so far."

"Great. What are you focusing on?"

"Well, I find a magic sword, and become blessed with warrior might, and I have to slay a dragon and two ogres, and then there's a time machine and some robots. It's all stuff that happened after *Cry Uncle*, before *Squeeze Play*."

Barry stares at me for a moment.

"I'm kidding," I say. "I haven't really started it yet."

"Oh."

"What were your ideas?" I take a bite of the egg. The yolk is so well done it's like talcum powder and I choke.

"Well, I think you've been spending a bit too much time on the early years. People are going to see 'Troma' on the cover, and they're going to want to hear about starting the world's oldest independent film company. And we haven't even gotten there yet."

MARVEL COMICS

The Cinematheque Français stated, "Troma put a new spin on the movie superhero of the eighties in the same way Marvel Comics put a spin on the comic book hero of the sixties." This is no surprise, considering the influence of the Marvel Universe on Kaufman.

"I first got turned on to Marvel Comics in the sixties at Yale," Kaufman says. "The same guys who turned me on to movies were also Marvel fanatics. The Hulk, Thor, Spider-Man, the Avengers."

The Marvel Universe officially began in 1961 with *Fantastic Four #1*, written by Stan Lee. This Universe was thrown into high gear by *Amazing Fantasy #15* in 1964, which included the origin of Spider-Man, also by Lee. The alter egos of DC comics' Batman and Superman were all too perfect and had little humanizing qualities with which readers could identify; Peter Parker, on the other hand, was an average ordinary high school student who had to deal with life's everyday travails.

"It was the commonplace in Marvel Comics that made them so special," Kaufman adds. "Like how Spider-Man would have to quickly defeat Doctor Octopus so he could get home in time to give his Aunt May her ear medicine. I was also turned on by how all the characters in the different Marvel books interacted and affected each other's lives. That sense of a real universe which could envelop young readers was a powerful influence on Tromaville."

After graduating from college, Kaufman struck up a friendship with his idol Lee. In the early seventies they collaborated on a script, *Night of the Witch*. This was a lesson for Kaufman in what the industry calls "development hell."

"The script was picked up by Cannon for a few bucks," he says. "At that time, of course, I was excited; I thought for sure it would become a movie. I was crushed when they put on another writer to rewrite it. I later put the moves on this writer, and then her lesbian lover called me at four in the morning and threatened to kill me. But that's, I guess, besides the point. . . . *Night of the Witch* ended up sitting around Cannon for months with nothing happening. It was never turned into a film. I learned that just because you sell your script, doesn't mean anything will happen with it. Again, I was propelled through this experience to keep control of my own ideas."

Later on, Stan Lee turned two Troma creations into popular Marvel comic book series: *The Toxic Avenger* and *The Toxic Crusaders*. In the nineties, Kaufman and Lee, now longtime friends, collaborated on another script, *Congress-Man*. The script is currently stuck in development hell within Troma Studios.

"Why do I need the studios to ignore my scripts?" says Kaufman. "When I can do it myself?"

Kaufman's three favorite superheroes: Toxie, Stan Lee, and Spidey.

"Right."

"And a lot of people think of you as part of a two-man team, with Michael Herz. You guys directed fifteen or whatever movies together. You founded the company with him. But you've hardly even mentioned him."

"I was going to talk to you about that," I say.

"What?"

"I was wondering if I could leave Michael out of the book."

"What?"

"He doesn't want to be in it."

"How can you leave him out?"

"I thought maybe I could just sort of work around it."

"Why doesn't he want to be in the book?"

"Michael's a little weird. He doesn't like the spotlight. I mean, back in the early days Michael used to do it, do interviews or whatever needed doing. He would do it, and he was great at it. But he always hated it. Now he won't even talk to reporters. He won't appear in our own little video and TV sketches. He just doesn't like it. He asked me not to talk about him in the book. Me, you know, I rather like interviews."

Barry is slumped over the table. His face is in his hands.

"Lloyd, you *have* to put him in the book. The book's about Troma. He's an intrinsic part of Troma."

"Michael pretty much wants to stay on the business side. He doesn't really enjoy the public part of it. You know what we did one time?"

"No."

"When we started *The Tromaville Café* TV show, we wrote one of the parts for Michael Herz. We planned on Michael playing himself. But Michael refused to do it. Now, Michael takes great pride in his body. He works out every day, and can bench-press over three hundred pounds. So we got a five-hundred-pound actor* to play Michael. Now people all over the world think Michael Herz is a big huge fat person."

Barry has slumped even further onto the table.

"That's very interesting," he says. "But we can't put a big fat person in the book."

"But I could say he's really fat to get back at him for his uncooperativeness."

"I thought you weren't going to include him."

"Well . . . I just don't know how to attack it. Even though we've been in business for twenty-five years, he's still sort of a mystery to me. Holy cow!"

"What?!" Barry, in a panic, swirls to look behind him.

"Check out that girl's body on the TV. I like those muscular arms."

"Oh." The soap opera actress seems to have a soothing effect on Barry. We watch her for a few minutes.

"Listen, Lloyd. I've got an idea."

"Okay. What?"

"The yin and yang thing that you've been doing. Apply that to you and Michael. Michael's sort of the grounded cofounder, and you're more of the visionary. It takes both of you to make Troma what it is."

"A company that hasn't had a single hit in twenty-five years?"

"No, an independent film company that's become a brand name. You're the independent spirit. Michael's the practical businessman. To-

---

*Troma action hero Joe Fleishaker—for more on Joe, see chapter 11.

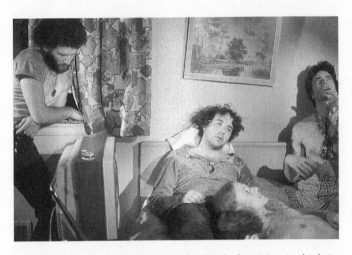

Frank Vitale (l., producer of Troma's *East End Hustle* and *Battle of Love's Return*) and Andy Kay (r., *Battle of Love's Return*) have decided that the hardest part of filming this scene from John G. Avildsen's *Cry Uncle* was between Lloyd Kaufman's (c.) legs and the naked young woman's head.

gether you make 'Movies of the Future,' right? Way ahead of Hollywood."

"Not bad. Except that's not the whole picture."

"Why?"

"Like, for example, I enjoy the business part a lot too. I definitely focus on it. If anything, I'm cheaper than Michael."

"I thought you said in the first chapter you didn't know anything about business."

"I sort of exaggerated to make a point. Also, I don't know if I'm really the 'independent spirit.' I like to think of myself as such, but really Michael's the one with the integrity. If someone fucks us over, Michael will never deal with them again, no matter how much dealing with them will benefit us financially. Me, if it means a few more bucks, I'm willing to sign on the dotted line with the Aryan Nation. And I'm always the one out there in Hollywood, trying to get meetings with the studio heads and bigwigs—degrading myself, basically—in an attempt to get us some bigger deals. For instance, we've been approached to get this big-budget version of *The Toxic Avenger* made. I'm dealing with Cassian Elwes, the William Morris superagent. He's talking to Warner Brothers and Paramount and Universal. I *say* I hate Hollywood, and I do, but still . . . Michael, he hates Hollywood so much he won't even deal with those places. He couldn't care less. So, really, he embodies more of the true independent spirit than I do. He's probably a better film director as well."

"Still, Lloyd, basically Michael is more of the no-nonsense type, and you're . . ."

"Nonsense?"

"Well . . . So, don't you think in Chapter 4 you should talk a little bit about how you guys met?"

"No."

SOME CALL HIM . . . HERZ!

First meeting? I can't quite remember. We shook hands in my doorway at Yale, or something, and that was that. Michael and my younger brother Charles were both counselors at a summer camp a few months before and now he had stopped by to introduce himself.

At Yale, we were both basically loners. We weren't friends with each other, and neither of us had many friends of his own. Michael claims that the only reason he ever talked to me at all was because I was the only one in the dormitory who had a TV—a small black-and-white that went blank every time someone walked past it. He would come over occasionally to watch it.

Also, Michael owned a pinball machine. He put it in the Yale commons area and charged 10 cents a game—an entrepreneur from the very beginning.

Besides that, the only concrete memory I have of him at Yale was humiliating him, er, uh . . . *filming* him in *The Girl Who Returned*. I didn't see him again until after we had graduated.

CUT TO: 1972— A young, attractive woman, Maris, is going for a night out on the town with her mother. They decide to see a movie. After they flip through the *New York Times* they agree upon a film called *Cry Uncle* because it has gotten pretty good reviews, and maybe also because it is rated X (though Maris holds her thumb over this part of the advertisement).

I neglected to say in the last chapter that I had an embarrassing role in *Cry Uncle* as a burnt-out hippie. Here are some of my lines:

- "You're hallucinating, Herbie. This is really strong acid."

- "Stay in the room, Herbie. *Please*."

- "It's the fourth hour, Herbie, the fourth hour. Dig it?"

In fact, those are *all* of my lines. Maris recognized me on-screen, and confirmed this by reading the end credits.

During this period, Maris' boyfriend, Michael Herz, was a law student at NYU. Although Michael loved the law, he was coming to dread the prospect of practicing it. It didn't seem like a fulfilling way to spend his life. Instead, he harbored a secret desire that he shared with only Maris: He wanted to be a screenwriter.* She took him to see *Cry Uncle* (which means Maris actually had to sit through the fucking thing twice). Shortly thereafter I received a call from a young and eager Mr. Herz, and I brought him onto the production of *Sugar Cookies*. It was at this point that I began to ruin Michael's life as well as my own.

VERTIGO, LESBIANS, AND OLIVER STONE

"*Sugar Cookies?*" Barry says.

"Yes. It was a disaster. Oliver Stone worked on that one."

"You said you were going to mention him in the next chapter."

"Yeah, but I don't know how much I want to talk about that either."

"You knew him?"

"He and I were best of friends growing up."

"Really?"

I nod.

"Now that's definitely something people would want to hear about," Barry says.

"We aren't so close anymore."

---

*All of this information, incidentally, comes from Maris. Michael won't talk about any of it to me (he seems to be afraid to say anything around the office recently, lest I include it in this tome), and I have the memory of a . . . what was I saying again? Anyway, I was surprised when Maris reminded me of Michael's screenwriting aspirations, because, outside of those first couple months, I don't remember him having ever brought it up again.

This picture proves the oft-contested contention that Kaufman's parents, Stanley (l.) and Ruth, were the original inspiration for Mickey and Mallory in Oliver Stone's (pictured at right, circa 1955, with camera in hand) *Natural Born Killers*.

"What happened?"

"I had one of those Vietnamese potbellied pigs a few years back. Have you seen those?"

"Yes."

"Well, Oliver and I were hanging out at my folks' town house one weekend, and I accidentally walked in on him while he was in the bathroom, and Oliver was raping my pig."

"*REALLY?!*"

"No. But I've been considering putting that in the book."

"Lloyd, that's exactly the kind of thing you have to stop doing. Now that I think about it, you should probably take out that thing about Meryl Streep in the second chapter too."

"You know, I get a little bored with my own life, so I want to start making stuff up."

"You'll get sued."

"That's okay. Penguin Putnam's rich."

"No, Lloyd. *You'll* get sued. There's a clause in the contract holding you liable."

"Excuse me?"

"Yes."

Long pause.

"Really, Lloyd, I think you should put Oliver in the book. We put something like that on the jacket, that means a lot more sales."

"I don't know. I'd feel like I was abusing my relationship with him."

"More sales means more royalties for you."

"I'll tell you anything you want to know."

"Did he get you into movies?"

"No, I got *him* into movies. We had been friends since we were kids. Our parents were friends, so we were often partitioned off together."

"So the world owes Stone's movie career to you! That's good stuff, Lloyd! What was he like?"

"Um, when we were little he made up this game with baseball cards. Which was just like Oliver, obsessive. It was part of this extremely intricate baseball league, which went into great depth with statistics and rules and everything. He was also very neat and organized. And very domineering, always controlling what was going on around him. By the time he was in seventh grade he carried a pocket notebook everywhere he went, taking down notes—his musings on the world, lists of things to do."

"What else?"

"Athletic. Oh, also, when Michael and I first started Troma, Oliver came to us with a very strange treatment called *La Chateau* that he wanted us to turn into a movie. It seemed to me to be autobiographical, all about a Vietnam vet just like Oliver. And, in the end, the character *ends up fucking his dad!* Though, of course, I don't think Oliver ever fucked his dad."

"Will you stop making stuff up?"

"That one's true!"

"Wow."

"I remember one time in fourth grade when I spent the night at his house on Sixty-fourth Street and he beat the crap out of me. I just left his house right there and walked home in my bathrobe. Oliver's parents were supposedly confused as to where I went, looking all over the house for me. He also used to like to fence me—only he'd take the little rubber tip off the end of his sword, while leaving mine on. Oliver was also very sophisticated—so sophisticated, in fact, that he turned me on to the night life in Paris when we were rather young."

"You might want to leave that out. And so you got him into movies?"

"He never seemed to be beyond a casual movie fan. He kept an eye on the films I was making at Yale, and after he came back from Vietnam and entered NYU he started helping me out. He had a small part in *The Battle of Love's Return* and assisted on the production. And then we made him associate producer on *Sugar Cookies*. From the start, he had a lot of foresight. He insisted we have a celebrity of some sort in the film. He got Monique Van Vooren. She was sort of a name back then. Me, I never saw much need for celebrities or had any attraction to them. To this day I prefer young new slaves . . . er . . . unknown actors. But Oliver saw what things would eventually become, with all the Hollywood pictures today relying completely on opening-week grosses fueled by stars' box-office appeal. He had a really keen business sense. At one point, he tried to get me to form a partnership with him. I was tied up with the producers from *Sugar Cookies* at the time. Oliver told me that the guys were no good, that they would fuck me, and that I should come along with him. But this was the early seventies, with a lot of notions about loyalty and masculinity, and I wasn't about to abandon those guys. In hindsight, he was right. I should have gotten out of that deal before it even started."

Sugar Cookies was a high dive into the teeming waters of Hitchcock's classic *Vertigo*. Unfortunately, no one told us the swimming pool was empty.

The mixed-up lovers were played by two women, Mary Woronov* and Lynn Lowry, instead of a woman and a man, Kim Novak and Jimmy Stewart (Stewart played the man). Theodore Gershuny, Ami Artzi, and I formed a company called Armor Films to produce the movie from my script.

"We're telling you, Kaufman," they said. "A hundred thousand bucks, we'll raise it like it's nothing. It will be like asking a farmer for a bag of dirt. See, Kaufman, we have friends on Wall Street. BIG MONEY PEOPLE. It won't take us more than a few weeks to raise the cash."

Right.

Eventually, we got the 100,000 dollars for the film. Unfortunately, all the investors came from *me* and my friends (Roger Kirby, Oliver, Garrard Glenn, Tom Sturges, among others)—soon to be former friends. The BIG MONEY PEOPLE Ami and Ted told me about were nowhere to be found. I should have known then that everything wasn't

---

Hollywood Boulevard (1976), *Rock 'n' Roll High School* (1979), *Eating Raoul* (1982), *Scenes from the Class Struggle in Beverly Hills* (1989).

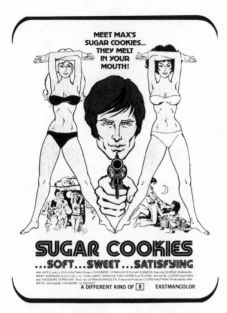

MEET MAX'S
SUGAR COOKIES...
THEY MELT
IN YOUR
MOUTH!

SUGAR COOKIES
...SOFT...SWEET...SATISFYING

AMI ARTZI and LLOYD KAUFMAN Present THEODORE GERSHUNY'S SUGAR COOKIES Starring GEORGE SHANNON, MARY WORONOV and Introducing LYNN LOWRY, MONIQUE VAN VOOREN as HELENE, Written By LLOYD KAUFMAN and THEODORE GERSHUNY, Music By GERSHON KINGSLEY, Executive Producer LLOYD KAUFMAN, Produced by AMI ARTZI, Directed By THEODORE GERSHUNY
A DIFFERENT KIND OF [R]   EASTMANCOLOR

going to finish as planned. But instead, I wanted to believe in Ted and Ami. I liked them. And out of my own desperation, I clung to this relationship, not for one film, but for two.

Like I said, *Sugar Cookies* is about a couple of sapphic love dolls, which, you have to admit, is a pretty good start. The way I saw the film, it was soft-core with a goofy edge. It would contain some melodrama like in Fuller's* *The Naked Kiss*, and a good dose of Russ Meyer wit. Unfortunately,† even though I wrote the movie, and assembled the budget myself, and wanted to direct it, I let "the older, more experienced" Gershuny take control. I regret it to this day, but I was a kid and perhaps not as strong as I should have been. Gershuny at this point invented a new kind of soft-core, called mushy-core, which really didn't have much of a core at all. He rewrote and cast his wife, Mary Woronov. Ted assured me Mary had a fair amount of passion for the women offscreen (they had an unusual marriage). However, on-screen she seemed to have more passion for leaning back and acting like a wooden plank. Lynn played her lesbian lover. She had never done nude scenes before. I convinced her that this was a good move for her career.

Sorry, Lynn.

Sugar Cookies is the ultimate seventies film in the Troma catalog, awash with bell-bottoms, pop art, and Vaseline lenses. There's a contrived artiness to the film, a slow-moving quality that destroys any wit

---

*Samuel Fuller, who also did *Pickup on South Street* (1953) and *Shock Corridor* (1963), is one of my favorite directors. In 1997 I had the privilege of meeting him. Even though Sam had had a stroke and could hardly speak, he still hated commies. He went crazy when I said I liked Castro. He ended the day by offering me his novel *144 Picadilly* to adapt and direct.
†This word's going to come up a lot this chapter.

that was in the original script. To screw ourselves even further, when the movie was released by General Films,* the sleazy poster art was about as sexy as a dog licking its balls.† Needless to say, the film did very little box office, appealing to neither the art-film audience nor the raincoat crowd. But at least I got to see Lynn Lowry naked.

Oh, yeah, and one more interesting thing. When a *Sugar Cookies* investor and I were at the Cannes Film Festival in 1971 with *Sugar Cookies*, we decided to pick up a couple hookers, which we did, and we took them back to our apartment. Without any provocation on our part, the two young women disrobed and indulged in a lesbian sex show right there on the rug. The investor and I eyed each other, reminded of the lesbians in *Sugar Cookies*, the film which at that very moment was underwhelming film buyers at the Ambassades Cinema in Cannes. What a *co-wink-ee-dink*!

After we left Cannes we went back to the States to raise money for another cinematic jewel, *Big Gus, What's the Fuss?*

BIG GUS, WHAT'S THIS PIECE OF SHIT?

"Big Gus, What's the Fuss?" Barry says. "What's that?"

"Christ," I say. "It was the most horrible film I've ever had anything to do with. We made it in Israel."

"Israel?"

"Yes. We had an English version and a Hebrew version, and it was a bilateral flop."

"Is it bad enough to be funny? Like *Croaked: Frog Monster from Hell*?"

"No, it's beyond that. Far, far beyond."

"People might want to hear about that. That could be exciting, how you overcame a catastrophe. What happened?"

"I'm not going to tell you."

---

*This distributor was in equal doses incompetent and dishonest. They played the tame *Sugar Cookies* at the Lyell Theater in Rochester, which had previously been home to *Deep Throat*. Luckily, the raincoat crowd didn't have their hands free to strangle us to death. General Films did teach me that signed contracts are meaningless in the movie industry (also see the New Line/Toxic Crusaders deal, chapter 13). We had to sue them to get our contractually "guaranteed" money.

†And if you think *that's* sexy, you're definitely reading the right book.

* * *

Big Gus, What's the Fuss? was the perfect plan. We couldn't fail. The film was GUARANTEED to make ten times its budget back. Or at least Ami Artzi told me so. Theodore Gershuny had dropped out of Armor at about this point, so it was just Ami and me. And Michael Herz.

During *Sugar Cookies*, Michael just answered phones and ran errands. But when *Big Gus, What's the Fuss?* came up, Michael saw it as his opportunity to become rich. He began raising money.

He believed in the plan too. Ami told him: *Big Gus, What's the Fuss?* couldn't fail. Ami introduced us to Menacham Golan, who was going to be our coproducer. All we had to do was raise the dough, and Menacham and Ami and the State of Israel would do the rest.

"First of all, you make it all in Israel. The Israelis are *dying* to make movies in their country," Ami told us. "And believe you me, when an Israeli film comes out in an Israeli theater, every single person in the country comes to see it, four times. They're loyal. Right there, just in Israeli box-office grosses, what do we have, Lloyd?"

"A lot of money."

"A profit, Lloyd. A PROFIT. Guaranteed. But it doesn't stop there."

"It doesn't?" said Michael, wide-eyed and smiling. Back before this film destroyed the financial futures of his entire family.

"It doesn't, my friend. Because we make *two* versions of the film."

"Two?" Michael and I said in unison.

"One in Hebrew and one in English. We dub some of the English, shoot some on set. Therefore, we are getting two films for the price of one! But really even more films than that, because the Israelis are dying so much to make films in their home country. So what do they do? They give special rates to filmmakers, and they give you some subsidy money back when you are finished, about 25 percent of all your money back, so really we are making two and a half movies for the price of one movie in America!"

"Holy moley!" said Michael.

"And guess, my friends, how much money is to be made in America."

"A lot," I said.

"Even more! Because, first of all, this film will be such a great hit—it will be a G-rated family film, not like *Sugar Cookies* at all—that it will make millions of dollars in theaters across the country. Theaters are *dying* for G-rated films! They can't get enough of them! And let me let you in on another little secret."

"What?" I said.

"Synagogues."

"Synagogues?"

"Synagogues! Guess how many synagogues there are in the country."

"Three hundred," said Michael.

"MORE!"

"How many more?"

"LOTS! And they are dying to show Israeli films in English in their synagogues. Just in American synagogues alone, guess what the box-office receipts will add up to?"

"A . . . profit?" I said.

"A PROFIT! GUARANTEED!"

Big Gus, What's the Fuss? was the biggest failure, monetarily and artistically, of my entire life.

The story concerns a pudgy Israeli running around from place to place in Tel Aviv, and . . . well, that pretty much says it all.

When I arrived in Israel I discovered that our original script, which Andy Lack,* Michael, and I thought was pretty decent, was rewritten in Hebrew by the Israelis and Ami. I received an English translation. I knew in my heart it sucked and that I should close down the production. But actors had been hired and I was told that it was "perfect for the Israeli market." So, again, I backed down. Today I wish I hadn't—it would have been much wiser to have followed my instincts, taken the remaining money, and made a smaller movie or given as much of it as I could back to the investors. I also wimped out when it came to directing. The Israeli coproducers insisted that Ami codirect.

---

*My childhood friend, now the president of NBC News and the creator of the MSNBC Network. I suckered him into raising moolah for *Big Gus* and joining me for the fun in Tel Aviv as associate producer. He advised me to leave *Big Gus* out of this book.

עמי והבלשים

מונה זילברשטיין | **ששי קשת** | **יוסף שילוח** | **בומבה צור**

יוסף שילוח (ימין) ובומבה צור, צמד הבלשים השלומיאליים

An Hebraic ad for *Big Gus, What's the Fuss?*—a film that arguably has done more damage to the Jewish people than *Mein Kampf*.

So now I share director credit with Ami. This is a credit I do not deserve, unless you consider slumping on the floor in the corner of the set with your eyes shut tight while pulling out small, bloody clumps of your hair "directing." On *Big Gus*, everyone hated everyone. The actors and Ami had an unusual working relationship: they refused to speak to each other. Ami would simply not listen to a single one of my ideas, and the crew wouldn't listen to a single one of his. Some days the crew would show up, some days they wouldn't. The actors had enormous egos, despite the fact that each had as much charisma as a dead frog in the sun. And the crew and Ami would *constantly* be screaming at each other in a language I didn't understand. Every day, I longed to be flayed alive. I prayed to be captured by invading Turks and have my toenails pulled out with pliers. That would be heaven compared to the set of *Big Gus*.

When we finally finished the movie, the "breaks" Ami and Menacham had promised us from the Israelis seemed to be hanging out somewhere with the BIG MONEY PEOPLE he and Ted had promised me before *Sugar Cookies*. Michael and I ended up *owing* the lab and just about everybody in the State of Israel a huge amount of cash. We couldn't even get possession of the English-language negative.

War broke out in Israel the day *Big Gus, What's the Fuss?* opened in theaters there. The fates wanted us to be sure we knew our movie was a bomb by actually dropping them.

Michael and I thought we could save ourselves and our friends' bank accounts with Ami's synagogue idea. So we sent letters to every synagogue across the United States, asking them to show our film. *One* synagogue accepted, somewhere in Detroit. After showing the G-rated film they refused to pay the $100 rental fee. They sent us a postcard stating that we, Michael and I—and this is no lie—were a disgrace to Jews.

The bad news should stop there, but it doesn't. All of our friends and relatives (again, Ami had put in nothing) lost almost every cent of their investment. If you ever see Andy Lack over at NBC and notice the empty space at the seat of his pants, that's because he lost his ass during *Big Gus, What's the Fuss?* Uncles, parents, college buddies: no one escaped the blazing fire of this film. There are few harder things than watching people around you lose large amounts of money on something you advised them to do. In the end, Michael and I were burnt worst of all, in finance, reputation, and spirit.

But we walked through it. And I guess that's one of the two biggest lessons out of all of this. The lessons aren't about how to interact with investors or crazy Israeli crews or mushy-core directors. The lessons are **NEVER GIVE UP CONTROL OVER SOMETHING YOU FEEL IN YOUR HEART,** like I did with directing both *Sugar Cookies* and *Big Gus, What's the Fuss?* And **IF YOU REALLY WANT SOME-THING, YOU HAVE TO STEP THROUGH THE FIRE TO GET IT.** Nothing comes easily. But if you are truly committed you will get something very much like the goals you set out to get.

There was a light at the end of the tunnel.

TROMA

For many years, I had admired Roger Corman. With Samuel Arkoff's American International Pictures, Roger had directed and produced hundreds of films. He had given career starts to such filmmakers as Jack Nicholson, Martin Scorsese, John Carpenter, John Sayles, and many more of today's finest. Roger made films on limited budgets with more than a dash of integrity. He was uniquely successful. He created his own industry and inspired armies of young filmmakers.

Michael and I were mimicking Roger when we first started Troma. We had the concept for a small studio that could turn out unique, quality films at a time when theaters actually needed them. Due especially to the proliferation of multiplexes, there were more screens at that time than there were movies being released. It was a lot easier to get into theaters. As a new studio, we would produce and distribute films that had predefined audiences—horror, sex, and science fiction. If you made a romantic comedy, there was a chance that absolutely nobody would see it. But if you made a monster movie or a movie with lots of breasts, there would be some sort of audience no matter what. From this base we would expand, in the tradition of the comics' Marvel Universe, to create an entire world.

We called it Troma.

For years we have been asked about where we got the name. Our stock answer is that Troma is the ancient Latin word for "excellence in celluloid."

The common response to this is "Oh, that's interesting," nodding, and then a double take: "Hey, wait a minute!"

There has been a rumor around for years that Troma is an acronym for "Tits R Our Main Asset." This is definitely not true. We are not that clever.

Just last year I found out that Troma is an actual word, for a metal alloy found in China. We deny any relationship to this Communist resource.

The truth, for the first time anywhere, is as follows:

Michael and I had kicked Ami out of the company, for obvious reasons, so the name Armor, Inc. was no longer an option. We needed a new corporation, and to incorporate in New York State you need to register the corporate name. Registration takes about six weeks to process. Now, since New York is a very old state, there have been literally millions of corporate names. We needed a company name that hadn't yet been registered, and fast. Zeus Pictures?—taken. Madcap Films?—no go. Barry Neville, Inc.?—sorry. I'm-Stuffing-A-Donkey-Up-My-Ass, Inc.?— No, there was an I'm-Stuffing-A-Donkey-Up-My-Ass for two weeks in 1923. Every time we came up with a name, we were struck down by the gods at the registration office, who maintained that every appellation, no matter how ludicrous, had been used.

So Michael suggested we make up a word. But not just any word.

"Let's think of the most ugly sounding word ever uttered by man," he said. The words started to form on his lips. "T-T-Tr . . . Tr . . ."

"T.R. is good," I said.

"Tro . . ."

"Trobo?" I said.

"Too sweet," Michael said. "Trom . . . Let's see . . . Trom . . ."

"Trom?"

"A."

"A? What happened to the T.R.?"

"TROMA!" Michael uttered, grimacing as if he had just laid a giant turd.

"It's not as catchy as I'm-Stuffing-A-Donkey-Up-My-Ass," I said. "But what the hell, it sure sounds horrible."

*   *   *

I look across the table at Barry. He is staring at me, obviously enjoying my story about how the name Troma came about. He leans over the table toward me.

"What are you doing?" I say, trying to get away.

Barry's tongue is coming out of his mouth and he is trying to kiss me.*

---

*EDITOR'S NOTE: Everything's going along fine, Lloyd, and then you have to put something like this in.†

†It's true, Barry, admit it. You tried to shove your tongue down my esophagus.‡

‡EDITOR'S NOTE: IT IS NOT TRUE!

A Chapter with No Sex

(OR, PREPRODUCTION: THE FOREPLAY OF FILMMAKING)

Our ever-smilin' editor Barry has told me that many of the people purchasing this book will be young filmmakers wanting to learn about the industry. Until that moment, I had mistakenly assumed that most people who bought this book would be using it as a masturbation aid—many people say they enjoy masturbating to pictures of me, and I had a planned outline of my sexual escapades with Jacqueline Bisset, Drew Barrymore, Ashley Judd, that girl with the nice breasts on the *Law and Order* TV show, and whoever the lead singer is of the rock band No Doubt. However, a few of these celebrities have somehow heard about my intentions through the grapevine (I suspect Barry) and have sent letters disinclining me to do so. In addition, Penguin Putnam, for some reason, has been afraid of the legal ramifications of knowingly publishing a book full of what they called "flat-out lies." I wouldn't want to say that they're being pussies about the whole thing—but, there it is, it's been said.

So, to appease Barry, this chapter deals with the brass tacks of preproduction. If this somewhat technical material is not your bag, simply hop through it, searching for the dirty words and vague humor that attempt to spice it up. As in the special effects chapter, many of the examples are from *Tromeo & Juliet*.

Remember, if you read this section and it bores you, it's all Barry Neville's fault. In protest, give Troma a call at 1-800-83-TROMA. We'll give you Barry's home address and you can go beat the bejesus out of him. Or you can do that thing with the paper bag on fire on his front porch and he comes out and tries to stomp it and the bag is full of shit and he gets shit all over his foot. I've never done that, but I've always imagined it would be hilarious. The only problem is that Barry lives in a building with a carpeted hallway, and if you set a fire there the whole building might go up in flames, and there are a lot of families with small children that live in the building, and you could possibly end up burning them all to death. That would make it a little less funny.

CASTING

I'll hire you as casting director. You place an ad in *Backstage*, looking for actors for a feature film, non-SAG. Mention that some roles require nudity. You receive thousands of 8 x 10 headshots in the mail. Wow, you think. Some of these look fantastic! You're brimming with hope. Separate the headshots into piles, a pile for each character in the movie. Set up appointments with the good headshots, giving them fifteen minutes apiece. "Wear something skimpy," you tell them on the phone, "a tight T-shirt and shorts, so that we can see your body." On the first audition, make them do monologues of their own choosing. At this point, you learn something very important:

MOST ACTORS SUCK.

There seems to be a certain type of sad cretin that lives in his parents' basement, watching TV, dreaming endlessly of becoming a star, who leaves his home only to audition for Troma movies. His headshots will show sparkling, clean skin; a wide smile; and perfectly coifed hair. In person, however, his face is covered with acne, puss dribbling from holes on his cheeks. His smile is crooked, with shit-colored teeth not clear in the black-and-white headshots. And his hairdo appears to be some sort of parasitic seaweed that lives on a steady diet of motor oil and lard. People like this, who come in both male and female models, will line up around the block to be in a Troma movie. On top of these other problems, their acting abilities pale in comparison to those of a plastic Troll doll.

BUT if you are very lucky, Troma Casting Director, you will find a few actors that have some talent. Next, you repeatedly audition them, to make sure they have the perseverance needed* to make it through a Troma film. Then you learn a second important lesson about casting:

TALENTED PEOPLE ARE USUALLY IRRESPONSIBLE OR INSANE.

Most actors are late. They "forget" appointments. They show up stoned. They try to strangle casting directors for no good reason. They forget to take their medication and start blabbering about how their uteruses have a direct pipeline to the Kremlin.

HOWEVER, if you are very, very lucky you will find a few hardy souls who consistently show up on time, sober, and are only slightly psychotic.

That's your cast.

They may not match the model thespians you imagined when you started this job, but at least they're competent.

As you walk home you see a cardboard box with a sign that says "free kittens." You peer in on their cute, fuzzy faces. They paw each other and clamor to get to you. You go to pick one up when something horrible churns deep inside you. You have an uncontrollable desire to step on their heads.

But don't worry, Troma Casting Director. That comes with the job.

HIRING PRINCIPAL PRODUCTION STAFF AND CREW

This takes place simultaneous to casting. The production manager is hired first, who then hires all of the below-the-line and some of the

---

*Rick Gianasi was called back to audition for the lead in *Sgt. Kabukiman NYPD* twelve times before he got the role. Jane Jensen came to over twenty Troma auditions to get the role of Juliet in *Tromeo & Juliet*.

above-the-line personnel.* When I interview people, I primarily stress how hellish it is working on a Troma movie. I tell them that they must be up at sunrise and can't leave until after midnight. I tell them I'm difficult to work for and they will likely end up hating me. I tell them that they will have to ravage their minds, souls, and bodies for little or no money.

If the person still wants the job, then I tell him how bad it really is.

I tell interviewees this in part to scare off those who aren't serious. But I mostly tell them this because it's true. Without exaggeration, only one out of every twenty production assistants at the beginning of a Troma movie is there at the end. Some people may be happy once they're done with the Troma experience, but hardly anyone is happy while they're in the midst of it (I'm naked as I write this).

REHEARSALS

At Troma we take a good month or more in rehearsals. This is uncommon for any picture, even big-budget ones.† On a low-budget film you save money this way: you don't need to spend expensive set time going over lines or blocking. John Avildsen taught me to rehearse on actual locations as much as possible; actors become comfortable with their surroundings and blocking is pertinent. Recording rehearsals gives you a chance to start composing shots. On *Squeeze Play* I actually shot the entire film on Super 8 during rehearsals. Because of the intricacies of depicting a ball game (strangely enough, more difficult in many ways than a complex action sequence), this Super 8 footage was helpful for keeping order. Today we plan some shots with a camcorder. I always try to get the DP and members of the crew to attend as many rehearsals as possible. In addition to getting some healthy feedback, you also quickly find out which crew members are most likely to punch you in the face during filming.

---

*BELOW-THE-LINE personnel includes craftspeople, technicians who make up the crew, and production staff. ABOVE-THE-LINE personnel includes everyone on the supposedly creative side: producer, director, writer, and actors.
†On *The Final Countdown,* due to the great expense of the stars, we only had two or three rehearsal days with Martin Sheen, Kirk Douglas, and Katherine Ross.

Rehearsals also test the script. On both *Sgt. Kabukiman NYPD* and *Tromeo & Juliet*, the screenwriters attended all the rehearsals. We were able to see what lines worked and what lines didn't. We were able to see if a character's lines needed to be altered to serve his personality. We were also able to incorporate into the script any funny or interesting lines either the actors or the screenwriters came up with during improvisational sessions.

LOCATIONS

This is the biggest hassle in preproduction. Here are a few reminders for LOCATION MANAGERS:

1 **Your job sucks.** It is possibly the worst in the whole film business, but you will be rewarded in heaven. I've been in location Hell myself on *Rocky, Slow Dancing in the Big City, Saturday Night Fever*, and *Cry Uncle*, etc. I love you all.

2 **Every location must have a contract signed by the *owner* or the *legal proprietor*.** No one else. Too many times I've gotten kicked out of shooting in a store that had the manager's or a goofy-salesgirl-who-happened-to-be-a-Troma-fan's signature and not the owner's, or a house where the permit was signed by the person renting it and not the landlord.

3 **Be honest.** Tell locations what's going to happen. No hard sells. It's better to lose the location immediately than halfway through shooting. Location proprietors usually imagine filmmaking as a glamorous star-studded experience with five or six people standing around with a camera and a single light. In fact, they will have fifty-six smelly, dirty, food-eating crew members trampling over their Oriental rugs. Gaffer's tape will be stuck everywhere, thick electrical cords will be tied into the fuse box, and things will get broken (that you'll have to pay for). It's noisy, and obscene, and there's nothing glamorous about it. But we'll give you 23 dollars. Sign on the dotted line.

4 **Sometimes, be dishonest.** We had an opportunity to shoot *Troma's War* at a real army barracks. One little snag: the U.S. Army wanted to read a copy of the script to make sure it didn't reflect

negatively on them. As you may know, *Troma's War* is one of the most extreme films in the Troma library. It spends a lot of time satirizing the armed forces. So we gave the army a *special script* that was written in a few hours, but that loved the U.S. Army very, very much. They gave us permission. This tactic is also useful for churches when you want to film butt sex on the altar.

5 **Get the owner of the location to feel sorry for you personally**. Form a personal bond with the person. Let him know how difficult your job is, how important it is as an early step in your film career, and *how you will get fired if anything goes wrong*. The person will be less likely to kick you out of the house when he discovers a disenchanted PA has dropped a turd in his Ming dynasty vase. I did this with the family who owned the house where John Travolta lives in *Saturday Night Fever*.*

6 **Get permits**. On *Tromeo & Juliet* the New York Public Library wouldn't give us permission to shoot the romantic naked couple having sex next to the stone lion, so we had to steal the shot. Sometimes you can get away with shooting without a permit. Often you can't. As a general rule, get a city permit for every location where you will be shooting. (This is a good reason to shoot in New York, where getting permits are easy and cheap, instead of expensive, pain-in-the-ass L.A.)

7 **As with everything else in low-budget film, when an opportunity arises, *take it*, despite the script**. This is the Tao at work: accepting the lack of control as well as you accept the control. Shortly before filming of *Cry Uncle* commenced, John Avildsen read a story in the *New York Post* about a bankrupt cruise ship that had been abandoned by its crew in the middle of Manhattan harbor. We tracked down the owner of the boat, and David Disick, the producer, and I were able to bargain an extremely reasonable rental rate. The addition of the ship in the film gave the film a grand look and much higher production value. Any time you have

---

*That is, I bonded with the family whose home it was, I did not drop a turd in their Ming dynasty vase. We actually only paid about $100 a day for that house—pretty good for a Paramount production, huh?

an opportunity to shoot someplace exalted or unusual, do it. So what if you have to change the second lead's occupation from someone who works at a 7-Eleven to someone who works in an alligator-skinning factory?

SCHEDULING

Scheduling is usually the responsibility of the Assistant Director, often in tandem with the Production Manager. First, they must complete a STRIP BOARD. This is composed of thin cardboard strips laid out on a flat frame. Each strip represents a specific scene and contains coded information: scene number, location, exterior or interior, day or night, number of pages in the script, actors in the scene. To do this, I know from personal experience, is very boring work. These strips can be moved around on the board to create a shooting schedule.* While scheduling, one must take into account weather and location conflicts. In addition to the primary location, every day of shooting should have a backup location planned as well.

On *Squeeze Play* I instituted some basic scheduling precepts that would become part of the Troma Bible (a screwy bit of religious arcana which replaces the Holy Spirit with Tromie the Nuclear Rodent).

1 Shoot sex scenes first.

2 Shoot all exteriors second.

3 From there on, shoot in sequence as much as possible.

After one actress backed out of being naked during *Squeeze Play* (which you'll hear more about in chapter 7), I decided in all future films I would shoot the nude scenes first. Generally, I have stuck to this rule. The reason is simple: The erotic contents of a Troma movie are important to sales. I cannot continue making movies without that

---

*Actually, there are now computer programs that do this, the most popular of which is the Movie Magic line of products, but I still like the grassroots approach. The strips also look cool.

insurance. Therefore, if one of the main actresses on a film backs out, our geese will be flambéed. If we know they are unwilling to do it on the first day of shooting, we can replace them without having a lot of useless footage. In fact, today, we always shoot the sex scenes fully naked on Hi-8 before we shoot on film, to make sure that everyone's comfortable. Another reason to shoot sex scenes first is to get it over with for the actor. If the actor is nervous about it, he or she won't have to worry about it for the rest of the film.

The second rule is common outside of Troma. It's a basic film maxim to shoot exteriors first. In this way, you won't back yourself into a corner concerning weather. If you plan an outdoor scene a few days before the end of the shoot, and suddenly you're beset with rain and flooding for forty days, you'll waste a lot of money going overtime on the film. Plus, you'll have to buy an ark to store the equipment in, which would be a pain, especially with two of every animal eating your scrims* and urinating on your Inkies.†

The third rule, shooting in sequence, is extremely unorthodox. I do it because I like to keep things loose. I want to be able to change the story at any time. If someone pisses me off halfway through shooting, I can simply kill him off in the movie and tell him to pack his bags. Also, because we work with so many amateur actors, it's easier for them to get a line on things if we shoot in sequence. Same goes for most of our crew members, who are usually autistic.

Finally, I always schedule a day of preproduction filming, sort of a dry run for cast and crew. I usually choose a scene that requires little effort from the actors and that would probably be considered a second-unit shot in Hollywood. There's less at stake, at least dramatically. In *The Toxic Avenger*, the famous head-crushing scene was shot in preproduction, as was the close-up of the nipple-piercing in *Tromeo & Juliet*. These set the tone and got everyone charged up. On larger-budget films this isn't done, due to union rules and the expense of picking up and returning equipment.

---

*SCRIM: a lighting accessory made of wire mesh, silk, spun glass, or plastic translucent materials. You place it over a light source to diffuse or weaken the light.
†INKY-DINK: the smallest focusable studio lamp, with a bulb up to 200 watts.

GET THE BASICS DOWN

Preproduction is your chance to get all the supposedly little things ready for your shoot. Make sure there's enough toilet paper, pancake makeup, and tampons. Quite often on a production the newer and younger Troma Team members will be surprised how much I focus on the "small" aspects of filmmaking as opposed to some loftier vision. But, in truth, if you don't have electricity on a set it suddenly becomes more important than actors. And if you don't have enough bathrooms for the crew, you'd be surprised how much it affects their work product. Visions and ideals and art are important, but they don't come until after you have the mundane, basic groundwork laid down for *getting it done*. Before you can make a movie *good*, you have to be sure you can make it at all, or at least be sure the crew can make a doody. Preproduction gives you a chance to get to know each other, to learn, and to fight.

I'm bored with this chapter, Barry. Can I go on to the next now, please?

I Was a Teenage six Studio Slave

Our First Office: Michael and I sublet a broom closet from *McCall's* magazine for $87 a month. It wasn't just small. It was literally a broom closet. It was a prerequisite that they continue holding their cleaning stuff in there, and that their janitors retain a key. Steel buckets, mops,* and spongy things hung from the walls. Troma came into the world with 300 bucks in the bank,† so a closet was the best we could do. We bought ourselves a little desk. We set it up with an old typewriter that didn't have a "d" and that for some reason printed the capital "L" upside down, and we began to distribute. Movies. Most people in the building thought we were distributing drugs, I guess. Back in '74 Michael and I weren't exactly the picture of corporate America. We both sported shaggy beards, and my curly hair, when longer than ¾ of an inch, begins to have a sort of Chia appearance.

When we started, we only had a few movies. There was *The Battle of Love's Return*, of course. We continued to send it out to art houses,

---

*I remember a mop seemed to stare at me, beckoning me, crying, "Lloyd, Lloyd . . ."
†Today, with $327 in the bank, we're rolling in profits.

colleges, and occasional sub-distributors* around the country. Sometimes theaters would think because it had the word "battle" in it that it was an action movie, so they'd take it. We'd make ten bucks here, fifteen there. Paid for the typewriter. And we'd do what we could with *Sugar Cookies* and *Big Gus, What's the Fuss? Sugar Cookies* would play sporadically. *Big Gus* continued its streak of theatrical virginity.

Eventually we picked up another film, *Sardu: The Incredible Torture Show*. The film was directed by Joel M. Reed, the proud progenitor of soft-core sex opuses like *Summer Farm Girls* and *The Career Bed*, which had shown on the grind-house circuit a few years before. We changed the name to the Chekovian *Bloodsucking Freaks*.

Bloodsucking Freaks has been cited as the "most tasteless, repulsive film of all time"; the film is sadistic and has no redeeming social values. Therefore, as the first *real* Troma movie in the Troma library, Michael and I concluded that it was perfect.

Bloodsucking Freaks is the gripping tale of Sardu, a guy who looks like a cross between Anton LaVey, Ming the Merciless, and a heroin addict, and his repulsive midget† assistant, Ralphus. They would mount Grand Guignol–type sex and torture shows for the Social Register types in the community. Little did these snobs know, but the torture shows they were enjoying were *real*. They also didn't know that behind the scenes Sardu and the midget guy kept naked women imprisoned in a basement cage. They would routinely abuse these she-freaks in such novel ways as employing them as footstools, extracting their teeth with pliers, and, in a scene reminiscent of *Terms of Endearment*, removing the top of a skull and slurping the brains out with a straw.‡ There's a cursory plot of a stand-up guy whose ballerina girlfriend§ is kidnapped by these fiends. But the majority of the film

---

*Before the eighties, distribution was often done through sub-distributors—small, localized distributors who would take up certain territories. For instance, there was a guy in Kansas City (John Schip) who would distribute our movies (and steal our box-office receipts) in the Kansas City territories.

†I'm a fan, to be PC, of the "astoundingly short," which is one of the reasons they appear in *Stuck on You, The Toxic Avenger,* and *Sgt. Kabukiman NYPD.*

‡Well, at least that's how *I* felt during *Terms of Endearment.*

§And not a very good ballerina—just watch the dreamlike dance sequence if you don't believe me.

A NEARLY LIBELOUS KAUFMAN EDITORIAL

Bloodsucking Freaks has a reputation as one of the most offensive films of all time. I admit: I feel a queasiness myself when I watch Sardu use a woman's back as a dartboard. And the camera seems to *enjoy* these activities. Disturbing? Yes, extremely. Just plain wrong? Perhaps. Offensive?

In comparison to Hollywood films? Give me a break.

Bloodsucking Freaks has a warning label on it because of its graphic content. Children cannot see it without their parents' permission.

However, a few years ago when I was flying back from France with my eleven, six, and four-year-old daughters we had to sit through the only slightly censored *Pretty Woman*. This made me realize how much more offensive the messages of most Hollywood films are than the sex and violence in Troma movies.

Case #1. *Pretty Woman* has very few of the things deemed "offensive" by mainstream society and the MPAA ratings association (aka Satan's Disciples). It doesn't have any pubic hair or perky nipples or bloody scenes of the type you see on the network news every night—"horrors" all. And thank God it doesn't have many bad words. Instead, *Pretty Woman* teaches my young daughters who have no choice but to watch it on the plane that the life of a prostitute—not a high-class escort, but a bargain-basement streetwalker—isn't all that bad. She will probably end up marrying a rich prince anyway. A telling exchange reputedly occurred early on in the preproduction of *Pretty Woman*, when the fine actress Jennifer Jason Leigh was auditioning for director Garry Marshall.

After Leigh turned in a dramatic reading from a page of the script, Marshall asked her if she couldn't read it again, only do it lighter and more fun this time.

"Lighter?" Leigh responded. "This woman has been giving blowjobs to strange men in parked cars for five bucks."

"Yeah," Marshall said. "But she hasn't been doing it for that long."

Case #2. Even more crafty is the beloved *Forrest Gump*. I like to describe Troma as Anti-Hollywood, Anti-Elites, Anti-Forrest-Gump. This doesn't sit well with many people, including my own normally sophisticated wife, who think of *Gump* as the moving story of a simple man's triumph.

But what's this movie really saying? Forrest Gump acts exactly as the mainstream and the government tell is made up of the "laff riot" vignettes of torture and humiliation.

Bloodsucking Freaks is the single film in the Troma library of 150 films that I feel queasy about distributing. I may have possibly secured my place in Hell by just watching it. It's one of those rare films that is actually *more* offensive now than it was twenty-five years ago.* However, simultaneous to that, I believe one hundred percent in free speech, and if someone wants to see *Bloodsucking Freaks* they should be able to see *Bloodsucking Freaks*.

That said, *Bloodsucking Freaks* came to us with a terrible reputation and a very short length. Joel Reed told Michael and me that there was a lot of footage that had been removed be-

---

*Peckinpah's *Straw Dogs* also comes to mind.

him. He follows orders, becomes a hero in the Vietnam War, and meets U.S. presidents. He becomes Ping-Pong champion of the world with absolutely no effort, not to mention a member of the Forbes 500. His life is directly contrasted to that of the woman he "loves," played by Robin Wright. This young woman, who acts independently, often as a part of underground culture—including protesting the Vietnam War—dies of AIDS. The lesson to our young people is obvious: DON'T THINK FOR YOURSELF. DON'T ACT DIFFERENTLY THAN THE HERD. GO ALONG WITH BIG BROTHER, ESPECIALLY IF YOU'RE A WOMAN, OR YOU WILL GET AIDS AND DIE.

Forrest Gump won six Academy Awards, including Best Picture.

Case #3. The PG-13 *Reality Bites*. It's the delightful modern day tale of a young woman choosing intelligent substance over surface. Isn't it?

Winona Ryder (aka act-cute-and-giggle-so-as-to-receive-rave-reviews-for-nonexistent-acting) is the protagonist who has to choose between two lovers. One is Ben Stiller (who is also, strangely, the director of this film), who works for an MTV-like cable station. He indulges in one of the things this movie most despises: he works for a living. Stiller treats Winona kindly, with tenderness and unselfishness, and even offers to give up his job for her. Stiller is the BAD GUY. The GOOD GUY is hunky, van-dyked Ethan Hawke. Ethan's a slacker. He reads Heidegger conspicuously at diners, the title proudly exposed. He never displays his feelings, and constantly makes fun of Winona's intelligence and choices. He's cruel but hip. Near the end of the film he is playing on stage with his cool rock and roll band when Winona walks into the bar. He begins to sing about how all she meant to him was just a fuck. The movie ends with Winona kissing this piece of shit. Oh, and, this is supposed to be a happy ending. You see, Ethan's DEEP.

The film is an evolutionary fable: BE COOL AND YOU'LL GET THE CHICKS. It also teaches, PRETEND TO READ CLICHÉD PHILOSOPHERS IN PUBLIC PLACES AND YOU WILL AUTOMATICALLY TAKE ON THE INTELLIGENCE OF A SCHOLAR.

Unlike *Bloodsucking Freaks*, which is honest about its malicious intent, these films attempt to surreptitiously prescribe a culture that benefits the elites.

To speak in a coded language just as these films do, I'll say that I hope all these filmmakers die by way of a bicycle pump to the urethra resulting in internal hemorrhaging. After all, they deserve it. Some of them probably protested the Vietnam War.

cause it was too graphic, so we, feeling some amount of debt to the Marquis de Sade fans of the world,* promptly proceeded to put back the missing scenes. The "Director's Cut" of the movie that you see today is actually the cut that Michael and I did under Joel Reed's direction. After it was reedited, the film, though never a blockbuster, did fairly well on the 42nd Street circuit (the seedy, sticky exploitation cinemas around the country as well as on the actual 42nd Street). Together with some production work and fees for preparing budgets, *Bloodsucking Freaks* brought in enough money to the company that we were able to move out of the supply closet.

---

*Who you would think would want to show *Big Gus, What's the Fuss?* at their dinner parties and gatherings.

* * *

Troma, Inc. relocated to the roof of the Actor Equity Building on 165 West 45th Street. This is the only time in history that the word "actor" and the word "equity" have ever been side by side within a three-hundred-yard radius of Troma.

To get to our office, we had to take an elevator to the top floor and hike up two flights to the roof and tread across the roof to where we were housed in a gardener's shack. I even had my own little tomato garden up there (like most of our movies from that period, the tomatoes were inedible). The crew at that time consisted of Michael, Maris, my wife Pat*, me, and an endless string of put-upon low-pay or no-pay interns and employees. The times were good, simple, and Spartan. Michael and I were healing from the wounds inflicted upon us by *Big Gus* and regaining our energy to reenter the game. After *Bloodsucking Freaks*, we picked up another movie called *Getting Together*. We retitled it *Feeling Up*. There was about as much sex in it as in Mary Poppins,† but the title sold tickets.

To supplement our income, we linked up with the establishment. Like a three-dollar crack whore stepping into a limo, I went to work for Hollywood.

YES, I DO DO GREEK

I did freelance work for numerous productions. Often this would mean doing the budgets‡ for films in the early stages of preproduction—I did this for Sean Cunningham, Barbara Koppel, Elliot Kastner, Sidney Beckerman, and many others. In addition I took on line production, location, and production management work for such films as *Rocky*, *Saturday Night Fever*, *My Dinner with Andre*, and *The Final Countdown*. This was a time of fear for me. I wanted to direct films; I wanted to work on the creative end. But I was only being offered the

---

*Maris and Pat worked during our salad days at no pay, a major factor in Troma's success.

†Which could be more than you think. I, for one, have had my fair share of fantasies of Lynn Lowry in that sexy governess outfit.

‡"Doing the budget" = In a budget, you take a script and figure out how much everything will cost from xeroxing scripts to actors' rates to sound editing.

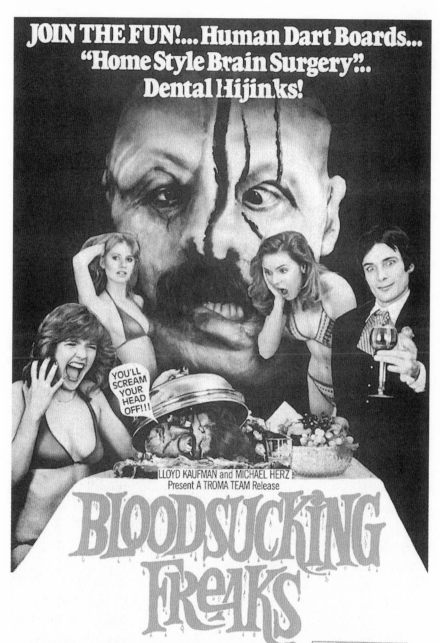

nitty-gritty production jobs. I was afraid that *Big Gus, What's the Fuss?* had sunk my chances of directing another picture. Oliver Stone and some of the other guys from *Sugar Cookies* had gone on to make *Seizure* with Herve Villechaize*—that was a train that had left without me on it and wasn't going to come back. All I could do was hope and, for a while, become a slave to the studios.

THE NEXT MARTY

"Avildsen loves him," I said. "He has a mug like a guy in one of those old Italian Renaissance paintings."

"He can't speak. If he's going to be an actor, he should learn to talk," Maris said. She went on to imitate him: "Blugga bluh bluh ruh."

"He's a nice guy," I said.

"This is going to be the worst movie ever," Michael said.

"My mother-in-law read the script," I told them. "And she said it was going to be the next *Marty*."†

"This is no *Marty*," Maris said.

Maris was right—*Rocky* was no *Marty*. It was ten times bigger. Not only did it make a $100 million or so domestically, it won three Academy Awards (Best Picture, Best Director, and Best Film Editing) and was nominated for quite a few more. In addition, it won the Golden Globe Award for Best Dramatic Film, the Directors Guild of America named Avildsen Best Director, and the Los Angeles Film Critics' Association named *Rocky* the Best of the Year. And Sylvester Stallone, the actor whom the Herzes so much maligned, went on to become, for a number of years, the biggest movie star in the world.

A SHORT BREAK FOR TWO DEFINITIONS:

DAILIES: Simply, the filmed 35 millimeter and recorded ¼-inch sound tape of dialogue for a single day. These materials go to the lab, where a work print is created from the negative, and a 35 millimeter magnetic soundtrack is made from the ¼-inch tape. "Dailies" also refers to the daily projections of these materials shown to the director and other primary members of the crew. Depending on the production, this footage will be from either one day or two days previous. On a Troma movie,

---

*Tattoo from *Fantasy Island*.

†1955 Paddy Chayefsky–scripted film starring Ernest Borgnine that swept the Academy Awards.

everyone in the crew is invited to watch dailies each day, except the cast, who I believe have a tendency to change their performances once they witness themselves on film. Dailies can be viewed either silent, which is commonplace on low-budget films, or synced to sound.

SYNCING TO SOUND: The work print and the 35 mm magnetic soundtrack go from the lab to an editor to be "sunc up" or "synced up." That is, the sound is aligned to match the picture. This is the real use for the clapper board (that black slate that clacks down at the beginning of every scene with scene and production information written on it in chalk). By syncing the clack, the rest of the picture and sound should fit as well.

Michael and Maris synced the sound for *Rocky*. The dailies would be delivered from Philadelphia to the Troma office every day. That means, believe it or not, that the Academy Award–winning rags-to-riches story was synced to sound on the same ancient Troma upright Moviolas later used on *Squeeze Play, The Toxic Avenger*, and *Sgt. Kabukiman NYPD*.

While Michael and Maris did their part, I acted as "Preproduction Supervisor" on the film.

Although *Rocky* ended up as a big Hollywood affair, it didn't begin that way. This was a film from the hearts of Avildsen and the screenwriter, a guy named Sylvester Stallone, who was also slated to star. Sly was far from famous. Only a spattering of cinephiles would recognize him from his roles in *The Lords of Flatbush* and *Death Race 2000*. It was risky to make a movie with such an unknown, but Avildsen strongly believed in Stallone.

Rocky was originally supposed to be shot entirely in Los Angeles, but both Avildsen and Stallone insisted upon real Philadelphia locations, so the production was split up between the two places. For the most part, interiors would be done in L.A., and exteriors in Philly. Avildsen asked me to put a crew and locations together for the Philadelphia part of the shoot.

"Veracity, Lloyd," Avildsen said to me. "That's what I'm looking for in locations. *Veracity*." I use that word a lot today (some accuse me of using it because "veracity" is cheaper than "set design").

Only a minimal amount of the low-budget million-dollar film was allotted for locations. But I was still able to get some pretty cool stuff, including the museum steps Rocky jogs up while "Gonna Fly Now" plays. At Avildsen's behest, I assembled a crew that included his cinematographer Ralph Bode and most of the same folks who worked on

Cry Uncle. We did the Philadelphia shoot nonunion to save cash, and kept this secret from the L.A. contingent.

FOUR TROMA FUN FACTS:

1 Rocky's pet turtles in the film were purchased in a pet store on 47th Street in New York and brought to Philadelphia by my wife, Pat. The exotic turtles were actually illegal to own in the United States. This is, to my recollection, the only time I had Pat transport illegal contraband. Oh, yeah, except for that time I had her running "ice" back and forth across the country for a little extra dough.*

2 Before filming, I had to search for gyms. This got me into going to the gym and being more health conscious. Going to the gym is what eventually gave me the idea for *The Toxic Avenger* (original title: *Health Club Horror*).

3 I appear briefly in the film as a bum, for which I get royalty payments occasionally (about enough money to keep me in dog biscuits for a week).

4 Stallone was a great guy and seemed genuinely happy, years later, when I reprised my role as a drunken bum in *Rocky V*. He actually set a Troma Times† on fire while I was on set.

I watched on my TV at home when John Avildsen received his Academy Award as Best Director. After picking up his trophy, he said, "A few people deserve special thanks." I was startled and touched that John mentioned me. This may not seem like an unusual occurrence, but it is. The next time you watch the Awards ceremony, listen closely to who people thank. They normally thank *people who can help them*. They thank producers and studios and billionaire investors and megastars. I talked to a mathematician at Columbia University while writing this book, who calculated that each "thank you" on the Academy Awards

---

*EDITOR'S NOTE: To be responsible, it must be noted that the author's wife, Patricia Kaufman, presently the Film Commissioner of New York State, and a dear, sweet, beautiful, and respectable Southern lady (far too good for the author in every respect) has never once run drugs for cash . . . that I know of.

†*The Troma Times* is the Troma paper that's issued a couple times a year; comparable to *The New Republic.*

Kaufman claims John G. Avildsen (pictured left, with Frank Stallone's brother and Talia Shire) was a major influence on Kaufman's filmmaking style. Avildsen was unavailable for comment.

is worth approximately 23.4 blowjobs to the thankee.* But here I was, a nobody, a schmuck, and Avildsen chose to use two of his twenty precious seconds to thank me. Very rarely, amidst all the shit, somebody like John Avildsen will come along to let you know at least one person in this industry has a soul.

SATURDAY NIGHT FEVER BLISTER

It was Avildsen, Travolta, my wife, and me. We were in our fifth discotheque of the night, and a fifth of vodka was in me. I watched as Travolta disco-danced with Pat. I have to admit I was getting a bit jealous. After all, *I* was the one who really wanted to dance with John. I was a much bigger Sweathog fan than she was.

Because of his *Welcome Back, Kotter* celebrityhood, John Travolta was *the* reigning teen dream of the day. He deserved it—he was a charming guy, fun to be with, and extremely polite. Because of his stardom, and the fact that Avildsen was just coming off winning an Academy Award, *Saturday Night Fever* had a "bigger feel" to it than *Rocky* during

---

*EDITOR'S NOTE: Where the Hell did that come from? This chapter sucks.

preproduction. Avildsen, who had been hired by producer Robert Stigwood to direct, hired me as "executive in charge of locations."

The script was based upon an article in *New York* magazine about
the seedy underworld disco scene in a Brooklyn club. However, the
club that the article was based upon was nothing more than a big
warehouse in Bay Ridge, in no way cinematic. It was my responsibility
to locate a discotheque that would have the flavor that Avildsen and
Stigwood desired. So Pat, Avildsen, and Travolta and I would go disco-
hopping, to find the right place and to get a feel for the world of the
movie. Travolta, who had never done any professional dancing before,
was taking lessons from the master of "The Hustle" and getting better
every day. Although, let's face it, getting better at a kind of dancing
that at best looks pretty stupid.

From the beginning, it appeared to me, there was friction between
Stigwood and Avildsen (who was again working with Norman Wexler on
the screenplay). Stigwood was in large part producing the film to spotlight a band he managed, some angelic-faced Aussie brothers called the
Bee Gees who had a couple of chart-topping U.S. hits, "How Can You
Mend a Broken Heart" (1971) and "Jive Talkin' " (1975), but had never
come close to superstardom.* Unfortunately, Avildsen disliked the Bee
Gees' music. The problems grew from there, an exponentially growing
series of disagreements between director and producer which would lead
to the eventual departure of Avildsen as director. Avildsen recently informed me that the real reason he was fired was that he had begun dating Judy Buie, the executive producer and Kevin McCormick's main
squeeze at the time. Since McCormick and Stigwood were very tight, the
pissed-off McCormick had Stigwood dump the Oscar-winning Avildsen.
I, on the other hand, always encourage my directors to date me.

When that happened, I did something unprecedented for an Executive in Charge of Locations.† I cabled Stigwood. I said that I needed
to meet with him immediately.

---

*To contrast all that, the soundtrack to *Saturday Night Fever*—a double album—
would eventually sell over thirty million copies, becoming what is still today the
largest-selling soundtrack of all time. In the year 1978, songs penned or co-penned
by Barry Gibb, the Bee Gees lead singer, spent a combined 25 *WEEKS* at *NUMBER
ONE* on Billboard's Top 100!
†In fact, "Executives in Charge of Locations" are kind of unprecedented. Because I
wasn't in the union at the time, Avildsen would give me these hoity-toity sounding titles.

Stigwood called me into his office. I tried to conduct myself in the proper manner, but my big mouth has no control. Avildsen, I said, was one of the greatest living film talents, and he, Stigwood, had made an astronomical mistake by letting him go.

"You fucked up," I said. After speaking, I was sure I would be fired. Surprisingly, Stigwood sat back in his chair and smiled.

"Boy, do you have a great set of balls," he said.

"Like in a good way?" I said.

"That took a lot of courage. It shows you're loyal."

"Fantastic. Does that mean you'll be hiring John back?"

KIRK DOUGLAS & THE FINAL COUNTDOWN

Kirk Douglas once told Lloyd Kaufman: "You can't be Jewish. You're too stupid." Despite this, Kaufman continued to admire the man who hired him to help produce *The Final Countdown*.

"Kirk taught me more than anyone else that you could be a great businessman and still have artistic integrity," Kaufman says. "Kirk owns the rights to many of the films he's made. He owns *Spartacus*. He's hard. He's gruff, and he's tough to work for. But of all the major stars I've known well, I respect him the most. I also respect him for having a marriage that's lasted all these years. How many big stars can you say that about?"

Kaufman's feelings about the rest of the *Final Countdown* crew aren't quite as positive.

"The Final Countdown, which we shot in 1979, I think, was the film that made me say I never wanted anything to do with a major studio film again. And, besides small favors for friends, I never have."

Kaufman found rampant corruption among the production staff, including one teamster who would bring in handwritten receipts for truck parts that had been replaced. When Kaufman called up the shops where the truck was supposedly worked on, the mechanics did know what he was talking about.

"And it wasn't just that guy," says Kaufman. "A lot of people were taking advantage of the guys that were shelling out the money."

The Final Countdown is the story of a U.S. nuclear-powered aircraft carrier that gets stuck in a time warp, sending it back to Pearl Harbor 1941 a few hours before the bombing. The commanders are faced with the decision to leave history intact or stop the incident. Despite the movie's on-set problems, it stands today as a respectable piece of mainstream filmmaking. Without it—and without Kaufman's rejection of what it stood for—Troma would not be what it is today.

Stigwood thought that was pretty funny. The answer was, of course, no. He had already hired John Badham to take Avildsen's place.

John Badham had really only done one theatrical film, *The Bingo Long Traveling All-Stars and Motor Kings* (1976), with Billy Dee Williams, but he would later go on to such classic mainstream fare as *WarGames* (1983), *Blue Thunder* (1983), and *Stakeout* (1987).

I was ready to quit. Avildsen told me I shouldn't. He said it was a good opportunity to continue my education. Forge ahead, he told me.

* * *

An interviewer said to the great comedienne Madeline Kahn: "Boy, your movies are so fun to watch, they must *really* be fun to make!" Kahn looked at him, cocked her mouth, and said: "And Twinkies are fun to eat. But I doubt the folks in the Twinkie factory are having a good time."

Likewise, working on *Saturday Night Fever* was as much fun as getting your tongue pierced with a harpoon.

I had to put together a whole repertoire of Brooklyn locations. This sucked. I had been to Brooklyn only once in my life, to see the Dodgers play at Ebbet's Field as a kid. My big resource was Maris' mother, Edith Gotleib, the only person I knew from that faraway land. She received thrice-daily calls from me. To make matters worse, I'm terrible at sports. I mention this because I consider driving a sport. Ask anyone who's ever ridden in a car with me at the wheel: It's like the Disney Matterhorn, only there are no tracks to keep you in place. I made more than a few wrong turns, and ended up in places that made the barrios of Brazil seem like New Jerusalem.

I liked Badham, but the production staff was full of the Hollywood crap you hear about: laziness, envy, back-stabbing, pettiness—things that I only knew from marriage.* I didn't much get along with any of my contemporaries and some of my superiors.† One of the reasons for the friction was that I was one of the few leftovers of the Avildsen people (another leftover was the cinematographer, Ralf Bode‡). At one point the negative treatment became so overwhelming that I threatened to quit if I didn't get a raise and if the attitude didn't change. By then, I had acquired a huge amount of responsibility and information. I had gotten all of the locations for next to nothing, which they might have

---

*Joke.

†Some of my more talented superiors, however, such as Mike Hausman, who went on to produce *Amadeus* and other Milos Forman films, and Milt Felsen, who fought in the Abraham Lincoln Brigade of the Spanish Civil War, went on to become my lifelong friends.

‡As an interesting side note, this DP, whom I had known since *Joe*, and who was later nominated for an Academy Award for *Coal Miner's Daughter*, lit a single scene in *Battle of Love's Return* as a favor to me; it's the best-looking scene in the film. For starters, you can see people.

lost without me, the contact man. They would have had to pay tens of thousands of dollars to find similar properties. I got the raise immediately, and quit getting shit. Another important lesson: the person that does the work, the nuts-and-bolts guy, wields a lot of power.

What was most interesting to me about *Saturday Night Fever* was watching Badham work. I noted many differences between his style and Avildsen's. I find it interesting to see how, when I direct films today, I have picked up qualities from both of them.

- Badham, in many ways, was easier to work for than Avildsen. When Avildsen called for a location, he had a very clear picture of it in his head, and you had to go from place to place until you found the world's closest approximation of this nonexistent reality. Badham was happy with almost any interesting location, and could bend the script to fit around it.

TODAY, I SWING TOWARD: BADHAM

Though I often have a clear picture of a location beforehand, I'm usually willing to settle, if it's inexpensive enough. Also, if someone finds an interesting location for free, I try to fit it into the script.

- Badham was much less involved with the production end of things. You did your thing and he did his. Avildsen was intimately involved with every part of the process, a micromanager who had to know even the most minor details—including things like permits and the model numbers on the Johnny-on-the-spots.

TODAY, I SWING TOWARD: AVILDSEN

Without a doubt. Because I work with so many people new to the business, almost every decision on set has to be passed before me. In addition, I am a control freak.

- Badham struck me as being more in search of the mainstream "blockbuster" film, whereas Avildsen seemed to think less about the commercial or noncommercial potentials of his work. John Badham added a car crash and a fight scene to the *Saturday Night Fever* script, knowing that the audience might crave a little action in addition to the drama and dancing. He was right. The crowd loved it.

TODAY, I SWING TOWARD: BADHAM

I constantly add elements to the script that I think the audience will enjoy. These things usually have to do with sex, violence, stunts, special effects, or increased production value. Also, monkeys.

· Avildsen, on set, moves quietly from place to place, taking care of business in a subtle way. Badham is perhaps more what people think of as a director— quickly and expertly calling out orders.

TODAY, I SWING TOWARD: BADHAM

I am more like Badham, except that I replace "expertise" with "having a big fucking mouth." Subtlety isn't my strong suit.

· Both get their way, but Avildsen is less adept at managing his superiors. Badham is better equipped to play the Hollywood game. Avildsen always fights for what he wants, and has left quite a few projects in addition to *Saturday Night Fever*, including *Serpico* and *Private Parts*, because of a lack of freedom.

TODAY, I SWING TOWARD: AVILDSEN

I am not adept at anything, especially managing my superiors. And I'm better at the Chinese game of Go than the Hollywood game. I have never played Go.

The most important thing I took away from Avildsen and Badham, however, is that they both love movies more than anything else in the world. They are both willing to give everything they have to make a movie great, while simultaneously being decent and loyal people.

I almost got fucked one last time on *Saturday Night Fever*. When I had been hired by Avildsen my contract stated that I would receive a "prominent screen credit," no less than ½ screen. I flew out to L.A. during postproduction to make sure that my credit would appear properly. As I had guessed, they weren't going to give me the full screen. I showed the clause to the newly hired postproduction supervisor, a walking penis, who said, in essence, "Location managers never get that kind of credit." When I explained that I had received bread crumbs for salary and that the large credit was part of my contractual compensation, he said, "So what?" Again, some Hollywood guy was going to screw me. Luckily, Ron Stigwood, the producer's nephew, interceded on my behalf and forced the supervisor to give me the proper credit. I could never figure out why the guy tried to fuck me out of my credit other than that he seemed to be a jealous, mean-spirited turd.

Years later, Gene Siskel outbid everyone else at an auction to buy the famous white suit worn by Travolta in *Saturday Night Fever*. Nevertheless, if God came down to earth and said, "Either Siskel or Ebert must die, you must choose," I would easily pick Siskel as the victim. Ebert has given more favorable reviews to Troma movies, and he wrote *Beyond the Valley of the Dolls*. But I would be most pleased if God killed them both.

WHAT *MADAME BUTTERFLY* AND A BOTTLE OF VODKA WILL DO TO YOU

Pat was down South visiting her family. I was home alone for the weekend. I had just finished my stint on *Saturday Night Fever*. Although the movie had come out great, it was oddly unfulfilling.

I fixed myself a large Three Stooges souvenir goblet of Popov vodka. I lay on the ragged convertible sofa. I sipped the vodka. Puccini's *Madame Butterfly*, one of my favorite operas, was blasting from the hi-fi. My eyes sprung tears. I looked at my distorted reflection in the Three Stooges goblet.

I was aching to get back into it. I could feel it. Here I was, over thirty years old, and I hadn't made what I considered to be *my* movie yet. It was 1978, four years since starting on *Big Gus, What's the Fuss?*, almost four years since the inception of Troma. But there hadn't been an actual Troma movie, just movies with the word "Troma" on them.

I was scared. *Big Gus* and *Sugar Cookies* had frightened me into subservience. Making another film would be a risk. I'd have to get another set of investors, and perhaps disappoint them the way I'd disappointed the other investors. I'd have to put my all, my soul, into something, and perhaps have it turn out as embarrassing as my past few efforts.

But I couldn't continue making excuses. I couldn't continue to rationalize doing budgets and production managing as "learning experience." I was fully educated. I had worked closely with two master directors. I was equipped.

Must. Make. My move.

The Puccini soared, filling the room with beauty.

I thought of softball.

A softball. A baseball bat.

I said the word: "Softball."

I couldn't figure out why it was on my mind.

seven

A Holocaust of Fart Jokes:
The Making of Squeeze Play

oxicity didn't come first. Before Troma became TROMA, with all the bubbling green goo and mutations that the name today conjures, there came the films that I call "Sexy Comedies." John Waters once said that whatever your first film may be, make sure it has a lot of sex and violence. That way, even if they hate you, you'll at least be spotted. Michael Herz and I went just for the sex. The violence would come later. . . .

Recently, I was invited to the world premiere of Howard Stern's film, *Private Parts*, at Madison Square Garden. Well, saying *I* was invited is something of a fib; in truth it was Pat, the New York State Film Commissioner, who received two tickets. I was only her date. Here I am, I've run a New York–based movie studio for twenty-five years, one of the oldest independent film companies *in the world*, and still I have to rely on *my wife* to get me a ticket to the season's most momentous engagement. To even pretend I'm part of the entertainment society scene* I have to grovel.

---

*Recently, at a classy dinner party, I was seated next to a middle-aged wife of a Warner Bros. studio executive. She asked me about myself, whereupon I told her about Troma and my films. "Whoo hee hee!" she exclaimed. "No matter where I go, they always seat me next to the pornographer!" She thought this was funny. As you would imagine, my amusement was less than overwhelming.

All of New York's glitterati attended the premiere: politicians, movie stars, rock 'n' roll idols, TV celebrities. An immense gathering of Howard Stern fans crowded around the Garden as the procession of limousines arrived. Pat and I tailed a three-block, Jacuzzi-enhanced Mercedes model in our beat-up dial-a-ride.

"CHEAP LIMO! CHEAP LIMO!" a Stern fan yelled at us. Pat ducked her head below the dashboard.

"Lloyd, why do you always have to be so economical?" she whispered.

"A real limo would have been at least thirty bucks!" I said. "This was only twenty-three!"

"That's only seven dollars!"

"A whole pizza!" I exclaimed.

Pat and I waltzed down the long red carpet toward the theater. KGB-like security guards kept the fans at bay. Flashbulbs flashed. Soundmen shoved their microphones into stars' faces. Some of the stars ignored them and kept walking. Others bounced pitifully from one camera to the next, shoving their mugs in any lens that would accept them. I won't mention names (David Lee Roth).

A hand grabbed the sleeve of my tux.

"Who are you?!" an attractive woman reporter asked.

"Lloyd Kaufman."

"Who?"

I extracted a *Tromeo & Juliet* 8 x 10 mini-poster from my pocket (the film was, coincidentally, opening in New York the next day). I was ready to deliver my spiel when the reporter whipped her head to the side.

"Isn't that Jo Ann Worley!!!??" she said, and darted away.

Another reporter stopped me.

"Who are you?" he said.

I lifted my arms out to the side.

"Jackie the Joke Man," I exclaimed. "Listen to me every morning on the Howard Stern Show!"

Bulbs and cameras clustered around me, blinding me with light.

"LLOYD!" Pat screamed. Hellfire in her eyes, she yanked me away.

I was almost to the door when a scraggly, bearded man stopped me. He was holding a Hi-8 camcorder and a Radio Shack microphone.

"Hey, you're Lloyd Kaufman," he said.

STUCK ON YOU

Stuck on You was the third of the four Troma sexy comedies, and thought by many to be the finest. The movie tells the story of a young couple engaged in a palimony suit, and incorporates the stories of famous lovers throughout the centuries—Adam and Eve, Queen Isabella and Columbus, King Arthur and Lady Guinevere, etc. It also has a classic Troma scene of chickens on a farm being shown chicken pornography so that they will lay more eggs. Although this is Kaufman's favorite sexy comedy, he also thinks of it as a major conceptual blunder:

"Here we are, a company trying to make movies on low budgets, and I come up with the most overwrought, impractical idea ever. I would have never considered doing a Troma period piece, but for some reason I thought it would be okay to do *ten period pieces at once*—and that's what it really was, going through the stories of all those historic lovers."

Stuck on You was also greatly inspired by the musical satire and writings of Tom Lehrer and Stan Freeberg, whom Kaufman admired. Also featured in the film was a sublime dance scene choreographed by Kaufman's friend, New York Ballet star Jacques D'Amboise. D'Amboise was Ballanchine's favorite male dancer; he can be seen in *Carousel* and *Seven Brides for Seven Brothers*. Kaufman had earlier directed a full-length documentary, *The Event of the Year*, on a pro-bono basis for D'Amboise's foundation, The National Dance Institute.

"I think it was a bit of a shock for Jacques [internal rhyming seemingly not intended]. In true Troma democratic fashion, we treated him no differently than we did

"Yes."

"TOXIE!" he screamed.

"Yes." This time I held up a *Tromeo & Juliet* air-freshener. The smell of coconut, seemingly mixed with the thick scent of peep-show jism, permeated the plastic wrapper.* "*Tromeo & Juliet*—the movie with all the kinky sex, car crashes, and body piercing Shakespeare always wanted and never had—opens tomorrow night!"

"TROMEO!" he screamed. "Hey, Lloyd, why are Troma movies so great!?"

"Because—"

David Lee Roth jumped in front of the video camera.

"Going to see *Private Parts*!" Roth hollered.

"DUDE, GET THE FUCK OUT OF THE WAY!" the scraggly man yelled. "THAT'S FUCKING LLOYD KAUFMAN YOU'RE BLOCKING!"

This scraggly man, I thought, deserves a hug. I was moved. Screw this movie! I'm going to go hang out with this scraggly guy, down a few Popov martinis, discuss the various levels on which my Troma career has affected American culture.

"LLOYD, COME ON!" Pat yanked me into the Garden.

---

*These things, which we had made as publicity giveaways, smelled so bad that I've actually had people stop talking to me after they opened them up in their offices, homes, or cars.

* * *

Inside, I stumbled into Kevin Bacon.

"I'm writing a book, my autobiography, for Penguin Putnam," I told him.

"That ought to be great," he said. "You must have a lot of interesting stories."

"Sure. In fact, you're in the book."

"Really?"

"Because of the Kevin Bacon game."

"Oh." He smiled.

"So next time you see Roger Kirby you have to thank him."

Kevin smiled more, nodded. He didn't know what the hell I was talking about. He probably had never heard of

any other Troma talent. He had worked out a hilarious extravagant dance sequence, and I guess we made a few too many 'improvements' on his work. Also, we cut it up in the editing room to suit our needs—moving bits and pieces around. That didn't really make him jeté for joy. Though I do admit, the best thing about rehearsals had to do with Jacques: Michael Herz was chosen to rehearse the dance numbers with him so we could block for camera. Although Michael's in good shape, he definitely looked a bit ridiculous dancing the female role with Jacques. Whenever Michael gets too pissed off today, I throw that memory up in my mind, and it sort of relieves any fear I might have."

Kaufman also had a unique run-in with a car dealership during *Stuck on You*. It concerned a joke about the first three vessels that arrived in the New World: The Nina, the Santa Maria, and the more economical Pinto:

"We had a hard time tracking down a Pinto dealership that would let us borrow a car in exchange for a credit at the end of the film. Eventually, though, we found somebody. The thing they didn't know was that we were going to have this car driving onto the beach as if out of the ocean. The car got stuck in the sand and, as the tide came in, filled with seawater. A few days after that, we had Columbus and Isabella driving along, and Isabella cried, 'Look out for that school crossing!' and we pelted the car with a school of a hundred smelly dead fish. The car dealership wasn't too happy with their improved Tromatic Pinto."

Troma gave them the credit at the end of *Stuck on You* despite their ingratitude.

Roger Kirby, had no idea how he and Roger linked up in this great plot of life. Pat and I walked into the theater.

We were seated in the front row. I had been working hard at Troma that day, so I fell asleep for a few minutes. Pat elbowed me. I awoke to see Howard Stern and the director, Betty Thomas, leaving the stage.

"They say anything interesting?" I asked.

Pat scowled.

The movie started.

Me: amazed.

Fart jokes, vulgar humor, huge breasts, and women in bikinis. The crowd, people like Sherry Lansing, Tony Bennett, Henny Youngman, the mainstream of the mainstream, was in hysterics. For years Pat has said to me, "Lloyd, you're so witty, you're so amusing, why can't you make a movie without all the vulgarity? Can't you just once make something that's not so puerile?" Meanwhile, Howard Stern passed gas on screen and Pat threw back her head and laughed as if she's never seen a fart joke. Christ, I thought. All of this stuff was in *Squeeze Play* twenty years ago.

"It's just so delightful!" she says later. "So funny!"

Three months earlier, Pat ran out of a prescreening of *Tromeo & Juliet* halfway through, furious that we had shown an extreme close-up of a nipple-piercing on screen. "Why do you have to be so crude?!!" she yelled at me.

Without a doubt, David Spade or some similar "comedy genius" will show a nipple-piercing on the screen in the year 2017, and it will be the toast of the town.

"Did you see the way the needle popped through that ripe bud and a little blood spurted out?" they'll say. *"Wasn't that delightful? Wasn't that marvelous? I can't wait till my kids see that!"*

I reflect on the *Private Parts* extravaganza because there are so many aspects of the film similar to *Squeeze Play*, the first of the Troma sexy comedies. And, since the *Squeeze Play* chapter is the chapter I must write now, it was on my mind during the Stern film.

Barry Neville told me, after reading chapter four, that I should go more in-depth in terms of how I was able to make these movies. Where did the money come from? How did I, brass tacks, get things started? Obviously it wasn't as simple as some financial backer just saying, "Hey, here's a hundred grand to produce and direct a film." Was it?

THE IDEA

QUESTION MOST OFTEN ASKED ME BY REPORTERS: "Lloyd, where do you come up with the ideas for your movies?"

MY STOCK ANSWER TO THIS QUESTION: "Most of our ideas come from newspaper articles or current events. For instance, I was reading an article in a newsletter on toxic waste dumps and came up with the idea for *The Toxic Avenger*. A news story will be the seed for the entire thing."

TRUTH QUOTIENT: 5 on a scale of 10.

My answer isn't entirely honest for two reasons. First, a few movie ideas *were* spurred on in this way, but certainly not "most." Second, how can anybody say where an idea comes from? They just come! Suddenly, the idea of Toxie just popped into my mind. It came from my cerebellum! In this way, creative people often feel—and I'm being so bold as to include myself in that category—that they don't so much "create" as allow themselves to be channels for ideas from God knows where. My best ideas come when I don't expect them. When, like the Tao dictates, I simply flow.

That said, I didn't come up with the concept for *Squeeze Play*. That idea came from a sub-distributor in Boston who told Michael and me, "You ought to make a movie about a women's softball team and their amorous adventures. You're sure to make money." Michael and I added the comedy element. I was also intrigued by the women's lib movement of the time and the controversy surrounding it—this is where the news of the day really did come in—and I wanted to incorporate some of that.

It seemed like a commercial idea to me.* Coming off *Rocky*, sports movies were in. I had never heard of one about softball. The women's lib movement was topical. And, sprinkle in some R-rated sex, and the guaranteed bottoms would give you a guaranteed bottom line—at least *some* people would be interested in seeing it for the spice alone. Michael and I concurred this would be especially helpful in selling the rights to foreign territories.

I set upon writing a four-page treatment. Writing is, to me, Hell. I have a difficult time staying still. Treatments are essentially for plot, which is not my strong suit. The *Squeeze Play* treatment was primarily

---

*All said, *Squeeze Play* wasn't an *entirely* commercial prospect. It's different today because the market is glutted with product, but at the time, *any* action movie could make money. It didn't matter how high the quality or the budget, you could sell any piece of crap fist and bullet *jambone* and make cash. But comedy was risky—what's funny in NYC isn't necessarily funny in Nepal. Although Michael and I knew this, straight action never appealed to us. The yin and yang of Troma once again: We refuse to make a film that's commercially safe (action) to make a commercially unsafe one (comedy), YET we insert extremely commercial—some would even say "sellout"—properties into the noncommercial film (nudity, etc.)

"A SAUCY, SPICY, ROLLICKING COMEDY!"
-KATHLEEN CARROLL
New York Daily News

"It's seven innings of 'Animal House' and 'Meatballs' in the wildest softball game of the year!"
Softball Power Magazine

A Lloyd Kaufman Michael Herz Production

SQUEEZE PLAY!

IT'S THE WORLD SERIES OF LAUGHS!

Starring JENNI HETRICK · JIM HARRIS · DIANA VALENTIEN · HELEN CAMPITELLI · SONYA JENNINGS · MELISSA MICHAELS · RICK GITLIN · RICK KAHN · ALFORD CORLEY
Produced by LLOYD KAUFMAN and MICHAEL HERZ · Directed by SAMUEL WEIL · Associate Producer IRA KANARICK · Director of Photography LLOYD KAUFMAN
Watch for the soon to be released Sound Track Album "SQUEEZE PLAY" featuring the new Disco single "LAST LICKS" · Screenplay by HAIM PEKELIS · Executive Producer WILLIAM KIRKSEY
A TROMA INC. Release   © Mountain Productions/Troma Inc.   R RESTRICTED

a list of things I found funny, along with a few interesting sexual situations—some upside-down sex, a girl whose bikini top comes flying off, a guy who is locked out of his apartment naked. The bare basics of a story were sort of tossed in.

At root, the story was: Female softball team challenges male softball team to battle of the sexes. Females lose. The end.

But, oh, the fart jokes! The wet T-shirt contests! The topless nudity! The nose picking!

THE FINANCIAL BACKING

Bill Kirksey was one of the *Big Gus, What's the Fuss?* investors with whom I had stayed on friendly terms. Bill owned a yacht.* He invited me on it for a weekend cruise. Normally, I'm not fond of boating. This is because I'm not fond of vomiting, and I'm prone to seasickness. I'm also a city person and prefer the joys of graffiti and bum-urine to fresh air and trees, which, you have to admit, are rather disgusting.

But I liked Bill, and I went on the cruise. I mentioned the treatment about the amorous adventures of a women's softball team. Michael and I were calling the project *Squeeze Play.*

"We came up with the title referring to the squeezing of women's breasts," I told him. "I was very surprised when I found out that, coincidentally, this was also a strategy in softball."

Although Bill had been supportive of my ambitions, I didn't think he'd want to take part in another film scheme. After all, he was practically missing the whole left side of his body from being burned so badly on *Big Gus.* But to my astonishment he immediately set about raising money for the film.

And that's the thing about finding a budget, Barry. Sometimes it's instantaneous, other times it takes forever. There are a lot of moneyed people out there interested in being a part of the film world. But to bring the right idea to the right person at the right time requires luck. With *Squeeze Play* we got the money quickly. With *Tromeo & Juliet*, a harder sell, it took about four years.

---

*I had met my wife, Pat, on this same yacht a few years before.

THE SCREENPLAY

As *Squeeze Play* approached reality, I entered a state of panic that didn't end until the film was released. I almost entirely ceased sleeping. I was constantly on the phone with investors, trying to get a little more money, trying to make sure the money we already had was actually in place. Michael, though he had a calm exterior, was frightened as well. We had struck out big, twice. Troma was hardly an enormous success as a distributor. I had no real reason to believe we would succeed on this movie or any other for the rest of our lives.

Because of my proclivity toward listing gags and situations as opposed to having a cohesive story, I needed a coscreenwriter with some control. Since there was so much at stake, we threw in a few more bucks than we normally would have. I'm talking big money. Over three figures.

John Avildsen recommended a writer named Haim Pekelis. He lived in a shack in Malibu. I went to live with him for three weeks. I brought a stack of index cards with dumb jokes and sight gags. Haim found them about as funny as leukemia, but, hey, I was footing the bill. He only put up half a fight.

The director Paul Williams* lived next door to Haim, in an actual house. I had met Paul in my Yale days, and had also once been hired to do a budget for one of his films for Ed Pressman. I admired his work. He stopped by one day.

"I hear you're writing a screenplay," he said.

"Yes!" I said.

"How's it coming along?"

"Great!" I said.

Haim groaned. Loudly.

"You don't think so, Haim?"

"It depends," he said. "How fond are you of bodily functions?"

"Well, listen," Williams said. "No matter what kind of film it is, put a gun in it somewhere."

"What?"

Miss Right (1981). No relation to the short munchkin-like creature who starred in De Palma's *Phantom of the Paradise* (1974). Also no relation to Anson Williams, known for his touching portrayal of Potsie Weber on TV's *Happy Days*.

"It doesn't have to do anything. Even if it doesn't go off. Just throw one in. People love 'em."

"What if it's a kids' movie?" I asked. "Like about dancing raccoons or something?"

"Throw a gun in," he said sternly. "If raccoons can dance, they can goddamn well pack heat."

Then Williams left. We ignored his dictum. There is no gun in *Squeeze Play*. But, you know, we might have been one step closer to true Tromaticism if we had listened.

Haim and I continued to battle it out over the vulgarity and corn-ball humor. Almost everyone I've ever written with has opposed the Troma extremism as well as the Charlie Chaplin, Three Stooges, and Borscht Belt influences. Still, I push these things through, time after time. As long as I am in charge of Troma, *I promise that extreme sex, extreme violence, and extreme stupidity will reign supreme.*

Haim focused on minutiae—logic and plot—whereas I focused on the grander scheme of things—like jokes about women's boobies. Eventually, after long, hard hours of me running around the beach chasing seagulls while Haim worked his fingers to the bone, we had a draft that we thought was in good shape. Haim's job was through. I took the 75 pages back to New York. There, my brother Charles and I began to rework the whole thing.

Mostly we did this by visiting the locations and thinking of jokes that interacted with the surroundings. For instance, we went to the ball field.

"Imagine someone sliding into home," said Charles. "And then his face slides on the baseline, and he gets up and he has a big white line down the center of his face."

We laughed hysterically for a few minutes.

"We could have a groundskeeper who is working the machine that puts down the baseline," I said. "Only he has a limp—which is funny enough in itself—but his back leg is swiping over the fresh line behind him as he walks, smearing everything!"

We laughed for a few more minutes.

"Damn!" Charles exclaimed. "We can probably have a good thirty, forty jokes just having to do with the baseline."

"And I plan on it," I said.

Even though Haim wasn't dead, I was sure he was turning over in his grave. He later became a stockbroker.

In a Troma tradition we've kept to this day, *Squeeze Play* never truly had a final draft. Even while shooting, the script would change from hour to hour. Charles and I wandered around the set in between shots thinking of gags. To the chagrin of the actors and script supervisor, we would generally rewrite whatever the next scene would be.

KILL BAD SEEDS (DON'T BE AFRAID TO FIRE PEOPLE)

Throughout production, you will be faced with problem members of the cast, crew, or production staff. These can be people that are stupid, untalented, lazy, or have a bad attitude. To me, finding a person with a bad attitude early in production is like finding malign cancer cells; without a doubt it will grow; remove it before it spreads to others. One reason *Tromeo & Juliet* was successful was because the early production crew, composed of James Gunn, Franny Baldwin, Andrew Weiner, and Bob Bauer, were only willing to work with people who were competent and had dedicated themselves completely to the project. Almost frightening in their intensity, they fired anyone who showed signs of unwillingness. Heartless? Perhaps. Cult-like? They were. But they efficiently streamlined an incredibly talented cast and crew. Breaking hearts was a secondary consideration.

They could have learned this from Woody Allen. More actresses and actors have won Academy Awards under Allen than any other movie director. Obviously, he's a master director who works well with performers. But there's a second reason for his string of successes: Allen isn't afraid to fire someone when they're not working out. He is known for such acts as cutting the young actress Emily Lloyd out of *Husbands and Wives* and replacing her with Juliette Lewis *after* filming was completed. He actually had to reshoot all the scenes. Allen has done this on numerous occasions with numerous thespians. It may be because their performances aren't up to par, or, more likely, that after seeing them in the roles, he discovers they weren't the right choice. Whatever the case, Allen bites the bullet and does the deed, even though it must be emotionally trying.

Anyway, I fucked up *Squeeze Play* because of a distinct lack of testicle-hood in preproduction.

The erotic nature of the film was extremely important to the project. We had talked to the actors and actresses about the nudity and lovemaking scenes, making sure that they were comfortable. They all assured us that, yes, they were fine. This was the seventies, they would say, and the modern actor had no problem with nudity.

But two days before we were to begin filming, the second lead actress, Melissa Michaels, changed her position.

She said, upon contemplation, doing nudity would "break her mother's heart." She didn't want to go through with it, although she had earlier said she would. She had no problem showing her back, and pretending to be naked, but she absolutely would not show her breasts or her bottom as the script required.

> **FIVE TROMA PICK-UPS YOU SHOULDN'T MISS**
>
> Most Troma fans consider the movies produced and directed by Michael Herz and Lloyd Kaufman the most entertaining. But these five films rank with the best of Troma in-house productions:
>
> *COMBAT SHOCK* (1986, Buddy Giovinazzo)
> *CHOPPER CHICKS IN ZOMBIETOWN* (1989, Dan Hoskins)
> *MONSTER IN THE CLOSET* (1986, Bob Dahlin)
> *MOTHER'S DAY* (1979, Charles Kaufman)
> *RABID GRANNIES* (1988, Emmanuel Kervyn)

Many people feel as Melissa did. That is good. Everyone should do as his or her heart professes. However:

THIS WAS TWO FUCKING DAYS BEFORE SHOOTING!!

HOLY CHRIST! The WHOLE IDEA of the movie was THE EROTIC ADVENTURES OF A GIRLS' SOFTBALL TEAM! And she wouldn't even show her butt! Not even a single buttock! Hell, I'd show my butt to anyone who asked! As Melissa related her feelings, I must admit, I was fuming. I saw my dreams of an oh-so-sexy comedic adventure swirling down the drain. Not even a guy with a white baseline on his face seemed funny to me now. But I kept my protests to a somewhat moping look of disappointment. "That's okay," I muttered. "You don't need to do the nudity."

This, of course, was a lie. It *was okay* that she didn't want to do nudity. It *wasn't okay* that she waited until the last minute to tell me, when it was seemingly impossible to replace her. I believed and still believe that she had made up her mind about the nudity long before she had told me, and had waited because she didn't want to be fired.

What would I do differently today?

I'd say:

"I understand completely, Melissa. And perhaps we can find a place for you in the film that doesn't require nudity. However, in this role, nudity is important, and we'll have to replace you with someone else."

Situations like this have come up a few more times since then, and I have been able to find the courage to act correctly. Two specific situations spring to mind (neither of these happened in preproduction, mind you, but what the hell—I'm not a fascist):

First, in *The Toxic Avenger II*. The actor who originally played Toxie in this film was not, to say the least, a team player. He asked for privileges the other actors didn't have, he liked to have the PA's carry his bags, and we needed to constantly track him down and phone him to make sure he'd be on set. One day, after a string of negligent acts, the actor didn't show up. We had his stand-in, Ron Fazio, take his place for the day. Michael Herz and I watched Ron.

"Hey, this guy's just as good," Michael said.

"And the beautiful part is, he's wearing a mask," I said.

From that moment on, the original Toxie was gone, and Ron, a trouper and a true gentleman (now, I believe, a nurse in New York City), took over the role for most of *The Toxic Avenger II*, as well as *The Toxic Avenger III: The Last Temptation of Toxie*.

Second: after two days of shooting *Tromeo & Juliet* we discovered that the guy playing Cappy Capulet, Juliet's father, wasn't going to work out. He had insisted throughout rehearsals he would be available twenty-four hours a day during the shoot. As we began shooting, and were seemingly locked in because we had footage of him in the can, he changed his point of view. He listed days he would be available and days he would not. His schedule, he said, could change at the last minute.

"Hey," he said. "I'm a working actor. What do you expect me to do? Give that all up when you guys are paying me next to nothing?"

"But you promised that the movie would come first," I said.

"I don't know what you're talking about, man."

On a large-budget film, these types of restrictions might be possible. But on a low-budget production, the actors must be available at all times. A schedule is inflexible—you may only be able to get a location for a couple of days. If an actor isn't available for one of those, you're screwed.

James Gunn and I went over our options. We could tell the actor to shape up or be fired. He'd probably choose "shape up." But how could we be sure the same thing wouldn't happen again? I admit, I almost made the same mistake as I had on *Squeeze Play*. But James said we had no choice but to find an actor to replace him immediately.

"But who?" I asked him. "Every actor that has tried out for Cap has been atrocious."*

James called Stevie Blackehart,† one of the actors in the film who was experienced on the New York stage. At 10:40 that night, he gave us the number of a Shakespearean actor, Maximillian Shaun. At 10:50 we called Max. He rushed down to the production office and read for James. Max was wondrous. After three months of repeated shit actors, we found a dazzling one in a single hour. By 11:30 he had the role of Cappy. He was on set at 8:30 that next morning.

The original Capulet was disappointed by this information. He admitted he was seeing how far he could push us, and apologized.

WE DON' WAN' NO STINKIN' WET T-SHIRTS

The *Squeeze Play* actresses were staging a rebellion.

I was up in arms. I was more out-of-control back then. I screamed more often. I was screaming now.

"It's a WET T-SHIRT CONTEST! You can't wear those! They're as thick as potato sacks!"

"Well, that's all we're gonna wear," said one of the actresses. "Take it. Or leave it."

---

*It's difficult to find decent actors over the age of thirty-five to act in low-budget films. Most professional actors have signed on to SAG by that age, or they've given up the calling for an easier lifestyle. So many of the non-SAG actors over thirty-five have been deluded by dreams of stardom for years and years, but don't have the self-awareness to realize they don't have the talent to back up their hopes.
†And also the star of Troma's *Rockabilly Vampire* (1997).

Famous RACK focus shot from *Squeeze Play*'s wet T-shirt contest.... Tromettes in their '70s formative stage.

"I'LL LEAVE IT!"

"Too. Bad."

I had made a bigger mistake than I had thought by not firing Melissa. It was like a virus. Just the day before, in homage to the AIP Women in Prison films, we shot a group shower scene. Nothing better than a bunch of sensuous women standing naked in the shower, lightly brushing each other, giggling—but they refused to get naked! Now *Squeeze Play* had the first shower scene ever where the women are wearing bathing suits!* Since Melissa didn't have to part with her skivvies, why should anyone else?

Now we're supposed to be doing the wet T-shirt contest. The costume designer had provided the actresses with thin T-shirts to wear on stage in the bar. However, Melissa and the others determined that the thin T-shirts were "demeaning to women," and they showed up wearing non-director-approved T-shirts of a very thick material—what appeared to be Formica. Not only that, but instead of pouring buckets of water on the shirts, they had a little bottle of spritz. Now it was a "sort of damp" T-shirt contest.

Again, my dreams were being dashed. From the beginning, I had

---

*Some say this inspired Courtney Love's entirely clothed striptease in Milos Forman's *The People vs. Larry Flynt*.

been obsessed with this wet T-shirt contest. These mythic, valiant battles of popular culture had been taking place all over America at the time. I thought I had an opportunity to perform the true cinematic interpretation of the event. This could be Kaufman's "Odessa Steps." To my knowledge, there had never been a decent scene in any movie featuring a wet T-shirt contest. Now that the actresses were rebelling, that would continue to be the case.

Today, I am afforded some respect. The Troma brand name has become a recognizable quantity to those in the industry. On *Tromeo & Juliet*, many of the young actors were children when *The Toxic Avenger* had come out. James Gunn had snuck into a movie theater to see *Squeeze Play* when he was just a boy. And, even if they have never heard of Troma, all it takes is one stroll through the Troma Building to see the placards and posters on the wall: A) We have many, many films that have been released all over the world, B) We're legitimate enough to have been favorably reviewed or reported on by such hallowed institutions as *The New York Times* and *The Wall Street Journal*, and C) We've been invited to an amazing number of Film Festivals, where our films have been Official Selections or subjects of retrospectives.

So, because of all this—and perhaps because of the fact that I'm now a stately fifty years old—on a Troma set today there aren't many rebellions. Most cast members actually listen to what I have to say. And, if there's griping about the script, my directing, or conditions on set, it's out of my earshot.

But on *Squeeze Play* I had never directed a film that had a real theatrical release. No one knew what a Troma was, and they definitely didn't know what a Kaufman or a Herz was. And, because of my past creative disasters, I didn't have complete confidence in my abilities. As director/DP, I liked to hide behind the camera lens as much as possible. On *Squeeze Play* that was my only safe haven. I preferred to talk to the actors through David Alexander, the AD, as much as possible.

The actors and crew sensed my insecurity. They often came upon me like ravenous animals.

Such as:

"I refuse to say that. It's too ridiculous," said the actor.

"But it's funny!" said Kaufman.

"It's a pun. I hate puns."

OR:

"Okay, then could you please move over to this part of the bedroom, where you kiss passionately," said Kaufman.

"Okay, but . . . I'm not going to actually . . . you know . . ." said the actress.

"What?"

"You know, touch his tongue."

"Put your finger on his tongue? Why would you do that?"

"No . . . you know what I'm saying—"

"No."

"You know . . . the French kissing thing. I'm not going to actually do that!"

"What?! Why not?! It's supposed to be a passionate kiss!"

"I've got a boyfriend, Lloyd!"

"Yeah, but you told me you didn't have any problem with sex scenes on camera!"

"But not where parts of us are touching! Geez! What is this, a porno?!"

OR:

"Lunch," said the (very large) grip.

"What?" said Kaufman.

"Yeah. It's a fucking movie set. We want to be fed fucking lunch."

"I can't . . . you know . . . afford, exactly . . . lunch."

"You know, Kaufman, you're a little guy."

"Yes . . ."

"How'd you like it if I tear your fucking face off your fucking skull?"

"What kind of cold cuts do you like?"

OR:

"You want me to do what?" said the actor.

"You put the piece of popcorn in your nose," said Kaufman. "You push down on your open nostril, and then you blow the piece of popcorn into this girl's mouth over here while she's laughing."

"Into my mouth?" said the actress.

"Yes."

"Give me a break! I'm not about to have him spit his booger into my mouth."

"No, no. It's not a booger. It's a—it's a piece of popcorn."

"That's not funny," said the actor.

"It is. It is funny."

"Oh, yeah, right. Like, how would you like to have a person blow his booger into your mouth? You think that'd be funny?"

"You misunderstand," said Kaufman. "It's not what I would like to happen to me. It's what I would like to see happen to somebody else. Trust me. It may not be funny now. But on screen, it will be hilarious."

"I don't care if it's hilarious," said the actress. "I just don't want his snot on me."

"I don't care if my snot goes on her," said the actor. "I just don't think it's hilarious."

"But it doesn't matter what you think is hilarious! I'm the director!"

"Not when you're having a booger jump out and land in my mouth.* I'm going home."

And so on.

The film set became a debating society on what was or wasn't funny. It could have been an NYU class on the philosophy of humor. According to the cast and crew, slapstick was not funny. Nor were puns or sight gags. Anything to do with bodily functions, picking your nose, or a sexual act was not amusing. Women's breasts were not a joke. If we cut out all "unfunny" bits in the script according to their philosophy, the *Squeeze Play* screenplay—which they had all read weeks before shooting—would have been two pages long. I liked to call them "The Humor Nazis." Theirs was a holocaust of fart jokes.

A LESSON ON WHY TO LISTEN TO THE DIRECTOR

The scene that got the biggest laugh in the film is this: One of the men on the male softball team pulls down his pants to moon the female batter, hoping to destroy her concentration. Instead she hits the ball, and it gets stuck in the crack of his ass! You and I, I think, will both

---

*My brother Charles and his girlfriend Nancy ended up doing the gag, and it got one of the biggest laughs in the film.

agree that this is undoubtedly one of the funniest motherfucking things we've ever heard! But the actor set to do it refused to have a ball taped to his hairy ass and yanked off (we did the "upside-down and backward" effect here). A minor character volunteered and, as we all know, cemented his place in world history.

SOMETIMES YOU NEED TO BREAK RULES

In *Squeeze Play* we actually shot the big finale—the softball game with the men against the women—at the end of the shoot, despite that it's an exterior. I did this because this scene was more complex than the rest of the film. The only professionals on *Squeeze Play* were the focus-puller* and the soundman. Even our production managers were fresh out of high school. Therefore, everyone needed as much practice (the easier scenes were like rehearsals) as they could get before the complex final game. And it was a climax toward which the

> LLOYD KAUFMAN'S FAVORITE FILMS OF ALL TIME
>
> *PRINCESS YANG KUEI-FEI* (1955) KENJI MIZOGUCHI
> ANYTHING BY CHARLIE CHAPLIN
> ANYTHING BY BUSTER KEATON
> ANYTHING BY JOHN FORD

actors could build their performances during the previous four weeks of filming.

Luckily, as I mentioned in chapter 5, I had figured out every shot of the final scene on 8-millimeter.† This was like having a celluloid storyboard. This was important, as it gave me something to completely and utterly ignore when I went to shoot it for real. Shooting a low-budget film is a lot like war. I hear that when one steps onto a battlefield, despite any amount of training, he goes crazy and shoots in every direction. This is why such a large percentage of people die from

---

*The guy or gal who keeps the picture in focus.

†John Avildsen had advised me to use primarily long lenses in the softball game. Long lenses make the camera's object seem closer than it is. They compress the action, heightening the tension, for example, when someone's heading for home plate. The person seems to be running with much more effort.

friendly fire. Troma movies are the cinematic equivalent of friendly fire. You just lose your head and start shooting in every direction.

POSTPRODUCTION

Everyone, take a very deep breath and enjoy it: Fill your lungs. Now let the air flow free, blowing it out slowly between pursed lips. Refreshing, is it not? Now, imagine that pleasant feeling increased by, say, a billionfold. That's what it feels like going from production to postproduction. The stress, though still there, has decreased greatly.

Postproduction is divided into eleven basic sections:

1 EDITING

2 OPTICALS

3 NEGATIVE CUTTING

4 LOOPING

5 SOUND EFFECTS

6 THE MUSICAL SCORE

7 THE SONG RIGHTS

8 THE EROTIC COMPONENTS OF COLOSTOMY BAGS

9 THE SOUND MIX

10 THE COLOR TIMING

11 THE RATING

Editing is the most time-consuming aspect of postproduction. Today most editing is done on computers, usually the Avid system. On Avid, it's easy to cut, move clips around, toss in a musical background. You can even add animation and special effects without much hassle. Perhaps because it's so easy, Troma has never cut a movie on Avid. I imagine we'll use it on our next film, but everything up to and including *Tromeo & Juliet* has been done on our ancient flatbeds on the top floor of the Troma Building. Up until *Sgt. Kabukiman*, a large portion of the films have even been cut on our fifty-year-old Moviolas. Every cut is cut by hand. There's logging, and constant rewinding and reconstitution. I look forward to the bright future, when Troma is using editing equipment that was common to the rest of the film industry in 1982.

The director's relationship with an editor is quite difficult. For instance, editors often take the splicer* and shove it into the director's eye, attempting to slice open his eyeball. Other times they scrape his face against the concrete floor.

On second thought, maybe those are just the ways that editors interact with *me*.

I admit, I'm not easy on them. Most of the fellows are so patient— you have to be patient, working in such a tedious medium. But editors still often lose their patience with me, since I want to see a scene cut every possible way it can be cut. "I really won't know what I'll like until I see it," is not something an editor wants to hear, but with me, it's true.†

A WARNING: Editors are generally *weird* people. Anyone who wants to be locked up in those little rooms watching the same visual images over and over must be unusual. When hiring one, look out for the ones that appear normal. Those are the ones that rape animals.

Opticals range from the very simple—fade-ins, fade-outs, dissolves, wipes‡—to the more complex, such as animation/live action mixes. They also include the superimposition of credits, and the credit roll at the end of the film. Troma doesn't get involved in complex opticals because they're costly. A simple example is in *The Toxic Avenger*, when the mop boy Melvin is transformed into Toxie. Here we used a negative flashing effect combined with the frame shaking up and down. In *Tromeo & Juliet*, you can see a different approach when Juliet transforms into a cow-creature while beautiful, colored lights flitter around

---

*The utensil used to cut film and then join it onto another shot.
†Editing giant Ralph Rosenblum, who edited *Annie Hall*, edited *Stuck on You*. He was a tireless creative worker who taught me to keep cogitating on and rewriting the script, and reshooting the script even after the film is wrapped.
‡Where the film cuts out of a scene by a shot scooting across the frame and being replaced by another.

her. With that, we were attempting to go against the typical horrific transformation scene by making it beautiful.*

Negative Cutting begins once the editor has completed reels. Every film is divided into reels. Each of these reels is initially ten minutes long, but when they go to theaters every two reels are spliced together to form twenty-minute reels. When the editor finishes a work print† reel, he sends it on to the negative cutter. There, the negative cutter pieces together the actual negative using the editor's cut as a schematic. Theoretically, using this cut negative, final prints can be struck that go on to theaters. The occupation of negative cutter makes the job of editor as exciting as that of a World War I fighter pilot. There is no creative input necessary, just a connecting of the dots while being constantly overcautious so that the priceless original negative isn't chafed, smudged, or scratched in any way. Negative cutters can cost anywhere from a couple thousand bucks to the tens of thousands. Because Troma goes with the lower end of this spectrum (to say the least), a print will usually come back with a wonderful, glowing scratch or two. There's nothing I like better than visiting a negative cutter as he hovers over our neg, lipping a cigarette with two inches of ashes. Sometimes he'll get a little sick of paying close attention and he'll accidentally put a shot in the wrong place. You will see, in the middle of a beautiful sex scene, a tattoo needle entering a man's eye.

I speak from experience.

And then there are a few things that have to do with sound.

---

*The *T & J* animated effect, though, is not entirely successful, for a technical reason. The opticals guy, instead of placing the animation effect directly onto the negative or a copy of the negative known as an "internegative," put it onto an actual copy of the positive print. Therefore, when you see the animated shots you're seeing a film of a film, which stands out notably against the shots around it. Had we not been in such a rush to finish the film, I would have had it done again. If the shoddy quality of this scene decreased your pleasure of *Tromeo & Juliet* in any way, call 1-800-83-TROMA. We will give you Barry Neville's home number, and he will refund your money for the price of your ticket, the rental, or tape.

†WORK PRINT: The actual film that has been manually spliced together from the original footage. By the end of editing, a work print looks horrible, scratched up from months of splicing and re-splicing.

* * *

Looping, also known as dubbing, is when an actor rerecords his lines after the editing is completed. This happens if the actor's original dialogue is too quiet or jumbled and you can't understand it. Many Troma actors seem to say their lines with large chunks of shit in their mouths, so looping is often necessary. Dubbing is also often done on films in foreign languages. There, dialogue is overdubbed in English by American actors. In some countries, most notably Italy and Hong Kong,* it is common to shoot entire films without sound (M.O.S.). Although it seems strange to American filmmakers, all the dialogue and sound effects are added afterwards. At Troma, we shoot some days like this as well—but it is usually by accident, say, someone forgets to turn on the tape-to-tape deck, or someone has mistakenly placed a large wad of gum over the microphone.

During dubbing sessions, the Troma Team adds a lot of background dialogue. Much of this is simply "walla"—that is, the indecipherable murmur of a crowd. But we'll also gather three or four of us to throw in little whoops and hollers and reactions to whatever is going on on-screen, supposedly coming from background characters. Many of these are little jokes, almost inaudible, that no one but us will ever know are there. In *Tromeo & Juliet*, a man with his arm over a woman's shoulders passes behind the primary characters. You can't understand exactly what he's saying, unless you listen closely:

"Please, come on, let me stick it in your butt."

It's that type of intellectual humor that lies beneath the surface of every Troma film.

Seems like a good place to bring up *Ferocious Freedom Female Fighters*. FFFF was an Indonesian martial-arts film that took itself very seriously. Troma bought the U.S. rights to the film, and we completely redubbed it. Not an unusual occurrence, you might think—except for the fact that it was originally produced in English. My brother Charles wrote the new dialogue, adding numerous instances of farting, bad sportsmanship, and a chronically masturbating little boy who was singularly obsessed with his ejaculate and the size of his mother's breasts. We also changed the serious kickboxing hero to Elvis Presley, and the

---

*Much of this has actually changed in the past couple years, and both these countries will most likely, eventually, sooner rather than later, have primarily sync sound.

Indonesian mom to a stereotypical Jewish mother. It was all, of course, done in good taste. The Indonesian producer of the film, extremely happy that his film was being distributed in the U.S., came to see a screening with some of the "little changes" we had told him about. Now, Indonesians are a joyous people, but when the producer saw what we had done he wasn't at all pleased (for one thing, being a Muslim, he didn't find the Jewish mother particularly hilarious). He left abruptly and told us if the actors ever saw this film, they would, well, kill us. That's one of the dangers of dubbing.

Sound Effects: This is where you add the *"Boooinngg!"* sound that breasts make when they're unleashed from a brassiere, you know the one, or the *"Ding!"* that happens when you come up with a new idea, or the tweeting bird sounds that surround you when you fall to your knees after being kicked in the crotch. These are all sounds that commonly happen in Tromaville but that may not happen in your world (they *do* happen in mine, but, then again, I hear voices telling me to kill). All sound effect work was once done by the Troma Team. Our foley room* would be the editing room. We'd stomp around doing a very poor job of matching footsteps. Today, we farm out the work. On *Tromeo & Juliet* we used Jeff Kushner and Pete Conlin,† from the renowned Shooting Gallery. With these guys, as usual, I became obsessed with a few areas.

First, the sound of farts. Jeff and Pete originally made fart sounds that were too dry. There is no humor to a straight *"Plit!"* Rather, there should be a softness, a tenderness, like *"Plissh!"* so that you know the fart is wet, and therefore smelly. However, if the fart is too wet the audience may mistakenly think that the character is letting go a little

---

*The name for the room where the sound effects are created. You've probably seen the common example on TV, where a man is using two blocks of wood to re-create a horse's hooves, or splashing around in a baby pool to re-create the sounds of the ocean, or frantically fucking a grapefruit to re-create the sounds of lovemaking. Oh, wait a second—that last one was me last night when Pat wasn't home.

†These guys also did the sound work for Billy Bob Thornton's *Sling Blade* (see Billy Bob's earlier, better work in *Chopper Chicks in Zombietown*). A little known fact: The screeching voice of the Penis Monster in *Tromeo & Juliet* is a mixture of the voices of Larry Maestrich, the famous head of the Shooting Gallery and producer of *Sling Blade*; Nick Gomez, the critically acclaimed director of *Laws of Gravity* and *New Jersey Drive*; and heroin addict and pedophile James Gunn.

doodie into his drawers. Obviously, from a point of view of plot, this could be disastrous—people will be wondering about the character's embarrassment at having shit in his underwear when they should be concentrating on, say, the dramatic confession of adultery. Therefore, it is wise to keep just an edge of the dryness—"*Plitsssssh!*" In the words of a poorly subtitled Hong Kong martial arts movie I recently saw:

"You made fart noisy and stink!"*

I also related to Pete and Jeff the important mantra of Troma fist-fights—every punch has THREE basic components: the grunt of the puncher, the punch itself, and the grunt of the punchee. Every time Pete and Jeff left out one of the three sounds, I would remove one of their knuckles. We don't fuck around in Tromaville.

Which segues into my other sound effects obsession on *Tromeo & Juliet,* the sounds of battering human bodies. In the first round of breaking bones, Jeff and Pete came to me with sounds that were largely loud cracks.

"Not violent enough," I told them. "In addition to the crack, you need the sound of something sort of wet and splishy."

"Splishy?" Jeff said.

"I'm sorry. I'm getting too technical. A slightly less accurate adjective would be squashy. That way, you get the sound of the flesh splitting open along with the bone cracking. And there is one more addition—break celery. This adds a third important, crunchy layer."

"So—something splishy on top of something crunchy on top of something cracking. What part of the human body makes a crunchy sound?"

"Cartilage."

"But there's no cartilage on the top of someone's head."

"In Tromaville, every human being has a thin layer of cartilage over their entire body. A little known medical fact."

In the end—and I'm telling the truth here—Jeff and Pete purchased a dead pig and brought it into the foley room. There they cracked his neck every which way, stabbed him with various sized knives, and beat him with shovels and clubs and tire irons. Being pro-vegetarian, I was grateful they did not eat the pig afterward.

---

*From *Don't Give a Damn* (1994) starring Samo Hung.

Now, when you watch *Tromeo & Juliet*, and see Sammy Capulet's skull strike the fireplug, or Tyrone Capulet's arm get ripped from his body, or bobby pins thrust into Cappy Capulet's eardrums, you know what dear animal to thank.

Babe. Yes. We bought the frisky little talking porcine wholesale from George Miller's production company after they had finished filming the movie.

The Musical Score comes after the picture is locked—that is, when all the editing is completed. Composing music for a film is quite different from composing a piece with no restraints. That's why so many great musicians can't pull off a film score. A film composer needs that unique ability to write lively music within a rigid format, moving along with every movement on screen.

As I have stated, I often enjoy playing with the high art/low art dichotomy within Troma movies. Therefore, I have customarily used versions of classical music in the scores: *Waitress!* uses a Tchaikovsky violin concerto, *Sgt. Kabukiman NYPD* utilizes the Un Bel Di aria of *Madame Butterfly*, and *Tromeo & Juliet* uses a piece by Delibes as well as an old Negro spiritual, "Yes, We'll Gather at the River." The Delibes was used in the original Cukor version of *Romeo & Juliet*, and the Negro spiritual has been used in numerous John Ford films. I must admit, I now doubt my decision to incorporate these themes. The score of *Tromeo & Juliet* was put together by Willie Wisely, an extremely talented musician out of Minneapolis. The score was wonderful; however, the pieces that Willie composed himself were noticeably more enthusiastic and fitting than the pieces based on the works of others. I believe this is because Willie, although an accomplished musician, was new to the film composing scene. Working within the confines of the movements of the film *and* the confines of someone else's music was too much. I also imposed my specific musical concepts on the composers of *Kabukiman* and *Troma's War*, and I probably harmed their work as well. In the future, I am going to consider letting the composer "have his way" with the film . . . well, on second thought, Stravinsky's *Firebird* would be a perfect theme for *Schlock & Schlockability*.

The Song Rights: We've had everyone from the Smithereens to the dBs to Alex Chilton to Motorhead to Sublime to Superchunk on Troma soundtracks. Normally rights for a song from a popular band cost a film around thirty grand, often even more. But because there

are a lot of Troma fans out there, we regularly get our songs for between nothing and $100. Recently, the Ass Ponys gave us the rights
to their song "Mr. Superlove" for a check for $9.95. The lead singer,
Chuck Cleaver, said he didn't care about the money. He just wanted
to frame a Troma check for $9.95 and put it on his wall. (Unbeknownst
to Chuck, as soon as I found out the check was going to be hanging
on his wall, I, of course, canceled it.)

The Erotic Components of Colostomy Bags*: My favorite sexual aspects of a nice full colostomy bag is that the hole is the perfect
size to be

after a good cleansing with a disinfectant.

The Sound Mix: Expensive. A week (five days) of mixing costs,
on the low end, is about $30,000 dollars. To mix in stereo as opposed
to mono, which Troma has never done (why have two *small* sounds
when you can have *one big one?*), would cost twice as much. To go
any lower would mean going to a house with less-than-exemplary facilities.

Mixing consists of balancing the volume levels of about thirty
tracks. Each track is a different recording of a different series of
sounds. You'll have at least two tracks for primary dialogue, at least
one for background voices, at least two for sound effects, at least one
for the composer's score, and at least one for songs not by the composer. On *Tromeo & Juliet* we had twenty-four tracks. This combined
the numerous digital tracks we had for the sound effects and the score,
and the mag† tracks we had for the dialogue and the songs we had
transferred from compact disc or DAT tape.

The only moment more relieving than the last day of shooting is
the last moment of mixing. When you hear that last song running over

---

*EDITOR'S NOTE: Uh-uh. This time I refuse. We just ain't gonna go there.
†Magnetic tape.

the end credits, it's a truly euphoric moment—with just a tinge of sadness. Almost every single bit of creative work has been completed on the film. What is there is all that will ever be there—for all practical purposes, nothing can ever change. You're finished. Except for:

The Color Timing: The color timer is a gruff guy (they are *always* gruff guys) who sets the color levels on every shot in the film. You can set the exposure so that a shot that was over- or underexposed can look normal (within limits). This is also where you can turn day into night. When shooting a film, especially exteriors, each shot has a different quality light. What you're doing, in addition to making the whole film look crisp and attractive as possible, is making all the shots seem continuous—same colors, same amount of light from shot to shot.

With Troma movies, the color timer usually does the first run-through on his own. Then what's called an "Answer Print" is struck: this is basically the first draft of a print. The Troma Team makes notes on the answer print. Then one of us will go into the booth with the color timer and guide him through changes. You can end up repeating this process a few times.*

If you think that sounds boring, you have to go through the whole fucking thing again before it comes out on video, with video color timing.

The Rating: Here's where the MPAA gets their grubby little mitts on the work of art you've been toiling over, putting every last ounce of your soul, breath, and sweat into for over a year, and they decide to give it A LETTER that will be stamped upon it till the end of time. Back during *Squeeze Play* there were three ratings—G, PG, and R. Today they throw PG-13 and NC-17 into the mix.† Here are some of

---

*Though, because prints are expensive (a few thousand dollars each), we will probably end up using the earlier "drafts," excepting the first answer print, to send to the smaller film festivals, or to the low-end piece of shit theaters like the Embassy 2-3-4 in Times Square.

†X isn't really an MPAA-approved rating. It can be used by anyone to show that the feature is "for adults." Almost thirty years ago some "respectable" movies, like *Midnight Cowboy* and *Cry Uncle*, chose to use the X. Today it's used only to show that something's pornography. Despite popular belief, there is no difference between X and Triple X. It's all advertising (and, as I walk home now with my video copy of *Anal Rampage 12* in my pocket, I know that it must work).

the things the MPAA deemed were so horrible in *Squeeze Play* that no one under 17 could see them, even with a parent or guardian:

1 A guy holding up a cucumber in a goofy phallic manner. Dear God! Don't let your children see that!

2 A man pulling a straw out of his nose. Pornography!

3 A baseball flying into a butt and sticking. Lord! Children might start throwing baseballs into each other's asses all over America! Rectal injury on a nationwide scale!

Unbeknownst to Michael Herz (well, until the moment he's reading this), I removed the bits the MPAA deemed too extreme so that we could get an R rating. After they gave us the R, I put them all back in. We released an unrated movie under an R-rated banner and the MPAA never discovered. A couple years later, a shit kicker theater in the Bronx was playing a double feature of *Bloodsucking Freaks* and *I Spit on Your Grave*. The R-rated version of *Bloodsucking Freaks* is 51 minutes long. The unrated version is about 45 minutes longer than that. I decided to send the unrated print to the theater with the R rating on it. An enraged woman, who had brought her four-year-old child to the theater (who brings a little kid to a movie called *Bloodsucking Freaks?*), called up the MPAA and complained. The MPAA charged Troma with "copyright violation" (they own the little box with the R in it). We ended up paying a pretty hefty fine. I remain unrepentant.

If I could do so, and not be in any way legally responsible, I would tell all of you to get your films rated by the MPAA, and then change them back however you want them; screw the MPAA, a moralistic, discriminatory plague on the independents. But I can't tell you that, so I won't.

THE RELEASE

Back to *Squeeze Play*.

The movie's finished. Michael and I watch it. We think it's hilarious. Great, right?

Wrong.

Everyone hated it. I showed it to Bill Kirksey. He's kind about it but tells me, in so many words, that the movie's as funny as a thorny branch up your ass (which may be part of my problem—I consider that sort of humorous). I showed it to other friends and members of my family. Not only did they not like it, there was a lot of looking away in shame going on.

I approached an old friend after a screening.

"What'd you think?" I asked.

"Great. Great. *I gotta go!*" And out the door he went, his lie wafting in the air around me like a fart, noisy and stink.

We showed the film to the folks at major studios to see if they would distribute it on a larger scale. No one was interested. More than that: We got angry letters about how we had no place in this business.

"The director, Mr. Samuel Weil,* should consider an occupation in janitorial work, perhaps," read the letter from one Director of Acquisitions. Two of the executive producers on *Squeeze Play* saw the movie and asked to be removed from any and all credits.

Theaters around the country refused to show the film, telling us it was unreleasable. Finally, Michael and I took the film to the sub-distributor in Boston who came up with the idea. At least that was one city where we knew we could get booked.

"Um, that wasn't exactly what I meant," he said. "I was thinking more just sex, you know, with the girls having baseball caps on. But you actually have a *game*."

"Well, it's about softball! There has to be a game!"

"Yeah, but I was thinking more about, you know, just how sexy the uniforms are and all. Those red pinstripes. Those socks with the strand that goes down under the heel. I mean, these girls are just wearing regular clothes. And all the comedy and everything. I mean, you know, I have guys coming into my theaters, they want to see something hot. All that comedy is just going to distract them. It's just going to, you know, make them sad."

Michael and I left Boston, no theaters booked.

We took the film to Cannes. Hell, *Squeeze Play* didn't cost that much—$115,000. We never really expected to make that much money in the States anyway, we told ourselves. All we need are a few sales in

---

*The pseudonym I used as director for over ten years, because of being a member of the Director's Guild of America. More on this in Chapter 11.

MADONNA: TROMA STAR THAT NEVER HAPPENED

In 1981, Melanie Mintz and Ilan Cohen were the casting directors on *The First Turn-On*. Like every Troma casting director before and since, Melanie and Ilan worked long, torturous weeks. During daylight hours, they would oversee the auditions of hundreds of potential future celebs (like Vincent "*Full Metal Jacket*" D'Onofrio, who had a small role in *The First Turn-On*). In the evenings, they would trot from bar to club to bar, dispensing business cards with the Troma number to people they found "interesting-looking." By extracting individuals from the disco underground, they were able to populate Troma films with the extremes of beauty and oddity. One night in May of '81, Melanie and Ilan spotted an unknown young woman in the discotheque *Danceteria*.

"She was attractive and wild-looking," said Ilan, years later. "But I wasn't sure about giving her the number. I thought she might be a little too 'punk' for Michael and Lloyd."

Despite this, Ilan and Melanie handed the woman a card. Her name, she told them, was Madonna Ciccone.

"She was dressed exactly like she later would be in *Desperately Seeking Susan*," added Ilan. "She mentioned to us that she was about to make a record. We politely nodded. Everybody was making records back then. It didn't seem like a big deal."

Two days later, Madonna came in for a casting call. Both Michael Herz and Lloyd Kaufman were present (today Kaufman has no recollection of meeting Madonna). To Ilan's surprise, they both liked her. They told him to set

key territories overseas, and we'll make our money back. Those countries love anything with a bit of nudity, as long as it has some sort of hook. And we had a big hook—the softball. There was only one problem.

PEOPLE IN OTHER COUNTRIES DON'T KNOW WHAT THE FUCK SOFTBALL IS!!!

I couldn't believe I could have been so stupid. And Michael too—the smartest human being I have ever met, and this one simple fact never occurred to him. In France, Germany, Sweden—everywhere—they didn't have baseball, much less softball. It'd be like England trying to sell a movie about snooker in the States. No one wants to see a movie about snooker! But we had actually done it! We had made a movie about snooker!

Four months went by. *Squeeze Play* didn't bring in a single dollar.

I had screwed up again. Another failure as massive as those before. I looked forward to a life of drawing up budgets for shitty films starring half-baked celebrities, calling the folks at Days Inn, trying to get good deals for the cast and crew.

The phone rang. I picked it up.

"Troma," I said.

"Yeah, I'm down here in Norfolk."

"Virginia?"

"Ummmmm . . . yeah, that's right. Anyway, I'm in kind of a bind here, and I was wondering if you fellas could do me a favor."

"What's that?"

"I got this here new Peter Falk movie, *The In-Laws,* playing in its Virginia debut. And my goddamn second feature just bailed out on me, and I need a new one right quick. I don't really got much to spend on it. I hear you guys got a movie on some girl's baseball team?"

"Softball."

"Yeah, yeah. Well, I know it's short notice. But if I could have that thing in the next couple days, I'd definitely appreciate it."

up a second audition, and that she should wear something sexy and suitable for camping.

On the second audition, however, only Michael Herz was present—Lloyd Kaufman was at the Cannes Film Festival. Madonna showed up in a new wave version of a camper's outfit, which she said she made herself—an outfit that showed off her ample bosom.

"I want this role," she told Troma's vice-president. "I really want a role in a Troma movie. I will do anything for this role. *Anything.*"

However, Herz didn't see her as the right actress for the part. After the audition, he told Ilan to thank her, but that they had chosen someone else.

"You're making a mistake," Madonna told Ilan. "I'M GOING TO BE A BIG STAR."

Ilan nodded, with gentle condescension. A year later Madonna Ciccone graced the cover of *Time* magazine.

"I stand by my decision," Michael Herz says today. "She was trying out for the role of a Jewish princess. She acted more like someone's Italian grandmother."

It is no secret that *Sizzle Beach, U.S.A.,* starring Kevin Costner, is the most successful Troma movie in terms of expense-profit ratio. Undoubtedly, a Madonna *First Turn-On* would have pulled a similar coup. On the other hand, *The First Turn-On* could have possibly turned out as shitty as the boring sentimentalizing of fascism that *Evita* is, as opposed to the classic sex comedy it is today.

"I'm still pissed off at Michael about it," says Kaufman. "I bring it up as often as possible."

Then Lloyd makes a little sailor hat out of a *Curse of the Cannibal Confederates* mini-poster and puts it on his head.

Norfolk, Virginia. 1979. *Squeeze Play* made its theatrical debut on a double bill with *The In-Laws,* a Saturday night sneak preview. Michael and I didn't think much about it. We already knew people reacted poorly to the film. We would make a few bucks at least. I went to sleep early that night.

Early Monday morning. The phone rang. It was the booker down in Virginia again.

"Hey, you the guy that made that movie?" he asked.

I almost lied, but instead told him the truth. "Yes."

" 'Cause I just happened to be in the theater when that movie of yours—what's that called, *Squeeze Box?*"

"*Squeeze Play.*"

"When that movie of yours played. I watched it."

"I'm sorry," I began to utter.

"*Goddamn!*" he shouted. "*That is some funny shit!* People were fucking dying, man! The guy next to me, he vomited a little blood he was laughing so damn hard! I mean, *everybody*, that whole theater, going crazy."

"What?"

The booker started to laugh. He could hardly get out his words. "You got that fucking guy, baseball flies and sticks into that man's ass! Goddamn, I told my wife—Jean, hit my goddamn chest, I'm having a goddamn heart attack right here! I swear to God!"

I was speechless.

"How did you do that, man? How'd you throw that baseball just right so it'd stick there between that man's butt cheeks! I'm thinking, Ouch! That man there, that is one damn trouper. I don't know if he's a baseball player or some sort of actor or what, but I admire that motherfucker, I tell you that, standing there and having someone toss a baseball up his motherfucking poop chute!"

"It was a special effect. . . . We turned the camera upside dow— We didn't really . . ."

"Hollywood! Goddamn! I tell you something else. You have that man pull a straw out of his nose that once? I goddamn had some shit come out into my drawers I'm laughing so hard!"

My eyes welled up with tears. It was, and still is, the happiest moment of my life.

"I tell you, man! You are one motherfucking comedy genius!"

For better or worse, the Troma fan was born.

We flew one of the stars, Jennie Hetrick,* down to Norfolk. She went to shopping centers, bars, and theaters, signing mini-posters and 8 x 10s of herself. Norfolk wasn't used to "celebrities" visiting. They ate it up. It taught me a lesson that I'd later act out more completely with Toxie, Kabukiman, and even to some extent, Brick Bronsky and Jane Jensen—if you can't afford real movie stars, make your own.

---

*Years later, she was a returning character on *L.A. Law*.

The film played in a few theaters in Norfolk. Business was incredible. Word got out, and theaters all over the country wanted the film: Chicago. L.A. St. Louis. Detroit. Dubuque. Everywhere. We played ninety-two theaters in New York alone. Every time we made enough money in one city, we'd buy more prints and send them on to the next. The gatekeepers may have felt as if *Squeeze Play* was a pile of shit, but the audiences loved it. Most of the reviews were terrible, but a few, like Janet Maslin's at *The New York Times*, took a favorable stance.

We marketed the film feverishly. The media picked up on it quickly. Even though we only had a few people working in the office, we dealt with newspapers and magazines all over the country.

EXPLOIT YOUR HOOKS became our rallying cry. Every Troma movie has some sort of hook to get the media interested, usually something topical. And if it doesn't, we make one up. *Squeeze Play* had the "women's softball" angle. It had the "moviemaking on a low budget" angle (a hook we've used for the company as a whole since). It had the "women's lib" angle.

Later on, *The Toxic Avenger* would have the "ugly superhero" hook, the "a monster movie—where the monster's a good guy" hook, the "mixture of comedy and violence" hook (also known as "gore slapstick" and shared by many Troma movies since), and especially the "environmental message" hook. *Sgt. Kabukiman NYPD* had the "economic and cultural war between the U.S. and Japan" hook. *Class of Nuke 'Em High* had the "New Teen Comedy" hook as well as the nuclear power plant stuff, and *Bugged* had the "Troma movie from an African-American perspective" hook. *Tromeo & Juliet,* coming on the heels of a lot of other, serious-minded Shakespeare adaptations, had more hooks than a tackle box: "The most extreme Shakespeare adaptation of all time" hook; the hooks of its many current and popular subjects, including tattoos, body piercing, and sex CD-ROMs; the "alternative soundtrack" hook that put us on MTV. I'm not even mentioning the Penis Monster and the lucky stroke of debuting during the 400th anniversary of *Romeo & Juliet*.

But although these other, later films are more well known than *Squeeze Play*, received more press, were more critically accepted, and made Troma a lot more famous, none of them did as well theatrically as *Squeeze Play* (and its follow-up, *Waitress!*). *Squeeze Play* was perpetually in *Variety*'s top 50 list. Later on, *Squeeze Play* was sold to cable

TV for about a million dollars. That's ten times the budget of a film we'd already made a stunning profit on. It was *Squeeze Play*, in fact, that helped buy the Troma Building. It was *Squeeze Play* that let me know I was on this world to be making movies after all. It was *Squeeze Play* where I saw, for the first time ever, someone laughing hysterically at a movie Michael and I had made.

And despite all the money or accolades or whatever else being a moviemaker brings you, there is nothing else, not a thing in the world, that can ever compare to making an audience happy. Even if you're an atheist you can't help, for that one brief moment, believing in God.

Squeeze Play made everything worth it.

Oh, yeah, and one more thing. Those two executive producers who had their names taken off the film? They called us a couple months later, asking to be put back on. We told them we'd see what we could do.

Two final notes I can't leave the chapter without stating:

The theme of *Squeeze Play* has to do with the women's liberation movement. At the end of the film, the women lose the ball game, and then they go off and have sex with the men. I once read a feminist critique of the film that said this was "my warning" to women everywhere that they should stay in their places, act as sexual toys, and refrain from competing with the male of the species.

That wasn't the intent. I chose that ending first and foremost because it's exactly what the audience doesn't expect. All through the movie you're led to believe that the women will have a triumphant victory. It's fun to pull the rug out from under the audience at the end. Feminists, not known for their senses of humor, seem to miss the point that IT'S FUNNY. Second, it's because, yes, women are, in fact, not as adept as men at playing softball. Having them win wouldn't have proved a thing about their place in the socioeconomic community. Third, if there is any gender-political point at all, it's this: Women can compete with men *and* be feminine. Sexuality and sexiness are not the opposite of power.

Occasionally I have lectured at Milos Forman's class at Columbia for my friend Michael Hausman. Twice I have shown *Squeeze Play* and spoken about it. The first time, in the early eighties, I was verbally at-

tacked by some women who found the film demeaning. The second
time, in the early nineties, there was no such protestation. The women
were amused by the movie. There were also more women in the class.
They were knowledgeable on the history of low-budget films. They
wanted to know the practical points. How did I get this shot? Where
did I get the money? How did I distribute it? The values of *Squeeze
Play*, as well as all of the sexy comedies, are closer to the values of the
postfeminist feminists of today than those feminists of the seventies
and eighties.

My last little piece is another example of my assholicism. One of my
biggest weaknesses in life—and I think one of the reasons I have never
been able to work with the larger studios on projects—is that I enjoy
pissing people off. I found that out when I showed the movie of the
pig being slaughtered and enjoyed the negative reaction. This is why,
from my point of view, so many movies today are limited in the emotions they elect to elicit. As a filmmaker, you're *allowed* to get someone's adrenaline pumping, to make someone feel romantic, to make
someone laugh, but you're not allowed to piss someone off, to disgust
someone, or to make someone groan. I believe movies would be on a
much higher plane (I'm getting pretentious here, but it's late and I've
been drinking coffee) if they would allow themselves to extract from
the audience a wider range of feelings. True artists do this. Even bore-
dom, in the films of Warhol and Brakhage, has been examined. And I
guess I get a kick out of offending people.

So when Michael and I returned to Yale to show *Squeeze Play* to
an absolutely silent crowd, I can't say it was my worst moment ever.
Afterwards, I took the podium. I stared out at the sea of faces who had
just paid a dollar each to see the movie.* Michael was standing beside
me.

"Any questions?" I asked.

Not a peep. Still waters don't always run deep—sometimes they
run into the minds of zombified, academic peons.

Finally, a young man in the back stood up.

"Yes?" I said.

---

*Michael and I didn't make money—it went to the Yale Law School, dammit!

"WE WANT OUR FUCKING MONEY BACK!"

I stared at him for a moment. I must admit, I was a bit giddy with the energy.

"OH, YEAH?" I cried. "COME AND GET IT!"

The crowd stood up in unison, like Nazi youth in *Triumph of the Will*. I knew I was in trouble when I saw Maris and Pat, in fear for their lives, escaping out the back door. Michael Herz physically threw me out of the way and took the stand.

"Hold on!" he bellowed. The crowd slowed. They stopped. Michael began to explain why the movie was the way it was, and answer questions, and thoughtfully debate with the audience. He won them over, and in the end received a round of applause.

To me, he didn't say a word the whole ride home.

Caught! eight

I arrived at my town house on the Upper East Side. It had been a long day—a fellow from Malaysia wanted the money back he paid for *Tromeo & Juliet*, even though the movie was already showing in theaters. He thought he was buying the film with Leonardo DiCaprio and Claire Danes. I told him DiCaprio did the voice for the Penis Monster. He didn't believe it.

I set my jacket on the love seat in the front hall. A clanging echoed from the kitchen, along with the odor of soup. I entered the kitchen. Pat was lifting a pot from the stove. Her face was stern. She didn't look in my direction.

"Hi, Pattie-pie," I said.

Pat didn't answer. She set the pot down on the counter.

What did I do wrong? I tried to remember. She was angry at me about something, but I couldn't be sure of what. I *had* replanted the stolen ivy around our dog toilet tree like she had asked. Had I forgotten to pick up some cleaning? No. I couldn't think . . .

"The food smells delicious," I uttered.

Pat glared at me. She walked over to another pot, one filled with carrots. She stirred, quickly, battering them and squashing them against the sides of the pot. I had definitely fucked up somewhere.

"What's wrong?"

"Nothing," Pat said.

"Nothing?"

"Not a thing, Lloyd. Not a thing."

"Oh. Good." I grinned.

Pat looked hard into my eyes.

"Except for the fact that you're trying to ruin our lives," she said.

My face became a stupid, clueless thing.

"I read the chapters," Pat said. She slammed the carrots from one burner to the other for no apparent reason.

"You . . . read . . . the chapters?"

"From your book, yes, Lloyd. Some of them were a bit different than the chapters you first let me read. It seems, for me, you did some creative editing."

"A . . . bit . . . different."

"Quit talking like a moron." Pat shoved a wooden ladle into another pot, one filled with something green and mushy. She thrashed it wildly.

"Pat, please stop cooking. You never cook, and besides, you're going to destroy the food."

"How could you write those things?" The mushy green stuff splattered onto Pat's apron and to the kitchen floor.

"Like what?"

" 'To get laid in Africa it only cost five bucks or a bar of soap.' "

"Well, uh—"

"Or what about your beautiful reminiscence about masturbating to Lynn Lowry? That certainly deserves a place in a how-to book on filmmaking."

"Hmmm. See—"

"Or 'Now every time I see the Zapruder film I get an erection'?"

"That's funny, don't you think?"

"I don't think so, Lloyd."

Pat wiped the green mush from her hands with a towel. "Really, it's just embarrassing!"

She stomped toward the family room.

"It's just a joke!" I said.

"I'm not laughing!"

"I don't want to put out just another boring how-to-get-in-the-movies book. I want it to be fun to read. I want it to have a personality."

"And the personality you want it to have is John Wayne Gacy's?"

"Doh!"

"And it's riddled with inaccuracies."

"Like what?"

"I didn't 'run out' of the *Tromeo & Juliet* screening 'halfway through.' You know that, Lloyd. I had an appointment with the governor, I had to be there."

"Yeah, but you left."

"Even if I had liked it I would have left."

"But you didn't like it."

"You had the best script and the best cast you ever had, and you had to make it disgusting!"

"But you thought Howard Stern's movie was hilarious!"

"Please. There's a world of difference."

"How?"

"He didn't have a talking penis come out of his crotch."

"But he will! In fifteen years, Howard Stern will have a penis monster coming out of his crotch!! He'll have lots of 'em!"

"And all the same jokes, over and over again. I masturbated to *this*, then I farted, then I looked at her big boobies, then vomit came out, blah blah blah. It's so repetitive, Lloyd. Hitting the same key on the piano over and over *does not* make a song."

"Oh, yeah, what about Philip Glass? Huh?"

"You're not Philip Glass."

"That's the problem, Pat. You're not being supportive. You think I'm not Philip Glass, I'm not Howard Stern—you refuse to give my artistic vision any sort of authority."

"Just grossing people out is not art!"

"Some people think it is!"

"Do you?"

"Maybe! Just maybe!"

"Making everyone angry is art?!"

"Maybe!"

"Come on, Lloyd!"

"What?"

"Whenever we argue about this, you give the answer that serves you best. When we talk about 'art' you say it's part of your artistic vision to be puerile. When we talk about movies as a whole, you talk about how it's something you do to compete in the marketplace. You say that it's what people want to see and it's the only way you can compete with the big studios. You have to make up your mind."

"No, I don't!"

"And you can see it in the book too. Its point of view changes. Sometimes you're puffing yourself up like some great artist, and other times you talk about the 'bottom line' and making a dollar."

"I don't try to puff myself up."

"Please . . ."

Pat brought her hands to the sides of her face and stopped. She seemed flustered, speechless, even regretful. She lowered herself onto the couch. She peered up at me sadly. I fiddled with a Charles and Di collector plate on the piano. We have a lot of these types of plates, many from the famous royal marriage. I buy them when I'm out of town and bring them home to Pat as gifts. They're cheesy. I love them. She has grown to tolerate them. I walked over. I sat down beside her.

"I'm sorry if I embarrassed you," I whispered.

"It's not that, Lloyd."

"It is, I know. I embarrass people. I don't mean to, but I do. And I appreciate it, Pat. You've stood by me for twenty-five years trying to live a respectable life while I've marched beside you doing an idiot dance. But, to be honest, I don't really know how to write a book, and I'm just trying to do something that would interest me."

Pat nodded. She took my hand in hers.

"Well, can you please just do me a couple favors?" she asked.

"Okay. What?"

"Take out the stuff about the hookers. The ones in Chad, and the other ones too. My mother will probably read this book."

"All right."

"You promise?"

"I promise."

"And I'd really rather not have you write about our personal relationship."

"All right."

"Lloyd . . . ?"

"Yes?"

"What's that in your pocket?"

"Nothing."

"What is . . . IS THAT A TAPE RECORDER?"

"Uh—"

"YOU'VE BEEN TAPE-RECORDING US THIS WHOLE TIME?!"

"Uh—"

[*Footsteps. The sounds of a struggle and falling furniture. Bone-crunching noises. A scream. Footsteps retreating. The sound of carrots and green mush whizzing through the air and splattering on human flesh. A slam.*

Tape ends.]

· THE TOXIC AVENGER was created by Troma's Lloyd Kaufman in 1982 and has since become recognized worldwide as the definitive, youth-oriented monster-hero. The Toxic Avenger's name and likeness are similarly notorious. The words "Toxic Avenger" have become part of the modern lexicon, used in *New York Times* editorials, TV shows, rock songs, and other mainstream media.

· Three low-budget, live-action Toxic Avenger movies had theatrical releases in the U.S., Europe, and Asia, including runs of about one year in cities like New York, and 120 prints released in Japan by Shochiku, 50 prints released in Germany by End/Ufa, etc.

· Major U.S. home video releases resulted in more than 250,000 rental cassettes sold through Vestron, Warner Bros., LIVE, and Troma Team Video. All three Toxic Avenger films continue to perform well in the sell-through (lower-priced, direct to customer) market.

· The Toxic Avenger films spawned a popular Saturday-morning cartoon show, *The Toxic Crusaders*, which penetrated 96% of the U.S. television market and was often the top-rated show in its time period. The show also appeared in Europe, Asia, Latin America, and Australia. Most people who were children when *The Toxic Crusaders* aired (1990–1993) also know who the Toxic Avenger is today; TOXIE, as he is affectionately called, is a part of youth culture's mythology.

- Major worldwide movie-related licensing: there were over one hundred licenses for Toxie merchandise in the U.S. and abroad, including a line of Playmates action figures; two Marvel comic book series; Topp's trading cards; Nintendo and Sega video games; Thermos lunch boxes and thermoses; Colorforms play sets; International Games board games; CD-ROMs; model kits; Halloween masks; and so on.

- Mainstream worldwide television exposure, including USA Networks/Sci Fi Channel (U.S.); HBO/Cinemax (U.S.); Showtime/The Movie Channel (U.S.); *Entertainment Tonight* (U.S.); ABC's *Prime Time Live* (U.S.); ABC's *Nightline* (U.S.); *American Journal* (U.S.); MTV's *The Big Picture* (U.S.); *Tonight with Jonathan Ross* (UK); E! Entertainment Television (U.S.); HBO Olé (South America and Brazil); Canal + (France); Telepiu (Italy); Bravo (UK); the BBC (UK); CNN (International); 24 Stunden (Germany); FilmNet (Europe); and many, many more.

- TOXIE is the icon of Troma Entertainment, Inc.—he is the Mickey Mouse of Troma Studios. He is a star of *The Troma Basement* and *Tromaville Café*, television blocks featured throughout Europe, the U.K., and more. Toxie appears at the head of most Troma Team Video releases. He marches in the Macy's Thanksgiving Day parade every year, and he's been a favorite with modern rock musicians.

- The Toxic Avenger's image and name have been pervasive in the environmental movement. For example, he has been utilized by the EPA, the Armed Forces, the Green Party, and a group of young environmentalists in Brooklyn who call themselves "The Toxic Avengers."

THE PRECEDING IS PROPAGANDA. It was accumulated by the Troma Marketing Department (a guy named Ed James) because William Morris superagent Cassian Elwes wants to show the Hollywood Studios that the Toxic Avenger is a ripe subject for a large-budget remake. The Troma Team and various mega-studios have been flirting over this possibility for a while. Although exaggerated a bit here and there, the above facts are accurate. I thought they would be a good way to open the chapter on Troma Studios' most famous creation, the Toxic Avenger. Or, if not a good way, at least an easy way.

"Lloyd," you might say, "you've been so honest and intimate with us thus far, even being open with us concerning your masturbation fantasies about Lynn Lowry, which, in truth, disgusted us all. Why would you start a chapter on such a personal topic from such a distant viewpoint?"

He was 98 lbs. of solid nerd until he became...

A
LLOYD KAUFMAN
MICHAEL HERZ
PRODUCTION

THE TOXIC AVENGER

The first Super-Hero...from New Jersey!

Starring ANDREE MARANDA • MITCHELL COHEN • PAT RYAN, JR. • JENNIFER BABTIST • ROBERT PRICHARD • CINDY MANION • GARY SCHNEIDER • MARK TORGL
Directors of Photography JAMES LONDON and LLOYD KAUFMAN • Written by JOE RITTER • Edited by RICHARD HAINES • Associate Producer STUART STRUTIN
Music Consultant MARC KATZ • Directed by MICHAEL HERZ and SAMUEL WEIL • Produced by LLOYD KAUFMAN and MICHAEL HERZ   From TROMA, INC.
©TROMA SALES CORP/THE HCH CO.

To that, let me go to Jimmy Lang, a young man in New Hampshire who sent me a fan letter a few months back:

Dear Mr. Kaufman,

I am writing to thank you for all your movies by Troma over the years. I most like the three Toxic Avenger movies, mostly the first one, and that one is my favorite movie of all time. I thank you from the bottom of my heart for this Toxie and his movies. I am sixteen years old and in a wheelchair after being paralyzed from the waist down when I was eight. My legs are smaller than the rest of me. When the other kids at school make fun of me, I know that if Toxie was here he would kill them. I love the Toxic Avenger. Thank you, thank you, thank you, Mr. Kaufman.

Sincerely,
Jimmy Lang

Now you say: "Again with a point of view other than your own, Lloyd. What's up with that?"

And I reply, "It's because of Walker Percy."

The late writer Walker Percy,* in his fantastic essay "The Grand Canyon," wrote about—yes—the Grand Canyon. But, more broadly, he discussed mentally "framing" subjects. It is impossible to see a clear and true picture of a person, object, or place once the vision of it has been predefined by the media, word of mouth, or reputation. If you go to the Grand Canyon, Percy maintains, it is impossible to look down upon the natural wonder and see it for what it is. Your assessment of the Canyon, your "vision" of it, has already been adjusted by postcards, TV shows, your Aunt Trudy's reaction, history books, the souvenir shops outside the site, and a vomitous movie starring Kevin Kline and Steve Martin. This affects memories of things as well as conceptions of things not yet seen; when you recall seeing the Grand Canyon as a child you're unable to filter through everything you've been told about

---

*Novelist, essayist, philosopher, physician. Wrote such extraordinary novels as *The Moviegoer, Love in the Ruins, The Last Gentleman,* and *The Thanatos Syndrome.* Although Percy was from Louisiana and most of his novels take place in the South, I refrain from calling him a "Southern writer" for the same reasons I wouldn't want to be only referred to as a "Jewish filmmaker." Incidentally, in a recent article in a Belgian magazine I was called "The Jew Pope of Trash Cinema." I believe—I think—this was meant as a compliment.

it since. The Grand Canyon was certainly an overwhelming sight to those Native Americans who first set their eyes upon it—but everyone since has had the image "framed" in their minds by others' evaluations and manipulations. Now, alas, it is impossible to see its pure, unadulterated beauty.*

I'm certainly not maintaining that the Toxic Avenger is one of the Seven Wonders of the World (though, this *is* a thought—perhaps there's some way Ed James can work it into the aforementioned list of distinctions). What I *am* saying is that because of the success, and especially the *fame* of the Toxic Avenger, it is impossible for *even me* to see the character clearly. Toxie doesn't belong to me—he's come to mean too much to other people. My memories of what he *was* have been hampered by what he's become. Even though *Squeeze Play* earned millions of dollars and showed on TV all over the world, there's still something secret about it. It hasn't acquired cultural significance outside itself. It's still just a movie, and therefore an easy subject for me to tackle in this book.

The Toxic Avenger *has* acquired significance outside the celluloid it's on, and because of that I've been having a hard time writing this fucking chapter. Even though I'm running behind schedule, I find myself walking around the house doing anything else to avoid doing it.

I guess I'll start somewhere around the beginning . . .

SOMEWHERE AROUND THE BEGINNING

I entered my and Michael's office. Michael was standing behind his desk, looking at a copy of *Weekly Variety*. He was laughing.

"What's so funny?" I said.

Michael held up the *Weekly Variety* so that I could see. The headline was large, bold:

---

*This is another reason why I enjoy making movies without celebrities. When you see a movie with Tom Cruise you already have preconceived notions about him as a character, and you carry with you into the theater all the movies you've seen with him in the past. When you see a poster for the movie with a big picture of Tom's sweet mug, already you've had the experience of the film framed for you. When I see a film with all unknowns, I'm able to see them as *characters*, not as stars. This can ultimately be a much more rewarding experience. The answer? After a person has had a starring role in a film—kill him.

"THE HORROR FILM IS DEAD"

"Holy Christmas," I said. I assumed that some reporter at *Variety* had lost what little of his/her/its mind the journalistic trade had left him/her/it to lose. Or, perhaps, some rabid PMRC Tipper-Gore type fundamentalist had taken over the *Variety* presses to spread this rumor and halt production of violent (i.e., fun) movies.

Whatever the case, it was impossible that someone could have actually come to this conclusion. The horror film had been a staple since the days of the silent movies. George Méliès' *Le Manoir du Diable*, made in 1896, is commonly considered the *first* horror film. J. Searle Dawley's *Frankenstein* (1910),* the first screen attempt at interpreting Mary Shelley's classic myth, was important in furthering the form. And Robert Wiene's *The Cabinet of Doctor Caligari* (1919) and F. W. Murnau's *Nosferatu* (1922) would stretch the boundaries of what not only horror movies but *all* cinema could be.

THE KAUFMANS: A FILMMAKING FAMILY

In addition to Lloyd, both his brother Charles and his sister Susan have been involved in the film industry. Charles today runs a bread company in California, but in a previous Tromatic life he wrote, produced, and directed three Troma movies: *Mother's Day* (1979), *When Nature Calls* (1985), and *Jakarta* (1988). Some critics consider *Mother's Day* and *When Nature Calls* the two finest films in the Troma library, bar none.

Susan Kaufman is a well-respected production designer. She went on to help create the look of mainstream films such as David Mamet's incredible *Homicide* (1991) after working on Troma films like *I Was a Teenage TV Terrorist* (which she produced) and *Squeeze Play*.

Lloyd's family has also *acted* in many films: His father, Stanley, made his screen debut in *Battle of Love's Return*, and went on to appear in many films his son directed up to and including *Sgt. Kabukiman NYPD*. Lloyd's mother had a cameo in *Waitress!* Likewise, Lloyd's wife, Pat, who helped to run Troma for twenty-five years, had speaking roles in numerous Troma movies. It's also a tradition for at least one of Lloyd's daughters, Lily Hayes, Lisbeth, or Charlotte, to appear in every Troma in-house production. They are fondly remembered for being mutilated at the beginning of *Kabukiman*, blown up into a tree in *Toxic Avenger III*, kidnapped by terrorists in *Troma's War*, and playing the mutant children—the "dawn of the twenty-first age"—in the final scene of *Tromeo & Juliet*.

---

*A Thomas Edison production, which attempted to retell the tale in *16 minutes*. Strangely, Frankenstein in this film looks very much like Sgt. Kabukiman's head grafted onto Tromie the Nuclear Rodent's body. I'm not kidding.

Here's What The Critics Across The Nation Are Saying About "THE TOXIC AVENGER"

"...maniacally farcical sense of humor..."
-Stephen Holden
THE NEW YORK TIMES

"...a wicked sense of satire that stays just this side of the maniacal."
-Peter Stack
SAN FRANCISCO CHRONICLE

"It's made to order for gross-out addicts."
-Jay Carr
THE BOSTON GLOBE

"...gross food jokes and a sweet romance..."
-Richard Freedman
NEWHOUSE NEWSPAPERS

"...a genuninely satiric vision of America..."
-Ron Rosenbaum
MADEMOISELLE MAGAZINE

"Hilariously tasteless... jawdropping violence... we would watch it again in a minute."
-Jay Maeder
THE NEW YORK DAILY NEWS

"...a mix of special effects, sadism and insanity... will probably become a cult movie"
-Pia Lindstrom
WNBC-TV

"...a cheerfully tasteless science-fiction comedy. This is surely a...cult movie..."
-Scott Cain
THE ATLANTA JOURNAL AND CONSTITUTION

"If there's a hall of fame ...THE TOXIC AVENGER belongs there."
-Michael Heaton
SAN FRANCISCO EXAMINER

"...fast-paced action sequences inspired sight gags and rapid-fire lowbrow jokes."
-Dan Perez
THE HOUSTON PUBLIC NEWS

"Raunchy, vulgar and frequently funny"
-Judith Crist
WOR-TV

"...a hilarious high-camp cult hit..."
-Joyce Kulhawik
WBZ-TV 4, BOSTON

"...I liked it..."
-Katie Kelly
WABC-TV

"...often funny...cult following potential ...off-the-wall spirit."
-William Wolf
GANNETT NEWS SERVICE

"...un rire enorme."
-La Presse
MONTREAL, CANADA

"...sneakily funny...the Avenger acts like a combination of Charles Bronson, King Kong and Alan Alda... Should do brisk business among the cult movie crowd."
-Harper Barnes
ST. LOUIS POST-DISPATCH

MOVIES OF THE FUTURE

TROMA, INC. 733 Ninth Avenue, New York, N.Y. 10019 · (212) 757-4555 · Telex 645615 TROMA UD

The Horror Film Is Dead! Preposterous! I had never been a huge horror fan, but the genre did hold meaning for me. I remembered with reverence, as a kid, watching the seminal horror movie host Zacharly on TV. James Whale's *Bride of Frankenstein* (1935), Edgar G. Ulmer's *The Black Cat* (1934), and the Corman films based on the work of Poe (Edgar Allan, not the pop singer) were all extremely powerful experiences for me. And William Castle: As a kid, I would go to the theater every time Castle put out a film with one of his ludicrous gimmicks—the skeleton that came swinging toward the crowd during *The House on Haunted Hill* and the theater seats equipped with electric shocks (basically, muted joy buzzers) in *The Tingler*. Sure, it was a disappointment when the actual devices didn't live up to the ads. But, as David Friedman would later point out, it was all about selling the sizzle instead of the steak—and the sizzle itself smelled so good! It was an important lesson to learn. Troma would need to sell a little sizzle now and then just to stay in business.

So, yeah, this headline pissed me off. However, Michael's reaction may not have been the most levelheaded one.

"I think it's time Troma made a horror movie," he said.

HOW MOVIE MARKETING IS GENERALLY DONE BY STUPID IDIOTS

Hollywood's like a little fucked-up planet all its own. Everyone there's a fortune-teller, trying to foresee trends, tell the future: What type of film is going to be big over the next year? What type of movie are people going to want to see?

- HOLLYWOOD EXEC: "I hear Steven Spielberg's making a film about a kid with Down's syndrome who can see through walls. Let's make one just like it, only our Down's syndrome kid can see through doors."

- *ENTERTAINMENT WEEKLY* ARTICLE: "This year, every major film director—from William Friedkin to Brian De Palma to Penelope Spheeris—is making a film about a guy with fish falling out of his ass."

- HOLLYWOOD STUDIO HEAD I: "Disease pictures are BIG BIG BIG! I want young wives riddled with leprosy! I want wide-eyed brats with Lou Gehrig's disease!

> I want animals with face cancer—their faces are falling off all over the forest!! Hunters come in—'Whoops, I slipped on a fuckin' face!' Then the hunters come to love the animals and they get all weepy over the skeletonized bastards!"
>
> · HOLLYWOOD STUDIO HEAD II: "Movies with people with two heads are huge this year." HIS ASSISTANT: "Should we make one?" HOLLYWOOD STUDIO EXECUTIVE II: "Hell no—let's make seventeen of 'em!"

When one of these two-headed romps flops, the studios whip out a "logical" reason. Their film came in "just a moment too late," they may say. Or they come up with a ridiculous rationalization of why their marketing "science" was off, such as: "People like it when the second head is growing out of the left shoulder, not the right one. Unfortunately, we made an erroneous conclusion, having the head come out of the wrong shoulder, and that just blew the whole thing."

The lower-budget "B" movie companies are really no better; they follow the trades religiously, wanting to know what the studios are making so that they can churn out cheaper versions of the same films.

The arty independent films, God bless 'em, usually see none of this. In fact, they often have trouble seeing anything besides what's directly in front of them. It's hard to turn when you have a huge stick up your ass.

BUT THE TRUTH IS THIS: *These supposed "trends" rarely have anything to do with the reality of the general populace. They are instead ways for giant studios to wave their giant pricks in public, and for marketing executives to pretend they actually have some practical use within the system.*

[place large raspberry here]

A SECTION ABOUT *DANTE'S PEAK*
IN THE MIDDLE OF A CHAPTER
THAT IS SUPPOSEDLY ABOUT *THE TOXIC AVENGER*

I just recently attended the Brussels International Festival of Fantasy, Thriller, and Science Fiction Films, one of my favorite festivals in the world—*Tromeo & Juliet* was an Official Selection. While there, I had the unfortunate experience of watching a movie entitled *Dante's*

Peak, a volcano disaster film starring Pierce Brosnan and Linda Hamilton.

I would have rather a garbage disposal had its way with my penis.

Dante's Peak is a bomb. The film reputedly cost—get this—100 million dollars (or two hundred *Toxic Avengers*). It is often the assumption of Hollywood that the world's moviegoers are stupid. This may be true, but *Dante's Peak* proves that the world's moviegoers are not *really, really* stupid.* The film is simply a conglomeration of devices utilized in other megahits. There's a narrow escape by a dog in *Independence Day*, so there's a narrow escape by a dog in this film as well. There are two kids in *Jurassic Park*, so there are two kids in *Dante's Peak*.

Dante's Peak was made after *Independence Day* and *Twister* became big hits. Now there are dozens of "disaster films" being made in Hollywood. Some of them are enjoyable, and they make money. Some of them aren't, and don't. Hollywood continues to pretend their system of trends has some reliability, that it is a science, when, in fact, it could have probably been making any type of big-budget film and had the same ratio of success. The same thing happened a few years back when Clint Eastwood's *Unforgiven* was a big hit, and suddenly there was a flood of floppo Westerns. Someone in marketing forgot to point out the Eastwood vehicle was a hit because it was a *good* movie.

The reason I bring all this up is because whereas other B-film companies try to copy the majors, and other independent films simply ignore them, Troma actively tries to do *exactly what we aren't supposed to do*. Sure, we listen to what the experts have to say—and then we do the opposite. Sometimes this works to our monetary benefit; we get lucky and fill a niche market that's been abandoned by the studios. But mostly we do it because we hate the status quo, and we like to shake things up. We have a bad attitude. We wear spiritual leather jackets. That was the primary reason we began making *The Toxic Avenger*.

---

*After all, there's hardly any lava in the movie. What's a volcano movie without any fucking lava?! The big threat is smoke. A big burst of smoke comes out of the volcano and falls over cars and stuff.

TIME FOR A CHANGE

Michael and I had just released *The First Turn-On*, the last of the four Troma-produced sexy comedies. Although *The First Turn-On* is in many ways the funniest of these raunchy classics, it was not successful at the box office. The film prior to that, *Stuck on You*, had done poorly, and now *The First Turn-On* had underwhelmed box offices everywhere. The problem was that the major studios had gotten into the business of producing like-minded films: *Porky's, Spring Break, Hot Dog, Going All the Way*—all were based upon the successful template of *Squeeze Play*. They all featured a young cast indulging in goofy, often lowbrow humor and light romantic dalliances, which would undoubtedly result in some above-the-waist nudity. Often competitions (like the male-female ball game in *Squeeze Play*) would play a substantial role.

To make matters worse, these Hollywood productions took unfair advantage by using proper lighting and good scripts and decent actors—the cads!

Michael Herz had been complaining that Troma was making the same film over and over again. He was bored with the sexy comedies, and now that they didn't seem commercially viable, he wanted to indulge in something new. Therefore, he was enthusiastic about making a horror film in response to the *Variety* headline.

"How about a mummy movie?"

"Mummies aren't frightening," I said. "They're too slow. Mummies are the guy at school whose glasses you steal and throw them over his head. Fuck mummies. Stupid cunts."

"Okay, then. Something else."

SORT OF LIKE WRITER'S BLOCK

We originally planned a conventional horror film. Ever since working on *Rocky*, Michael and I were interested in setting a film in a health club. Like Hitchcock, who set terrifying situations in banal locations, we thought we could do the same with the horror genre. I wanted to deal with America's mania over creating young, beautiful bodies. Plus, I knew we could think of a way to have those weights really do some damage.

The basic concept was simple. There would be a monster in the

health club, who instead of killing good people killed *bad* people.*
Despite the various sexual proclivities of the characters in *Friday the
13th*, they were still good people for whom you rooted. We wanted our
film, which we started calling *Health Club Horror,* to be different. The
other thing we knew we wanted was a disgusting-looking monster.

So I spent a few weeks mulling over the different possibilities in
my mind. But nothing seemed to click. It didn't *feel* right. The idea of
a horror movie seemed so good when we first thought of it, but now
it was fraught with problems. First, if the monster was BAD and the
people it was killing were BAD, why would the audience care? Sure,
the gore and violence might keep folks enchanted for a while, but no
matter what, a movie needs characters that the audience cares about
for it to be successful. Second, the movie just seemed so *done*. It was
1983, and low-budget slasher horror films with hideous monsters had
been put out there time and time again through such fare as *Funhouse*
and *My Bloody Valentine*. Certainly others, like *Halloween*, were minor
masterpieces. I didn't want to have to do the same thing everyone else
had, but besides the fact of intermixing the horror theme with the
health club, I couldn't think of a way of making it original.

I would roll these problems around in my head constantly, while
taking a shower in the morning, while jogging to work, while having
business meetings, while changing Lily Hayes' diapers, while being interviewed about *The First Turn-On*. I thought so hard my brain hurt.
Nothing, nada, zip. My career, I thought, is over (this thought comes
to me a lot in case you're noticing a trend).

AN ANSWER APPEARS

The Cannes Film Festival, 1983. I was on my way to a meeting
with a Venezuelan distributor who controlled about half of that country's theatrical and video markets† when I suddenly stopped. I stood
completely still in front of the Carlton Hotel, where the Troma busi-

---

*This harkens back to the script I wrote with Stan Lee in 1971, *Night of the Witch,*
where the witch only kills bad people.
†Video pirates have since cut into his share—they control about 60% of the Latin
American videocassette market. Unless you consider Australia Latin America, which,
unfortunately, much of the Troma Team does.

THE DOG AND THE MONKEY

THE DOG

Troma has received disappointingly little hate mail over the years. The film that incited by far the most anger was *The Toxic Avenger*. The scene that brought this animosity on was *not*, as you might think, the child's head being run over by a car. Instead it was when Sarah's seeing-eye dog was shot.

"It wasn't real," says Kaufman. "Obviously we didn't shoot a real dog. But letters and phone calls kept coming in, cursing us out for shooting a dog on film. People who had been fans for years said they would never again see a Troma movie. But we had just crushed a kid's head in the same film!"

Herz and Kaufman were actually upset about the dog scene as well.

"We wanted it to be more real," said Kaufman. "I asked the PA to find me a piece of fur that matched the grayish color of the dog. Instead he brought me a three-by-four-inch piece of brown floor rug. When you see the close-up of the bullet entering the dog, that's what you're watching."

And what about afterward, when the dog slides across the floor?

"That was a trick his trainer did with him," says Kaufman. "He'd throw the dog across the newly waxed floor. Then the dog would run back to get thrown again. He could get thrown all day."

ness office was. People rushed past me on both sides: beautiful women, aging execs with sunglasses and too much tanning lotion, wanna-be stars, boobs in gray suits, and boobs jumping out of halter tops.

"Make it a comedy," my brain said to myself.

"Not a bad idea," myself said to my brain.

"You've gone in the wrong direction," said my brain. "*Of course* you can't make a horror-monster-slasher movie like everyone else. It doesn't interest you. But if you make it *a comedy*—now that could be something to sink your teeth into."

Finally, after all the thinking, I had squeezed something out of my slightly impaired slice of gray matter.

I jogged back up to the Troma office. Michael Herz was there with a Japanese man who, for some reason, was wearing a hillbilly's straw hat.

"Michael, I have the answer," I said.

"Why aren't you with Mr. Blanco?"

"Never mind that. Listen—"

"Never mind that?! You were supposed to be there ten minutes ago!"

"We should make it a comedy."

"What?"

"*Health Club.* We should make it funny."

"Not scary?"

"Exactly."

Michael's eyes lit with the fire of religion. He saw it too. We were going to make a horror-comedy.

"American comedies," said the Japanese man in the straw hat. "Are funny!"

JOYCEAN EPIPHANY

From there, the pieces of the puzzle came together. This often happens on a creative journey when the project begins to gel. You think long and hard. There seems to be no answer. But, if you remain open and fearless, and go to the very edge with an idea, all

THE MONKEY

It was one of the last scenes to shoot in *Sgt. Kabukiman NYPD.* The scene took place between a monkey (Toyota in the movie, Daniel Boone in real life) and the star, Rick Gianasi. Crouched behind a car, Gianasi was supposed to hand Daniel a pistol. Because Daniel had a tendency to stray, he was attached by a leash to Gianasi's wrist.

There were other animals on set as well, including a tiger and a lion. The lion had never seemed dangerous; like a big Siamese, he loved the attention of his trainer and the crew. But, earlier in the day, the monkey had been teasing him while he was in his cage. So now, as his trainer walked him in the opening shot of the warehouse scene, the lion decided to make a good go at eating the monkey.

With the camera going, the lion grabbed Daniel Boone in his mouth and pinned him to the ground.

"And I'm attached to the monkey!" says Gianasi. "The lion is chewing on him, and I'm getting pulled along. I'm not sure how far up the leash the lion is going to go. I'm mortified!"

The animals' trainers were there quickly. They held the lion down and Daniel Boone escaped. Somehow, he wasn't at all harmed. Not physically at least. Mentally was a different matter.

"The monkey's catatonic," says Gianasi. "We're going to go on with the scene anyway. But he just sits there, staring blankly, forgetting everything he was trained to do. I'm supposed to hand him the gun. He won't take it. I'm scared of *the monkey* now. He looked like he might lunge for my neck in revenge or anger."

In the film today you can see that the monkey, lively throughout the film, is a zombie in the last scene. Later on the monkey got his revenge on the lion by biting actress Susan Byun.

the elements that initially seemed so disparate conjoin and become one.

Now it seemed so simple: The movie could still take place in a health club, which seemed a more natural place for a comedy than a horror film. In addition, the monster's ability to sense evil now made sense: He would be *good.* This would finally give us someone to root for. The monster would be a hero. I jumped for Joyce!

THE BASIC STORY

All right, so many of you who have bought this book already know the story of The Toxic Avenger. But for those of you who don't, here it is:

There's this guy, he's a mop boy at the Tromaville Health Club. His name is Melvin Junko. He's not too bright (Leonard Maltin describes him as "retarded" in his movie review), a little strange, perpetually horny, and extremely nerdish. The bullies and bimbettes that work out at the club perpetually tease and torment him. These same jerks also like to drive around Tromaville hitting innocent pedestrians and bicycle riders in a game for "points."

Melvin's only friend is his mother. The relationship is slightly Oedipal.

At one point, Melvin is tricked into wearing a tutu (getting to that point is sort of involved, so let's just leave it at that). To escape the laughter of everyone at the health club, he runs and leaps out a window. Hey, their laughter was really bugging him!

Unfortunately, on the street below the window is a vat of toxic waste. Melvin lands in it, ass in the air.

Some bystanders pull him out. As Melvin lies on the ground his skin begins to bubble and smoke. People look on, surprised.

Then his body inexplicably catches on fire and he runs home.

At home, he mutates into a hideously deformed creature of superhuman size and strength (in case you're on the slow side of the readership, the Toxic Avenger). Still dressed in a now-charred tutu, his only weapon is a mop. In addition to being ugly, and pretty strong, Toxie also has the power to sense evil—and it enrages him (and though no genius, he also seems a little smarter than he was as Melvin). He commences to murder those who are evil. Along the way, Toxie falls in love with a beautiful blind woman, Sarah, who is able to love him in return (she can't see how disgusting he is). Simultaneous to all this stuff, there's a corrupt and environmentally unsafe mayor (who, you'll be happy to hear, is extraordinarily fat!). In the end, Toxie vanquishes the bullies, goons, and mayor (he shoves his fist into the mayor's big, fat belly), and is embraced by the community (just another parenthetical phrase).

SOURCES OF INSPIRATION

Unlike *Squeeze Play*, which was just three basic ideas melded together (boobs + softball + women's lib = *Squeeze Play*), the inspiration for *The Toxic Avenger* came from numerous and various sources of pop culture, the mainstream media, and the underground. Every idea seemed to lead to ten more, and I remembered things that hadn't crossed my mind in years, all to throw into the stew. Here are some of the most important:

- FRANKENSTEIN: Frankenstein was always my favorite of the Universal Horror monsters. Unlike Dracula he wasn't an out-and-out bad guy. You felt sorry for him. Beneath it all, you knew, he was a victim. At the end of the movie, while the villagers chased him with flaming torches, I always wished he would get away. Of all other monsters, our monster would be most like him. The difference would be: We'd let him live. The other influence of *Frankenstein* was that of the inclusion of the little blind girl who befriends him (simultaneously a tribute to the blind girl in Chaplin's *City Lights*). There's a slight difference in that Michael and I thought we'd update the little girl into a well-endowed blonde who'd wear a bikini and have rampant sex with the monster she couldn't see. That made it much better.

- *HAIL THE CONQUERING HERO:* This Preston Sturges movie, among others, would be important in the evolution of Troma. *The Toxic Avenger* is the first film in which there would actually be a Tromaville, which was based in large part around the small-town ensemble atmosphere in the Sturges films. In addition, the screwball nature of the comedy was all Sturges (in *Lady Eve*, Sturges didn't have Barbara Stanwyck's arm get ripped off and have her beaten over the head with it like in *Toxic Avenger*, but I'm sure if he would have thought of it...) Also like Sturges, I went for *mugs** when casting. Unlike Sturges, I had to learn the hard way that most non–Screen Actors Guild mugs can't act.

- NEW JERSEY: Though I had been born and raised in Manhattan, there was always something uniquely exotic and human about this land across the river. Distinctly noncosmopolitan, I thought of New Jersey as true America much more than I did my home city. Small-town suburban life both attracted and

---

*Meaning unusual and unforgettable faces, not receptacles for coffee.

repulsed me. So does Tromaville, where everyone is either beautiful or hideous with no in-betweens. Also, I liked how New Jerseyites lived relatively without airs, especially in comparison to New Yorkers.

· THE ENVIRONMENTAL MOVEMENT: This was a big one. I was nauseated with what was going on around me. Pat and I drove on a trip across the U.S., and I remember seeing miles and miles of nonbiodegradable McDonald's Styrofoam boxes* on the side of the road. Many people believe I was jumping on the environmental bandwagon in creating Toxie, because the environment shortly thereafter became a fad. Although I *was* trying to exploit the health club fad, it was nowhere in my mind to do this with the environment—it wasn't a fad yet. In 1983, when we filmed, there was very little stink being made about nuclear waste or pollution, or their harm to our bodies and natural resources. I didn't see that the future would bring along such interest. Even when Toxie was released on a wide scale in '86, environmentalism was still an underground movement.

· *SILENT SPRING: Silent Spring* was a nonfiction book, written by American biologist Rachel Carlson in 1962. It warned of how the persistent use of pesticides such as DDT could bring enormous dangers to wildlife. I read it in high school for extra credit, and it made an indelible impact.

· *MONDO CANE: Mondo Cane*, by Gualtiero Jacopetti, was the first (and the best) of the "Mondo" films, which were documentaries (often faked) reveling in the more unusual aspects of the planet we live on. In *Mondo Cane* (it means "Dog's World") there were some little frogs or fish in an area where nuclear testing was going on. These frogs had mutated and taken to *living in trees.* I hadn't thought of this film, or this segment of the film, in years until I started working on *Health Club.* For some reason the frogs popped into my head while I was in the initial stages of planning the film. They are therefore direct ancestors of Melvin the mop boy who mutated into the Toxic Avenger.

· PIXIE DUST: I read an article in I. F. Stone's *Weekly* about how South American children had been playing with what they called "pixie dust" in a city dump. The dust was irradiated waste from X-ray machines. The children had

---

*That's McDonald's 1982, not biodegradable McDonald's 1997. Incidentally, a McDonald's just moved into the building next door to Troma. For some reason they found it acceptable to *cut into the Troma Building* to fit their enormous sign. Also—and I swear to God this is true—rats have been seen running through the Troma basement for the first time in twenty years.

fun frolicking in the beautiful, shiny sparkles, and it ended up killing them. To this day, I find this chilling.*

· RUNNING OVER MY SISTER: When I was fourteen I used to drive the car around the property, even though I didn't have my license. I got in the car, and backed out quickly. I heard a loud thunk. I ran around the back. My four-year-old sister, Susan, was sprawled out on the ground. For a minute I thought she was dead, but then she got up and walked into the house. This may be where I first discovered my desire to run over a child with a car. ALSO: When I was about five, we had a pet dog, a little Hungarian Poolie. All it did was bark and bite and chase cars. A counselor had just dropped me off at the end of a day of day camp. As I walked toward the door, I turned and saw the Poolie attacking the car. First it was yipping, its usual nastiness, and then I heard a piercing squeal. I turned and saw it, stuck in the wheel, getting ground up, flipping up over the wheel and into the space between the tire and the car, and then out again. The camp counselor stopped and yanked the dog from the car. It looked like a floor rug that had been sitting in a pot of tomato sauce. It was pretty dead. I don't really know what this has to do with *The Toxic Avenger*, but it was awfully disgusting.

· *THE ROAD WARRIOR:* This wonderful George Miller film had just been released. Since Michael and I had never really shot action or car chase sequences before, we studied this film to get it right. The famous Toxie-on-top-of-the-car scene was definitely informed by this work.

· YOU WILL BE JUDGED ON A POINT SYSTEM: In the New York *Post* there was an article about some kids who had gotten arrested; they were playing a game, trying to hit people with their cars, and they got a certain amount of points for every person they hit. If you smashed your car into an old woman it was worth only 2 points, but a pregnant woman was worth 15. It was such a beautiful, touching American story—one about the triumph of humanity and love over the travails of the postindustrial world—that I knew I had to some-how incorporate it into the film.

· C. WRIGHT MILLS: C. Wright Mills defined the politics of Tromaville and be-yond. Especially in his groundbreaking tomes *White Collar* (1951) and *The Power Elite* (1956), Mills harped on the conspiracy of the elites. These elites have effectively joined forces to cut off the common people from any sort of wealth, comfort, or power. It is these elites Toxie battles to emancipate the

---

*Pat, thirty years earlier, used to dance and play in the DDT clouds sprayed in her Charlotte, North Carolina, neighborhood. In 1993 she was diagnosed with breast cancer.

little people of Tromaville. The philosophies of Mills can be seen in almost all Troma movies, especially the Toxie films, the *Nuke 'Em High* movies, and *Troma's War*. Whereas Mills was concerned with the military-industrial linkage, my basic belief was that the labor, bureaucratic, and corporate elites conspired to suck dry the little people of Tromaville of their spiritual and economic life fluids. This is directly parallel to the way Warner Bros., Paramount, Universal, Columbia, and the MPAA-CARA ratings board attempt to suck dry Troma Studios.

· GRANNIE KAUFMAN: She told me about C. Wright Mills, among others. (She also told me how strontium 90 is put into food and will cause men to grow breasts [as in *Class of Nuke 'Em High*], how Nixon was the devil, and how Mao and Castro were good for getting rid of the drug lords, whores, and effete elites.)

AN INVESTOR

The way Michael and I figured, we needed about $500,000 to make *Health Club Horror*. We assumed it was going to be a struggle.

A young man approached Michael and me at a party for *When Nature Calls*.* He claimed he had a guy who wanted to invest in a movie of ours. Once you've been in the film industry long enough, you discover that this is something you commonly hear. Everyone in the movie business is constantly trying to impress everyone else. Everyone constantly feeds off everyone else's dreams. These promises of money and support almost always lead to nothing. But, in fact, we met with the investor a couple days later and had the money almost immediately.

We also got the investor's girlfriend. Andree Maranda ended up playing Toxie's blond, blind, bimbo girlfriend, Sarah.

SIDENOTE: After the film had been in distribution for a while, the investor asked Troma to buy him out. We let him know that there was a chance that a cartoon series was going to be made from the movie (*The Toxic Crusaders*—which was where the really big money would come into play), but he still wanted to go through with it. Therefore, today Troma owns all rights to the Toxic Avenger and his films.

---

*We would "give parties" by getting a club to give us a free venue and about an hour where lousy champagne punch was served; after that "our guests" had to purchase their own beverages (and, if they had any manners at all, treat me to a few as well).

A SCREENWRITER

Avildsen introduced me to one of his camera assistants, Joe Ritter. Joe was interested in screenwriting. Together we sculpted out a basic plot, and Joe set the first draft down on paper (which we pretty much ignored while filming—everything in the film was changed, up to and including the ending). Joe also worked on the production as a utility cameraman.

A SPECIAL-EFFECTS ARTIST

Upon leaving the era of the sexy comedies, a new role of influence on all future Troma movies was born: the special-effects artist. Jennifer Aspinall was the woman who created the look of the Toxic Avenger.*

I had a very specific image of Toxie in my mind. I related this to Jennifer carefully, making sure that she took precise notes. I told her I wanted a face extremely disgusting, with bubbling pustules. I wanted part of the skin around his mouth torn away so that we could see the teeth below. I wanted the face to look like a Picasso cubist face, like this:

---

*Perhaps it's because it was a woman who originally molded his face that Toxie is so often called "sexy." Many women seem to have a strange sexual reaction to Toxie's ugliness. This has often been mentioned in letters and e-mails from our female fans. It's also a fact that men who wear the Toxie mask and costume out in public almost always end up getting the phone numbers of four or five women. No lie.

Jennifer listened carefully; then she went out and created something entirely different.

She brought in the first set of sketches. I was shocked.

"He seems more lumpy than bubbly," I said.

"I think it gives him more character," Jennifer told me.

I told her I wanted him to look how I originally described him. She went off, did some more sketches, and brought them back to me.

"They look exactly the same as the last ones," I told her.

"No, they're different," Jennifer said. "Very different."

I told her to change them again. This time she brought back the molds, which looked exactly the same as the sketches.

"But . . . but . . . What about the fact that part of his face should be torn away to reveal his gums and teeth?" I asked. "What about making people vomit?"

> ## MOVIES OF THE FUTURE
>
> Although the Troma Team claims to be business amateurs, the Troma catalog proves Messrs. Kaufman and Herz to be remarkably prescient and—purposeful or not—savvy.
>
> Artistically, their forward-thinking is obvious. Their early *Squeeze Play* and *Waitress!* predated later blockbuster sexy comedies like *Porky's* and *Spring Break* by years. Likewise, *The Toxic Avenger* took advantage of the gore and comedy mix long before *RoboCop* or *Scream*. Numerous filmmakers have professed admiration of the Kaufman-Herz vision: Quentin Tarantino, Peter Jackson, Kevin Smith, Mike Judge, Trey Parker, Dario Argento, Shinya Tsukomoto, Stuart Gordon, and Sam Raimi are among them. Troma's extremist elements have opened the doors for their mainstream films.
>
> Herz and Kaufman acquired the Kevin Costner films *Sizzle Beach USA* and *Shadows Run Black* before Costner was a star. Kaufman knew Costner was the dead body in *The Big Chill*, and had "a good feeling about him becoming a star." Troma has made about 150 times its investment on the two films. Many relatively unknown films have made similar profits, such as *G.I. Executioner*.
>
> Troma has chosen to *own* their negatives and build a library; Kaufman and Herz were influenced by Charlie Chaplin, who owned all his negatives and lived a prosperous life, as opposed to the equally talented Buster Keaton, who did not own his negatives and was unable to continue directing films. The ever-growing Troma library exemplifies Troma's keeping one eye on the future.
>
> Troma Studios, over the past twenty-five years, almost certainly has a higher rate of profit-making productions than Universal or Paramount or Miramax or any major studio. Luck? "Falling into success?" The power of the Tao?
>
> Possible, but not probable.

"If we did that, he couldn't smile," Jennifer told me. She went on to show how, with her design, Toxie could give a world-lovin' grin. From then on, it would be a large part of Toxie's allure. The ugly

In this production still from the set of *The Toxic Avenger Part II*, Toxie (r.) mistakes gaffer's tape hanging from the belt of special-effects artist Tim Considine (l.) for toilet paper. The somewhat messy consequences resulted in the loss of a half day of shooting.

creature with a beautiful smile. I didn't agree with her back then, but today I can see she was right.

Jennifer did retain the Picasso influence, however. I thought the perfect hero of the modern age should be based in part on the paintings of the preeminent modernist painter. That is why Toxie's face is disjointed, why one eye is so much higher than the other. Honestly, I thought that Toxie's face should be even more chaotic—but Jennifer knew how to strike the right balance.

After the movie, Jennifer went to work for the Metropolitan Opera Company, the logical next step after Troma.

A CAST

Mitchell Cohen: Mitch played the Toxic Avenger. He had a great deal to do with adding comedic grace and a kindness to Toxie's more monstrous side. Like so many people who play inhuman creatures in films, Mitch, with Jennifer Aspinall, would have to go through four hours of makeup applications every morning. Unlike most of these other actors, such as Robert Englund as Freddie Krueger or Doug Bradley as Pinhead in the *Hellraiser* films, Mitch was getting paid very little. There are very few actors that have had to put up with the hardships that Mitch Cohen did and yet never have their faces on-screen. He was a hero in every way.

This year Troma Team Video has released the Director's Cut of *The Toxic Avenger* (with the full head-crushing scene) on video. At the end of the film, we tagged on some scenes exorcised from the original work print. One of those is in honor of Mitch: his cameo from the movie, the only known footage of his face on-screen. Toxie throws a Drano and Crisco sandwich out the window, only to have it hit himself (Mitch Cohen) in the face in a window across the street.

Andree Maranda: As mentioned, Andree was the girlfriend of *The Toxic Avenger's* primary investor. However, Andree got the role of Toxie's love interest fair and square after auditioning against countless others—she was simply the best for the role. Like the inheritors of her reign, Phoebe Legere and Jane Jensen, Andree's primary area of expertise was music, and she sung professionally around the country. The only drawback to Andree was that she was unwilling to bare her breasts on-screen—but unlike the actresses in *Squeeze Play*, we knew this before we hired her. Andree was a hard worker and totally devoted to the project, even spending time with the Lighthouse to learn as much as possible about how to portray a blind person.

Jennifer Babtist and Robert Prichard: I mention these two together because they fell in love on set and got married, and I believe they are so entwined to this day. Jennifer played Wanda, the dark-haired bulliette, who masturbates over the Polaroid of the child with the crushed head. Robert played Slug, one of the bullies who chases poor Melvin the mop boy out the window. Which brings me to . . .

Mark Torgl: Mark was the script supervisor on both *The First Turn-On* and *The Toxic Avenger*, and he assisted in writing and re-writing scenes as well. He played pre-Toxie Melvin Junko and was wholly responsible for the fact that many people think Melvin is re-tarded. He also acted in *The First Turn-On* in a hilarious role as a demented boyfriend. Mark's, uh . . . *unusual* acting added a lot to the insanity of the film. I do remember one moment, however, when he was pushed too far.

We were shooting the scene in *The Toxic Avenger* where Mark rolls around the street and passersby stand around him as his skin begins to bubble and smoke. Green goo falls out of his mouth.* Mark, I no-ticed, was having trouble getting as fully into it as he had in earlier scenes. Finally he stood up and defiantly lifted his chin.

"I'm being exploited!" he said.

He stood there in his tutu. Green stuff dripped down his chin and from his hair. Air-pump-activated patches of skin stuck to his body, bubbling and receding as the special effects people tried to work out a bug. A circle of actor persons stood around him, watching his agony.

You need to have a certain mentality, I thought, to act in these movies. I guess you need to, well, go beyond your everyday definition of "dignity." We left the scene with the footage that we had and went on to whatever was next.

Mark today works as a writer and a trailer editor in Los Angeles. We wanted him back for *Toxic Avenger Part III*, where Toxie tempo-rarily becomes Melvin once again. But I was cheap and said we couldn't afford his rates, which amounted to about 50 bucks a day. Today, I regret that choice. I didn't think the fans would care. They did. Torgl IS Junko.

Pat Ryan: Pat played the corrupt and fat mayor. He reprised his role as an evil member of the power elite in *Class of Nuke 'Em High*.

---

*Incidentally, this is the first time that the Bromo-Seltzer trick was used in a Troma movie.

He was probably the most accomplished actor in *The Toxic Avenger* cast and was especially adept at changing terrible dialogue into something not quite as terrible (he would, with my and Michael's blessings, change all of his lines). Although Pat went on to star in the film whose director we at Tromaville hate more than just about any other (I won't condescend to say the film's title, but I'll let you know its initials are S.T. and it rhymes with "Wreet Wrash"), I have to say he was great to work with.

A funny side note concerning Pat:

The Toxic Avenger was going overtime. Michael, always with one eye on the budget, decided it was time to pull the plug. So, we just stopped. After we got into the editing room, we found out that the film didn't really end—the mayor didn't get his just desserts and Toxie didn't triumph.

We shot a new ending, where Toxie punched the fat mayor in the stomach and pulled out his intestines. The only problem was Pat Ryan had had some sort of fat guy surgery and had his fat vacuumed out of his body. The other problem was Mitch Cohen wasn't around. So we had some skinny fellow in the Troma office throw on the Toxie costume. Therefore, if you watch the ending closely (all right, you don't have to watch it *that closely* to notice), you'll see a lot of close-ups of very thin Toxie legs approaching a skinny fat mayor before Toxie pulls out his guts. At least everything was proportionate.

Norma Pratt: Norma Pratt had played the role of the mother-in-law in *Stuck on You*. Norma was overjoyed with the role, and she personally thanked me shortly thereafter. She said it was the first time in her life that she had ever been cast in a role that had absolutely no reference to the fact that she was a small person. I was moved by her gratitude, and promised to use her again.

When it came time to do *The Toxic Avenger*, we called Norma. In the film, Norma has to hold up a pair of jeans with what was supposed to be ejaculate on them. The white goopy stuff didn't seem to show up too well through the eyepiece, so I kept screaming for more to be globbed on. I wasn't in a particularly good mood that day.

"THIS IS TRULY ASSHOLE TIME!" I said. "PUT ON MORE OF THE COME!! MORE JIZ, MORE!!"

Norma didn't find this as enlightening as her time on *Stuck on You*. Next, I had Toxie pick her up and shove her into a clothes dryer.

We shot her through the little round window tumbling around in the dryer as it went. It was funny, you know, because she was a dwarf, right? A dwarf inside a dryer! I laugh now even thinking about it.

Norma never returned our calls after that.

TOXIC AVENGER: PROM KING

Of course I've pondered what makes *The Toxic Avenger* so popular. One reason, of course, is that audiences had never seen anything like it before. I say this without claiming it as positive or negative. Many of the slasher films of the early eighties had a sense of humor about their gore. But none of them had taken it to its logical extreme and turned it into slapstick. The *amount* of blood in T.A. was ludicrous and knowingly so—a live-action cartoon. "Violence as good, clean fun" is a scary statement, but truer in *The Toxic Avenger* than most any other film up until that time.

Also, in addition to humor, the movie has a rawness and a messiness about it that gives it a sense of veracity. Here was a movie with the seams showing, which made it all the more approachable from an audience's point of view. In the late sixties, Pete Townsend purposely used feedback for the first time on a rock and roll record. Shoddiness in Troma movies can be employed in the same way.

Then, of course, there were the "hooks" the movie had.

But what is it, I sometimes ask myself, that makes the *character* of Toxie so enduringly appealing? Again, it's tied up in the yin and the yang: Toxie has a dual nature.

First, Toxie is both completely INNOCENT, and yet he TEARS PEOPLE'S HEADS OFF. He is a *good* character who only attacks evil, yet does so in gratuitously horrifying ways. Toxie's tenderness comes out in his relationship to his mother and girlfriend and the children of Tromaville. This may seem silly or trite at times in the movies, but I promise you that I'm sincere about his warmer side. Very similar to this, Toxie has both a FEMININE (bone-crunching) and MASCU-LINE (protective, mothering)* side. The fact that a woman special-effects artist originally designed him and another woman cowrote the scripts to the sequels probably enhanced this.

---

*EDITOR'S NOTE: Lloyd never did understand conventionalized ideas too well.

In between movies, Toxie takes his devilishly witty and sophisticated ventriloquist act on the road, playing across the Catskills and beyond. Toxie is pictured here with "The Great Charlotteo."

Also, Toxie's a combination of both FANTASY FULFILLMENT and NIGHTMARE. He's Chaplin's tramp and Frankenstein's monster in Steve Reeves' body. A member of his audience can both wish to be him and be utterly afraid that they are perhaps like him. He's a muscular symbol of power, something desirable. Simultaneously, he's an outsider, something ugly and unwanted.

In the outsider quality, though, I think we find Toxie's core. No matter how much attention he's given, he'll never really belong. And, whether or not we admit it, I think most of us feel the same way.

THE TITLE

In the film, if you notice, the character is only called "the Toxic Avenger" by characters offscreen. We never had a title for the picture until we were nearly done editing—we had to add characters saying the name in late-stage dubbing sessions. Even before we were done shooting, *Health Club Horror* just didn't seem right anymore. The proponents of the creature wear T-shirts that have "The Monster Hero" on them near the end of the film. But *The Monster Hero* as a title? Too bland. I began to toy with the word "Toxic."

"The Toxic something," I thought. "Toxic Man. The Toxic Creature. The Toxic Brute." I walked around for a couple of weeks putting Toxic at the beginning of every noun I could find. "Toxic Cereal Box. Toxic Pit Bull. Toxic Pencil. Toxic My Leg." Nothing had the right zing.

Then our longtime business associate, mentor, and friend, the late Walter Manley,* mentioned that films with the word "Avenger" in them were doing well in the foreign market. I tried that noun on, it seemed to fit perfectly, and everyone that heard it agreed.

THE STORY BEHIND OTHER TITLES:

CLASS OF NUKE 'EM HIGH: Codirector Richard Haines had originally deemed the movie *Atomic High School,* which I changed to *Nuke 'Em High.* Not sure of this, we did some purposeful research and discovered that *Class of 1984* (with Perry King, the star of *Rappaccini*) was magnificently profitable in every territory where it was sold. We changed the title again to *Class of Nuke 'Em High.* This is one of the only times in the history of Troma where we set out to use the copycat ploy. And it worked—*Class of Nuke 'Em High* became our biggest video title ever (see next chapter).

SURF NAZIS MUST DIE: This film was a pick-up from its director, Peter George (who later went on to do the more serious *Young Goodman Brown* for us). Peter's title was just plain *Surf Nazis.* The problem with this was that people originally thought that the Surf Nazis were supposed to be the good guys. We thought that changing the title to *Surf Nazis Must Die* would let people know that no, we at Troma aren't anti-Semites (Michael Herz is only anti-Semitic when it comes to me). Although this spelled it out for most people, video retailers are often dimmer than your average bloke; many were still afraid to carry it because it had the word "Nazi" in the title.† Despite this, the film went on to be the most popular Troma title not produced in-house.

TROMA'S WAR: The working title of this film was *War,* but we changed it at the last minute by adding the *Troma's.* Unfortunately, many people who went to see it were regular middle-aged action movie fans who thought it was about a guy named Troma. They were probably a little surprised by the Siamese twins attached at the head and Señor Sida and the AIDS Brigade. It did dismally in its theatrical release, so in a couple test cities we changed the name to *1,000 Ways to Die.* Under that name, it performed equally poorly.

FAT GUY GOES NUTZOID: The Troma Team originally named director John Golden's great comedy *Fat Boy Goes Nutzoid.* Then we received a call from

---

*Producer of *The Green Slime.* Later masterminded *The Toxic Avenger*'s intro into foreign markets.

†Speaking of Nazis, Leni Riefenstahl used to stay with my stepmother and father when she visited New York in the seventies and eighties.

the lawyer of the rap band the Fat Boys, who threatened to sue if we used this title. I'm sure the thousands of overweight kids across America will be happy to know that the bullies calling them "fat boy" could be sued. In the Troma Team Video opening for this movie, I went on a rant against the rap group, yelling "Fuck the Fat Boys!" The day after it was edited and off to the video dubbing house I discovered that one of the Fat Boys had just died—by falling off of a couch (this is not a joke. It's funny, but it's not a joke.).

THEY CALL ME MACHO WOMAN: Although this film is truly Tromatic, the filmmakers originally tried to market it by calling it *Savage Instinct*, and designing the ads as if it was a run-of-the-mill erotic thriller.

NYMPHOID BARBARIAN IN DINOSAUR HELL: This Brett Piper/Alex Pirney production was originally called *Lost Fortress.* We tagged on a new scene at the beginning, announcing this mythic land as Tromaville of the future, and changed the title to something Andrew Lloyd Webber might want to someday redo as a musical. We also changed the name of one of the dinosaurs to a Tromasaurus.

STAR WORMS II: ATTACK OF THE PLEASURE PODS: I can't remember the original title of this film. But I *do* remember that there was never a *Star Worms I.*

HOUSE OF THE RISING: This dramatic feature is shot in the same style as Hitchcock's *Rope*, seemingly in one shot. The title comes from a character's T-shirt, which once read *House of the Rising Sun* but has had the bottom ripped off.

CANNIBAL: THE MUSICAL: This movie was originally entitled *Alferd Packer: The Musical.* The film was released in the United Kingdom under this name. Alferd Packer was the first and only person convicted of cannibalism in U.S. history. He's a famous figure in Colorado, where Trey Parker and his band of merry upstarts made the film, but he's unknown in the rest of the country. After kicking around hundreds of other possibilities, we settled for this title, which Troma art director Noah Scalin had come up with early on. Shortly after this film, Trey Parker created the Comedy Central cartoon series *South Park*, as well as the film *Orgasmo* (in which he gave me a part).

TROMEO & JULIET: This was the initial title, but before we started production I promised both Michael Herz and James Gunn that we would change it. They both hated it. They thought it would appeal only to Troma fans, shutting out a larger potential audience. Michael wanted to call it something with "Bang" in the title, preferably *Bang in the City.* James wanted to call it simply *Romeo & Juliet* (this is before we knew about the Baz Luhrman production). But we got a lot of press attention early on, and the film became known as *Tromeo & Juliet* before we were done filming.

A CLOSE CIRCLE OF FRIENDS AND FAMILY

When *The Toxic Avenger* was done being edited and mixed, about eight months after the end of production, we decided to have a screening for a close circle of friends, family, and various other Troma supporters.

I was excited. This was our best film yet. I knew it in the bottom of my soul. It was funny and, what I liked about it most of all, it had heart. Despite the violence and weirdness and insanity, there was still something lovable about the monster.

I stood near the theater doorway as the crowd started to arrive. My father and stepmother were two of the first to show up. They introduced me to a stern-looking woman.

"She's a justice on the Supreme Court in Germany," my father said to me when the woman took her place.

The *Toxic Avenger* investor showed up, along with Andree Maranda as his date. He chuckled, shook my hand. He was glad to see that it was all over.

Eventually, almost all the seats were filled. Everyone was talking, excited about what was to come.

The lights dimmed.

The movie started.

Mark Torgl came on-screen, doing his ridiculous performance. No one laughed. A couple stood up and left the theater.

"Stupid," one of them muttered on the way out.

One of the actresses bared her breasts. A few more people left. Then came the first big fight scene, with Toxie bashing the goons.

"Christ Almighty!" someone yelled out at the sight of splattering blood. He moved quickly out of the theater. More of them got up and left—they evacuated in droves.

I looked down the aisle and saw the German Supreme Court justice. Her mouth was wide open in horror: her face stayed like that, frozen as if she was encased in a block of ice. I kept watching her. She didn't change.

I sank lower in my seat. My ass hung off the end. I held my hand over my nose and mouth.

The credits began to roll. The lights came on. The theater was less than a third full.

People nodded at me as they walked by, but they wouldn't look me in the eye. The ones that did shook their heads in disgust.

My father ushered the Supreme Court woman out of the theater. He whispered to me as he passed: "Good God, man! You *backed up and ran over the kid's head AGAIN?*"

Then everyone was gone.

I sat alone in the theater, listening to the projectionist rumbling around in the booth behind me. I looked down at a flyer for the movie I had had in my hands when I entered. I had twisted and torn it into a long ragged string. I gazed up at the blank movie screen. It was a relief to not be seeing the movie up there anymore.

Vince, the guy that ran the theater, poked his head in the doorway behind me.

"Mr. Kaufman, I'm afraid we have to close up now," he said.

"Okay," I said.

But I could hardly move. I continued to stare at the blank screen. My legs were heavy as iron.

Vids, Squids, and the Nuke 'Em Kids

ten

hat's how you're ending it?" Barry asked.

"What?"

"You're ending the Toxic Avenger chapter as if it's a tragedy?"

"Well, yes. But see, in the next chapter I'll talk about how successful the film was after all. At first no one wanted to buy it, and none of the theaters wanted to take it. But then one small theater in New York, the Bleecker Street Cinema, took it to play midnights. The next day, one of the Troma Team members came in to tell me that there had been a line around the block waiting to get in. The movie ended up playing there for more than a year, which led to more theaters across the country and all over the world. The reviews were much better than we had ever received before. In Japan it was huge: When it played at the Tokyo Film Festival the crowds went insane—it was the first time I had ever been treated like a star. It was an incredible triumph. See, Barry, it's a clever literary ploy. I bring them *down* in one chapter only to bring them *up* again in the next."

"It's basically the same story as *Squeeze Play.*"

"Well, yes, but this time it's completely unique because I end the chapter differently."

"I don't know if that counts as completely uni—"

"Also, the reaction to *The Toxic Avenger* was much stronger. People were crazy over it. They went to see it repeatedly. We started to get fan mail. This was the birth of the true Troma, with all the elements in place."

"Did it make a lot of money theatrically?"

"Well, no. Not too much. By this time it was extremely expensive to promote a film, and the majors had monopolized most of the theaters. But this was the golden age of video, and we made a huge amount there. And that's not even mentioning the TV rights, the sequels, or *The Toxic Crusaders* TV show."

"Is that what's going to be in the next chapter?"

"No. I think I'm going to have *Class of Nuke 'Em High* next."

"That warrants its own chapter?"

"Yes! Definitely! There's a lot for filmmakers to learn from that experience."

"That's one of the reasons I wanted to meet today. It seems we're straying a bit from the original goal. This is supposed to be a work that travels step-by-step through your career in such a way as to serve as a how-to manual for young filmmakers. But presently it's nothing like— Lloyd, so far you have twenty-two jokes having to do with masturbation."

"Barry, not to put you down. But counting my references to jacking off is the best way you can find to spend your time?"

"If I read another one, I'm going to lose it. So, before you start writing the next chapter, why don't you tell me how information about *Class of Nuke 'Em High* is going to help filmmakers."

"First of all there's how I came to codirect it with Richard Haines."

"Yeah? How?"

"Originally Richard was supposed to direct by himself. Richard was cool, I liked him. He was a walking pop-culture encyclopedia."

"Yeah, right. So?"

I stared at Barry. He stared back. He seemed to be getting exasperated.

"I feel like you're testing me," I said.

"I'm not *testing you*. I just want to know *why* it warrants a chapter. The book is long, Lloyd. You were worried about making seventy-five thousand words? It's already that."

Readin'...Writin' and Radiation!

A LLOYD KAUFMAN/MICHAEL HERZ PRODUCTION

CLASS OF NUKE'EM HIGH

"Great!"

"No. It's un-great. The book needs to sell for $14.00. That means it can't be too long. Putnam is hard-core about keeping the paper expenses down."

"Really?"

"Yes."

"We have tons of paper all over the Troma office. You can use that."

"Are you joking? That's ludicrous!"

"Smaller print?"

"*Lloyd! You—*"

Barry stopped himself. He sucked his lips into his mouth and clenched his fists. He must be having problems with the girlfriend, I thought.

"Please," he muttered. "Just go on about Haines."

"He had been editing films for us for a long time. He edited *Toxic Avenger*. He wanted a chance to direct. Michael and I thought we owed it to him. But there were some problems."

"Like what?"

"I don't know. I mean, Michael and I are abusive, I guess. But Michael's that way because that's how he gets something done and people respect him, and I'm that way because I get nervous. And not to say that Richard was abusive, but we had only filmed one day of preproduction shooting when some of the actors came into our office. They said they were going to quit if Haines continued directing. Michael and I decided that I should come on board to codirect."

"Was Haines upset?"

"I think he was a little relieved. It was a lot of pressure on him and having me there made it easier."

"Yeah, sure."

"Another interesting thing about *Nuke 'Em High* was that it played for the first time at a market screening during Cannes. As it did, the radiation cloud from the Chernobyl explosion floated directly over us. Children were told not to go swimming, and everyone was told not to eat rabbit. Another thing: we have a shot of an imploding building in the movie. It's a good example of using an opportunity. Jersey City was destroying this building, so we went and filmed it, and used that for the school blowing up at the end. It looks totally different from the school that's in the movie."

"Terrific," Barry said flatly. "Did this movie make money?"

"Oh, yeah. Barbara Javits from Media Home Entertainment watched it on the flatbed in the Troma Building. She only saw about twenty minutes of it when she offered us a deal, basically the budget of the film, as an up-front advance for U.S. video rights. She said it was going to be a big hit. She was right. It was our biggest success on video for a long time thereafter. And there's also something about Montgomery Clift that I wanted to include."

"Montgomery Clift?"

"He was a neighbor of mine growing up. One day he came over to my house very drunk. I was the only one home. I was about eighteen. He kept getting closer and closer. He kept commenting on my belt buckle, saying what a great belt buckle he thought it was. It was just this crappy metal thing. Eventually, he started putting his hands on the belt buckle. I didn't know what to do! He was Montgomery Clift! He started asking me how you work it, and then he unbuckled it. At that point I sort of jumped away and said I had something to do. Monty looked sort of embarrassed and he left."

"That's another thing you've made up, right?"

"No. That one's true. But I was thinking I could make up a story about how he gave me a blowjob. It's not like the Whitney Houston thing. We were the only two there, *and he's dead*. It *could* have happened. Including that seems pretty commercial to me. Perhaps Putnam will give us some more paper."

"Lloyd."

"Yes?"

"*What does that have to do with* Class of Nuke 'Em High?"

"Well, nothing. I just don't know where else in the book to put it. I don't know how to arrange these things. I'm not a *book writer*. What do you think? Do you think I should do the blowjob thing?"

"NO!" Barry shouted. Then he closed his eyes and regained his composure. "Listen. Just do me a favor."

"What?"

"This stuff isn't—It's not too interesting. Let's leave *Nuke 'Em High* as one of the periphery movies, okay?"

"But it's important!"

"Will you listen to me? We need to publish a book that has at least some rudimentary information about the film industry instead of just,

TROMETTE: A PRETTY LITTLE WORD THAT MEANS DON'T FUCK WITH ME
by Andy Pennington

As for *Webster's*:

Tromette (trô'-mĕt) *noun* 1: the archetypal heroine of a Troma film 2: a proactive, intelligent female self-starter who appeals on all levels to both sexes (as well as to genderless space mutants) 3: a thick linguine noodle with a creamy calamari sauce most common in the northern-most provinces of the Middle East 4: a fiercely pointed mind in a lushly curvaceous body; a beautiful woman with a large mind and small clothes

From the softball queens of *Squeeze Play* to Tromeo's pierced, bisexual, patriarchy-smashing Juliet, audiences have come to cherish the Tromette. SHE is a brazen in-dividualist who is stunning in both her physical and men-tal resources. That so many of these sensuous revolutionaries handsomely fill out a D-cup may just be good luck. Well . . . maybe.

Lloyd Kaufman's maiden film effort, *The Girl Who Returned*, features the embryonic Tromette. Gretchen Her-man stars in the title role as a world-class athlete whose T-shirt becomes world-class the minute she goes jogging. Thus, *The Girl Who Returned* features a lot of Gretchen jogging. And that T-shirt has never received a single bad review.

On the other hand, *Squeeze Play* was initially criti-cized as exploiting its female cast. In reality, the first real Tromette movie championed a group of dynamic, self-determined women. That this was lost on some boobs dis-tracted by playful nudity and locker room jokes says more about the critics than it does about the film. The public took to *Squeeze Play* right away, however, proving that there is nothing quite so closed as an intellectual's open mind. (Except maybe Kevin Costner's mouth when *Sizzle Beach USA* comes up.)

Funky, slinky, sexy, subversive Phoebe Legere was a major figure in Manhattan's booming performance art scene of the eighties. Since Troma had long glistened at the vanguard of Gotham creativity, Ms. Legere's destiny as Tromette was inevitable. Lloyd Kaufman caught Leg-ere's nightclub act in a murky downtown locale and rec-ognized her as a genius. He cajoled her immediately, then, into moving to a waste dump and doing topless love scenes with a tutu-clad monstrosity. As Toxie's blind, blond, bomb-shell girlfriend/spirit-guide/mop-changer in *Toxic Avenger II* and *III*, Legere brilliantly honored the Tromette tradi-

you know, this insane anecdotal stuff. What I really want in the next chapter is for you to go into some detail on video releases."

"*Elggh!*"

"Lloyd."

"God! How bor-ing! That'd be like go-ing into detail on the retail market for men's shirts!"

"COME ON, LLOYD!" he exploded. "YOU'RE NOT WORKING WITH ME ON ANYTHING HERE! ALL YOU WANT TO TALK ABOUT IS MASTUR-BATING AND URI-NATING! REALLY, I NEVER TOOK MUCH STOCK IN FREUD! BUT NOW I DO! I REALLY DO! YOU'RE STUCK IN LIKE SOME ANAL EXPULSIVE PHASE FROM WHEN YOU WERE THREE!"

Everyone in the diner was staring at us.

"Barry," I whis-pered. "Chill out."

"You're driving me crazy."

HELLO VIDEO

When video was first introduced into the American home marketplace, it was a strictly ancillary means of profit for film companies. Over the years, however, video became increasingly important, and for a while it was *the primary means of income for independent film companies.*

In more clichéd terms, a gold mine. *Class of Nuke 'Em High*, as I told Barry,

tion. Like Lynn Lowry in *Sugar Cookies*, her mind was her sexiest feature. Like Carol Drake and Carol Bever in *Waitress!*, her comic dexterity was awe-inspiring. Like the awesomely oiled-up Jessica Dublin in *Troma's War*, she could kick irradiated ass with the best of them. And like Lisa Gaye in *Class of Nuke 'Em High Part III: The Good, the Bad, and the Subhumanoid*, she had a hairdo with a dressing room of its own. Most importantly, Phoebe Legere inaugurated a new standard for the Tromette. She was a self-invented original.

Jane Jensen, the titular Tromette of *Tromeo & Juliet*, epitomizes modern feminist principles. Not coincidentally, she may be the ultimate Tromette. Outside of Tromaville, Ms. Jensen is yet another renaissance artist, as the star of numerous independent films and stage plays, as well as an internationally successful rock star. As Juliet, Jane is far more intriguing and energetic than Tromeo, not to mention that she is capable of delivering a lesbian sex tussle with tattooed cook Debbie Rochon far better than he ever could.

In the fifties, a woman was required to hide her intellect to heighten her erotic presence. In the seventies, women concealed their bodies to be taken seriously as scholars and thinkers. The nineties woman is, at last, free to celebrate all aspects of her being, just as the Tromette has been all along. Troma has always made movies of the future, but it's exhilarating to know that in terms of the Tromette, the future is now.

was one of the largest-selling videos Troma has ever released.* On its initial release there were over 100,000 copies sold at about 100 simoleons a piece, just for rental alone. This is not because it was the best or most beloved of Troma Films. This is just because it came along at the right moment.

THEATRICAL GOES BUST

In the early eighties, theatrical profit became nigh impossible for independently distributed films. During Ronald Reagan's big-business-ass-sucking, Alzheimer's-riddled reign as U.S. Chief Executive, the antitrust laws were altered and it suddenly became legal for studios to own movie theaters. This aided in initiating a monopolistic theatrical

---

*After some time, *Toxic Avenger* surpassed it.

landscape. Mom-and-pop-owned movie palaces were wiped off the map one by one. It became virtually impossible to find a theatrical venue willing to carry product from independent distributors. If the studio didn't *own* the theater, they could still use other means to ensure that films from their studios were the only films theaters would take (i.e., "We'll let you have our mega-budget Tom Cruise blockbuster this summer *only if* you take our shitty Judd Nelson movie *now*"). In addition, since independent studios were so desperate for distribution, they would take a lower percentage of the door. In the seventies the film would take perhaps 50–65 percent of the door, and the theater would take 35–50 percent. Later, that changed to 50–50, and today, in some of the more popular theaters, they'll only give *10 percent* to the film and keep 90 percent for themselves.

The final tap on the wooden stake in the heart of independent films was skyrocketing advertising costs. Newspapers + TV + billboards and so on all doubled and tripled their costs. Simultaneous to that, the large studios began octupling their own advertising budgets for films. Today a film's advertising budget is often equal to its production budget.* The days of low-budget, by-the-seat-of-your-pants, grassroots, dance hall, grind house distribution were over. To make matters worse, TV networks owned by Disney, Warner, etc., continually do so-called "news stories" that amount to billions of dollars of advertising for the big studios. Independent films are ignored. Joel Siegel confirmed to me that he "doesn't review Troma movies." Gene Shalit has the same policy. They both even refused to review Troma's national release of the animated, G-rated classic *My Neighbor Totoro*.

THE TROMA AMENDMENT: Troma continued *and continues* to pride itself on creating films meant to be watched in an actual cinema. ALL of Troma's in-house-produced films, including later productions such

---

*Not only that, but the percentage of spending on advertising is much, much higher in the film industry than almost any other business. Although it may *seem* as if you are besieged by Coca-Cola ads and ads for the newest Chrysler, in truth, most companies, including soda, car, and beauty aid companies, spend, at the most, 5 percent of their budgets on advertising (usually closer to 1 or 2 percent). Hollywood studios, however, can spend upwards of 33 *percent* on advertising. Seem stupid? It isn't. Movie advertising is some of the only advertising that is statistically proven to *work*. In these other industries, the effect of advertising is negligible, if it indeed has any effect at all.

Liz Caiten, another stellar example of the early Tromette, demonstrates why the ahead-of-it's-time *Squeeze Play* is far superior to the overrated *A League of Their Own*, which was produced fifteen years later.

as *The Toxic Avenger III* and *Sgt. Kabuki-man NYPD*, are shot on 35mm film in such a way as to promote optimum enjoyment while being viewed on a forty-foot screen. It irks me when Troma is referred to as a straight-to-video outlet, though we continue to release films theatrically. Of course, I know that the majority of people who will see these films will see them at home. And I admit: this could be yet another sign of my refusal to do what is most beneficial to my pocketbook. Other low-budget film companies—including my friend Roger Corman's company, Concorde—completely eliminated theatrical release from their budgets long ago. But I still love projectors and popcorn and faulty speakers and floors where your shoes stick to the dried-up cola.

AND THENCE CAME THE VIDEOCASSETTE (OR, WHY *CLASS OF NUKE 'EM HIGH* RAKED IN THE BUCKS)

As previously stated, video was initially an Elysian Fields for movies like *The Toxic Avenger* and *Nuke 'Em High*. The reasons for this were numerous.

FIRST, video stores had a need for product—any product. In

In this publicity still from *Tromeo & Juliet*, Jane Jensen, who plays Juliet, searches the set for her contact lens.

1982 you didn't have 30 billion Blockbuster stores scattered across the landscape like so many elephant droppings, filled to the brim with thousands of videocratic choices. You had a few video stores with a lot of empty shelf space. Once a VCR owner rented the few major releases available on tape, they didn't have anything else to rent. As the big studios are in every trend, they were *late* to realize the potential for video. The stores simply needed *something* to put on the shelves.

"You got a documentary on elephants farting? We'll take it."

"A biopic called *God's Favorite Son: The Kirk Cameron Story*, starring Corey Haim? Yessireebob— give me two copies of that bugger."

"*Tiddlywinks: The Movie*? An *Over-the-Top*-esque feature about two six-year-olds in a class tiddlywinks play-off made for twelve grand? Yes, thank you."

If the stores didn't get new movies, their customers would get pissed off about the amount they had to pay for memberships and/or the player itself. When they were *most* in need of something, *Toxie* and *Nuke 'Em* came along.

SECOND, the stores purchased nearly equal amounts of all new movies. Therefore, a shot-on-16mm-in-my-parents'-backyard slasher movie could theoretically make the same amount of money as *Grease*. It was at first a truly democratic environment.*

THIRD, films that were commonly grouped in the category of "exploitation movies"—that is, films with catchy titles and (the promise of) lots of sex and violence—were tremendously popular. Much of the

---

*As it is equally fascistic today. Those who care about the continued purity of the Internet, take note of this historical catastrophe and don't let it happen again.

Fully evolved Tromette of the 90's, Stephanie Stokes models the look that all Tromettes will be wearing in the near future.
PHOTO BY BARBARA NITKE.

public, who may not have wanted to spend six bucks to see low-budget
fare like this in the theater, were more than willing to check it out for
two bucks in the privacy of their own homes. Also, the "party-nature"
of Troma films and the like was more acceptable at one's own residence, where a group of friends could sit around the screen interacting
loudly and doing something else during the boring parts.

FOURTH, many of Troma's fans are criminals.* Whereas they may
not have the cash to buy a movie ticket, they very likely have, at one

*We get a large amount of fan mail from inmates.

point or another, stolen a VCR. They would also sign up for video memberships in the name of a relative, rent movies, and never return them. This was another reason *CNH* did so well: So many copies were stolen, the stores would have to buy more.

FIFTH, *Class of Nuke 'Em High* was widely and unanimously considered, in the words of Roger Ebert, "Even better than *Citizen Kane.*"*

A TIP OF THE HAT TO AMELIA EARHART

Since *I know* that the great publishers Penguin Putnam are going to do their best to buy a few extra reams of paper on which to print this book, I shall take a few moments to mention some historical facts in honor of them.

George Palmer Putnam (1814–72) was the founder of G.P. Putnam's Sons—the precursor to Putnam Berkley—and *Putnam's Magazine* in 1848. He had two sons: George Haven Putnam (1844–1930), the person primarily responsible for instituting the international copyright laws, and George Palmer Putnam† (1887–1950), a world-class explorer who led two expeditions to the arctic. In addition, G.P.P. II, the second son, was adept at getting the babes. He married the great aviator Amelia Earhart (1897–1937) in 1931.

Earhart was, of course, in 1928, the first woman to fly across the Atlantic. She was also the first woman to fly it alone four years later.

In 1937 she and famed drunkard navigator Frederick Noonan set out to fly around the world using the longest and most difficult route. They had covered about half the length when they began to fly the 2,556 mile distance between New Guinea and Howland Island (now known as Thurston Howell Island). After a few enigmatic and broken radio messages to Howland air base, Amelia Earhart and Fred "Blotto" Noonan disappeared forever. Theories abound about what happened: perhaps she was taken captive by the Japanese, or crashed on a small island, never to escape. Most likely, though, Earhart simply plummeted into the sea and died a horrific death. Perhaps, as they hit the water, her limbs were torn from her body with great amounts of blood spurting from the gaping wounds. The front of her body could have possibly

---

*EDITOR'S NOTE: Uh, do I even need to say that he's making stuff up again?
†Putnam, like George Foreman after him, seems to have named all his sons George.

ripped open on the steering wheel or something and, as the plane sunk more and more quickly, she could maybe see her intestines drifting up in front of her. "Dear God!" she might have thought. "I can see my own innards passing before my eyes! This is the most horrible thing I can imagine! I am in terrible pain!" And then she glanced over to see Fred "The Lush" Noonan, and his head had been ripped from his body. The head bounced around the cabin, off of little dials on the dashboard (I don't know much about planes), until his eye got impaled on a shard of glass along the broken window. The head just stayed there, stuck. "Fred!" Amelia tried to say, but a flood of water and part of her own intestine entered her mouth. And then she gagged to death on her intestine. I can see it quite clearly. It all goes to prove the unfortunate fact that girls just aren't as good at flying planes as boys.*

The end. Thank you, Penguin Putnam. Who's Penguin?

VIDEO TODAY

Today, video is no longer the booming business it once was. It is rare one makes a film's budget back by video alone. Stores are filled with titles released over the past twenty years, so the need for new product isn't as strong. Second, instead of buying equal copies of all video releases, they buy thirty copies of the new John Travolta movie and then, maybe, if they have a little bit of cash left over, they'll buy one copy of a new independent release. If they have any money left over after that, they'll get a Troma movie. The older public—that is, the folks who were renting videos at the form's inception—are admittedly gun-shy about independent, unknown product. Because of the barrage of "any and everything" when video began, most people have rented more than their fair share of crap. Therefore, today they're less likely to rent a video they haven't read about or seen on theater marquees. The younger audience, raised on video, are more brainwashed by sixty-million-dollar ad campaigns than ever to watch only that material featuring big stars. That way, you'll safely know that a movie sucks before it begins rather than find out after you start watching it.

Another reason for video's downfall—especially in the case of Troma

---

*All of the above information is either from the *Columbia Concise Encyclopedia* or *David Wallechinsky's Twentieth Century*. Or I made it up.

and other alternative cinema—is the screwy morality and traditionalism of certain tight-asses out there in the industry. It doesn't matter how many people want to rent Troma movies—they won't be able to if store owners refuse to buy them. I won't mention the name of the primary offender, a huge chain started by a Christian fundamentalist, which is, in many ways, the world's ultimate evil (I'll drop a hint—it rhymes with SCHLOCKBUSTER). Not only does this largest-video-chain-in-the-world not allow NC-17 films in their stores, but they only want "Soft R's"—that is, movies that don't rub too hard against the edge of that rating (unless they star Arnold Schwarzeneggar, Sylvester Stallone, or another huge celebrity). They are known to have versions of movies in their stores which have been altered from the original, with no warning whatsoever on the box. Who can forget the famous buttery anal sex scene in Bernardo Bertolucci's great *Last Tango in Paris*? Well, a lot of people who've rented the Blockbuster version (whoops, it slipped out) notice that a GIANT LAMP has been superimposed over Marlon Brando's butt! Yes, thanks to Blockbuster, the United States' tradition of Puritanism and prejudice continues to thrive.

SO, IF THEATRICAL HAS BEEN DEAD FOR A WHILE AND VIDEO IS RECENTLY DECEASED, HOW IS IT THAT TROMA MAKES MONEY ANYWAY?

Good question. The truth is, it's a miracle that Troma keeps staggering along. There isn't much money to make out there with low-budget films.

Luckily, TV sales have taken over some of the gap. With *so many* channels out there all over the world, TV brings in more money (though not as much as has been lost in these other travesties). In fact, one of the video-killers not mentioned above is the ever-increasing popularity of pay-per-view, which is a newly meaningful market.

In 1995 Troma Studios initiated a new wing of the company: Troma Team Video. We wanted to keep with our own tradition of doing everything backasswards. So we started a video company right when the video market plummeted. Still, the company hasn't been doing too poorly—now we're able to control how our films are marketed, spread the use of Troma as a brand name, and take the profits ourselves. We sell films at both rental prices and sell-through prices. The rental tapes sell at a much higher price, between fifty and eighty dollars, and are sold almost exclusively to stores where you rent videocassettes. Originally, in the first part of the eighties, these were the only types of tapes sold—usually for about 100 smackers. The consumer, or sell-through, tape is priced so that your average fan can buy it to watch and rewatch at his or her leisure. Consumer tapes sell for between ten and twenty-five dollars. These have been an asset to Troma Team Video, since we can now market directly to our fans.

Newly important in the sell-through market, and to the continued survival of film companies like Troma, is the World Wide Web.

AND NOW YOU TOO CAN OWN A TROMA VIDEO

All you have to do is turn on your computer and go to: http://www.troma.com

There you can see a variety of Troma films available on tape—great movies like:

CLASS OF NUKE 'EM HIGH!
SURF NAZIS MUST DIE!
THE TOXIC AVENGER!
DEF BY TEMPTATION!
BLOODSUCKING FREAKS!

And many more!

All available for less than twenty bucks! You heard me right! Less than twenty dollars!

"Boy," you may say, "I'm a bit too lazy to, you know, like, write out a check and write out Troma's address on an envelope and, you know, lick the envelope shut and send you the check for a video and everything."

And we say: Great! Now Troma offers a way to buy videos tailor-made for lazy fucks just like you! All you have to do is enter your credit card number on the Web Site, and check off the Troma movies you want to BUY, and then, like magic, you'll have your new Troma movies in just a few weeks! Do it AGAIN and AGAIN and AGAIN! Hell, that's the great thing about credit cards! They're not like *real money!* You can't even see the money—it's just out there, some amorphous thing—AND YOU CAN GIVE IT ALL TO TROMA!

Isn't the Net fun?!

BUY TROMA MOVIES NOW!

eleven

There's Nothing Like a Good War to Make Heroes of Us All

THE STORY OF TROMA'S LONG IGNORED MASTERPIECE, *TROMA'S WAR*

It was 1986 and I was getting a hard-on to make another movie. *Toxie* was a hit, *Class of Nuke 'Em High* was a hit, and our audience was clamoring for more Troma booty. We were ready for the next level. We would make a movie that fully utilized the Troma feel, that would catapult us into the mainstream of moviemaking. No film is more Troma than the resultant *Troma's War*. Unfortunately, the only place it catapulted us into were warehouses of unsold videotapes.

Troma's War was Troma's answer to Reagan and Rambo. After two decades of peace power, WAR was back in style in America. In *Troma's War*, an airplane crashes on what appears to be a deserted island. Some of the passengers survive, including a low-level rock and roll idol, a blind woman, a Vietnam vet/used car salesman, a mother with her baby, an assassin, and a priest. Each of them is an ordinary inhabitant of Tromaville—one of the "little people." While on the island, they uncover an army barracks, where elitist terrorists and businessmen are preparing an offensive on the United States. It is the Tromavillians' responsibility, they realize, to indulge in some undercover terrorist work of their own, to save the world from this evil conspiracy. With guns, bombs, mutants, full-frontal assault, and full-frontal nudity these ordinary folks must salvage democracy.

I have long maintained that *Troma's War* is our undiscovered masterpiece, with only *The Toxic Avenger* and *Tromeo & Juliet* in its league.

Less well-known than *Toxie, Tromeo, Nuke 'Em High, Surf Nazis, Bloodsucking Freaks,* or even *Sgt. Kabukiman, Troma's War* is my personal favorite. However, like anything of great personal worth, you wind up having to overcome seemingly endless hurdles to achieve it. Like all Troma films, it started as a burst of inspiration and ended up a practical yet frantic exercise that just needed to *get done.* Get that shot! Say your line! There's only two hours of daylight left, goddammit! Move that fucking sandbag out of the frame! Get that machine gun barrel out of your mouth!

INSTINCT VS. DELUSION

I believe there's a certain dichotomy within the life of every artist. On the one hand, as an artist, it is important to withhold ego and to *listen* to the opinions of others. The artist who says, "I don't care what other people think, I only create my art for myself," isn't really an artist at all. Art is simultaneous acts of creativity, expression, and communication. If you don't care how the art affects others, you're expressing very little and communicating nothing at all. I think the need for others' opinions is especially true in the world of film, which is not only the most collaborative of arts, but is also the art that financially necessitates speaking to a broad spectrum of people. I have seen too many expensive, horrible films that were hurt by their creators refusing to listen to input from others. Better that one should get opinions on his or her screenplay early on.

On the other hand, an artist must heed his gut and be courageous enough to act upon instinct. Sometimes this means blocking out the words of everyone around you, and doing what you need to do.* Unfortunately, pride and vanity are clever foes that sometimes manifest themselves as instinct, and it is only wisdom, experience, and a rigorous self-honesty (not self-doubt) that allows one to distinguish between true instinct and its impostors. I felt compelled by instinct to make *Troma's War,* which meant I had to frequently turn a deaf ear to those who disagreed, even when those who disagreed were people I loved.

> ### WHAT'S THE MOST EXTREME TROMA MOVIE?
>
> Despite the many claims of this book, it's not *Bloodsucking Freaks* or *Troma's War* or *Tromeo & Juliet.* Instead, it is the 1996 release *Beware Children at Play,* directed by Mik Cribben. "They love their parents . . . with ketchup," the ad proclaims. Then: "Patricide! Matricide! Fratricide! None of the kiddies are on *YOUR SIDE* in *Beware Children at Play!* Scarier than Death! THIS IS NO GAME!" Although this movie isn't extreme throughout, it features a shocker ending where children who are zombies (but look exactly like normal kids) are killed in myriad and graphic ways by their own parents. One child has a gun shoved in his mouth and his head blown off. When the uncut trailer for this movie played before *Tromeo & Juliet* at the Cannes Film Festival, over twenty-five people left the theater in protest.

HURDLE #1: MY PARTNER, MICHAEL HERZ

Michael and I support each other in our business as well as our art. Together the two of us can act as a mighty blockade against outside invaders and the establishment. Our secondary purpose, however, is to act as each other's nemesis. Michael will attack me when I am weak or when my thinking is wrongheaded. I despise his actions while they're occurring, but I also know that these actions force me into being stronger, making my life better in the long run. One of the things we most often clash over is the direction Troma should take.

---

*An example: MGM executives tried three times to remove the song "Over the Rainbow" from *The Wizard of Oz.* Producer Arthur Freed followed his instincts and said, "The song stays—or I go!" It ended up winning the Oscar for best song—and, even better, it was recorded by the talented and sexy Kathie Lee Gifford on her smash album *Sentimental.*

"But we just made a film, Lloyd."

"I know, Michael. But we're a movie studio. We should keep making movies, right?"

"Wrong."

"We have the money! A clean million! And I've got the first draft of a script—it's called *War!*"

"Think of all the other things we can get for that, Lloyd."

For a long time, Michael has seen a more practical possibility for Troma. That is, instead of spending a million and a half dollars on making a single film, you can buy the distribution rights to 150 low-budget films for 10,000 dollars a piece. This is a far less risky investment. However, with the recent successes of *The Toxic Avenger* and *Class of Nuke 'Em High* as exhibits, I was able to convince him we should once again set out on the path of moviemaking.

One hurdle overcome. My partner was behind me.

HURDLE #2: THE SCREENWRITER, MITCHELL DANA

Mitchell Dana cowrote the screenplay with me. Mitchell had been a fellow student of mine at Yale, and when we met up years later he showed interest in writing a screenplay. Unfortunately, what had become a tradition with my co-screenwriters was true once again: Mitchell wasn't enthusiastic about taking the Tromatic road.

"I think we ought to go about doing it a bit more straight than that, Lloyd," he told me after I had added copious notes to his first draft.

"Straight? It is pretty straight."

"What?"

"Even *The Longest Day* had some jokes in it."

"Well, yes, but in *The Longest Day* you didn't find out that the evil force behind the Nazis were misshapen Siamese twins attached at the head—"

"Think how interesting it would have been if John Wayne had walked in on that! Or, better yet, *The Longest Day* could have revealed the *truth* about Hitler."

"The truth?"

"That he used to have Eva Braun shit on his head."

"*What?*"

"It's supposedly true. Do you think, as sort of a nod to that, we ought to have somebody shitting on Pig-Nose's head?"

"No. That's what I'm talking about. All these things you've added. Here, on page seventy-two, girl gets hit in the mouth and you have her spitting out an endless number of teeth."

"Why can't you have that?"

"I wrote a realistic script."

"Even *Platoon* had jokes in it."

"Like what?"

"That slow-motion shot of Willem Dafoe crying as he got killed? That was hilarious!"

"I don't think it was supposed to be funny."

"Intent has nothing to do with it!"

"But, here's the problem—most of these things aren't funny at all. The *AIDS* Brigade?"

"That's not funny, that's frightening. Just imagine if that really happened."

"Okay, Lloyd. Whatever. But the truth is I wrote a realistic script. I think you're making a mistake by screwing around with it."

Mitchell, from a financial perspective, was probably right. *Troma's War* made money when it was finished, almost exclusively because it was an "action movie" with a certain amount of explosions and machine gun blasts (and because we had a video deal with Media Home Entertainment before we even commenced filming). But it didn't make *a lot* of money because it was a bit too weird for your average foreign territory (and also, in the States, the MPAA disemboweled it—we'll get to that in a little bit).

Still, despite its lack of huge profits, it's worth much more to me than the sales some bland, boring action movie would have generated. I feel a deep, warm pride when I think of *Troma's War*. You have to ask yourself, how much is *that feeling* worth?*

---

*After *really* asking myself this question, I have come to the striking and unfortunate conclusion that the deep, warm sense of pride is worth slightly over forty-seven thousand dollars. Undoubtedly, if I had made a straight action film we would have made at least a few hundred-thousand dollars more in sales. Therefore, fuck me— Mitchell Dana was right. I am SUCH a stupid cunt.

HURDLE #3: GUNS AND SQUIBS

Despite the fact that Paul Williams had once advised me to put a gun in every movie I ever make, I had dealt with them very little. I knew zippo about weapons. I thought an AK-47 was a classic novel by Joseph Heller.

Luckily, there was Rick Washburn. Rick was a Vietnam vet who wanted to get into the business of supplying weaponry for films. He gave us a deal on the guns and blanks in the movie, in part because we gave him one of the lead roles—the used car salesman (a role in which he was fantastic*). Rick trained the rest of the cast and me in the use of guns. By the time we started filming, I was an expert.† Rick was also helpful with his knowledge of Vietnam—it was his idea to have his character collect the ears of his victims and wear them as a necklace (an actual ritual in the war), sort of "counting coups."

The shoot-out sequences in *Troma's War* were difficult from a technical perspective. I hadn't really shot anything more complex than gang fights and softball games, and now here I was with an entire war; huge stunts, countless people killing each other at the same time, naked women running through the forest (this last one was easy). For much of the shoot we had three crews shooting simultaneously: one shooting the primary action, another shooting gags and close-up details, and another shooting cutaways and minor effects (squibs, etc.) It has been said that *Troma's War* employs more squibs‡ than any other movie outside of *The Wild Bunch* and the films of John Woo. Whether or not this is true, I have no idea. But I do know that *Troma's War* was the first film to squib each of a woman's breasts and have them burst upon being "shot," which is far more historically significant.

---

*This is another tactic to save money on a low-budget film—GIVE YOUR SUP-PLIERS ROLES. Most people want to be on-screen, and will give you a good deal on a truck rental to be so.

†Years later, my enthusiasm for guns dwindled when I was brought up on charges for attempting to bring a pistol onto an airplane. (Oh, wait a second. That wasn't me. That was Christian Slater. Damn. I always get the two of us mixed up.)

‡A minor explosive and blood packet, most often used when a bullet hits someone.

HURDLE #4: MY PREGNANT WIFE, PAT

Pat and I made the mistake of going and getting pregnant with our third daughter before we filmed *Troma's War*—about nine months before, to be exact. The baby was due any time, and I was in the boondocks of New York State,* awash in mud and forest, filming in the trenches.

Pat was less than appreciative of the Skinner-boxian treatment of our fourteen-month-old daughter Lisbeth. Lisbeth plays the role of the young baby who survives the plane crash. Brenda Brock, an experienced soap opera actress, plays her mom. Brenda was a profoundly dedicated actress, who chose to do everything she could to bond with Lisbeth. She did this to make her performance as a mother more realistic, and to help out Lisbeth's performance as well. Although today, at the age of eleven, Lisbeth's a pretty good actress, as an infant she was really shitty. You just didn't *believe* she was a baby who had been through a plane crash. She seemed like, you know, a regular baby. For weeks before the shooting, Brenda would often come over to our home and spend time hugging, holding, and playing with the baby. Eventually, Lisbeth became familiar with her. Her pudgy little face would brighten up every time Brenda came to visit. Unfortunately, Lisbeth didn't know we were preparing her for the truest form of method acting.

In one of the first scenes we shot, murderous thugs wearing ski masks surround the mother and steal the baby from her. I guess I didn't adequately explain the scene to Lisbeth. She saw the masked men coming down on her, blasting guns, and began to freak out. All the bonding that Brenda had worked so hard to set up suddenly, ironically, worked a bit too well. The kidnappers snatched her from her surrogate mother and darted with her into the woods. Lisbeth began to wail. After we finished the take, *everyone* was angry with me. Pat snatched Lisbeth, saying I wasn't allowed to use her anymore. Brenda was distraught. And the "tough guys" in the ski masks began to curse me out.

"Kaufman, you motherfucker, look what you made me do to that poor little kid!" said one cauliflower-eared guy.

---

*Actually, outside the great and friendly city of Peekskill, NY—the *real* Tromaville.

Obviously, if they had been looking through the camera's viewfinder like I had, they wouldn't have been complaining. The shot was absolutely beautiful!

Soon, Pat had another kid. We named her Charlotte. When Pat went into labor she was in NYC and I was on the *War* set in the middle of nowhere filming burning men. Luckily, Jeff Sass, our production manager, cowriter, and longtime Troma employee, had been lugging along a Cro-Magnon version of the mobile phone* for that very purpose. Pat, again exemplifying an understanding beyond compare, knew that we were shooting a magic hour† shot and waited until nightfall to call. Sass had a PA ready who had pre-driven the quickest route to the hospital ahead of time. The PA got me out of the forest and there as quickly as possible. I was able to stand by Pat's side while the baby was born. (I don't know if you've ever seen this, but it's really disgusting. If I saw something like that coming out of me, I'd hit it with a hammer.) I took one day off, on which Michael Herz took over all of the directing.‡

I remember holding my newborn daughter in my arms for the first time, looking down upon her vulnerable, beautiful face, her heartbeat pounding lightly beneath my thumb, and thinking, "Christ, I hope the weather doesn't fuck up our crash site scenes!"

HURDLE #5: THE CAST

The cast on *Troma's War* was the best I had up until that time. The group of young actors put themselves into it 100%, and their morale stayed strong throughout a hellish and messy shoot. However, perhaps because they cared so much, they were also exceedingly willing to argue with me over everything from plot points to makeup to stunts.

---

*A huge fifty-pound device with dials and gadgets that appeared to be out of some old Buck Rogers serial.

†Magic hour is simply the time of day around sunset (there's another magic hour at sunrise). As far as time of day for filmmaking goes, these things are gold. Tenuous gold—if you set up the shot and screw it up, there may not be time to do it again. Even large-budget productions can get screwed in this way.

‡Incidentally, the footage from this day was some of the most exemplary footage in the film. I can't tell you how great it was to return to set and have everyone in the crew tell me how much better it was having Michael set shots than me. What a joy!

Famous Troma action hero Joe Fleishaker (l.) smiles nervously upon being found in hotel linen closet with unidentified Troma groupie.

One of the great pleasures of *Troma's War* was working with ass-kicking senior citizen Jessica Dublin, a star of many spaghetti westerns. Once, while Jessica was trudging through the mud in high heels, I screamed at the crew:

"Can we get some help over here *now*—I got a seventy-year-old woman about to have her ass broken!"

I could tell Jessica was offended by my remark.

"I'm sorry, Jessica. I meant to say 'butt.' "

"Fuck that!" Jessica said. "I'm only *sixty-nine!*"

The other great discovery in the *Troma's War* cast was Joe Fleishaker. Joe was a five-hundred-pound extra—excuse me, actor person—to whom I took an instant liking. I saw the potential in him of a Troma action hero. The cast complained that I was spending too much time focusing on this "background character," giving him lines and action-oriented scenes, even though there was no such character in the original script.* "You're just focusing on him because he's fat," said one of the actors. Which, of course, was completely untrue—another five-hundred-pound actor person had also been on set, who I wasn't nearly as

---

*On Troma sets, actors often get jealous because I spend more time on the goofy second unit shot of a background guy tripping in the mud than the dramatic climax of the romantic relationship. This is probably one of my great failings, but what the Hell—it's more fun this way.

drawn to. Since *Troma's War*, Joe has appeared in both Toxie sequels, *Sgt. Kabukiman*, and *Tromeo & Juliet*. He also plays the character of Michael Herz in the *Tromaville Café* TV series and other video projects.

My primary problems with the cast, though, came during the scenes with Señor Sida and the AIDS Brigade. The AIDS Brigade had been a bone of contention from the very beginning, when Mitchell Dana claimed it was too extreme. I have said before, and I will say again, that I did not think of this as being demeaning to people with AIDS. A recent conversation with screenwriter/water sports enthusiast James Gunn emphasized that perhaps, yes, there are some ways in which I view the world differently:

> TROMA'S UNSUNG CLASSICS:
> 5 MOVIES YOU DON'T KNOW ABOUT BUT
> WANT TO SEE
>
> *STORY OF A JUNKIE* (1984, Lech Kowalski)
> *DEAD DUDES IN THE HOUSE* (1988, J. Riffel)
> *SCREAM BABY SCREAM* (1969, Joseph Adler)
> *SCREAMPLAY* (1986, Rufus Butler Seder)
> *THE GEORGE PAL PUPPETOON MOVIE* (1986, Arnold Leibovit)

"I mean, Lloyd, come on. In all the offensive things I've seen in all Troma movies, this was the peak. I have to admit even I blushed a bit when I saw it. Nothing in *The Toxic Avenger* shocked me, but this I just couldn't believe."

"I didn't think of it as shocking."

"How could you—?"

"I just thought of it as frightening. It was one of the more serious parts of the film—this could actually happen."

"Wait a second. You don't have these people acting like humans with a horrible, debilitating disease. They're hunched over, growling and spitting, sticking out their tongues, scrunching up their faces, they're acting like, well . . . monsters."

"Yes, well, you know the PAs showed up wearing the makeup, the bursting boils, the pustules—"

"Those were PAs?"

"And a few members of the crew," I said. "The actor persons casting people screwed up. The AIDS Brigade was supposed to be about fifty people, but we only ended up with six or seven."

"Hm. I'd think a brigade would be at least nine people."

"Yeah. Anyway, they showed up in this ridiculous makeup, and everybody in the crew just started cracking up."

"So you decided to have them act like monsters?"

"Well, you know—On the one hand it was funny. . . . On the other hand it was horrible. . . . I didn't really connect the two."

"You know what the most offensive scene in the movie is, don't you?"

I shook my head.

"It's where the leader of the AIDS Brigade—"

"Señor Sida."

"Yes. Him," James said. "He takes that sexy girl into that wooden shack and rapes her. And then, when he's done, she jumps up, topless—these huge breasts bouncing around—and she yells out, 'I've got AIDS! I've got AIDS!' I completely freaked when I saw that."

"Why?"

"*Why?* First of all, you're making a joke involving *rape* and AIDS at the same time, and then, because you have a chance for some gratuitous naked titties, you just sort of throw that in on top of it."

"You didn't like it?"

"No. It was my favorite thing in any movie ever."

"Thanks."

"After every time I had sex with my girlfriend over the next few weeks, I would jump up and down yelling, 'I've got AIDS! I've got AIDS!' "

"Really?"

"She didn't find it as funny as I did."

"Well, to tell you the truth, that scene was the one *nobody* wanted to do.* The actress said she didn't want to say the 'Got AIDS' line, the DP said he didn't want to shoot it, everyone on the crew thought it was stupid."

"But you knew that you really wanted to take this movie over-the-top?"

"No."

---

*NOTE: This is where that hurdle comes in—I'm trying to keep this as relevant as possible.

"No?"

"I just wanted to make sure that people understood."

"Understood what?"

"That she had AIDS."

"She just got raped by a guy with AIDS-spurting boils all over his face! It was obvious!"

"I was afraid the audience wouldn't get it. It was purely for plot."

"I'm not saying this in a bad way, Lloyd. But there is something very, very wrong with you. Why'd you throw the boobies in?"

"I don't know. Again, nobody wanted her to do that. So, to appease the crew, we shot it two ways, topless and not topless."

"And you knew all along—"

"And I knew all along which one I was going to use, sure."

"And you figured, you know, if a woman's willing to bare her breasts, you shouldn't pass up that opportunity."

"You're the one that said it."

"But you didn't realize that your thinking process is kind of weird. Again, I'm not saying this in a bad way—this is why Troma movies are so unique. But most people would say, 'Okay, we have this gratuitous nudity. We'll put that over here in *this* scene. And then we have this horrifying rape situation—so we'll put that over in this *other, different* scene'—you see what I'm getting at here? 'And then, we have a silly joke, so we'll give that guy his own scene too.' See what I mean? But in Troma movies, you just throw all that stuff in one scene together. It's like emotional gumbo."

"I sort of see what you're saying."

"But it's what makes the movies great, Lloyd."

"Thanks."

"It makes you insane at the same time, but you know—"

Although James did point out to me some unusual zags of my thinking process, I must say that I did care about the AIDS theme quite a bit. What was important to me wasn't so much making a broad statement on the nature of AIDS in our society, but to push the disease itself in people's faces. It was 1986 and the issue was being swept under the carpet by the media and by popular culture in general. AIDS hadn't been dealt with at all in movies, with the exception of a TV movie, *An Early Frost*, which was just the old *Brian's Song* disease movie transposed with a new disease.

Many have criticized us, saying that although *Troma's War* was the first movie to deal with AIDS, all that is nullified. They say Troma "makes jokes out of things that just aren't funny." In addition to AIDS, these things also include violence, sex, and toxic death. I would agree that these things are not funny—but that is why I make jokes out of them. Humor, I believe, is one of the human spirit's healthy ways of dealing with pain. As I believe strongly in both free speech and the fact that ideas in and of themselves cannot in any way be dangerous (only the preclusion of them can be), I do not believe in stifling humor because it's based around something "too heavy." And, now that I think of it, toxic death *is* funny. By the way, here are my four favorite quotes on humor:

- "All humor is based in cruelty."—Al Capp, great cartoonist, creator of *Li'l Abner*

- *"That says a lot more about Al Capp than it does about humor."*—George Herriman, greater cartoonist, creator of *Krazy Kat*, upon hearing the above quote

- "Life is a tragedy when seen in close-up, but a comedy in long shot."—Charlie Chaplin

- "Tragedy is when I fall into a manhole and break a leg. Comedy is when you fall into a manhole and die."—Mel Brooks

HURDLE #6: THE CREW

On the first day of shooting, Troma employee Phil Rivo was working the craft service table* when an assistant cameraman punched him in the nose. I wasn't sure exactly what the scuffle was over.† Whatever the case, it was certainly a sign of things to come with the crew.

---

*Craft services are the food services on set. This is the second worst job after location manager.
†This was not the only time Phil got a fist in the face—at the Cannes Film Festival he stuck a Toxie sticker on the back of someone's silk suit and got similar treatment. And again, on the set of *Toxie II*, special-effects artist and *Redneck Zombies* creator Pericles Lewnes downed him, saying, "I just had to do it, man. I had to do it. I hope you don't fire me."

Before I go on to complain about the crew, let me fess up: My temperament on *Troma's War* was not exactly Dr. Andrew Weil-esque. As a director, part of your job is to control your surroundings. One unfortunate caveat to this is that there are always some factors you cannot control. On *War*, I was learning this. The size of the production promoted numerous anxiety-fueled moments of rage and illogic. Throwing things, screaming, making forty-year-old men cry—all of these were common occurrences. Yet it was still surprising to me when the crew, who had been living in barracks on set for weeks, decided to indulge in a sit-down—an actual strike—refusing to work until certain requirements were met. Jimmy London, the DP, took me aside.

"Lloyd, it seems there's a little problem."

"Why aren't they setting up? *Hey, you, Gruenwald, get your ass on that HMI!*"*

"No, uh, Lloyd, see, they're refusing to work until—"

"*What?!*"

"Until—"

"That's asshole time! Tell them to get back to work, or else they're fired!"

"They just want one thing."

"What?"

"Chicken. They'd like to have a little fried chicken at the end of the day. Maybe a little pizza on alternating days."

"Blackmailing pigs!"

"We're having sixteen- and seventeen-hour days, Lloyd. They're a little hungry at the end of the day. They want food."

"We already give them lunch! What do they want out of me!? My blood!?"

"It doesn't really seem like it's that out of line."

"I guess I should have someone here to shine their shoes in the morning as well!"

Eventually, due to Jimmy's calmness, I acquiesced. If we had fired them all at once, the movie would have had to stop. I opted instead

---

*HMI: Hydrargyrum Medium Arc-length Iodide—large lamp that gives off light similar to daylight.

WHY THEY CALLED HIM SAMUEL WEIL

In 1977, Lloyd Kaufman had to become a member of the DGA—the Director's Guild of America—to get credit on *Slow Dancing in the Big City*. Thereafter, by the rules of the Guild, he was not permitted to direct nonunion films. Directing credit on the Troma movies from *Squeeze Play* through *Troma's War* was given to Samuel Weil (along with, in many cases, Michael Herz—who wasn't a member of the DGA). Samuel Weil was the name of Kaufman's great-grandfather, a founding member of the Board of Directors of Armour Meats and Manufacturers Hanover Trust. A few times Kaufman was charged with breaking the Guild rules, and threatened with charges. But he maintained that "Samuel Weil" was the name for the Troma Team as a whole, not him personally. Then, in 1986, a *New York Daily News* article had him interacting with Pig-Nose and a large-breasted female soldier (played by Troma art director Alexis Grey) on the set of *Troma's War*. The article said Kaufman "directed [Pig-Nose] to snort" and quoted Kaufman as saying, "Moan! Moan louder!" to the soldier. Because of the article, Kaufman was brought in front of his DGA peers. The article was evidence of Kaufman's breaking of union rules.

"Gentlemen," he said. "If THIS is what you call directing, God help our profession."

He was found innocent of directing.

He resigned from the DGA shortly thereafter. His letter of resignation cited the racist and sexist discrimination of the Guild—which at the time was almost 100 percent white males—as a motivating force. Today, due to the Guild's vast improvements, it only seems to be about 98 percent white males.

for the healthier option—to walk around from day to day with a burning resentment that I would act upon with vague mumblings and passive-aggressive behavior.

Not too long after that, though, one of the PAs drove a van to pick up a shitload of fried chicken. Even though drinking on a Troma set is strictly prohibited, some of the crew thought the PA might have been intoxicated. Whatever the reason, he got into a car wreck. Fried chicken was strewn all over the highway. The PA, not too seriously injured, had to go to the hospital. I, of course, blamed this, vocally and often, on the crew for needing a third meal so badly. The blame, however, was truly my own self-centeredness and lack of tranquillity, as I was about to find out.

Jeff Sass, probably the best Troma employee ever, quit in the middle of *Troma's War*. He told Michael that he couldn't take my behavior any longer. It had been ten years since I had been mistreated by the higher-ups on *Saturday Night Fever*. Now things had come full circle—it was me who was being unfair. I knew that if I was scaring away even this most tolerant, capable, and intelligent of individuals, there must be something very wrong with the way I was acting. Michael said I would be crazy not to beg to have him back. Which I did, including promising to change my behavior. Jeff claims that I did improve slightly. Today, although I am still in a constant state of explosive paranoia while on set, I hope it is a somewhat kinder, gentler explosive paranoia.

HURDLE #7: BODILY FUNCTIONS

Troma is far too cheap to lug around Johnny-on-the-Spots when we're filming in deep woodlands. Therefore, taking a shit became somewhat of an issue.

HURDLE #8: ACTS OF GOD

Ninety percent of *Troma's War* was shot outdoors. One problem with this was the constant, overriding concern of weather. Rain can be an almighty boon.

One of the most important scenes in *Troma's War* is when our group of heroes sit on a high rocky ridge and decide to fight the terrorists. You'll notice, however, upon watching the scene, a streak of Kaufman-Herz flair. One shot will feature a torrential downpour, which will cut to another where the sun will be shining bright. You may think that the Troma Team spent countless hours setting up rain-machines and bright lights, a potent act of weather as symbolism, showing how quickly our lives can change from dark to light, from "cloudy" to "bright," the yin to the yang, and how the whole outlook of our lives can change on a dime.

Unfortunately, it is truer that we had very little time. The rain was coming down in sheets, and then suddenly disappearing, off and on. We didn't have any choice besides just continuing to shoot. The cast deserves hearty accolades—they were given the choice to disband, but decided to do what was best for the movie.

Another act of God concerned the character of Colonel Jennings, also known as Pig-Nose. Pig-Nose was one of the leaders of the terrorist conspirators. His whole character was based around the absolutely hilarious concept that he had a—*get this!*—a nose like a pig! The hilarity was cut short, however, when Rick Collins,* the actor who was

---

*Rick went on to play the Chairman/Devil in *Toxie III*.

playing this modern-day Diabolus, was in a car accident while driving to his first day on set. There was only one, small part of his body that was injured in the wreck. You guessed it—his schnozz. The prosthetic nose the special effects artist had created was too painful too apply. It had to be replaced with a simpler, less-hilarious version.

Some dreams die quickly and with absolutely no accounting for whatsoever.

HURDLE #9: TIME IS NOT ON MY SIDE

A Troma tradition started on *Troma's War*: we shot way too much film. The first cut of the movie came in at OVER FOUR HOURS LONG. Many people have commented that *Troma's War* (which had a budget of 1.3 million) has the highest production values of any Troma film. Again with the yin and yang: We got a lot for our money, but we could have gotten a lot more. Almost half of our budget was strewn on the cutting room floor. Fortunately, we had one of the greatest editors it has been my privilege to work with, George Norris. George actually takes part in the creation of a film—like all the best editors, he is a storyteller and innovator as well as a technician. With his help, we were able to cut the film down to under two hours.

The trait that, unfortunately, both George and I share is an inability to stop. Therefore, we continued to cut and cut, fine-tuning, trying new ways around a problem, rearranging scenes. We did this for over six months, until Michael Herz finally said we had no choice but to stop where we were. We begged him for the chance to go on, but he wouldn't let us. The madness was over.

HURDLE #10: THE FUCKING MPAA

But not really. Actually, the madness hadn't even started. That began on the day we turned the film into the MPAA-CARA ratings board.

Like all arms of the established elite, the MPAA obviously saw it as part of their duty to destroy Troma when we were at our strongest. As I said earlier, *Troma's War* is my favorite Troma film. Both Michael and I believed, because of the recent success of *Toxie* and *Nuke 'Em High*, the superior *Troma's War* would deliver us to an even broader audience. The theaters were waiting for it, the media was waiting, and so were our newfound fans. After watching our final cut, Michael was relieved: "That's not going to have any problem getting an R," he said. It shouldn't have: Michael and I had paid close attention to mainstream films like *RoboCop* and *Die Hard*, making sure that none of our violence went farther than that. And, since in those days the theater chains we were playing would not accept unrated movies, we *needed* the R. We also needed to deliver an R-rated version to the video company, Media Home Entertainment, by a certain date, or risk losing our guaranteed advance payment in the hundreds of thousands of dollars.

After we had sent the film to the MPAA, one of the Tromites called up to see if we had gotten our rating.

"Forget it," the MPAA rep said. Then added, "This is a horrible film."

The Tromite told me what had happened.

"It's horrible?!" I yelled. "What does that have to do with anything?!* They aren't supposed to be critically evaluating things, just seeing how adequate it is for children under seventeen."

I told Michael. Michael got Richard Hefner on the horn. Hefner was head of this part of the rating process. Hefner said, quote, "We will never give you an R."

We're ruined, I thought. Troma is over. No theaters. No money from Media Home Entertainment—our contract for about half a million called for an R-rating. I wondered if I should shoot myself alone, or take my family out with me.

In the end, we convinced Hefner to watch it again. But this was only after we turned it into mush. Everything that made *Troma's War*

---

*To this day, it is common for MPAA reps to comment on the quality of a film. Recently, they've said they've liked two films—*Cannibal: The Musical* and *Tromeo & Juliet*. Not so coincidentally, these are two of the films which got past their scissors fairly uncut. *Cannibal* was given an R with no changes, and *Tromeo*, the most extreme film we've yet produced, was given thumbs-up with under two minutes cut out. *Beware: Children at Play*, rated at about the same time, and which they said negative things about, had enormous chunks removed from it, including a heart being pulled from a chest similar to that in the PG-13 *Indiana Jones and the Temple of Doom*. You might think that I'm proud when they compliment a picture of ours— actually I find it reprehensible. If quality is such an important part of their viewings, their ability to fairly assess the content of films is nullified.

so great had to be changed. As we tore it apart, it felt as if I were clawing out chunks of my own flesh. Even the scene where the woman spits endless teeth out of her mouth (each of the teeth was a cartoonish two-inches long) had to go.

I must admit, much of my battle against the MPAA and their unfair practices against independent films is inspired by revenge.

HURDLE #11: THE PUBLIC

When *Troma's War* was released into theaters, it performed dismally. Our fans were pissed because it was so bland. They thought it was our attempt at selling out. The media didn't catch on to it—to them it was just a slightly quirky action movie. It didn't have a prominent monster or an overtly sexual theme like the other movies.

Media Home Entertainment released the video in both an R-rated and an *almost* uncut version.* It sunk like a rock because there was no positive theatrical publicity behind it. The rare few who saw the uncut version seemed to like it. Our market screenings were the best they had ever been. The reviews for it were as good as they were for *The Toxic Avenger*, and today it has a very small cult following. But, because of the theatrical fiasco, most people have never seen it, never even heard of it. I hope that some day, in a future edition of this book, we will be able to amend this chapter with a more positive outcome. I hope that there's a brighter day yet ahead for *Troma's War*.

---

*The completely uncut version is a newly available sell-through on Troma Team Video.

Stunts Gone Wrong

twelve

On Troma movies we hang up posters on every set and in each production office that read:

Rules of Troma Production:

1 Maintain Safety to People
2 Maintain Safety to People's Property
3 Make a Good Movie

Michael and I take these principles seriously. Making a good movie is not worth killing people (unless those people are U.S. senators or studio executives or people that you don't like). We decrease the chances of injury by taking every precaution available. However, in the past we *have* fucked up. In the next few pages I provide six examples of stunts that have not gone as planned. In addition to a few cheap laughs, I hope that these mistakes will provide the novice filmmaker with a vivid illustration of what not to do.

1

MOVIE: *The Toxic Avenger*
THE STUNT, IN SCRIPT: In the midst of a chase scene a car crashes, flips, and rolls.

THE STUNT, AS PLANNED: The car comes rushing down the road and zooms up a ramp. On the ramp, the car's right side rises up while its left wheels stay low. The car then rises high enough to flip over and roll across the street.

It has been my philosophy that, if you want, you can hire hack writers, hack directors, hack actors—but you can't hire hack stunt people or pyrotechnics. You shouldn't even *be* a hack stunt person or pyrotechnic. In a world of ridiculous legal regulations on virtually every aspect of life, this is the one area which has practically no restraints.

On *The Toxic Avenger*, we hired stunt people with long lists of past credits, many of which were Hollywood movies.

The dangerous part of this stunt would be hitting the ground upside down and rolling. If you did this in a regular car, the nonreinforced roof would crush in, leaving the driver with a head akin to Sylvester's after Tweety hits him with a frying pan. But our professional Hollywood stuntman had taken precautions. He had set up the car with a "roll bar"—that is, a bar that went around the inside of the car and over the roof, reinforcing it so the car could roll without being crushed.

Three people were involved in the stunt: the stunt coordinator, the guy who put the roll bar in the car, and the driver, Russell.

Michael Herz was directing the scene. He had been taking control of all the stunt sequences in *The Toxic Avenger*. I was behind one of the cameras.* We were filming with four cameras, as we had been doing with all our major stunts. That way we would be able to cut from angle to angle without having to redo the stunt. And if something went wrong with one of the cameras, the stunt wouldn't be lost forever. We also set the cameras at different speeds, getting some angles in slow motion for increased drama, and some in fast motion to exaggerate the feeling of speed.

Michael was standing on top of a truck. He had a megaphone. "Action!" he cried.

I watched through the eyepiece as the car came rushing down the street. Looks great. Beautiful. The car runs up the ramp and into the

---

*I always place myself on the camera closest to the dangerous action—but, still, never in any true danger. Well, almost never (see #3).

air, flying there against the backdrop of the blue sky. Then it falls. Rolls. Gorgeous! Fabulous! Perfect!

Then, suddenly, while the car is upside down, it flattens like an accordion. The roll bar didn't hold.

Russell is dead!

I dropped the camera. I ran toward the car. Michael was ahead of me.

"RUSSELL!" I yelled. "RUSSELL!"

No answer. Through a crack in the metal I could see part of his body, part of the brown jumpsuit he was wearing. He didn't seem to be breathing. Christ, he couldn't have been much more than twenty-five years old.

Michael and I looked at each other. I knew we would never, ever make another movie again. This was our fault, the two of us.

I was too old to go to dental school.

Then a small sound came from inside the car: "Elggh."

"Russell? Is that you?"

"Shit. Ow."

He was alive. My body swayed for a moment. For a second I could have sworn I fainted, but I stayed upright.

Soon the ambulance arrived. They used the jaws of life to cut open the car like a tuna can and remove Russell. He was miraculously unbroken.

I inspected the car: The motherfucker who had installed the roll bar simply screwed it into the floor of the car. As soon as any pressure was applied on top of it, it popped through the bottom like a fork through a wet paper bag. The guy who built it was an idiot—the floor was obviously unstable.

Whose fault was this?

It was *his* fault for claiming to know what he was doing. It was the stunt coordinator's fault for hiring such an idiot, and for not checking out his work. It was Russell's fault for not checking out the car before doing a stunt like this and putting his own life in jeopardy. And, finally, it was my fault because I also should have checked it out myself, and I shouldn't have hired guys who were shitheads.

LESSON: Don't hire shitheads.

ALSO: A Hollywood pedigree does not preclude shitheadism. If anything, it ensures it.

2

MOVIE: *Troma's War*

THE STUNT, IN SCRIPT: The bad guys are on a huge cruiser leaving the pier on their way to America to enact their wretched conspiracy. One of our heroes drives a jeep up a ramp, out over the water, and directly into the ship. At that point the ship explodes, killing the baddies.

THE STUNT, AS PLANNED: The boat is filled with explosives. The jeep (with no one inside) goes up a set of tracks,* flies over the sea, and into the boat†—when they collide, the pyrotechnic detonates the bombs with a trigger on land.‡

If you've heeded the call of Rule #1 and you've chosen adequate stunt people, they should know a lot more about doing stunts than you. Therefore, most of the primary decisions should be up to them. On *Troma's War* we hired Scott Leva as the stunt coordinator and Will Cabane as the pyrotechnic. Leva was always extremely responsible, safe, and accurate. He had used a complex series of mathematical equations to figure out exactly where to place the boat so that the car would fly into it. Cabane was likewise trustworthy—when he set off an explosion, he could tell you to the very inch how far it would go. He stood by with a detonator to charge the explosives.

---

*The script calls for "the cynic" to drive the car and suddenly become a suicidal hero. The stuntmen wanted to drive the car and escape underwater. Michael refused. We had done a similar stunt on *The Toxic Avenger* with a driverless car. There was no reason to risk a stuntman's life. A couple months later a stuntman drowned doing the exact same stunt on a major Hollywood film.
†The boat that the jeep would actually fly into was about a tenth of the size of the huge cruiser we just saw the bad guys board, but, you know, Troma is a hearty and active supporter of the suspension of disbelief.
‡To make things even more difficult, this was set up on the Brooklyn waterfront. There was only a thin sliver of space we could use to film—if the camera panned slightly to the left or right you would see buildings where there is supposed to be only remote tropical island. To blot out some of the buildings we set some of our borrowed potted palm trees in the foreground on the sides of the frame. We obtained a truckload of these potted palms from a New York florist in exchange for a credit. We would have to return them at the end of shooting. After dragging them around from location to location for over a month, with days of sitting in 95° sun and little bits and pieces being smoked by the crew along the way, they ended up looking like large, furry Krazy straws. The florists were not pleased.

The cameras were set. The jeep was revved up, ready to go. Suddenly, Michael Herz stopped the whole thing.

"Move the boat closer," he said.

"If we move it closer, the jeep will just fly over it, not into it," Scott said.

"No way," I told him. "Michael is a hundred percent correct. I can see. The boat is too far away from the land. The jeep's going to land in the water in front of it. Move it closer."

A minor debate occurred, but, as usual, Michael and I prevailed. They moved the boat closer to land.

The jeep revved up. There were four cameras—four cries of "Rolling" came out, one after the other—the last one from me, on camera four. "Speed!" yelled the soundman. "Action," Michael cried.

The jeep took off. It went up the ramp. It flew over the water in a clear, clean arc. And then it flew directly *over* the boat.

"Oh, shit," I said.

Will Cabane, thinking quickly, set off the explosives as soon as the jeep was over the boat. The result on film looks rather humorous. The boat explodes *beneath* the jeep, without even touching it. But at least we got our explosion, and the *idea* of what was supposed to happen was shown on-screen. Thanks to Will, but no thanks to either Michael or me.

LESSON: Let the experts be the experts.*

3

MOVIE: *Sgt. Kabukiman NYPD*

THE STUNT, IN SCRIPT: Harry Griswold unintentionally transforms into a Kabuki-clown and is chased around the city by Brick Bronsky† and other hoodlums. Two of the hoods crash their car into the rear end of another, propelling their car to flip in the air, turning in circles, landing and exploding.

---

*I know this whole section seems to completely oppose "Never Trust a Pyro" in Chapter 3. This contradiction goes to prove two additional points: "Lloyd often doesn't know what the hell he's spouting off about," and "A funny little story is far more important to Lloyd than actually making any sort of sense."

†Brick, a professional wrestler and consummate nice guy, later went on to star in *Class of Nuke 'Em High II: Subhumanoid Meltdown* and *Class of Nuke 'Em High III: The Good, the Bad, and the Subhumanoid*. After that, he appeared with Jean-Claude Van Damme in *The Quest*.

THE STUNT, AS PLANNED: The stuntman drives up a very steep ramp, flips over in midair, and lands on the ground. Later on, we shoot a similar (but different) car exploding and cut them together.

In addition to being a classy stunt, this provided me with a chance to steal a Brian De Palma* shot from *Carrie*. At the end of *Carrie*, John Travolta and Nancy Allen get into a car wreck, flipping over. De Palma shot the two actors in a stable car while twirling the camera around in circles. I would use this same shot with the hoods as their car spun in the air.†

We shot on a street in Hoboken, New Jersey (although it was supposed to be Manhattan, it looked more like Boise). We set up five cameras around the area of action. As usual, I took the camera position closest to the danger, nearest where the car would land—but 100 percent safe according to the stunt coordinator. When everything was in place, I yelled, "Action." This was relayed to the stunt driver by walkie-talkie. The car took off. It zoomed up the ramp very fast . . . too fast. It flew into the air, drawing a perfect arc. Everyone was in awe. It was truly beautiful. As I looked through the viewfinder, I noticed something unusual. The car seemed to be coming straight at me.

Either someone had misjudged or they hated me.

It's hard to say what happened next. I only remember the car landing ten feet away from me. Bits of gravel and metal shards struck my body. I was in shock.

Everyone was clapping. The stunt driver jumped out of the car and did a little football dance, wiggling his legs around.

"Wonderful!" the crowd shouted. "Fantastic!"

I wondered if they were referring to the fact that he had almost killed me.

---

*De Palma's first movie, as well as Robert De Niro's first movie, is *The Wedding Party*, which is owned by Troma.

†Another shot of De Palma's in *Carrie* "inspired" me. When Carrie and William Katt are dancing at the prom, De Palma put the actors on a large lazy Susan, spinning them around as the camera spins around them. In *Tromeo & Juliet* Jane Jensen and Will Keenan have their first dance (and first kiss) on a large lazy Susan, as the nighttime stars stay stable behind them. At one point our production assistant began spinning the lazy Susan too fast and the two actors fell off of it. Because of Troma's emphasis on safety, we had spotters there to catch them; neither one was injured.

I told the DP that I ran away from the camera, that I didn't get the shot. Strangely enough, though, when we watched the footage in the dailies I had stayed with the camera the whole time. The shot looked perfect.

LESSON: Don't let a car fall on you.

The shot looked *so* perfect, in fact, that it would be a waste to use it in just one movie. Which brings us to:

A Special Money-Saving Tip from Troma:

Tromeo & Juliet had the lowest budget of any Troma production since *The First Turn-On*. It was the cheapest of all Troma films that required any sort of real stunts or special effects. Therefore, we had to think of new and novel ways to save money. One of those was REUSE STUNTS—namely, the car-flip stunt from *Sgt. Kabukiman NYPD*.

The scene in *Tromeo* is perhaps the most exhilarating scene in the film. The head Capulet baddie, Tyrone, is hit by a car and then tossed through the air and onto the end of a flatbed truck. His head is decapitated, whereupon it flies through the air and lands upon the moving car of a clean-cut Happy Family—a mother, a father, and two children—who happen to be having a sing-along of "Found a Peanut." The family sees the head on the hood of the car. The parents are distraught; they weep. The children point at the head and begin to giggle. The father panics and turns, ramming into another automobile. Their car flies up into the sky, flips in midair, and lands. The mother and father dart from the car, sobbing profusely. The kids jump out, play catch with the human head for a moment, and then join the parents as they all watch the car explode. An all-American family portrait.

In the movie, most of this footage is new. However, the car flip itself is composed of the same shots as in *Sgt. Kabukiman*. In preproduction, the *T & J* crew found a car that (pretty vaguely, actually) resembled the car in the stunt. We shot the family* in the new car. We shot a new car crash since the old car crash distinctly showed the drivers in the *Kabukiman* scene. However, we used the same flip, as well as the same explosion. Once again, in honor of De Palma, we used his shot of the Happy Family flipping in 360° turns; on the day of shooting it, though, we were rushed. If you look closely you can see the brick of the wall behind the family as they turn. It flips along with them.

Ironically, although *Tromeo & Juliet* was actually shot six years after *Sgt. Kabukiman NYPD*, it was released on video first. Its theatrical release was also wider. Because of this, many people have been mistaken about the Troma film in which the shots originated.

---

*The father was played by *T & J* coscreenwriter and foot fetishist James Gunn.

4

MOVIE: *Sgt. Kabukiman NYPD*

THE STUNT, IN SCRIPT: Naked woman gets thrown out of window.

THE STUNT, IN PRACTICE: Stuntman jumps through a candy glass* window, wearing obviously fake wig and nude bodysuit, and falls fourteen stories to land on a huge inflatable target.

One of Michael Herz's favorite pieces of advice for people in the film industry is, "Assume everyone's an idiot." Unfortunately, most everyone *is* an idiot. When you're dealing with new employees, especially people inexperienced in film, it's important that you make sure they understand instructions. This usually means having them repeat to you the directions you just gave them. Many people find this humiliating. Mostly because it is. But over fifty percent of the times I've had new people repeat instructions, they repeat them to me wrong. This is sometimes because I failed to properly communicate the message, sometimes because the person is extremely stupid, or, most often, because a new person becomes so frenzied and nervous on set that he loses the ability to *listen*.

You may think that this doesn't apply to your professional stunt people. As I said in example #2, you should trust your stunt people in decisions pertaining to the expertise of stunt work. However, when it comes to *the practical information concerning how you and the stunt person are going to interact during the filming*, you must check, double-check, and triple-check that the two of you are in sync. Otherwise, you won't have any need for fake heads on your set. You'll have enough stunt people heads to go around.

Case in point:

Sgt. Kabukiman: A stuntman was on the top floor of a building in Harlem. He was dressed up to look like a naked woman (shortly before I noticed that he had a big black hairy mustache and forced him to

---

*Candy glass, also known as sugar glass, is a fake glass used on movie sets. It smashes into safe blunt pieces. Many stunt people today prefer to work with BEADED GLASS, which is the kind of glass used in most modern car windows. This glass smashes into beads and looks more realistic, and it's cheaper—but it's more likely to damage the individual jumping through it.

shave it). Now, like most stuntmen, he had psyched himself into an energized, animalistic, goldfish-eating frat-boy frenzy, ready for the jump.

I communicated with him through the assistant director, by walkie-talkie.

"Tell him we'll do it like this," I said. "First we'll cry, 'Speed.' Don't jump. Then we'll say, 'Ready.' Again, don't jump. Just get ready to jump. Then we'll cry, 'One-two-three—action.' On 'action,' jump out the window."

The AD relayed my information through the walkie-talkie.

THE FIVE WORST TROMA MOVIES

Okay, we know you're out there. Those of you reading this book looking for the worst in cinema. Well, folks, when you're talking about the worst in the Troma library you're talking HARSH competition. But we've pared it down. Watch at your own peril.

BIG GUS, WHAT'S THE FUSS? (1972, Lloyd Kaufman, Ami Artzi) Kaufman wasn't lying. This film has no peer. It is *impossible* to sit through. See chapter 4 for more gory details.
CAPTURE OF BIGFOOT (1979, Bill Rebane) The best film ever about a man in a fur coat falling down in the snow . . . again . . . and again . . . and again . . .
CURSE OF THE CANNIBAL CONFEDERATES (1982, Tony Malanowski) The only Civil War film containing not a single Confederate uniform. But it is faithful to the period in other ways. For instance, the quality of the cinematography.
CROAKED: FROG MONSTER FROM HELL (1981, Bill Rebane) Rebane strikes again. Even the thousands of frogs were embarrassed to be in this thing.
PICK YOUR NERD MOVIE: Troma picked up more nerd movies than you can shake a pocket penholder at in the wake of *Revenge of the Nerds'* success. All of them share the quality of major suckage. *KILLER NERD* (1990), *BRIDE OF KILLER NERD* (1991), and *NERDS OF A FEATHER* (1991).

"Okay," the stuntman said.

"You got it?" said the AD.

"Yeah."

Five cameras. We aimed them at the top of the building. We began rolling.

"Speed!" I cried.

"Speed!" the AD repeated into the walkie-talkie.

"Ready!" I screamed.

"Ready!" the AD said.

The stuntman came jumping out the window.

"Shit!" I yelled. I tried to follow the fall with my camera, but I hadn't been ready.

The stuntman landed expertly into the inflatable bag. He jumped up, waving his arms triumphantly in the air. His fellow stuntmen ran over to him, hugging him, slapping him on the back, and exchanging high fives.

They were followed by five irate cameramen, cursing him for jumping on "ready" instead of "action." The stuntman just looked baffled. He was too psyched up before the stunt and hadn't really listened to the directions.

LESSON: Assume everyone is an idiot.

ALSO: Communication is the most important commodity on a movie set.

5

MOVIE: *Tromeo & Juliet*

THE STUNT, IN SCRIPT: London Arbuckle is horrified after seeing that his beloved fiancée Juliet has mutated into a disgusting cow-creature. Then she reveals an enormous penis beneath the skirt of her wedding dress. London throws himself out of a window to his death.

THE STUNT, IN PRACTICE: We film the interior scene with actors Steve Gibbons and Jane Jensen. Later, we shoot an exterior at a different building. There, stuntman Arthur Jolly jumps through beaded glass and lands on a large stack of cardboard boxes on a balcony two stories below.

Arthur and stunt coordinator Marcos Miranda told the production designer, Roshelle Berliner, to buy ¼-inch-thick glass to put in the window frame. Roshelle questioned this, wondering if it wouldn't be easier to jump through thinner glass.

"Of course it would be," the stunt guys told her. "But it wouldn't look as realistic."

The day of filming came. The DP Brendan Flynt and I stood on the balcony, each manning a camera. Next to me was Efrem, the still photographer, ready to get some publicity shots of the stunt. A third cameraman stood in the backyard getting a wider shot. Arthur Jolly was dressed to look like Steve Gibbons: sporting a tuxedo and curly blond wig. He stood at one end of the bare upstairs room, bracing himself for a run which would end in him crashing out the glass.

I cried, "Action."

With every bit of strength he could muster, Arthur raced across the room. He slammed his head into the glass as hard as he could. But he didn't go anywhere. The glass was too thick. Instead of breaking, the entire window frame was knocked loose. The glass and frame fell two stories—and the glass still didn't break. It was definitely too thick. Arthur remained standing in the upstairs window.

Arthur's hands slowly came to his blond-wigged skull to caress it. "Ow," he muttered.

After it was ascertained that Arthur was okay, we had to figure out how to salvage the scene. We didn't have enough time to buy new, thinner glass. Instead, we decided we'd shoot Arthur jumping out the venetian blinds.*

Again, Arthur stood at the back of the room. Again, I cried, "Action." Arthur darted across the room, and out through the venetian blinds. He sailed through the window in a graceful manner. But this time there was a new cause for grief. Arthur was supposed to be jumping onto the balcony below the window. Instead he had thrown himself out with too much force. He began to fly feet first to the edge of the gate—if he flew over it, it would be another two stories down for an overall four-story drop to hard ground. Luckily, something was there to stop him: the face of Efrem, the still photographer. As Efrem snapped photos, Arthur's feet collided with the camera, basically imbedding it in Efrem's forehead. Then Arthur fell back safely onto the cushiony cardboard boxes. Efrem, a large and hardy soul, was okay but for a few scratches on his face. His camera, however, was utterly destroyed. He had everyone sign it in indelible marker at the wrap party, and kept it as a remembrance.

When Arthur was asked why he jumped so far, he said, "I forgot there wasn't any glass in the window."

Life becomes more and more like a Dali painting all the time.†

LESSON: There are some stories that should have probably been left out of this book, lest I look too much like an irresponsible buffoon.

---

*This, despite the fact that when we shot the interior we shot Steve Gibbons running toward a glass window.

†I was particularly happy that three newspapers, a TV crew, and one of our key investors chose this particular day to watch and experience Troma efficiency.

6

MOVIE: *Tromeo & Juliet*

THE STUNT, IN SCRIPT: Benny Que scuffles with the rest of the Capulet family. Although Benny gets battered around a bit, he eventually triumphs.

THE STUNT, IN PRACTICE: Fight choreography between Stevie Blackehart as Benny and other cast members.

We were shooting the master shot* of a *Tromeo & Juliet* fight scene with three cameras. The foreground knife fight was between Tromeo and Tyrone.† In the background, Tromeo's tough older cousin, Benny Que (Stevie Blackehart), was taking on the entire Capulet clan. This complex background fight, which Stevie had coordinated himself, included a move where Peter (the dazzling Tiffany Shepis) "kicks" him in the face and knocks him over. While we were filming the scene, Tiffany kicked toward Stevie's face in the same way that she had done in every single rehearsal, which had always worked out well. But this time she struck his mouth and sent him to the hospital. How was this possible?

Because in rehearsals Tiffany had never worn high heels; when we filmed it, she did. The extra couple inches were enough to make contact. The impact, especially from a three-time jujitsu champion like Tiffany, was enough to knock Stevie for a loop.

Stevie finished the shot thinking he'd only been nicked. But as soon as the cameras stopped running, he collapsed and turned white. His lip gushed blood. It was the most frightened I had been since Russell's car had flipped over in *The Toxic Avenger.* My brain is always willing to go to the most extreme possibility, and now I thought Stevie had

---

*MASTER: a shot (or shots) of the entire scene or sequence, usually from a wide angle. You can then pick up "angles"—close-ups and medium shots. The editor cuts all this footage together to make a scene.

†After I finished shooting my handheld stuff of this fight, I picked up the enormous serrated "rubber" knife which had whizzed oh so close to Will Keenan's eyes and jugular vein. As I grasped it I noticed my hand was bleeding. They were fighting with a large, *real*, incredibly sharp knife. I complimented Marcos Miranda, stunt coordinator, on his witty practical joke.

sustained a neck injury that would kill him. *This was just like Bruce Lee.* The paramedics showed up, fitting him with a neck brace and carting him off in an ambulance.* Luckily, he was okay with a few stitches and some rest. But it could have all been avoided if Marcos Miranda, the stunt coordinator, had had rehearsals dressed in the clothes the actors would wear on film. Likewise, fights should *always* be rehearsed on location.

Incidentally, we still had to complete the fight scene. There were some actor persons on set, so we picked out the one that looked most like Stevie—which wasn't very much. This guy had a goatee, and was about a foot shorter and fifty pounds heavier than Stevie. Stevie had been wearing a red T-shirt. We tracked down a PA wearing a T-shirt that was *orange*, which is sort of like red, and used that. In the final cut, as you might imagine, we used as few shots of the short, pudgy, bearded, orange Benny as possible.

LESSON: Tiffany Shepis is a good kicker.

And that's the end of the chapter known as "Stunts Gone Wrong."

---

*This just happened to be the day that CNN was filming a day in the life of Troma.

His Fingers Were Bitten Off by a Gorilla!!

(AND VARIOUS OTHER ANECDOTES, 1987-93)

RENAISSANCE DINER. JUNE 1997.

Dominique sashayed away from the table. Her short skirt swished up over her thighs. Barry Neville pushed his glasses up his nose. He sipped his cup of coffee. He was nervous. I didn't know why.

"You're not sticking to the outline," he said.

"Yes," I told him. "I have trouble. My brain. It goes off in different directions."

"You just seem to throw in whatever you want. There's no rhyme or—"

"Same with Troma."

"What?"

"There's no rhyme or reason to Troma, either."

"Still—"

"It's just an accurate reflection, I think. Does that make sense? We don't always plan everything out. Things simply happen the way they do. I mean, the Tao. You liked that, Barry."

"As a theme. I think it's good to have themes."

"I have themes."

"Listen. Lloyd. Penguin Putnam hired you to write a book on Troma Entertainment. We wanted something simple, a work that dealt with the various movies you've produced, how you raised money to make them, how you did the special effects. A how-to manual, Lloyd, as I've told you before. Funny stories of stunts gone wrong and cheesy special effects, all that's okay. We wanted to hear about the famous people: Costner, Stone, Travolta, blah blah blah."

"Stella Stevens?"

"What?"

"Stella Stevens was in *Monster in the Closet*. There was a scene with her in the shower, where you see her breasts. Pretty nice breasts for an older woman. When the movie came out, though, Stella got angry. She said she was told that the camera would stay above the nipples. I mean, come on—"

"Yes, that's a good story."

"She was standing there naked! Do you really think that she didn't know?! All you need to do is put a couple pieces of tape—"

"Nice anecdote. Thank you. But you're missing—"

"Maybe I should put that in the book. You think?"

"You're missing the point, Lloyd. I'm sorry. You have *some* of the things we wanted, but most of the pages that you're turning in aren't what Penguin Putnam and I expected, nor what we asked for. You're throwing in things about Amelia Earhart that have nothing to do with Troma whatsoever. You're sharing parts of your personal life that no one asked you to share and, frankly, things the general population will probably find disgusting. Your sense of humor goes beyond the daring at points and into something darker—talking about hitting a baby on the head with a hammer if it came out of you, for instance. And lists of things—sometimes utterly unrelated things—often replace entirely any narrative thrust. What I'm saying is, I just don't think this is working out."

Pause.

"You're breaking up with me," I said.

"I like you, Lloyd. I think you can be funny. Really, I think this book is often funny. And I like your movies. Some of them. But I don't think this book is the kind of book Penguin Putnam wants to put on the bookshelves. It's not what people expect."

"Isn't that good? Giving people something other than what they expect?"

"Not this time. No."

Barry looked legitimately regretful.

"But you can't just . . . fire me . . ." I said. "There's a contract, Barry."

"You were supposed to have a first draft done by today, and now, here we are, with three chapters to go."

I slumped back in my seat, dazed. Barry looked embarrassed. He flipped over the bill, put some money on the table, and left.

I sat there for a few minutes, then asked Dominique for another cup of coffee. The coffee tasted like shit, but I got a glimpse of Dominique's thigh as she walked away from the table. At least that was something.

The Troma Building. My and Michael's office. Later that same day.

"They signed a contract, didn't they?" Michael asked me.

"Yes," I said.

"Well, how are they going to get out of that? They're going to have to pay you for the book, right?"

"I guess."

"Troma needs this money, Lloyd. You've done everything to uphold your side of the contract, right?"

"Sure, well . . . you know . . ."

"What?"

"Nothing. Technicalities. Minor things."

"Technicalities. What technicalities?"

"Little things. Like the first draft was supposed to be due yesterday. They're making a big deal out of that."

"And . . . you didn't have it done?"

I shook my head in embarrassment. Michael shook his head in disgust.

"That's great," he muttered. "So now you've basically breached the contract. They don't have to pay you anything. In fact, they can probably ask for the money back they've already paid us. You didn't uphold your side of the contract. They don't have to uphold theirs."

"I don't think Barry wants to end the deal," I said.

"What?"

"I think he's being put up to it."

"Let's not get into this."

"There was sadness in his eyes, Michael. Like the look of a prize-fighter forced into taking a fall."

"Now you're going to tell me it's a part of the conspiracy of the—"

"Bureaucratic, corporate, and labor elites. Yes."

"I'm not listening to this, Lloyd."

"It's the major studios. They're out to destroy us."

I looked down at my desk. There was a resume for a young man who had been working for the past five years with the "severely mentally ill." He wrote that he wanted a "change of occupations." Obviously, he didn't know much about the Troma Team. I looked back up at Michael.

"Michael, somebody got to Barry," I said. "I don't know who. But somebody from the studios is forcing him to ditch this book, to bury it."

"Lloyd, I'm done with this conversation."

"They know it will be a good thing for Troma if this book comes out. They're threatened by it. It denigrates the major studios. They don't want that."

"You know why Penguin Putnam's probably trying to get out of the book deal?"

"Because of the conspiracy."

"No. Because you're probably writing about those beliefs in the book, and Barry knows people will think you're crazy."

"People can think I'm crazy all they want. But I've seen, Michael. I *know*."

"It doesn't matter. The book's done. It's over. You lose. Maybe now you can get back to making some movies or deals."

"I don't believe it's over. I believe we can still win Barry back to the forces of good. I believe it."

Notes from my journal, that night:

It seems as if the book has been neutralized. Barry called me today, said it was over. But I'm going to continue writing. On almost every Troma movie there has come a time when I thought the whole thing was kaput, a time where I've wanted to close up shop and send everyone home. And every time, somehow, things have worked out. Because of my experience in those situations, I'm going to act *as if* nothing has changed—*as if* the publication of the book has not been halted in any way. I hope the creation of a book is somewhat like the creation of a movie. I will keep writing.

TOXIC BOX OFFICE SYNDROME: SEQUEL TIME!

Shortly after we had finished *Troma's War*, the Troma Team and I attended the 1987 Cannes Film Festival. By this time Toxie was an unqualified hit on video as well as a continuing cult hit in theaters across the country. Still, I had never really considered a sequel. So it was a surprise when a German buyer, Hans Hynek, came into our Carlton Hotel office in Cannes.

"I heard about the new movie, Lloyd," Hynek said. "When do you start production?"

"What?"

"On your good new film, *Toxic Avenger . . . Two!*"

"What?"

"I just heard. I am overwhelmed and gladdened by this news."

"Somebody told you we were making a *sequel*?"

"Everyone knows about it—they're screaming it up and down the Croisette.* Let me tell you, Mr. Lloyd. Perhaps you and I can work out a deal on the German rights before you sell them to a lesser company."

"To a Toxic Avenger sequel?"

---

*The Croisette is the main strip along Cannes. Most of the action takes place on this strip. All four of the primary hotels, where much of the business is done, are also on this strip—the Majestic, the Martinez, the Carlton, and the Noga-Hilton. There are some small coffee and sandwich stands along the strip, where you can get a good *jambon* (ham) sandwich for a much lower price than you can in the expensive Cannes delis. But, you know, Barry's been warning me about going into too much detail in these footnotes, so I guess that's too much. Sorry . . . But, by the way, there is one way you should know about to eat for free in Cannes; the rich people who stay in the Carlton never eat all the croissants that they get from their room service breakfast. When they're done with this $90 meal that morning, they put their silver trays out in the halls for the staff to come by and pick up. By trolling the hallways before the staff does, you can collect quite a banquet. Another important Troma Team find is the Carlton coffee machine, which is meant for the employees. It's down in some secret tunnels below the hotel. Although a customer coffee at the Carlton will cost you about 60 francs, a machine coffee only costs 8 *francs*. And the coffee is really delicious. I get turned off by a lot of European superiority, talking about Europe does this better, or Europe does that better—but the one thing they *do* do better is coffee. Their machine coffee is better than an expensive coffee house's product in New York. Another thing Europe does a lot better than America is genocide.

WHY DON'T YOU PUT STARS
IN YOUR MOVIES, YOU DIM BASTARDS?

Upon watching Troma movies, especially Troma-produced films, one can quickly ascertain that, although there are some famous people in Troma movies, they were distinctly not-so when they appeared in the film. Those celebrities who were celebrities at the time of filming are either the sub-Hollywood-Squares types (Professor Irwin Corey in *Stuck on You*) or they're famous for something besides acting (Lemmy, the main man of Motorhead, in *Tromeo & Juliet*).

Successful industry types often state the following argument against Troma's no-star policy: "If you throw in a couple of low-level stars, say, shell out another hundred-and-fifty grand to a four-hundred grand movie, you could probably double your sales. The math all works out, right? Just throw in an Alyssa Milano or a Jon Savage or a Shannon Tweed or a Joanne Worley and you got blockbuster profits."

However, it's not so simple. Troma films are able to keep their costs down by remaining nonunion. By putting in *one* celebrity the budget would increase in the following ways.

1) If one actor is SAG (Screen Actors Guild—all famous actors belong to the Guild) then the film would have to be a SAG film. That is, you'd have to pay *all* of the speaking roles something like $450 a day. $450 is approximately how much a lead receives for an entire Troma production.

2) SAG members also get a percentage of the money made from the film, getting huge cuts from the gross sales whether or not a profit has yet been made.

3) You have to hire SAG representatives, whose job it is to make sure everything you do fits into SAG guidelines. They hang around your sets and wear clothes with bad color combinations.

4) In many states the actor persons (i.e., extras) would also have to be paid a certain rate per day. One of the ways Troma keeps its production values high is by having literally thousands of actor persons. All of these folks kindly offer their services for absolutely free because they want to be in a Troma movie. Troma not only enjoys making money but also enjoys allowing ordinary nonactors a chance to be in a real live celluloid production.

5) It is very difficult getting a SAG production off the ground without having unions be a part all around, from crew members to teamsters. This adds, at the very least, another few hundred thousand dollars.

"Yes! We should talk."

"Well."

Pause. Hynek stared at me, his smile faltering.

"It is true, no?" he asked. "That you are making a sequel?"

"Oh . . . yeah," I lied. "Sure. It's true, Hans. We're making a sequel."

"And have you sold the German rights?"

"Well, there's a lot of interested parties."

"Is Ascot or Deutschland Studios one of the interested parties?"

"Could be . . ."

"Well, you do not want to work with them, Lloyd. You want to work with me! Did you know that the head of Deutschland Studios was once in the SS?"

"I didn't. No."

"It is true! He murdered thousands of Jews, such as yourself!"

"Hmm. You think he might murder me?"

"Perhaps! Perhaps! If you sell the rights of your very good sequel to him, that is a distinct possibility!"

And so from this rumor a bidding war resulted. Michael and I played along, pretending to have been in preproduction on a *Toxic Avenger II*. It was in the firmest of Troma traditions that one of the only films we've presold the video rights to is one that didn't really exist. It was an imaginary Troma film created by an industry's desire for it. I contacted Vestron out of loyalty (they distributed *Toxie I*), but they didn't believe other companies were really offering us big money. Lorimar snapped up the U.S. video rights at Cannes for about a million dollars up front. With the money from Lorimar and some of the money we had made from the first movie, we were able to put together a sequel. The budget was a little over a million dollars.

6) Fresh new talent work very hard and they know that the director has total control and total power—that he is, in fact, like a god.

7) Per diems: SAG rules regarding hotels, food, transportation, overtime, and travel time are an expensive pain in the butt.

So, spending another hundred grand on a semi-famous actor is actually spending another *million* or so on SAG requirements. Therefore, making "Twice as much money" is actually making much less in profits.

Currently, SAG is in the process of making some of its guidelines more open and lenient. If things keep changing in this direction, you may someday see an actual famous guy or gal in a Troma film. That is, if Troma can ever find a celebrity who doesn't totally suck.

I had a bug up my ass to shoot *The Toxic Avenger II** in Japan. After I had finished doing *Toxie, Nuke 'Em High,* and *Troma's War,* I felt as if I was in a creative rut, on the verge of shooting the same movie over and over again. Michael contended that this was already the case. Making a sequel could be even worse. Japan seemed a way to attack this problem. If I was going to make the same movie again, at least I could do it in a different *country*.

The fact that Troma, the world's cheapest movie studio, chose to shoot in the world's most expensive country struck my fellow low-budgeteers (of which there were more then than there are today) as ironic. Other productions traveled to the Philippines, Mexico, or Tai-

---

*I thought up the title. Pretty clever, huh?

wan so that they could save money. Everyone told me Japan couldn't be done. Even Japanese producers said it was impossible—there was no low-budget hustling there, no tradition of people working for the creative joy, experience, or credit instead of money. But this made me more determined.

I traveled to Japan on a prescouting expedition with our friend Tetsu Fujimura. Although his name sounds Italian, Tetsu was, in fact, Japanese—he had been born and raised in Hiroshima. At the 1985 Cannes Film Festival Tetsu was a Troma fan who would stop by the office to talk about our movies. He attempted to convince Michael and me that we needed a Japanese agent. He himself, he said, would be a prime choice for the job. Although he was unknown, he instilled in us a good feeling. We gave him the job. It was a great decision—over the next few years Tetsu would make Troma millions. Today, he's the head of the multimillion-dollar company Gaga Communications.

Tetsu located a production manager, who Tetsu said was the only one in Japan who understood the Troma production technique. We called him Binbun Furusawa—mostly because that was his name. Binbun wore a beanie, was small and quiet and smiled most the time. We told him we only had $200,000 to spend in Japan. Binbun told us he could put it together. While Michael and I readied things for the U.S. part of the shoot, we trusted Binbun to lay down the tracks for the Japan production.

THREE FUN FACTS ABOUT *TOXIE II* AND *III*:

1 In the Toxie sequels we changed the name of Toxie's girlfriend from *Sarah* to *Claire*. I have repeatedly wracked my brains to remember why we did this, but I don't have the faintest.

2 Toxie looks slightly different in the sequels than he does in the first film—a bit cuter and a bit less inbred-guy-from-*Deliverance*-looking. He is more brown and less pink. This was largely due to the new special-effects artists and the new Toxie mask. The new mask had a remote control eye that could move around—well, it was supposed to be remote control, but that part of it broke. We ended up only able to shoot the moving eye in close-up, because the guy that controlled it had to hide directly behind Toxie and manually work it like a puppet, using wires. I like puppets.

3 Beauteous Tromette Lisa Gaye was first discovered on *The Toxic Avenger II*. Lisa went on to act in four more Troma films—*Toxie III*, *Sgt. Kabukiman NYPD*, and *Class of Nuke 'Em High II* and *III*. The only other person to star in five Troma movies is 500-pound action hero Joe Fleishaker. Of course, because of his width, Joe counts each of his roles as *two*.

Gay Perrington Terry was my cowriter on *Toxie II*. Although she, like most of Troma's screenwriters, was skittish about the sex and violence quotient, she was extremely easy to work with. Because of her, the females in Toxie's life—primarily Claire and Toxie's mom—became more well rounded. Toxie became warmer and more human as well.

Unlike most sequels, there are no cast crossovers from *Toxie I* to *Toxie III* or *III*. Members of the original cast were offered roles, such as Mark Torgl and Pat Ryan, but they either wanted too much money, had joined SAG, were nowhere to be found, or were "busy washing their hair that month."

The most dazzling addition to the cast was Phoebe Legere. Phoebe was a singer and actress known for an unusual lingerie-driven lounge act on Manhattan's Lower East Side. A bond between Phoebe and me took root immediately. On the one hand, we had a great respect and concern for one another. On the other hand, we would be constantly bickering—a sort of nonsexually involved, mutant *Honeymooners*.

Phoebe was a consistent pain in the ass. She had a jerk of a boyfriend who enjoyed flicking a Bic lighter in the faces of the cast and crew.* She once refused to do a nude scene until we put a check for extra money beside her on the bed. She also liked to be seen on camera, and would constantly turn around so we could see her face when we were supposed to be shooting the back of her head and over the shoulder. Still, I have an enormous respect for her.

For instance, when *Toxic Avenger II* went to the Cannes Film Festival, we took Phoebe with us. She was fortunate enough to get a gig, performing her piano-lounge act at one of the most famous clubs in

---

*Phoebe told me that this spoiled brat was the only man who had ever been able to "ring her bell."

Cannes, La Chunga. The Troma Team and I showed up to watch her play. The place was packed with powerful industry folk—many of whom could have been helpful to Phoebe's career. I was sitting with Phoebe. She was ready to grace the stage when I turned and saw Jean-Claude "Baby Doc" Duvalier waddle into the club, along with a hoard of spooky associates and bimbos. The manager and wait staff crowded around Baby Doc and his cronies, lavishing him with attention and seating him at the best table.* I looked into his eyes. Most people have some sort of life or light in their eyes. He had nothing, only darkness. He was the devil.

"Do you know who that is?" I asked her.

"That creepy guy? No."

"That's Baby Doc Duvalier."

"A dictator, right? Where's he from?"

I told her:

"Jean-Claude 'Baby Doc' Duvalier was inducted with the 100 percent support of the U.S. as 'President-for-Life' of Haiti in 1971, directly after the death of his dictator father, Françoise 'Papa Doc' Duvalier. Papa Doc's Ton Ton Macoute had terrorized the country for thirteen years in a manner as despicable as Adolf Hitler. Baby Doc continued this reign of evil, looting the country's treasury and torturing and murdering political dissidents and others. In 1986—last year—Baby Doc resigned because of the outcry over his sadism and, considered even more despicable in this world of misplaced values, his theft of Haiti's national treasury. The five million Haitians rejoiced. However, his cronies continue to hold power in Haiti, and, through them, Baby Doc still pulls strings. The French, exemplifying once again their humanitarian values, kindly offered Baby Doc sanctuary in their own country."†

Phoebe stared at me. Stood. Walked over to La Chunga's manager.

"I'm not going to sing with him in here," she told him.

"Who?"

"Duvalier," she said.

---

*For several years prior Michael and I had spent thousands of dollars entertaining at La Chunga. The cheap French fucks never even offered us free bidet water.
†Well, maybe I didn't put it *exactly* like that at the time.

The manager told her that he would not ask Baby Doc to leave.

"Fine," Phoebe said. She, the Troma Team, and I all left the restaurant. I haven't been back to La Chunga in any of the ten Cannes Film Festivals since. That night, I had seen what Phoebe Legere was truly made of. She can refuse to do a hundred nude scenes for all I care.

In 1985 two likable Troma fans, Pericles Lewnes and Edward Bishop, arrived from Maryland to the NYC Port Authority bus station. From there, carrying huge backpacks, they walked six blocks to the Troma Building. With no appointment, they entered and plunked themselves down in the reception area. They had with them a film entitled *Redneck Zombies*, shot on video. The film was amazingly Tromatic, containing all the bubbling green goo and toxic waste a young Tromite could desire. It was also one of the most gory films I had ever seen. Although crude, the film was funny and the special effects were fantastic. Perry and Edward said it was their greatest dream that Troma distribute their film.

Michael and I got a kick out of their low aspirations, so we agreed to distribute *Redneck Zombies*, even though at that time (and still today) it was nearly impossible to get "films" shot on video into stores. Despite this, the movie is today a Troma Classic.

Part of the deal was that, for a nominal sum, Perry Lewnes would be a special-effects production assistant for *Troma's War*. Shortly thereafter Perry was on the Troma full-time production staff. By the time of *Toxic Avenger II*, he was the head of special effects. Perry would don the costumes of some of the monsters in the sequel.* He would oversee the constant churning out of masks (the Toxie masks wouldn't have much longevity and we'd have to continually be baking new ones). He also oversaw the continuous production of *agar*.

---

*Some of the more surreal moments on set were when I saw *three Toxies* wandering around: often an acting Toxie (Fazio), a stunt Toxie (Scott Leva and others), and the special-effects Toxie (Lewnes) would be on set at the same time.

agar (âʹ-gär', äʹ-gär'):

is a gelatinous material derived from marine algae—that is, seaweed. The word comes from the Malay, "agar-agar," the term by which some people refer to it to this day (even though this use is obviously illogical, considering that it takes twice as long to say). AGAR is used as a stabilizer and thickener in many food products like soft ice cream. But in the world of Tromaville AGAR is employed to resemble toxic waste—or at least the Tromatic vision of what we imagine toxic waste to be. On the sets of The Toxic Avenger films as well as Class of Nuke 'Em High, at least two PAs would at all times have as their sole responsibility cooking AGAR in giant vats. The results would be spilled in Toxie's dump/home or placed in giant "Danger: Toxic Waste" vats throughout the town of Tromaville. Because of all this cooking, along with the baking of masks, Troma sets often resemble a mad scientist's laboratory. This is one of the reasons we must have many, many naked women on Troma sets—we want the government to know we're a movie set and not some nefarious secret scientific agency out to destroy America. One unfortunate incident with AGAR occurred while filming The Toxic Avenger in Paramus, New Jersey. We were shooting on a flatbed truck* headed down the highway, carrying six barrels of bubbling AGAR and signs reading "Danger: Toxic Waste." We were unfortunately shooting without a permit. Several concerned citizens notified the police; they had seen the green goo dripping down behind the truck with the barrels and warning signs. Abruptly, three police cars pulled up around us, the officers' guns unholstered. Closely behind them were two fire trucks and an ambulance.

Black Rain, the Ridley Scott/Michael Douglas picture, was shot in Japan shortly before *The Toxic Avenger II*. The Japanese film industry had deep feelings of resentment for the *Black Rain* crew, because they shot the film in a distinctly American style: aggressive, overstated, and arrogant. Eventually, the American crew had such a difficult time that they moved the entire production to Hollywood, where they built sets approximating Kyoto. I had to admit to myself, normally Troma also shot in an aggressive American style. However, in Japan, Michael and I decided we would do the best we could to shoot in the manner of the Japanese. This was both out of respect and because we wanted the production to flow as smoothly as possible. We would live Japanese style, eat what the Japanese ate, and run the set in Japanese fashion.

Upon my arrival at the airport, Binbun Furusawa let me in on a serious problem regarding accommodations:

---

*The truck with the barrel that Melvin dives into, causing him to transform into Toxie.

"I don't think we can do two to a room on this trip," Binbun said. "Some of the actors refuse to share a room."

"What do you mean?" I asked, a bit aghast. "The actors always share rooms . . . that's how they get to fornicate."

"Have you seen the rooms?"

"No."

"They're small."

"I don't care if they're small. This is Tromaville."

"I mean, really small."

Binbun showed me the rooms. They were basically each the size of a single bed, only five and a half feet long, and a couple of feet across. They were small enough that if two men shared a room and one of them got an erection, it would have been an instant homosexual experience. For the first (and possibly last) time in the history of Troma Studios, each member of the cast and crew got his or her own room.

Our trust in Binbun had been well placed. Tetsu and he had assembled a marvelous Japanese crew and a cast that included Japanese television and movie stars—all for the price we had discussed. I thought, now, perhaps, we can get something really unique going, something to break me out of my pattern. A little bit of American-Japanese fusion just might help the world of Troma.

We had to sludge through some difficult on-set communication. Japanese culture maintains a steady ban on revealing bad news. This is unfortunate, considering, well, we're Troma. One day our lead Japanese actress, Mayako Katsuragi, wasn't on set. This was a problem—I was about to shoot Toxie meeting his father, and she was essential to the scene.* So I was extremely nervous about Mayako not being there. "Just flow with it," I repeated to myself over and over again. I didn't want to freak out in my usual "American" way.

I went about finding her. Yet I had to be careful not to ask the questions too directly—I was afraid of offending.

"I don't see Mayako around here," I said to Kazuo Ito, my first AD. "Hmm. That's interesting. I wonder where she is."

---

*As everyone who was with me on the production knew, I was obsessed with the idea of the Toxic Avenger killing his dad. I would froth at the mouth when I talked about it. After all, I wanted to get back at my own father for his crack of ten years before, stating that the only good thing about The Battle of Love's Return was the part where I died.

Kazuo would not look me in the eye.

"Oh, she will be here soon," he spit out. Then he abruptly walked away. It seemed unusual. I approached Binbun.

"*Ohio gozimus*, Binbun," I said, in my lowest, deepest voice.*

"*Konicheewa*, Kaufman-san."

"What a beautiful Japanese day."

"Yes."

"Mayako, she is a very fine actress. Thank you for getting her to do this film for us."

Binbun smiled. He nodded.

"Hmm," I said. "I wonder where she is. Wonder, wonder, wonder."

"Ah, yes," Binbun said. "She will be ready soon. Shoot Toxie's angles."

TROMA MOVIES AND SOME OF THEIR CELEBRITIES

- Kevin Costner *Shadows Run Black* & *Sizzle Beach USA*
- Marisa Tomei *The Toxic Avenger*
- Michael Jai White *The Toxic Avenger II*
- Billy Bob Thornton *Chopper Chicks in Zombietown*
- Shelley Winters & George Gobel *Ellie*
- Samuel L. Jackson, Kadeem Hardison, Melba Moore, & Bill Nunn *Def by Temptation*
- Vincent D'Onofrio *The First Turn-On*
- Willie Mays & G. Gordon Liddy *When Nature Calls*
- Oliver Stone *Battle of Love's Return*
- Paul Sorvino *Cry Uncle*
- Eric Douglas (Michael's brother) & Marlon Jackson (Michael's brother) *Student Confidential*
- Ron Jeremy *Class of Nuke 'Em High II: Subhumanoid Meltdown*
- Troy Donahue *The Love Thrill Murders*
- "Pistol" Pete Maravich *Scoring*
- Robert De Niro & Jill Clayburgh *The Wedding Party*
- Yvonne De Carlo *Play Dead*
- Karen Black & Jan-Michael Vincent *Haunting Fear*
- Russ Tamblyn, Michael Berryman, & Lawrence Tierney *Wizards of the Demon Sword*
- Joe Spinell & Caroline Munroe *The Fanatic*
- Calvert DeForrest (aka Larry Bud Mellman) *Waitress!*
- Rita Jenrette *Zombie Island Massacre*
- Lemmy Kilmeister *Tromeo & Juliet*

And then *he* walked away from me.

We guessed that Mayako was in her dressing room nearby. We shot all of Toxie's angles, and then sat around awhile longer. I didn't say anything, not wanting to impose, wanting the Japanese to do things in their own way.

"What's taking so long?" Michael asked me.

---

*We were informed that it is manly and attractive to say "ohio gozimus" in a deep voice. I also like to say "Ohio University" in a deep voice.

"I don't know. No one's telling me anything. But Mayako isn't on set."

Michael looked at the assistant cameraman, Taisei Konishi.*

"Hey. Taisei!" Michael said. Taisei turned toward us. He looked frightened.

"Where's Mayako?" Michael asked him.

"Be ready soon," Taisei said. He walked away.

Another fifteen minutes passed. Then an hour. Then another hour after that. Eventually, after lunch and 1,001 indirect questions, we got the truth out of Binbun: Mayako had had an argument with one of the production staff. She was at home. She had called at nine a.m. that morning and said she wasn't going to come to the set. No one wanted to give us the bad news.

If we had known in the morning, we could have shot an entirely different scene. Instead, we ended up having to shoot Mayako's angles at a totally different location. When cut with Toxie's angles they looked like what they were—in the same country but not the same street.

The final problem was the most serious. We had been assured that all the Japanese actors could speak English. And they did speak English, it was just incomprehensible English. When we saw the dailies, we couldn't understand a word. Michael, Pat, and I ended up post-syncing or dubbing all of the voices ourselves. Michael and Pat made me take the small roles, because I stink at dubbing.†

Besides these speed bumps, the Japanese people were wonderful. Our Japanese fight coordinator added a new element to our fight scenes, making them move twice as quickly as American fights. The precision of the crew as a whole, the ability for individual egos to work first and foremost as a group, was refreshing and made for a smooth ride. The Japanese ended up liking us as well, precisely because we did the opposite of what the *Black Rain* crew did; we tried to learn from the Japanese style. We ate Japanese box lunches on the set, and learned as much of the language as we could. Although we may not have always

---

*Taisei was the best focus-puller I have ever worked with; he was able to pull focus for complex dolly shots without rehearsal. He also did grip tasks, such as moving the camera and tripod, something unheard of in an American film for a first AC.

†Michael plays Toxie's Japanese father, Pat plays Miyako, and I play the sumo wrestler. My deep voice practice paid off.

been successful, our effort was apparent. Some of our crew even joined some of the Japanese crew for an excursion to "Soapland"—the area of Tokyo where you can get laid. I waved at them as they drove away, beaming like a proud father.

Upon completion of *The Toxic Avenger II*, the perennial Troma problem reared its ugly, pustule-filled head. The first cut was over four fucking hours long.

"I can't believe you've done this again," Michael said to me. "I told you we were overshooting."

I looked at the floor.

"And the plot isn't like *Troma's War*," Michael added. "It's not simple. I don't know any way you're going to be able to cut this down to under two hours. We're dead."

We were dead. I had killed us. The Holocaust, Hiroshima, Vietnam, and now *this*. Another tragedy in the long line of twentieth-century horrors. The worst part of all was that the footage looked *so good*. Jimmy London's cinematography was the best I'd seen yet (it was even in focus). We were working with a new lab, TVC, and the dailies looked more crisp, clean, and colorful than ever before. We had tons of expensive special effects and stunts; we actually drove a school bus over a cliff.* All for naught.

"Pat, it's all over," I told my wife in our bedroom that night.

"Come on now," she said. "You're overreacting. Everything's going to be fine. You'll think of a way out of it. You always do."

"Not this time. This time I'm dead. I'm going to blow my brains out. We better put the brownstone up for sale. If we fall on hard times, maybe your mom can adopt the kids."

"Lloyd, I don't think that will be necessary. Whatever happens, I think we can afford to keep the kids."

"Maybe she can adopt them anyway. I'm getting kind of sick of having them around."

---

*This is one of the stranger Troma phenomena. Although we pushed a real bus over a real cliff, the effect still comes out looking somehow like a miniature. Some of the reviews even mentioned the fakeness of it.

"Ha. Ha. Lloyd."

"Oh, Pat! Dear God! Making bad jokes is all I can do to stop myself from thinking what a ruin I've made of my life!" I threw my arms up in the air and began to cry. I looked ridiculous, I knew that, but I couldn't help it. I literally felt my life was over. If not for Pat I would have blown my brains out.

The next day I jogged to work. The adrenaline pumped through my body. The serotonin rushed to my head. I stopped at a fruit stand to buy an orange. I was breathing heavily. I sifted through the oranges for one that wasn't too bruised. I found a good clean one. Picked it up. At that moment I heard a giant "Whoosh!" sound above me. I looked up. I realized I was having a vision:

There in the sky above me floated a giant, human brain. The creases in the gray matter were so clear I almost thought it was real. The brain seemed to be dripping slime of some sort. I squeezed the orange in my hand.

"Fifty cents," the grocer said to me.

"A brain," I said.

The floating brain began to tremble and writhe when suddenly the left and right brain split apart. There, between the two halves, appeared a vague face. It was the Toxic Avenger wearing a top hat. My mouth dropped open in shock. I had gotten a runner's high before, but nothing like this. From the corner of my eye I saw the grocer hold out the palm of his hand.

"That'll be fifty cents, man," he said.

Beneath the head of the Toxic Avenger came a small scroll with the typewritten words: "Two movies."

"Two movies?" I said to myself. And then it struck me in one giant, brain-cell-popping burst:

WE CAN MAKE TWO MOVIES OUT OF ONE.

The plot lines instantly developed for me. It took no planning. It took no thought whatsoever. I could clearly see how *The Toxic Avenger II* could turn into *The Toxic Avenger II and III*.

I moved away from the fruit stand in a daze. I walked forward, an enormous, idiot's smile crossing my face.

We can do this, I thought. Out of the four-hour movie we can make two movies, with two different plots. Sure, there may need to be a fair amount of goofy voice-over narration to explain what the heck's going on, but we at Troma were masters of filling in plot holes with voice-over. With two movies we can make *twice as much money.* Lorimar had the video rights to the second film, but we could also sell the video rights to the third film. Instead of making one movie for a million and a half dollars, we've actually made two for that same price! This is fantastic! Fucking up was the best thing I could have done!

I couldn't wait to tell Michael. Again, I began to jog toward Troma, filled with a rare joy.

I felt arms sliding roughly around my waist.

"Wha-?" I exclaimed.

"You motherfucker! Come back here with my fucking orange!"

It was the grocer. He was tackling me. The orange was still in my hand; I had forgotten about it. I plummeted to the pavement. A group of bystanders gathered around us. The enormous grocer flipped me onto my back.

"Think you can steal from me, you cocksucker!?!?"

His fist flew down into my face.

"You yuppie bastards come along, stealing my fruit every fucking day! You think you own the goddamn world!"

Again, his fist came slamming down into my face. And then again, and then again. The red of my blood flowed over my eye. His fist came down again.

Still, none of it mattered.

Two movies! I thought. *How much more could God possibly love me!?*

It worked out beautifully. Vestron, who distributed the first Toxie, also ended up distributing *The Toxic Avenger III: The Last Temptation of Toxie* (Pat came up with the title). They paid an advance before we ever cut it, based on a treatment that I knew would work because we already had it in the can. Although you may not place the plot for either film with the best of Agatha Christie, they were fun and pretty much made sense—more sense than *Conspiracy Theory,* that's for sure. Most fans today still think the first film is top dog, but there are plenty of folks who like either the second film or the third the best (I myself

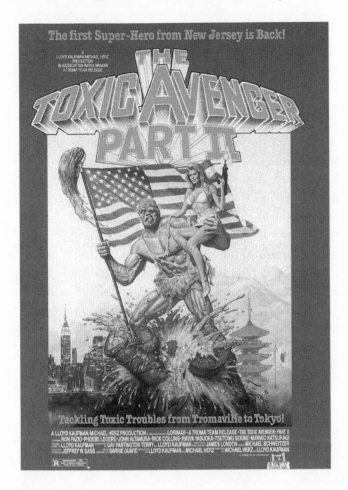

The first Super-Hero from New Jersey is Back!

A LLOYD KAUFMAN/MICHAEL HERZ PRODUCTION IN ASSOCIATION WITH LORIMAR A TROMA TEAM RELEASE

THE TOXIC AVENGER PART II

Tackling Toxic Troubles from Tromaville to Tokyo!

A LLOYD KAUFMAN/MICHAEL HERZ PRODUCTION ... LORIMAR · A TROMA TEAM RELEASE · THE TOXIC AVENGER: PART II
RON FAZIO · PHOEBE LEGERE · JOHN ALTAMURA · RICK COLLINS · RIKIYA YASUOKA · TSUTOMU SEKINE · MAYAKO KATSURAGI
LLOYD KAUFMAN ... GAY PARTINGTON TERRY ... LLOYD KAUFMAN ... JAMES LONDON ... MICHAEL SCHWEITZER
JEFFREY W. SASS ... BARRIE GUARD ... LLOYD KAUFMAN ... MICHAEL HERZ ... MICHAEL HERZ ... LLOYD KAUFMAN

have a soft spot for *Toxie III**). Each of the sequels had about 50 prints that played in theaters around the country, doing respectably. The video distribution, however, was not as good for either film as we had hoped:

Time Warner acquired Lorimar. Warner promised us *Toxie II* was going to be their huge release for the month. Michael and Toxie went to the 1990 VSDA† convention in Las Vegas, expecting big things.

---

*Pat may have come up with "The Last Temptation of Toxie" part of the title, but I came up with the "III" part.
†Video Software Dealers' Association.

There, Warner called a surprise press conference. They announced that they were going to release the Batman movie ahead of schedule—in the same month as Toxie. We knew they'd end up forgetting about us and focusing on Tim Burton's shittiest film. I continually called Warner to make sure we got some sort of attention. They stopped returning my phone calls.

At one point, Warren Lieberfarb, the head of Warner Home Video, called me from his car phone. He seemed angry, accusing me of harassing Warner. I tried to lighten things up and made a joke about how *I* was harassing a billion-dollar corporation. He became even more hostile. As with every other megaconglomerate we ever dealt with, Warner gave us the spiky dildo.

Vestron was a more respectable company, but by the time *The Toxic Avenger III: The Last Temptation of Toxie* was ready to be released, they were on their last legs. Our primary question was whether or not we were going to get paid (we did, for which we're eternally grateful). Eventually, Vestron folded. An equally destitute Live Entertainment took over and dumped *Toxie III* on a market that hardly knew it was coming.

THE TOXIC CRUSADERS: PART I

Shortly after we finished shooting the Toxic sequels, an agent and friend by the name of John Russo asked if we had ever considered turning *The Toxic Avenger* into a television cartoon for kids.

That's ridiculous, I thought. A violent R-rated horror-sex-comedy film famous for having some of the most extreme gore of all time turned into rugrat fodder?

But I said: "We've had a lot of offers. I just haven't met the right person."

Russo told us he had just the guy. He introduced us to Buzz Potamkin. Buzz worked with an animation company by the name of Murikami Wolf, who had had tremendous success with the Teenage Mutant Ninja Turtles cartoons. They told me that they wanted to make a Toxic Avenger cartoon show for kids.

"That only seems natural," I told them. "After all, we had a *kid's head* crushed in the first film."

The folks at Murikami Wolf studied up on the Troma movies. They thought they could capture the fun flavor of Tromaville without the normally requisite sex and gore. Not only could the Troma appeal be parlayed into a popular TV show, but a line of spin-off products would be a natural extension. The name, however, might be changed. "Avenger" seemed too violent. The Murikami Wolf people also thought it'd be preferable to center around a group of characters, as opposed to just Toxie. In that way, you'd have *many* action figures to sell. We added a character named Nozone, who had a large nose and radioactive snot; as well as a dog-man character named Junkyard (because there has to be a dog in *all* cartoons); a guy named Headbanger, who was based on the Siamese twins in *Troma's War*; and Major Disaster, a mutant vegetarian soldier who talks to plants.

The Toxic Crusaders were born.

Meanwhile, before the TV show debuted, I was working on a film.

FATAL SUSHI...LETHAL CHOPSTICKS... AND AS AMERICAN AS APPLE PIE

If you hang around actors for long enough—which is something I don't advise—you begin to get "hep" to their "lingo." One of their most common topics of conversation is "choices." As an actor, you make a choice for your character, whether it be a motivation, a movement, or a tic. You make that choice. And then you stick with it. You don't suddenly decide to change lanes in act two; a lisping character doesn't suddenly develop a stutter with no explanation. One thing you learn by hanging around these actors is that *every good actor* has some sense of these "choices."

The same is true with filmmakers. In retrospect, the largest problem with *Sgt. Kabukiman NYPD* was that I failed to make a choice and stick with it. I wavered. It was like if Robert Frost chose to take both the road less traveled and the well-worn road at the same time. Or he jumped back from one to the other, unable to make up his mind. Robert Frost would look like an asshole if he did this.

HOW KABUKIMAN CAME ABOUT

1 In *Toxic Avenger II* we had a character by the name of Kabukiboy. For some reason, the editors found this guy hilarious and would be on the floor with laughter every time he showed up. A little attention, for me, goes a long way. The name stuck in my head.

2 At a Japanese press conference on *The Toxic Avenger II* I joked that Troma was going to make a movie about a new superhero, Kabukiboy. Big laugh. Our old friend Tetsu Fujimura of Gaga Communications was attending the conference. He approached me afterward. "Lloyd, it's providence that you brought up Kabukiboy!"

he said. "I have been thinking about doing a production with some sort of Kabuki-type character."

3 Tetsu introduced us to Namco. Namco was the billion-dollar amusement corporation with their hands in video games and Japanese amusement parks. They were the company that unleashed the vicious dot-junkie known as Pac-Man* upon the world. Masaya Nakamura was the president of Namco.† He was impressed by how Troma had shot the Toxie sequels in Japan in a Japanese style for a small budget. He thought that a Kabuki superhero movie shot in America could make a lot of money. Namco, along with Gaga, became coproducers on the film. Straight up, we received a million and a half dollars to begin preproduction.

Sounds fantastic, you may say. How could it have gone wrong?

Well, at the time I just didn't get it. Namco wanted a mainstream film. They saw *Sgt. Kabukiman NYPD* as a chance to make a character that wasn't only in an internationally famous film, but also in toys, video games, cartoons, and in their amusement theme parks. They saw a character that was largely for kids, but could appeal to teenagers and adults as well. They saw a brightly colored, multicultural Batman. But I couldn't stay away from extremism. I saw a Troma movie. In the end, we satisfied neither side.

I wrote a treatment, called simply *Kabukiman*. Kabukiman, at that time, was an American college student who received ancient Kabuki powers. He drank beer, met chicks, saved the world. I showed the treatment to Michael. He claimed that, once again, we were making the same movie. It was his idea to change Kabukiman from a college student to a New York City cop. This way the character was older and a little more hard-edged, differentiating him from the Melvin Junko character in Toxie. The title became *Sgt. Kabukiman NYPD*.

Jeff Sass and I wrote the first draft of the script in my house.

---

*I actually met the gentleman who invented Pac-Man. Shockingly, he was just a salaried employee with another small cubicle in the Namco building, and no percentage of the dot-eater's fortunes.

†Nakamura was so rich and powerful that his son-in-law took the bride's family name.

INTERLUDE: SASS AND I STOP A CAR THIEF

I was walking around the room, imbued with Kabuki-spiration as Jeff typed out the script on my home computer. I pretended to throw chopsticks, fly, etc. I happened to gaze out the window and see a guy breaking into a car parked on the street.

"Jeff, get on the horn! Call the cops!" I said. "Somebody's breaking into a car down there!" I ran outside.

"Hey! You!" I screamed. Two neighbors also spotted the thief. The three of us tackled him. He was huge. He ran with the three of us attached to him. I streamed behind him like a little American flag stuck to a car's antenna. Eventually, we got him down. Although Jeff had called the police, they never showed. We finally flagged down a police car. A bored-looking policewoman took him into custody. She didn't even take my name. I doubt anything happened to him. She probably used him for oral sex and then sent him home. You know how policewomen are.*

I walked upstairs. Sass and I immediately put the guy into the script. He steals things from a few cars, and then Kabukiman kills him. The rest of Kabukiman is also a true story.

Jeff wasn't so fond of the sex and violence angle. Like Michael Herz, the Namco-ites, and my wife, he was beginning to feel that *Kabukiman* should be a mainstream film geared toward kids. None of them wanted this to be like *Troma's War*. They told me repeatedly. I kept forgetting.

After Jeff and I had finished the first draft we agreed there were a lot of problems. We hired a young writer to sort them out.

Andrew Osbourne deserves special notice for being the first writer I worked with who sympathized with my own desire for sex and violence. He was all for making *Sgt. Kabukiman NYPD* as extreme as possible. Since then, I have found it much easier to work with younger writers. He and I added a lot of stuff that Michael and Jeff didn't want in the script. Little things. Like we had two toddlers sliced up and mutilated in the first five pages. Little stuff like that.

Namco had some reservations about the script. At the Yubari Film Festival, in the sticks of Northern Hokaido, Japan, I met with Kuninori Onishi, Namco executive, Nakamura's right-hand man, and a Development Executive on *Kabukiman*. Kuninori informed me that he and

---

*EDITOR'S NOTE: Uh . . . no way, Lloyd. Remove.

the others were taken aback by a scene in which a man ate worms. "Worms are a good source of protein" I told him. He told me that this didn't matter too much, that people in Japan were disgusted by the devouring of invertebrate crawlers. It didn't even cross my mind what he was telling me: showing this scene would destroy *Kabukiman's* chances as mainstream family fare in Japan. I was simply focused on the worms I so dearly wanted. I somehow convinced him that keeping the scene in was okay.*

Incidentally, the character who played the old man who ate the worms, Fumio Furuya, was also on board for the entire shoot as "Japanese consultant." He helped us deal with the thorny cultural issues, since we didn't want to end up getting picketed like Philip Kaufman's† *Rising Sun* did a couple years later. We didn't want to accidentally offend Japanese sensibilities. We only want to offend people when we know we're doing it.

By this time, 1989, Troma had acquired a name in the industry. Therefore, when "The company that brought you *The Toxic Avenger* and *Class of Nuke 'Em High*" put ads in *Backstage* magazine looking for actors, the response was overwhelming. Thousands of headshots poured in. Because of this we were able to assemble the best cast we had had up until that time. The lead—Harry Griswold/Sgt. Kabukiman—called for a "Nick Nolte" type. We were lucky to get Rick Gianasi. Unlike most Troma actors, Rick wasn't a newcomer to the film industry. He had already had the lead in seven independent films. We were also fortunate to get Bill Weeden as head bad guy Reginald Stuart.‡ Bill brought the extra-added advantage of looking like MPAA head Jack Valenti, who is always the head bad guy of my dreams. The most difficult role to fill was that of Lotus, Harry Griswold's love interest and the *real* hero of *Sgt. Kabukiman NYPD*. Lotus had to be an Asian

---

*In the movie, recovering bug-eater Pericles Lewnes actually ate the worms, doubling for Fumio Furuya, who was supposed to be doing so.

†Director of *The Unbearable Lightness of Being*, *The Right Stuff*, and the great *The Wanderers*. No relation.

‡The other leading contender for the Stuart role was Maximillian Shaun, who later went on to play Cappy Capulet in *Tromeo & Juliet*. Max dropped out of auditions at the last moment to take a role in the stage play *Othello*, written by some hack.

woman who was beautiful, could act, could do heavy action sequences, and was willing to do nudity. It was hard to find actresses who fulfilled all of these requirements. In the end, we were blessed with Susan Byun.

I often hear directors declare that their stress increases the larger a budget gets. But *Sgt. Kabukiman* was the largest budget we had yet had, and I felt significantly *less* pressure. You don't have to worry about trivia. Because you can afford them, you're able to hire more competent people. *Kabukiman* was the first film on which Michael and I weren't the first ones on set every morning. Like most other directors, we had a call time that was an hour before shooting, a couple hours after everyone else. I was continuing to learn in my film career that things tend to get done, even if I don't take care of them myself.

There were some new problems to be faced, however. For Director of Photography, we used a union guy. He ended up using the name "Bob Williams" in the credits so he wouldn't get in trouble with his union or the ASC.* Here, however, I'll use his real name—Vilmos Zsigmond, Academy Award–winning DP for *Close Encounters of the Third Kind*.

Well, okay, not really. I can't tell you his real name. But "Bob" had been in the business for as long as I had. When I had first met him he was a third assistant cameraman. Now, eighteen years later, he was a . . . third assistant cameraman. To become a Director of Photography is perhaps the hardest job in the film business. There are fewer than 300 members in the ASC, so it's difficult to work your way up. Many people aspire to be a DP their entire lives but never have an opportunity since union members are limited to working in union films. Therefore, someone like "Bob"† would do most anything to take the reins on a project he could call his own. On *Sgt. Kabukiman* we had

---

*American Society of Cinematographers.
†Just so you know, "Bob" wasn't the first or last person to work on a Troma movie who was in a union. Almost every Troma movie has three or four false names in the credits who are actually in unions. These include actors who make their livings in sub-bit parts in union movies but are only able to find leads in smaller, nonunion films, as well as crew members who get a union job maybe once or twice a year and need to work on independent nonunion films to pay the bills or to gain experience.

to buy him a $400 fake beard so that when we shot exteriors no one would recognize him. The ruse worked. The first day he showed up wearing it, *I* didn't recognize him. There was this guy following me around, talking to me as if he knew me. I shrugged it off and pretended to know who he was. When I figured it out, I introduced him to Rick Gianasi as our new DP.

"New DP?!" Rick said. "What happened to 'Bob'?"

Sometimes larger budgets don't help, however. Jeff Sass said he absolutely refused to be production manager on yet another Troma production. So we hired the "best production manager in the New York independent film community" at the cost of $2,500 dollars a week.

"We've never paid anyone $2,500 a week!" I said. But I was assured he was worth it. Upon being hired the guy told us he needed an assistant. She was only $750 a week. And happened to wear skimpy outfits. After a month this production management team had done absolutely nothing. My first-time-barely-out-of-high-school production manager on *Squeeze Play* had done a better job. We fired the PM and his twinkie assistant and Jeff Sass took over once again, much to his chagrin.

Also worth mentioning is Edgard Mourino, whom we hired as stunt coordinator. Edgard was missing two fingers on one hand. Seeing that didn't inspire my faith in him as a stuntman. However, he told me— get this; I swear to God this is true—that *his fingers were bitten off BY A GORILLA when he put his fingers in a cage as a child*. I went home to Pat that night.

"Pat," I said. "Today at the office I met this guy WHOSE FINGERS WERE BITTEN OFF BY A GORILLA." She couldn't believe it.

In this entire book, no matter how many times I lie, I will never be able to top that.*

Rick Gianasi joined forces with Michael, Jeff Sass, Pat, and the entire corporation of Namco to make *Kabukiman* a mainstream film. Rick was an instrumental part of the movie. In rehearsals he would come up with many of his own lines. I trusted his judgment and consulted

---

*Coincidentally, Jeff Sass's daughter later had her finger sliced off at home in a folding stepladder. They took her and the finger to the hospital and they sewed it back on, good as new.

him often. He once expressed his desire to try his hand at directing, and I let him direct one of the scenes.* Rick was also the highest paid Troma actor ever. He was originally budgeted to make $50 a day, but he told us he needed $100 a day to cover his rent. Although it was extravagant, we gave it to him. However, when Rick protested a scene

CLASS OF NUKE 'EM HIGH II & III

"Today, of course, I kind of regret it," says Kaufman. "Not directing the two sequels. In the early nineties I felt I had to stay focused on the Toxic Crusaders cartoons and merchandise and development of the big-budget movie. One of the things that was stolen from me when that deal fell apart were the films I opted not to direct during that time. It's six years from *Kabukiman* to *Tromeo*."

Class of Nuke 'Em High Part II: Subhumanoid Meltdown and *Class of Nuke 'Em High Part III: The Good, the Bad, and the Subhumanoid* were given to director Eric Louzil. Like Fred Olen Ray, Dennis Adam Zervos, Bill Rebane, Will Zens, and Joel M. Reed, Louzil has more than one film in the Troma library. Unlike these others, Louzil has FOUR (the *Nuke 'Em*'s, *Fortress of Amerikkka*, and *Lust for Freedom*), and these films were produced by Herz and Kaufman. Kaufman also did a fair amount of writing on the screenplays.

where a rope turns into a snake that then crawls up a guy's ass and comes out of his mouth, *that* was going one step too far.

I had dreamed it the night before. That day we were shooting in a gym which, coincidentally, had a climbing rope. I was ecstatic about my "visionary dream" and told everyone about it: Kabukiman would somehow through magical powers turn the climbing rope into a snake, which would slide up the bad guy's ass, and exit from his mouth, thus killing him. I had imagined the cast and crew would see how providential this all was. However, instead, they all stood before me with slightly disgusted faces.

"What?" I said. "You don't like it? It'll be great!"

No one smiled. They just stood there, staring at me as if I were insane (this is not an uncommon occurrence, by the way).

"Lloyd, can I talk to you for a minute," Rick said. He led me away from the group. We stood face-to-face (or my face to his chin).

"You're doing it again," he said.

"Doing what?"

"Straying. Let me tell you something. The other day we were shoot-

---

*The one where Lotus gets interrogated in the police station.

ing second unit in the park. I was dressed up as Kabukiman. There were all these little kids there, and they ran up to me. There was something about Kabukiman that they were attracted to. They all wanted to jump in my arms, ride on my back. They found out Kabukiman's name and started chanting it."

"Hmm. That's interesting, Rick. You wanted to take me aside to tell me that story?"

"I realized then what a great movie for kids Sgt. *Kabukiman* would be. I think this is Troma's chance to move out of obscure cult, and up into the underground."

"I agree. I think kids will love it."

"So, then, you won't put this snake scene in?"

I stared blankly at him. He stared back at me, a little less blankly than me, but still pretty blankly.

"I don't get you," I said. "Where's the connection?"

"You can't have a kid's movie with a snake crawling up a guy's butt!"

"Ohhh."

"Yes."

"But it will be funny."

"It's not that funny, Lloyd. It's kind of weird."

"It'll be hilarious, Rick. It's a *rope* turning into a *snake* and then crawling up a guy's *ass* and then coming out of his *mouth.*"

"I know what it is. Put it in your next movie."

"I understand what you're saying. But I think I'll put it in this one," I said. I turned toward the special-effects coordinator. "Hey, Pericles! We have to figure out how to turn a rope into a snake!"

I got home from the set late that night. Pericles Lewnes had figured out a way to do the scene, but we hadn't had time to film it. We planned on doing it the following day. I wasn't home for long when the phone rang. It was Rick. He begged me again not to put the scene in. A week earlier he had asked me to remove another scene, where Kabukiman slices a prostitute and her pimp up into sushi. "Kabukiman's a hero!" he had said. "He's the good guy! He can't impose the death penalty for prostitution!" I had refused to listen, and kept the scene in. Now, tonight, I couldn't say no again. I told Rick I wouldn't film the rope-snake-ass scene.

The murder of the prostitute is in the film today. Countless people, upon viewing it, have agreed with Rick.

I, however, still have dreams about snakes going up my ass. If I had put the scene in *Kabukiman*, I probably would have purged myself of this nighttime delusion and lost my need to dream it. Fortunately, I enjoy this dream immensely.

One day, while we were filming outdoors on state-owned property in Harlem, Muslims visited the set of *Sgt. Kabukiman NYPD*. They called themselves the Sons of Islam. Their leader was a man named Mustapha Majeed, a tall, well-dressed black fellow wearing what appeared to be an oversized yarmulke. With him he had three or four other huge guys. They approached Jeff Sass and told him that they were with an organization called Communications Industry Skills Center. They said they wanted to go through the payroll list to make sure that we had enough minorities in our crew.

I interrupted.

"Wait a second!" I said. "What business is it of yours who we've hired?"

"It is our business, sir," said Mustapha. He got close to me. He was at least a foot taller. "I want to make sure that your hiring practices are fair. Last week we shut down the Sidney Lumet film."

"We're not going to let you see the list," I said. "It's not your business."

"It is our business. And there's not going to be any filming here until we *do* see it."

"That's bullshit!" I cried. "We are going to film! We'll film lots of things!"

"The only thing that that camera's going to get on film is my ass."

"Good! Because that's what I wanted to film today! A big ass!"

Mustapha and I argued. Although Jeff attempted to be diplomatic, I became more and more indignant. At one point Mustapha pointed to me, laughing, and said, "Man, *you* ought to be the actor!" But they refused to remove themselves from in front of our cameras. It was a standoff. We were losing valuable time; we had to throw a naked woman out of the building before we lost light. We couldn't wait until the next day. The cost of the sugar glass and spotters and stuntmen and the inflatable target went into the thousands.

Finally, Michael Green and Karen Ramos came down from the fourteenth floor where they had been preparing the sugar glass. They fessed up to being black.

Sekou Shepard, the chief sound engineer, came over and poked Mustapha.

"I'm black too," he said. "And this is my black assistant Fred."

Susan Byun, the actress who played Lotus, came over as well.

"I'm Asian. Do you take care of us?"

"We take care of everybody!" Mustapha said.

A hoard of PAs came over, along with camera assistants and actors: African-Americans, Japanese-Americans, Chinese-Americans, Arab-Americans, Native Americans. Over half the Troma Team were minorities. Mustapha began to laugh.

"Hell, this is the best set I've ever been on!" he exclaimed.

Mustapha and his crew ended up having lunch with us. He told me that he had a lot of connections at television stations and newspapers and that he'd call them to come down and do a story on how great we were.

A TV station showed up, as well as the *New York Post* and the *Daily News*. They asked me questions about our "confrontation" with Mustapha and his organization. It was obvious that they were looking for dirt—they wanted a face-off of some sort or a nifty race-hatred story. When they found out that Mustapha had called them down to do a *positive* story, they were visibly disappointed.

"Listen," I told them. "I know you're not going to do a positive story. I know you wouldn't do that. What you *should* write is a story on the sexism and racism in Hollywood. It's not that I'm a philanthropist of any type. I'm simply a good businessman taking advantage of Hollywood's prejudices. We have a soundman over here who's one of the best in the business. He ought to be making $6,000 a week on a Hollywood set. But he's black. So instead he can only get work with us, Troma, the shittiest company in the world, making one third of that. Half of our crew are women. Why? The same reason. I'm simply a businessman getting some of the best talent in the industry due to the system's corruption. Go ahead and do *that* story. Portray me like the old railroad tycoons who would hire Chinese immigrants for ten cents a day. But you know what? You won't write *that* story, and you won't air *that*, because you're all tools of the conspiracy of the bureaucratic, labor, and corporate elite, and none of them want you to touch this fucking issue. You can attack the racism in used car dealerships in Arkansas all you want, but when it gets close to home—the media, your boss—everyone's mouth is shut."

Nothing concerning this story showed up in the newspapers or on TV.

After *Sgt. Kabukiman NYPD* was completed, it took seven years to get a theatrical release. We had two versions—a PG-13 version and an unrated version (which would have actually been a soft R, but we didn't want to pay the MPAA the three grand it'd take to have it rated a second time).

We had the first screening of the PG-13 version for our Japanese investors, along with many Namco and Gaga employees. The disappointment was palpable. This was *not* a mainstream film. The film was confused: sometimes seeming lighthearted and general-audience

oriented, while other times it indulged in the violence or "trash aesthetic" that Troma was famous for. Unlike *The Toxic Avenger*, the differences in tone didn't seem deliberate. They seemed like what they
were, an inability to fully dedicate to either one vision or the other. It
was not what Namco expected, and it must have been obvious that its
child-geared spin-off potential was miniscule. One episode of a *Sgt.
Kabukiman* cartoon series was made, by Andy Heywood of DIC Animation, due to the hype about the upcoming *Toxic Crusaders* TV series
and the fact that Andy's kids loved the movie. But it led nowhere.

We tried for years to get a wide U.S. release of *Kabukiman*, but
neither theaters nor larger studio distributorships seemed interested in
the movie. For six years at the Cannes Film Festival we screened and
promoted the film, but there were few foreign sales. It played theaters
in Japan and Germany, but that was about it. We did get offers, but
they were never what we wanted, so we turned them down. At the
1996 festival we handed out promotional buttons—"Raw Fish in '96—
Kabukiman for President." Often, foreign buyers would think that we
were promoting a sequel to the first *Kabukiman*, which they had already seen years earlier.

In May of 1996 *Sgt. Kabukiman NYPD* was released at the prominent New York art house Film Forum.* Karen Cooper, the program
director there, called the movie "The best satire on New York I've seen
in years." The film did respectably, and ended up playing in a few good
theaters in the U.S. and U.K. The reviews were, overall, positive. But
much of the audience—most of them Troma fans—was disappointed.
Most of them want Troma to get more extreme as time goes on, and
this film was mild compared to the others.

This is not to say that I (along with many fans) don't like the film. In
some respects, quite honestly, it is one of our best. It's fairly well put together, well acted, and well shot. It's just that it could have been so much
more so if I had fully dedicated myself to one choice or the other. Michael Herz, Jeff Sass, Pat, Rick Gianasi, Namco, and Gaga all wanted me
to make a film that was more mainstream. All of these people are ex-

---

*At the time I was shocked—Film Forum is dedicated to art films. It was the last
place I expected a Troma movie to play. Until this time, most Troma films had been
played in more general establishments. Since, I am less shocked by it. *Tromeo & Juliet*'s comparatively wide release was almost singularly at art houses.

tremely talented and intelligent. With Gaga and Namco, Troma could have been propelled into a new stratosphere of interlocked media. Michael and Jeff have both shown nearly infallible heads for business. Rick had a feeling for children's entertainment that was profound.

Still, I am certain they were all wrong.

I miss the snake going up the ass. I am upset that we only intimated that the toddlers were mutilated at the start of the film, instead of actually showing it. I regret only having worms being eaten when we could have, perhaps, had someone chowing down on a water buffalo's penis. Not enough heads were sliced, there wasn't enough vomiting or pissing, and there wasn't nearly the necessary quotient of hot monkey love. Perhaps in forgetting these things I also, for a moment, forgot my place in the world.

THE TOXIC CRUSADERS: PART II

It wasn't difficult to get TV stations to carry *The Toxic Crusaders*. Kids action shows were in style. And though the Tromaville mystique was originally intended for adults, it flowed well into the world of children. This was no surprise to my friends, who know that I am extremely immature.

It wasn't long before Jeff Sass had lined up numerous merchandising deals for the characters, including action figures by Playmates, Colorform sticker sets, and a "Battle for Tromaville" board game by Mattel. Michael Herz was extremely enthusiastic—the most enthusiastic I had ever seen him. He saw this as our opportunity to enter the mainstream.

THE CARTOONS MOST PEOPLE UNDER 25 HAVE GROWN UP WITH ARE ACTUALLY INFOMERCIALS.

By the early 1980's, the FCC, under the Reagan administration, had relaxed its regulations on TV. A host of children's programming that was primarily commercials for toy lines, from *GI Joe* to *Thundarr the Barbarian* to *He Man*, were allowed on the air. Not long after, "barter

Troma cofounders Lloyd Kaufman (r.) and Michael Herz joyfully play with the full line of Toxic Crusaders toys. Seconds after this shot was taken, the idyllic scene was shattered as Herz's inner child kicked Kaufman's full-grown ass when Kaufman insisted upon wearing Toxie's Tick Tock Cleanup Time Watch.

syndication" became possible; that is, a toy company or animators would give their half-hour cartoon toy commercials to television for *next to nothing* or *free*, to the benefit of both parties. In the mid-1980s, Lorimar Telepictures broke new ground with *Thundercats*, actually paying TV stations a percentage of the sales the toys would reap in the broadcast area. TV stations became merchandising partners, saturating afternoon TV with kiddie brainwashing, while simultaneously selling commercial time within these commercials.* Classic animated efforts like Woody Woodpecker, Mighty Mouse, and the old Looney Tunes were gone forever. The elites had infiltrated the entertainment industry in secret ways to the permanent detriment of quality. I mention this because, although we did debut the Crusaders toys in specified areas simultaneous to the debut of the show, we didn't want our shows to be commercials. We cared about the quality of the cartoons. We were foremost in the business of entertainment, and we wanted it to stay that way.

The finest episodes were written by Jack Mendelsson and his wife Carol. Jack was well known for having penned episodes of *The Mary Tyler Moore Show* and, believe it or not, *The Show of Shows*. He also acted as story editor of the *Toxic Crusaders* series, cleaning up episodes

---

*Most of this information is from *Carnival Culture* (1992), by the great pop-culture historian and theoretician James B. Twitchell.

by other writers—including two episodes written by Jeff Sass, Andy Wolk,* and me.

I had my nose in all aspects of *The Toxic Crusaders*, such as writing with Jeff the captions for the Toxic Crusaders Topps trading cards.† I found myself having a great time in their world—one of the first times in my life I've been happy working outside of a film project. However, as Michael often reminded me, the toy companies knew a lot more about toys than I did, and Murikami Wolf knew a lot more about cartoons. Sometimes I'd get out of line. For instance, every cartoon script would have to pass over my desk before they filmed it. At one point I complained that I wasn't getting them early enough to make changes. It was then that I learned the twelve-hour turnaround time allotted for rewrites was normal. Television just moves at a much quicker pace than film does.

The TV show debuted around the country in June of 1991. Although the related merchandise didn't break any Cabbage Patch Dolls records, for a small company like Troma the royalties were enormous. They alone brought a couple of million dollars into the company. Even better, kids seemed to love the show: audiences and toy sales began to grow.

The large movie studios—everyone from Universal to Warner Bros. to Paramount—began to show interest in creating a live-action *Toxic Crusaders* movie. This was natural in the wake of a *Teenage Mutant Ninja Turtles* live-action film that did amazingly well at the box office, and upped the attendant merchandise considerably. It was an exhilarating time for Michael and me. For once in our lives the large studios were catering to *us*. We went to numerous meetings and expensive dinners.‡ There were drugs and hookers. Being that I'm a family man who likes to keep my debauchery on celluloid, I didn't indulge. But Michael had

---

*The UPS delivery boy whose bowels explode when Toxie squishes him in a folding wheelchair in *Toxic Avenger III*.

†Containing educational environmental information for kids, such as, "Conserve water: Don't bathe," and "Save paper: Blow your nose on your sleeve."

‡My longtime friend, Sam Arkoff, founder of AIP, got Fox interested. Joe Roth, boss at Fox, flew Michael and me to L.A. on the MGM Grand First-Class bullshit air-

sex with quite a few sexy prostitutes around that time. He received one horrible case of the clap, waking up the next morning and finding one of his testicles black and swollen to three times its normal size. Michael had to have his ball removed. Today he supposedly functions fully— but who the hell really believes that?*

Eventually we were offered a terrific deal by New Line. They guaranteed to make a big budget film that would propel the cartoons and merchandise to higher levels. Unlike the other studios, who mostly wanted to give us development deals (meaning there was a chance we'd get forgotten in the rush of larger projects), New Line offered us a Pay and Play deal. This meant that not only did they have to pay us, they were also obligated to produce the film by spring of 1993. New Line guaranteed that the film would cost no less than five million dollars, and that they would spend no less than an additional three million dollars in prints, advertising, and publicity. They paid us $100,000 up front, with $300,000 plus 5 percent of the budget to follow at the time of filming. Troma would receive a substantial percentage of the film's receipts in addition to the royalties from the film-related merchandise. Also, we had a fair amount of creative control. The script would have to be okayed by us. And I would direct if they didn't find someone more qualified.†

New Line seemed like the perfect company. They had started out as a small independent like Troma, distributing such classic films as *Pink Flamingos*. They had experience doing kids' films with cross-merchandising potential—they had made the *Teenage Mutant Ninja Turtles* films. I liked the people we were dealing with: Bob Shaye, the CEO; Michael Lynne, president; and Donna Bascom, a VP. Because they weren't as big as the larger studios, it seemed as if they'd give us

---

plane. Jean-Claude Van Damme, the nasty nontalent, was in the compartment next to ours. Later, Van Damme asked me to introduce him to John Avildsen, which I did. Van Damme said he'd sure return the favor if ever I needed it. However, a few weeks later, my brother needed to speak with Van Damme. The bastard never returned our calls—Hollywood rules.

*Okay, this is a lie. But after twenty-five years I really don't have much dirt to dish out on Michael, besides the fact that I suspect he's a cyborg. So I have to make some up occasionally.

†Like, say, if the New Line janitor turned down the job.

more personal attention and understand the independents' plight. We signed the contract in fall of 1991.

This was a mistake.

Like every time Troma attempts to enter the mainstream, we end up bouncing off an impenetrable hymen. And with New Line, even though we couldn't get through the hymen, we still got fucked.

They did some of the things they promised. They had the Toxic Crusader and NoZone characters show up at major New Line events. They made posters (as did we, with the New Line logo) to announce the upcoming film at markets. New Line commissioned a screenplay, written by a guy who wrote one of the Freddy Krueger movies.* They hired a line producer. They opened a production office in L.A.

But then things slowed. Spring of 1993 was quickly approaching, and the project didn't seem to be progressing. We, of course, called repeatedly. "Everything's dandy," we were assured.

Finally, the deadline came and went. No movie. I was at the Cannes Film Festival when Shaye and Lynne informed us that they weren't going to make the movie.

Michael, Jeff Sass, and I were distraught. From our point of view, it seemed that New Line, as opposed to having interest in making *Toxic Crusaders*, was using our characters for leverage. Here's how the situation looked to us:

At the same time they picked up our rights, they were also negotiating with the owners of the Teenage Mutant Ninja Turtles. New Line didn't yet have the rights to the third Turtles film. By throwing the Toxic Crusaders in their faces, it seemed that New Line could say, "See, we don't need your movie. We have these Troma guys if you don't give us a good deal on the Turtle rights." In the end they *did* get the rights for the third Turtles film, and we were screwed. It also seemed that, if they had another Turtles movie coming out, they wouldn't want a similar type film competing with it. So everything fell into place for New Line; they had the rights to the third Turtles movie, which they

---

*Which was, incidentally, 112 pages of papyrus about as enjoyable as used toilet paper. I wanted them to consider Jack Mendelsson as screenwriter, but they said he was "too old." "He's great!" I said. "He worked with Sid Caesar!" "Sid Caesar?" they said. "The guy from *Grease?*"

would make, *and* they had the Toxic Crusader rights, so no other studio would be able to make a competing Crusaders film.*

We hired a friend of mine from Yale, a powerful Hollywood lawyer named Peter Dekom, to work out a deal for us with New Line. New Line wasn't willing to deal. We took the Toxic Crusaders project to the other studios that had initially made us offers on the franchise, but they looked at us as if we were trying to hand them a used condom. "Lloyd, you should have gone with us," said the Warner President of Production. "Now it's too late." We had signed merchandising deals with over eighty different companies. They repeatedly asked us when the movie was due. They had agreed to make Toxic Crusaders products under the condition that a feature film was made. When they found out it wasn't happening, they began to drop away.

We had no choice but to sue. My father, the lawyer, was outraged by the situation—a major company who signed a contract and then just refused to abide by it. As we became more enmeshed in the legal process, we heard horror stories about other studios that would sign contracts with young, broke producers and then refuse to stick to them. If you couldn't afford to risk the huge sum it takes to hire lawyers, you'd have no way to protect yourself. With my father's assistance, we were hooked up with one of the most prestigious law firms in the country: LeBoeuf, Lamb, Greene, and MacRae.† A protracted and ex-

---

Entertainment Weekly reported that in May of 1997, director William Friedkin (*The French Connection, The Exorcist*) filed a multimillion-dollar lawsuit which claims that New Line had him develop a Jack the Ripper movie with an understanding from VP Richard Saperstein that if the studio didn't want to proceed that the rights would revert to Friedkin. Friedkin alleges that New Line froze the film because they were working on another Ripper film with the Hughes Brothers, but *still refused* to release the rights. Friedkin was quoted in *Entertainment Weekly* as saying, "I want the case to go to jury so that [New Line's] business practices are exposed. To me, these people are a disease."

†New Line put off going to court until 1996. We claimed damages of more than fifty million dollars. Taking all of the possible merchandising deals into account, that was the amount of money Troma could have been denied by New Line's refusal to abide by the contract. LeBoeuf, Lamb, Greene, and MacRae assembled a crackerjack team of lawyers for us, led by the legendary eighty-five-year-old Milton Gould (Milton was an old buddy of my father's; he was a founding partner of Shea, Gould, and Clemenko, which helped create the Mets and Shea Stadium; he also reorganized 20th Century Fox after Daryl Zanuck). The team included Jane Kober (most famous for playing the prissy lady who gets shot in the head at the beginning of *Sgt. Kabuki-*

pensive lawsuit would drain Troma faster than a shot of Dristan drains my sinuses. It didn't seem that things could get any worse.

In September of 1993 my father died.

A month later Pat was diagnosed with breast cancer.

BREAST CANCER

Throughout this book, I'm aware I seem somewhat flippant and irreverent. These are genuine aspects of my personality, but there are other parts of myself just as true. Because of the offhanded nature of this book I have been hesitant about discussing what was the most trying—and yet most enlightening—time in my entire life. Here it is anyway:

In 1993, Pat had a mammogram. The doctor saw something.

"It could be something, but it isn't anything," she said. "It's probably not cancer."

Nevertheless, she wanted Pat to get a biopsy. After the results of *that* test, Doctor #2 sat us down with the results.

"Seems like there's a bit of a cancer problem," he said. Pat, he told us, should have surgery as soon as possible.

Pat and I stepped outside of the doctor's office, feeling as if we had just had our ears boxed by God. My eardrums were ringing. I was off balance. The day was surprisingly sunny, it was warm, and so completely the opposite of what I was feeling. I reached out to touch Pat. I was hesitant. This was hard. I'm an American man, and we aren't known for the openness of our emotions in trying times. Yet I wanted to lend the support that she had always shown me. Years of stupid schemes and stupid movies and vanity and crudeness and belligerence, and yet she somehow put up with it. Even more: she had made me believe that my personality was a good thing and had a place in this world. And now, to even think that she could . . . I didn't want to think it, but I did.

We knew we couldn't go home to the kids without some sort of

---

man NYPD), Vivian Polak, and Ken Moltner. We were sure we would *win* the case; the fact that New Line breached the contract was obvious to us. The question was whether or not the New York jury would decide to award us a decent amount for damages. We could end up receiving less than our legal expenses.

plan. We went to a restaurant on Third Avenue, JG Melon, to have a drink and to sort out our thoughts. We entered at 3:30 in the afternoon. I was ashen and shaken, as was Pat. There was nobody in the place. The tables were empty. Pat and I took one in the corner. I held Pat's hands in mine. A waiter approached.

"What can I get you?" he said.

Pat and I ordered drinks.

"And what else?" the waiter said.

"That's it," I said.

"Unless you have something to eat, you can't sit here."

"There's no one else here."

"You got to sit at the bar."

"Please, can't we just—?"

"You got to move."

I was infuriated. All my emotions were crashing toward the surface. I know it wasn't just my anger at him, it was at everything. At life, at the fact that the world could steal from you the thing you cared about most. I wanted to throttle him, smash his head against the wall, scream out:

"CAN'T YOU SEE THIS WOMAN HAS CANCER!!"

Instead, for once in my life, I got the better of my emotions, and we left. I never went back there again, however. JG Melon: 1239 Third Avenue. Their windows look better with smashed, rotten eggs on them. I hope I'm not giving you any ideas.

A couple days later we went to a grief psychiatrist. That is, a psychiatrist who was an expert in grief. Normally, I would say that people who are experts in grief don't have any business giving anybody else advice. But we wanted to do everything we could to help the family through this, and a good friend had recommended her to us. The psychiatrist cost four hundred bucks for a half hour. We asked her how we should deal with telling the kids.

"Tell 'em straight," she said. "Then take them to this wonderful movie. It's called *Into the West*. I really think that movie will help the kids through their sadness."

"What's it about?" I asked her. After I did, though, I nearly hit myself. That question cost me ten bucks! I could go home and look it up in the newspaper for free!

"A white horse," the psychiatrist said. "But you'll see for yourself."

Pretty soon, the half hour was up. We went home. Finally, after summoning up all our courage, we told Charlotte, Lisbeth, and Lily Hayes about Pat. We didn't hold the facts back. Yet, we also told them about the hope; we let them know we were going to do everything that we possibly could to see that Pat got well. The girls took it better than we expected. We told them we'd take them to see a movie. They all wanted to see *Look Who's Talking Too*.

"No," I said. "There's this horse movie that's going to help you deal with your grief."

Into the West ended up being one of the most fucked-up movies I had ever seen. I don't remember exactly what happens, but it was something about a dead mother speaking to her kids and the horse ends up being the dead mother's spirit, and these kids get chased by some people, and then the horse and the kids jump off a cliff into the river and then they're drowning. And then the horse—the mother—DIES!

I have no idea what the crazy-lady psychiatrist was thinking. We were all devastated. We walked out of the theater, the $440 dollar ticket stubs feeling like lumps of lead in my pocket. I considered taking the kids to another psychiatrist who specialized in trauma resulting from films that suck, but thought better of it. To paraphrase the Who, I would not get fooled again.

Pat and I did everything we possibly could to safeguard her health. From the beginning, we obsessively utilized spiral-bound notebooks, just as I make PAs do on Troma films. I took down every word any doctor ever said to us. For the first time in my life I called on people for real favors. One of my fellow Trinity school board members, Evelyn Lauder, had built the new breast cancer center at Sloane-Kettering— one of the best units in the world. Although I didn't know Evelyn well, she came through for us immediately, finding Pat the best surgeon and oncologist in the world. Pat and I decided we wouldn't skimp on anything. When it came to my wife's health, I wanted the best doctors and the best facilities in the world. I wouldn't pay Mark Torgl the extra 50 bucks to appear in *The Toxic Avenger II*, but I wanted to be damn sure I got the Mark Torgl of surgeons, no matter what the expense. The first doctor we had was good, but not great. Without flinching, we fired him and got new doctors through Evelyn—ones that *were* great. I don't like hurting people's feelings. Oftentimes I'll make do with a less-qualified actor in a film because I don't want to let that person down. But, again, this was not a movie. This was life. And although I was forty-seven years old, this was one of the first times that I saw the difference.

Pat was set to have surgery only ten days after we discovered the cancer. Andy Warhol had recently died in a private room in a hospital. Apparently he had attempted to buzz the nurse as he was dying, but the nurse wasn't at her station. Once more I was influenced by Warhol: We put Pat in a semiprivate room so her roommate would be a safety check if something went wrong. On Pat's first night there, I slept in the hospital, on the floor behind Pat's bed. A nurse caught me. I was reprimanded. They told me I couldn't stay there at night anymore.

Pat's operation was set for nine in the morning. We had heard that it's best for the individual to be operated on first thing, because that's when the body is at its strongest and that's also when the surgeon's facilities are at their peak. However, the day before the operation a nurse came into our semiprivate room.

"Ms. Kaufman, we'll be in at eleven o clock tomorrow to get you," she said.

"Eleven?" I said. "She was supposed to be operated on at *nine*."

"No, no. You must be mistaken. I just read it on your chart. Eleven."

Pat and I exchanged a glance. We shrugged.

"I guess it's been changed," Pat said.

An hour later a four-foot nun stopped by. These religious people were always going in and out of the room: ministers, rabbis, priests. Not too many servants of the Dark Lord, but all the rest. Although I'm not a member of any organized religion, I do believe there is a spiritual as well as physical side that needs to be attended to in times of hardship. It was comforting to have these people around. They all had lists of the patients and their operation schedules. The short nun noticed on her schedule, she said, that Pat was having her operation at nine the next morning. She offered us her blessings.

"Wait a second," I said. "They told us she was being picked up at eleven."

The nun pointed out where it said on Pat's sheet that she was being operated on at nine, picked up at eight.

The nun and I traveled to the nurse's station. We teamed up for a bit of detective work, a sort of modern day Batman and Robin. (She got to be Batman, I guess, because she had the helmetlike ears). Eventually, we figured out the mystery. There was *another Kaufman* who was having surgery at eleven *with the same surgeon*. Only she was having surgery on her *right breast*, not the left like Pat. I looked at the little old nun. She smiled.

"Oh, my! That could've been a terrible problem!" she said.

"What if Pat came out of surgery tomorrow with the wrong breast cut off?!" I said.

"Ow!" the nun said.

I smiled. I felt grateful to her. I almost apologized to her for having people snorting coke and fucking on the altar of a Catholic church in *Sgt. Kabukiman NYPD* but reconsidered.

I ran around the hospital putting signs on the walls:

Warning! There are 2 Kaufmans!
PAT Kaufman = LEFT Breast, Surgery at 9:00!
OTHER Kaufman = RIGHT Breast, Surgery at 11:00!

Above Pat's bed I wrote:

NOTE!:
This is PAT Kaufman, not the other one!
LEFT BREAST, not right!
Please don't cut off the right breast!
↓

In the end, there was no mix-up, and there probably wouldn't have been anyway. But, like in filmmaking, you can never be too sure.

The surgery went as well as it possibly could have. But Pat still had to go through six months of chemotherapy. And we didn't know how permanent the cancer's remission was. I supported her as well as I could, and halted preproduction on a film I was considering (*The Troma Western*). They say that after five years, if the cancer doesn't show up again, it probably won't. The operation was October 29, 1993. Today is September 1, 1997.

We're keeping our fingers crossed.

*   *   *

"That's great, Lloyd," you may say, "although we're not used to you sounding sincere. But it doesn't have anything to do with *making movies*. So, really, we'd like our money back for these pages that have to do with cancer."

It doesn't so much have to do with making movies *directly*, I would tell you. It has to do with being a human being. And art has a great deal to do with that. I don't believe works produced by someone without any sense of his or her emotions, or, actually, love, have much worth. I've met hundreds of young people who've gotten trapped by using their "art" or "career" as an excuse for disregarding a full emotional life. "I don't need to have friends," I'll hear a young person say. "I've got my filmmaking to think about." It is true that you need to make many sacrifices if you decide upon the career of a filmmaker, especially sacrifices of time. And sometimes of relationships—I won't pretend that that's not true. But it doesn't mean that you completely deny yourself camaraderie, love, pleasure, or ethical behavior. In fact, quite the opposite—as an artist you have a *responsibility* to also be a human being. Time after time I see those who deny these parts of themselves fail at the success they most want. Balance is necessary.

Now, enough. I miss the fart jokes. Back to irreverence.

THE END OF THIS VERY LONG CHAPTER

Not long after I finished this chapter, I received a call from Barry Neville. He said that there had been no change; Putnam had decided to ditch my book.

"But listen, Barry, I have a new chapter," I said. "It's good. It goes over, pretty thoroughly, the way *Toxic Avenger II* became *Toxic Avenger II and III*. Then it talks about *Kabukiman*—I exaggerated some of the negative attributes of that film, to make a point about choices in filmmaking. There's, uh, Pat's breast cancer. And I go through the whole Toxic Crusaders thing, the fiasco with New Line, the—"

"I understand, Lloyd. But it's just a little too little a little too late."

Long pause.

"Barry," I said. "They've gotten to you, haven't they?"

"What?"

"Somebody from the studios. They got the thumbscrews on you. They heard about the book."

"Who? What are you—?"

"Yeah. Right. You don't know what I'm talking about. I can imagine what's going to fill the Troma book's slot next winter: *50 Years of Fascism with Walt Disney,* or *Dreamworks: How We Bought Penguin Putnam and Fucked Lloyd Kaufman.*"

"You're kidding, right?"

"Wrong. I know they hate the independents and if you're not part of a megaconglomerate, they'll do what they can to screw you."

"What are you talking about?"

"I read an article in the *New York Times* yesterday on Pat Robertson—he just sold his Satanic Broadcasting Network or whatever it's called to Rupert Murdoch. You know what Robertson said? He said, 'It's about time we got involved in consolidation.' As if *that* was a good thing! As if all businesses joining together into three or four huge monolithic,

---

WHAT'S IT LIKE TO BE A TROMA PA?

This question was put forth to Phil Rivo, who served as a production assistant on *The Toxic Avenger II* and *Troma's War.* Phil replied: "Well, the most important thing is, like, the sex. As a Troma PA you get laid a lot. On *Troma's War* some of us stayed in the barracks where we were filming. Well, at first no one wanted to stay there. But then, there was a cleaning woman that came in every morning. She was old and ugly and missing teeth, but man, she did this thing with her tongue! After a while, everyone wanted to stay in the barracks. I got it on with a couple other PAs during the shoot as well. I also got heavy with one of the actresses. She told me she loved my hair. Then she found out I was with the eighteen-year-old chick who got bagels for us every morning. She was hot too. Later, on *Toxie II,* the cool place to get laid was in Toxie's shack in the dump. I bet twelve, thirteen couples did it in there. You heard of the Mile High Club? This was like that, but not in a plane. In Toxie's shack. I'll try to think of a name for it that would be like the Mile High Club. Call me back tomorrow, and I'll give you a name for it. Okay?"

---

oppressive regimes was a good thing! Mr. Religion! Kill mom and pop. Kill the independent businessman. Kill the hearts and souls of the everyday people out there trying as hard as they can to grab just their own little tiny piece of the world. But really, for those everyday people, it's all just an illusion. There's nothing there to grab. Because the megaconglomerates won't let anyone have anything, whether the tools they use are theft, monopoly, intimidation, humiliation, or physical violence. There isn't really an America anymore. There's just those few super-companies that run the world. They're the only nations left. We're living in a time of war, a war fought by those who pledge their allegiances to the corporations, against those independent thinkers who pledge their allegiance to something a little more substantial, whether it be humanity, art, knowledge, or God. And you know what, Barry? Those of us on the independent side, we're losing. We're losing badly. I've seen the bodies of my fellow filmmakers strewn across the battlefield of art and ambition. We all cared at one point. But now they're all either a part of the mindless machine, or they're dead, gone, working in restaurants or babbling in an institution, sucking their fingers, pretending that they are what they should have been. Sometimes I feel guilty writing this book, Barry. Because maybe this book gives people a little too much hope. It may make them believe that these corporate superfuckers can be overcome. But at least it gives them a few of the rules. It gives them the rules and tells them to break them. Fuck them. Destroy them. Because in the end there are more of us than there are of them, Barry. And perhaps I'm grandiose in saying it—but I don't give a fuck anymore—this stupid and ridiculous book is one small splinter of light leading to something better. Even for me. I feel like there's something good about it, like I need to do it. It started with my own vanity—hey, a book about *me*—and the money I'll make from it, but now this book means something more. It's holy. And someone found out about the book, Barry, and they got to you, either directly or indirectly. Because that's what they're all about. Destroying light and putting absence in its place."

I stopped. There was silence on the other end of the line. Then a click.

"Lloyd? Lloyd?"

"What?"

"Are you still there?"

"What? Why?"

"I got cut off from you for a minute. We got this new phone system here. Something's wrong with them. What were you saying?"

"When did you . . . get cut off?"

"You started to say something about the *New York Times.*"

"Oh."

"An article in the *New York Times* said . . . ?"

"Never mind."

"Okay. All right."

My greatest speech ever, lost eternally to the wires of NYNEX. Another clicking sound.

"Lloyd, can you hold on?" Barry said. "That's my other line."

Barry pressed a button. It made a beeping sound.

"Hello," he said.

"I'm still here, Barry," I told him.

"Too many buttons. I can't get this thing figured out. Hold on."

Another beeping sound.

"Hello," Barry said.

I started to tell him it was me again, when somebody else answered.

"This you, Neville?" the voice said. It was dark and low.

It was obvious Barry had accidentally let me in on a three-way line.

"Yeah, this is me," he said. He sounded nervous. "Is Jessica all right?"

"Is what we talked about done?"

"Yes. I told him. You aren't going to hurt her, are you?"

"Meet me in an hour at the Suki Bar."

"Please. Tell her I love her."

The dark voice's phone went dead. Barry hit a button, I suppose to go back to me. Instead he cut me off. My line went dead. I stared at the wall.

I told Michael Herz what had happened and somehow talked him into going to the Suki Bar with me. There we hid in a booth beside Barry and a mountainous silver-haired gentleman. All of my suspicions were confirmed. Silver-hair and his bureaucratic associates had kidnapped Barry's girlfriend Jessica so that Barry would halt the publishing of the Troma book. He said that directly.

"Why are you doing this?" Barry said. "It's a good book. It's funny. Well-written. Chock-full of an irreverent and intelligent wit. A poignant statement on our troubled times."

Silver-hair said he did it because a major Hollywood studio PAID him to do it. FACT. Then Barry said he wouldn't do any more dirty work until he was sure Jessica was alive. Silver-hair led him out to a parking lot behind the Suki Bar. Michael and I followed. Michael kept apologizing for doubting me all these years. He actually licked my hand in submission.

In the back there was a limo. The rear window rolled down to reveal Jessica: beautiful, bruised, bound, and gagged. Barry caressed her face. It was touching. Then everything got ugly.

Luckily, I had brought guns with us, which I forgot to tell you about earlier. Michael and I came out with our guns blaring. Michael shot Silver-hair in the side of his head, and blood dribbled down over his Ralph Lauren silk suit. "Ow. Somebody did something to my eye," Silver-hair said. And then he died. I shot the driver in the face, replacing his nose with a big red sun. Barry opened the door and started to drag out Jessica, when three more thugs came out. A fat guy shot at me, grazing my face *in the exact place where I had had the skin cancer removed*. What luck! I thought. I could keep wearing the Band-Aid and no one would know the difference. Then I filled the fat fucker's belly with lead until he keeled over.

Like a jungle animal, Barry leapt onto the chest of another bureaucratic elitist, knocking him to the ground. Barry grabbed the man's throat and twisted it. With one mighty yank, he pulled the throat from the neck. Barry hollered. He waved the thorax over his own head, the blood dripping down onto his face and hair. It was sick and made Barry look a little pretentious.

The last thug said he was unarmed and begged Michael for mercy. Michael, who was going too far, shot him in the chest. The man tried to crawl away on his belly, but Michael stood over him and unloaded all the bullets into the man's back. Later on we found out that this guy was actually another kidnapping victim, which sucked.

Barry ungagged Jessica and they kissed. Then she kissed me, and then Michael, and then she kissed me again, and whispered in my ear that she was mine for the asking, but I told her that I loved my wife and also Barry was my good friend. I think she understood that.

"Thanks, guys," Barry said, a little embarrassed. "I promise never to submit to the bureaucratic, labor, and corporate elites ever again."

Then with no provocation whatsoever, Michael, Barry, and I jumped up and did a three-way high five.*

---

*EDITOR'S NOTE: This is, without a doubt, the most ridiculous thing that I've ever read. Reality stops somewhere around the time LK starts talking about Pat Robertson. Christ. (Though, I have to admit, I *did* like the part where I leapt up "like a jungle animal.")

Lloyd through a Fly's Eye: The Different Faces of Señor Kaufman

After my unrelenting pestering, Barry has surrendered and decided to forge on with the book. His decision was influenced, I believe, by the fact that Elizabeth Beier, director of Boulevard Books, found my manuscript in Barry's trash can. She decided to read it over, and she placed it back on Barry's desk. Her comments read:

> Publishable. There's a lot of freaks out there who might buy this crap.

I have finally been accepted by the literary community! Flowers! Great joy!

Barry, however, would only go forward with the project if he could include the following letters. He wrote to certain of my confederates, asking for an "honest assessment of the character and personality of Lloyd Kaufman." This is necessary, Barry maintains, since I am what he calls "an unreliable first-person narrator." The letters written to Barry are as follows:

PAT KAUFMAN, New York State Film Commissioner, and Lloyd's spouse:

THE CASE OF PATIENT X: "THESPIAN"

Recently, this Troma reporter contacted Forrest Dicker, Ph.D., a registered psychologist in the State of New York. I presented to him the case of one "Patient X," a semi-successful businessman and film director, who, although eminently untrained, continually forces himself as an actor into other people's movies. His performances, I tell the doctor, have been described as caricatures so broad they give new emotional range to sock puppets.

"Someone who exhibits these disturbing characteristics suffers from an oppo-Oedipal urge," said Dr. Dicker. "That is, unlike most people, who unconsciously have a desire to make love to their parent of the opposite sex, Patient X is so repulsed by his mother that he spends his life trying to 'turn off Mom,' so to speak. To 'stop her juices from flowing.' Therefore an automatic interior mechanism triggers an aggressive shame-seeking behavior."

"You mean he acts like an ass in public so that, no matter what, his mother won't want to fuck him?" I asked.

"Bingo," said Dr. Dicker.

PATIENT X'S EVIDENCE IS AS FOLLOWS:

1) *The Battle of Love's Return* Patient X directed and starred in this film. Showing that he himself has more sense than his friends, he did not appear in another one of his own films for twenty-five years.
2) *Cry Uncle* Patient X starts his personal tradition of taking advantage of his friends (in this case, John *Karate Kid* Avildsen) by forcing them to put him in their movies.
3) *The Love Thrill Murders* Patient X production-managed this film and gave himself another role as a hippie.
4) *Slow Dancing in the Big City* The second of four Avildsen-directed films in which Patient X appears.
5) *Rocky* Patient X plays a bum. Sylvester Stallone picks him up outside of a bar and brings him inside. The exterior of the bar was shot in Philadelphia, the interior in Los Angeles. Patient X is said to have gone so far as to have *paid his own ticket to Los Angeles* to be in the scene. "I am now a part of history," Patient X claims. NOTE: Extremely grandiose delusions.
6) *Saturday Night Fever* Patient X is the driver of John Travolta's brother's car service. Since Patient X is

Dear Barry,

Thank you for suggesting that I share my impressions of Lloyd and his book. Yeah, it's funny, yeah, it's full of wacky stories and outrageous Troma anecdotes. But it really misses the true Lloyd. Now I understand that Lloyd thinks it's funny to be raucous, raunchy, and, OK, sometimes gross. And he's certain that's what the people want in the book. But come on, I still have to take him to parents' night at our children's school. So let's get a few things straight.

First of all, the Lloyd I married and periodically take home does not use "that type of language." At least he doesn't in my or our children's presence, and certainly not in his mother's presence.

Second, he's unbelievably great with the kids. You may think this is because he's at their maturation level. That's true. But it's more than that. He adores our children. He walks them to school every day where all the fourth and sixth graders think he's a hoot. Even the eleventh grade likes him, but that may be because he watches MTV. More importantly, he cares deeply about what sort of people his girls are becoming.

And Lloyd is passionate about education. He's so loyal to Trinity, his prep school, that he has served as president of the Alumni Board and member of the school's Board of Trustees for the past ten years. He was awarded the Lawrence T. Cole award, which for Trinity Alumni is like an Oscar. HA! I bet he didn't include that in the book.

And I bet he doesn't bother to mention Fiftieth Street Films. Ah, so you think all the Troma films have mutants, gross humor, and girls in bikinis. That's because Lloyd won't admit to you that Troma's Fiftieth Street Films division was created so that Troma could distribute more mainstream films, including children's films and some art films. (Of course it could be that he also doesn't want to mention that it was my idea. I persuaded him to acquire Wildrose, a film by Sandra Schulberg. That's where it all started. Fiftieth Street also distributed My Neighbor Totoro.)

At the Junior League he's called "Lloyd the Saint." No joke. He was a terrific support when I served as president of the New York Junior League, a responsibility that kept me away from my family and in meetings many nights a week and required Lloyd's presence at many an event, often in a tuxedo. (Of course, even in a black tie Lloyd wears Day-Glo socks).

Furthermore, the chapter on my breast cancer, as sweet as it is, doesn't even come close to capturing

seen only on the very edge of the screen in a theater, the public is fortunately spared his visage on videotape, where the edge of the screen cuts him off.

7) *The Final Countdown* Patient X was associate producer on this film. His boss, the famous, butt-chinned Kirk Douglas, told him he shouldn't appear in the movie. Despite this, the sneaky sociopath stuck himself in a speaking role as a radio officer. Martin Sheen and Douglas are also in the scene. Douglas allegedly told Patient X, "You're a better actor than a producer." This reporter concludes the statement was more of a put-down than a compliment.

8) *Metropolitan* Again, Patient X took advantage of a friendship with a director. Patient X chose to play the role in Whit Stillman's neorealistic film, by his own confession, "in the manner of Fatty Arbuckle." Director Stillman showed a rare sense of taste in the film industry when, in 1990, he removed Patient X from the film. Patient X did not know that his scenes had been reshot with another actor until he attended the premiere at the Museum of Modern Art.

9) *Rocky V* Patient X was "called back" to reprise his role in this film. "Called back" = harassing the director until you get your way.

10) *Tromeo & Juliet* Cameo: spitting out water. According to the patient he "didn't want to do it" but was "talked into it by the crew." Assessment: Patient X is fibbing. His face takes to a movie camera as easily as a Smurf magnet to a suburban refrigerator.

11) *Cannes Man* Directed by Richard Martini. In the words of the star, Seymour Cassel, "[Patient X] has his gab down. He would go crazy, with his usual wacky off-the-wall routine. Then he would hit a speed bump, trying to think of what he was going to say next, going 'uh, uh.' Those moments of discombobulation were what Martini used in the film." NOTE: Martini's unique reaction may simply denote an internal defense against the horrible reality: HE HAS PATIENT X IN HIS MOVIE.

12) *Orgazmo, Cannibal: The Musical* director and *South Park* cartoon creator Trey Parker placed Kaufman in yet another speaking role, showing that the new era of filmmakers are as clueless as the last.

When Patient X is confronted with Dr. Dicker's theory, he responds:

"Disgusted by my own mother? That's preposterous! And I have the nude pictures under my mattress to prove it!"

The mystery remains.

what a soul mate Lloyd was through that terrifying period. He literally didn't leave my side for three weeks.* He made me believe I'd survive the ordeal. Most important of all, somehow he reached into his soul and found ways to make me laugh.

Finally, deep down inside Lloyd IS Toxie. Toxie is a creature of deep and abiding principle, loyalty and love. That's Lloyd! Toxie is devoted to his mother and loves his girlfriend/wife. Toxie is loved by little kids. And Toxie ALWAYS stands up for the little guy. My God, you should do an entire chapter on Lloyd and AFMA.† Every year Lloyd is elected to the executive board because he's the only one who really stands up for little guys who are true independents.

There's just no one more true-blue (or Day-Glo green as the case may be) than my Lloydie or my Toxie, and I love them both. . . .

JAMES GUNN, co-screenwriter, associate director, and executive in charge of production on *Tromeo & Juliet*; codirector and cowriter of *Tromaville Café*; the original Webmaster on the Troma World Wide Web; Troma's director of production, 1995–1997; and rubber enthusiast:

Hey, Barry:

So you want an objective view of Lloyd? It's impossible, man. Lloyd is too many things to too many people. He's a loving husband, affectionate father, cheap bastard, charismatic cult leader, camera hog, genius, tyrant, screaming crazy guy, loving mentor, father figure, delusional paranoid, guy who forgets his car keys a lot, narcissist, and a truly loyal friend. You can't pin him down. However, there are a few facts about Lloyd that may be passed over by your other witnesses, not to mention Lloyd.

Lloyd Can Be So Cheap as to Be Amusing.

We changed the actor who played Cappy Capulet after one day of shooting. The first Cap was skinny, bald, and not exactly John Barrymore in terms of his acting prowess. We had shot two short scenes: one of him pulling Juliet down the hallway, and one of him greeting Juliet's paramour, London, at the door. The next day we had the new Cappy, Max Shaun, who was about thirty pounds heavier, with darker hair. Max is a fantastic actor. Here's the kicker: Lloyd actually tried to talk me into not reshooting the scenes and using the footage of the original actor in the movie. As if no one would notice that the actor suddenly changed! "The hallway's pretty dark," Lloyd told me. There's a romantic aspect to Lloyd's willingness to utterly abandon preordained concepts of reality.

---

*EDITOR'S NOTE: No wonder it was a terrifying period.
†The American Film Market Association, the independent's trade association.

Lloyd Is Psychic.

On many different occasions Lloyd has foreseen tragedies. Some of this is due to twenty-five years in the film business, but I also believe he has a real sixth sense. He has known when actors or crew members are about to quit. He has foreseen tragedies on set. Once, when three actresses all turned down the role of a lead character in a TV show, Lloyd continually told me, "They've been talking" and "There's a conspiracy afoot." I considered this another of Lloyd's bouts of paranoia and told him he was crazy; all three of the women had good reasons for turning down the role, I said. After a while, though, I was able to elicit a confession from one of the women. The women had been talking, and one of them, who was insane, had made up a lot of ludicrous stories about Troma hiring hookers and physically mistreating employees. What she told them was untrue and wacky, but the other two had bought the whole thing. So, in fact, a sort of conspiracy did exist.

Lloyd Has a Hidden Reserve of Darkness.

Many people who have seen Tromeo & Juliet have realized, quite accurately, that I based Monty Que and Cappy Capulet upon Lloyd and Michael. I originally thought of Lloyd as the lovable old artistic drunk and Michael as the more evil business-minded character. Little did I realize what inner resources of darkness Lloyd Kaufman had in him. After that initial draft was written, Lloyd would come up with new dialogue for the evil Cappy at every script meeting. Something would happen to Lloyd's face: it would turn up in a snarl. His voice would become low and gravelly. And then he would start spouting out these horrible obscenities. He sounded like motherfucking Sybil! This evil was being spewed forth from Lloyd as if his throat was directly piped in to Hades. And the most chilling part is this: Cappy's nickname for his daughter is "little crenshaw melon." This was Lloyd's idea. I didn't even know what a crenshaw melon was. You know what Lloyd's nickname for his daughter Lily Hayes is? You guessed it. I feel creepy, I got to go on—

Lloyd Is a Genius.

Lloyd will like this one, but I sincerely believe it. When I first came to Troma I thought of Lloyd as part of the "Holy Triad" of Trash Cinema, along with Russ Meyer and John Waters. But I didn't quite know the depth of his prodigy. First of all, his production expertise is flawless—this is the reason he was so highly in demand as a production manager in the seventies. Secondly, his ability to act ludicrously in front of a camera is profound. How many of God's children are born without an ounce of shame? I consider that genius. Thirdly, and most importantly, his worldview is singular. There is no one else with such an amalgamated vision of toxicity, camp, the female body, and violence—it's utterly unique, amazing, and a wonder to see in action. And those words just skim it: Tromaville is a place in Lloyd's mind, placed there by God for who knows what purpose.

Lloyd is Gullible.

Lloyd, Mike Shapiro, and I were on our way to shoot a scene and do a guest appearance at Spookyworld, a horror-themed amusement park outside of Boston. On the way there, Mike and I told Lloyd that Mike was a former member of the musical group Menudo. Which was, of course, complete bullshit. Menudo are the singing sensations composed of fresh-faced teenage Latin American boys. Lloyd believed us, which surprised us, considering Mike is Jewish. Lloyd asked Mike how he tried out. Mike said he had to sing "A Spoonful of Sugar." He went on to make up more and more ludicrous stories about how the Menudo manager sexually abused him, but how it was worth it considering he had his own puffy sticker. Lloyd was amazingly impressed by this and took pictures of Mike to put in the Troma Times. Later, on stage at Spookyworld he announced Mike as a former member of Menudo and had him come on stage. Mike hooked his thumbs in his belt and stared at the floor. Everyone in the audience just stared blankly at him. Later, we told Lloyd the truth. He took it in a good-natured way. However, we've had a lot more fun with Lloyd since. I am the cat. Lloyd is my ball of yarn.

Some People Think Lloyd is Gay.

Last year at the Cannes Film Festival, Lloyd, Jane Jensen, and I went to a party thrown by Miramax. Lloyd came wearing his regular bow tie, and a special sport jacket covered with yellow flowers. I was dancing with a woman (she was a great chick, Barry, you would have liked her—these nice perky little breasts) who asked me, "Who's the flamer?" "What? Who?" I said. "The short guy," she said, and she pointed to Lloyd. I told her Lloyd had a wife he loved very much. I told her I didn't think Pat was a "beard." But, after thinking about it for a while, who knows? He does tell that Montgomery Clift story more often than one would expect. . . .

JOHN KOCH, *Tromeo & Juliet* production assistant:

Dear Mr. Neville:

Thank you for your note of June 18, 1997, asking for my opinion and recollections of Lloyd Kaufman, although I doubt you will want to print them in your book. I was hired by line producer Franny Baldwin to work in the Troma offices before the filming of Tromeo & Juliet. I was just out of college and looking for a way into the film industry. Not long after that I met Lloyd Kaufman. He was wearing a bow tie. He was friendly toward me, but seemed distracted. He asked my name and repeated it to me. This was the last time he ever got my name right, although he referred to me with every other possible name beginning with a J.

I noticed in him from the very beginning a tendency toward manic-depressiveness. Being that I had majored in psychology at Georgetown, its list of symptoms was fresh in my mind. One of the symptoms of mania is a tendency to make puns excessively, something that Kaufman couldn't seem *to stop himself from doing. He seemed to have in his head a prearranged set of word puns for every topic imaginable. Once someone was talking about dogs, and he instantly fell into it: "That's a very interesting TAIL," he said. "Now, let me PAWS for a moment." He would go on like this for twenty straight minutes. You just wanted to slap him. But, overall, in his manic moods Kaufman was not too bad.*

His darker moods were a different story. At one point, while I was eating pizza in the production office at the end of the day with some other PAs, Kaufman happened to stop by. I could tell he wasn't in a good mood by his dour expression. He saw we were eating pizza, and we ended up on the wrong end of a half-hour screaming fit about how we were having a cocktail party. He made it clear that making movies was not about having fun. On another occasion, I made a small mistake. I was supposed to show him some plans for the Penis Monster made by the special-effects artist, Louis. Being that it was extremely busy in the office, I forgot to do this. The next day Kaufman harangued me in front of everyone in the office. As a fully developed, well-rounded man, I am not afraid to admit that I began to cry. Everyone in the office looked on. Instead of looking contrite, Kaufman simply looked embarrassed. "Here is a man who has difficulty with his emotions," I said. Later that same day, I walked out of the Troma office and never returned.

Today, I have a good job as a sales representative at Kinko's, where the bosses are a bit more appreciative. . . .

MICHAEL HERZ, cofounder of Troma Studios, codirector or coproducer, with Lloyd Kaufman, of thirteen films:

Dear Barry:

Although I appreciate the chance to voice my opinion on Lloyd, I would rather not be included in All I Need to Know about Filmmaking I Learned from the Toxic Avenger. *Lloyd has promised me that I won't be mentioned in the book; I hope that this is still in fact the case. Thanks anyway. . . .*

SAMUEL FULLER, U.S. film director and novelist: *The Naked Kiss, Shock Corridor, The Big Red One* and more:

Dear Mr. Neville:

I try not to bother people and hope people don't bother me. But this Kaufman fellow, dressed impeccably with a bow tie, insisted on coming out to visit me at my home. He seemed pretty normal until he brought out a videocassette of one of his films, Troma's War, saying my films had inspired him to make it. That's when I started to suspect he was a little off his rocker. Then he gave me some goddamned awful-smelling car freshener that my wife insists on hanging from the rearview mirror in our car. I watched his films and I had a number of good laughs. This Kaufman character is crazy, in the way you've got to be nuts to do anything original. I like him. He's energetic, he's got balls and plenty of ideas. His own! I'm all for him and I wish him well in the fight to make original films. But I hope that he stops with those car fresheners. . . .

BETH ANNE JULIK, Troma fan:

Barry Neville—DUDE!

It was too fucking cool to get your note about Lloyd Kaufman! If I could really be in a book about Troma, I would totally freak out and it would be like the best thing in the world. The truth is YES I have met Lloyd Kaufman and he is the greatest fucking guy in the world. I met him at the San Diego Comicon and then again later at Dragon con in Atlanta. He's got a great sense of humor and he's making me laugh the whole time. He's like an old guy, but still he's able to make jokes about stuff that make a kid like me laugh. I'm nineteen. Later on I wrote a letter to Lloyd and he actually wrote me back. Not many famous people would do that, I don't think, although the only other person I ever wrote to was David Duchovny (hot!). I also must discuss Lloyd Kaufman's artistic qualities, because that's something that people forget. Many people wonder why I like Troma films and they say, like, those movies suck, which is totally untrue. Sgt. Kabukiman is the funniest movie ever made; I met my boyfriend the first night I saw that, and now it's like OUR movie. I just saw Tromeo & Juliet and thought that was the funniest thing that I EVER saw, but the weirdest part of it was how parts of it were serious, and that shows how Lloyd Kaufman is able to do EVERYTHING. And the best movie ever is The Toxic Avenger. Long live Toxie! What else should I say? Oh, yeah—I'D SUCK LLOYD KAUFMAN'S DICK HE'S SO COOL. Just kidding. He's a warm man. Great guy. And Forrest Gump sucks! Long live TROMA! If you want me to rewrite any of this, or make it neater, I will, but I really really really really really really really really want to be in TROMA BOOK. . . . *

---

*It's nice of Barry to end the chapter with the one truly accurate, well-rounded depiction of me. I hope this is the picture you'll hold of me in your mind while finishing this book. Thanks, Bar.

Tromeo & Juliet
and the Future of Troma

"During a retrospective on Troma done by the British Film Festival, I visited Shakespeare's birthplace in Stratford-upon-Avon. Whilst there, Shakespeare's spirit entered my body. I cannot reveal from which orifice Shakespeare's spirit exited my body, but it wasn't long after that that *Tromeo & Juliet* was delivered unto the world."

If you've read or heard an interview with me over the past couple of years, there's a good chance you're familiar with the above. When you're interviewed with some regularity, you stockpile a few statements that provoke a reaction. Here are some others associated with *Tromeo & Juliet*:

- "For years Troma has given people the bird—now it's time that we gave them the Bard."

- "*Tromeo & Juliet* has all the body piercing, car crashes, and kinky sex Shakespeare always wanted and never had." (Later manipulated by Mike Shapiro to become the tag line: "BODY PIERCING. KINKY SEX. DISMEMBERMENT. THE THINGS THAT MADE SHAKESPEARE GREAT.")

- "Rock 'n' roll on celluloid."

- "The most over-the-edge erotic-action-comedy since *Romeo & Juliet* debuted on the stage in 1596."

- "On Shakespeare's deathbed he had a dream. His dream was to rewrite *Romeo & Juliet*, a play that, although good, needed some improvement. His dream was to include a three-foot penis monster within the text. Unfortunately, he died. But now, four hundred years later, Troma has made Shakespeare's dream come true!!"

- "The most ambitious and important film to emerge from Troma Studios yet!" (Actually, this line has been used for every Troma movie since *Waitress!*)

Tromeo & Juliet came to me in a visionary burst. First the title, which I found humorous. Second, the desire to do a romance. True love has often been on the sidelines of Troma movies but never in the forefront. Third, I felt some debt to Shakespeare. I was bored with the baby-food adaptations that were being released. Shakespeare was a shit disturber. His plays had sex and gore* and risqué humor. They may be tame today but back then they weren't; it was even illegal for his plays to be performed within the city limits of London. The Bard was a regular 2 Live Crew.

Some of the essential aspects of *Romeo & Juliet* were as applicable today as they were in the time of Shakespeare. Today, the old are still feeding on the dreams of the young. My generation, the baby boomers, the largest segment of society, has manipulated the world to suit its own economic desires. The boomers trumpeted peace and emotional freedom in the sixties. Now they've given way to a blind elitism which preaches coolness over feeling. Meanwhile, they bombard today's kids with rehashed sixties music and movies and big-budget versions of sixties TV shows; these boomers have thus plasticized their own pasts, making the values they once trumpeted no more real than the Partridge Family, and therefore no longer dangerous to the status quo—that is, themselves. Contemporary Americans in their teens and twenties have turned inward, concocting their own universe of the cool, cold, and uncaring. To me, they can hardly be blamed. It's the same emotional response a man has after being repeatedly raped in prison. It's the natural reaction to being fucked.

---

*In the same way men played women on the Elizabethan stage, animal entrails played the roles of human entrails.

FIRST DRAFT

Spit out in 1992 by Phil Rivo and Andy Deemer—two Troma employees—and me. This version was pretty faithful to the original play, written entirely in verse. Most of the dialogue was directly from Shakespeare, although set in the modern day. There were, of course, Tromatic elements (the occasional fart and Toxic vomit, a lesbian situation between Juliet and the character of the Nurse). In this original draft, the role of Benvolio was replaced with The Toxic Avenger, and Mercutio with Sgt. Kabukiman NYPD.

We continually went over this script, but it seemed to be getting nowhere. In addition, Michael Herz had no intention of doing the movie.

"This is my life's dream project," I told him.

"Tromeo and Juliet?" Michael said. "That's stupid."

I approached numerous money people who had backed Troma films in the past. I told them we had a new project, *Tromeo & Juliet*, and were trying to raise the budget.

"You can't make money off Shakespeare," they said. "That's stupid. In fact, you're stupid."

Everyone thought the idea was preposterous. The employees in the Troma office read the first draft; they unanimously agreed that it had as much heart as a Joel Schumacher film and was as humorous as that kid that went into the polar bear pit at the zoo a few years back, high on angel dust, and was eaten alive. Not even that funny.

Still, some invisible apparition continued to crack the whip behind me. More than any other film, I was driven by a love for the project as opposed to commercial desire. There was something in me that felt it *needed* to be done.

"It's the will of God," I told Michael.

"Too bad for God then," he said.

"Don't blame me when you end up in Hell," I told him. But Michael didn't give a shit.

1994

The script was still a spattering of vowels and consonants without much of a center. I wondered how it was that I could plunder the work

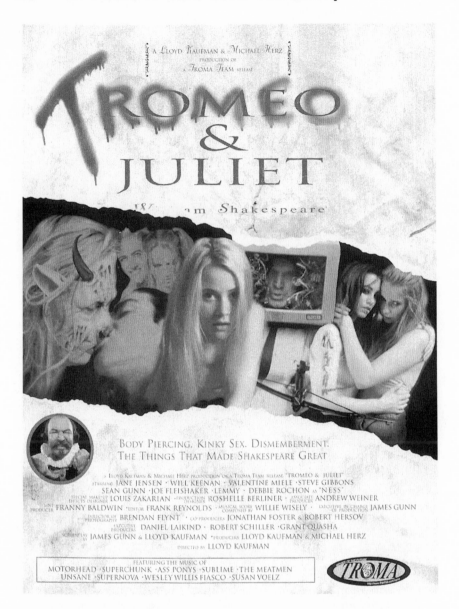

of history's greatest writer so directly, while filleting it of its soul. Still, I forged on, a good donkey plugging up the hill of fruitlessness. "Remember," I told myself. "Perseverance is the answer to everything. Remember how you and Michael didn't give up on *Health Club Horror*. That's how the Toxic Avenger was born. You can't stop now."

Still, despite repeated drafts with Andy and Phil, on the chart of artistic substance, *Tromeo & Juliet's* line remained flat.

I sent a draft to my old friend and mentor, John Avildsen. We had dinner at Talisai restaurant on Sunset Boulevard in L.A. John said that he didn't think the iambic pentameter was so bad, but using the original Shakespearean language didn't work. He thought that I should "get a young kid, and write how he or she speaks."

So that's what I did. The next writer was a nineteen-year-old named Jason Greene, a young man whom I had first met when his father brought him, at the age of twelve, to the set of *Sgt. Kabukiman NYPD*. Jason appeared as an actor person in that film, as well as some Troma TV projects. Jason turned in a script that was pretty close to the last. Although it used some of today's hep lingo, it still didn't work.

MARCH OF '95

We had finally raised the budget for *Tromeo & Juliet*: about $350,000. The movie was set to start filming in June,* but we didn't have a decent script.

I received a fax from Jill Champtaloup, a friend and supervising programmer at HBO/Cinemax. It was a resume from a young man who was a student in the Columbia University Masters program. His name was James Gunn. On it, Jill had written: "He's your man."

Something on Gunn's resume popped out at me: it was an attached article from *The St. Louis Post Dispatch* about Gunn's career as a performance artist. The article claimed that Gunn had vomited onstage. Whether it was from nervousness or for entertainment value or a critical assessment of Gregg Araki's career, it didn't really say—but *still!* A publicly vomiting writer! I felt like Zero Mostel in *The Producers* when he saw Dick Shawn audition for the play *Springtime for Hitler* and he screamed, *"That's our Hitler!"* I was pretty sure that James Gunn was ours.

---

*In Tromaville, we only shoot during the summer. If we didn't shoot by that summer, we would have had to wait another whole year.

Gunn Says:

I got a call in my apartment. I was still sleeping. It was noon.

"Yeah," I said.

"Hello, hello. Is this James Gunn? Is James Gunn there?"

"Yes. Who's this?"

"This is Lloyd Kaufman. Lloyd Kaufman of Troma Studios."

I didn't notice Lloyd's peculiar phone eccentricity of repeating every sentence twice with minor permutations (he does it to this day). Instead, I was amazed. The voice of the guy who made up the Toxic Avenger was in my apartment. I lit a cigarette.

"Big fan," I said.

"Thank you, thank you. So, Jill Champtaloup says you're interested in working for Troma. She said you might like to be involved with Troma."

We set up a date to meet the next day.

The next day I went to the Troma office.

Lloyd was a little short person. He was charismatic and likable, but his head always seemed to be somewhere else, imagining exploding heads and mutants tearing the tops off women in bikinis (that's exactly where it is).

"So, what kind of work are you looking for?" he asked me.

"Whatever. Some sort of stuff."

"You write?"

"Yes. I guess you're not allowed to smoke in here."

"No. What kind of things do you write?"

I paused. I basically considered myself an unpublished novelist, but I decided to fake it. "Screenplays," I said.

"Well, we have a few projects in the works, things that maybe you could become involved in."

"Yeah?" This was incredible, I thought. I was thinking I was going to have to file papers or something.

Lloyd sat there. He thought for a moment.

"How about you take a whack at a draft of *Tromeo?*" he said.

I nodded. I have just become a screenwriter, I thought. I once had more difficulty getting a job at Denny's.

Troma paid me $150 to do the screenplay. It was the most money I had gotten through legal means in a long time, enough to keep me in coffee beans for the one week they gave me to write it. Lloyd gave me a few drafts of the script to go from. I read a bit of them, thought they were pig shit, and threw them away. I started a new script. I had Juliet working as a stripper. Instead of having the love scene on a balcony, I would have it in one of those little booths where women do the live dildo shows while a man watches them through glass and talks to them through a speaker while

James Gunn, coscreenwriter of *Tromeo & Juliet* and coauthor of this tome, assures Kaufman that their intimacy of the night before and the resultant "icky feelings" are totally normal. The *de rigueur* midget in the corner looks on approvingly.

jerking off. That was romantic. I'd have Tromeo a crack dealer. Sounded good, real good. I wrote about twelve pages, read them. Pig shit. I threw them away. Started typing again. This time, God flowed through my fingers.

"Two households, as diff'rent as dried plums and pears..."

I was on my way. Whoo. I am the king of the world.

GUNN'S FIRST DRAFT

Came in a week later. It was a shock. He seemed like such a nice, clean-cut young man. But this was ... obscene. He had changed everything—very little of the original plot had survived. Although it was in strict iambic pentameter, there was no original Shakespeare. And he had changed the ending!* Also, he had fired Toxie and Kabukiman, and added a lot of wife beating, incest, and scatological humor. Could everything have come full circle? For

---

*Gunn had actually written three endings: the one we used, which has Tromeo and Juliet having a backyard barbecue with their deformed, inbred children; a second one, which had them driving away into the sunset, smiling while happy music played, whereupon they are hit by a truck and killed; and, finally, Tromeo and Juliet committing suicide after finding out they couldn't make it without Juliet's father's money. This last one was transmuted into a dream from which Juliet would wake into the happy ending. Although we shot it, audience reaction to it in the marketing screenings was poor, so we removed it and just had the happy ending. Look for it on the Director's Cut consumer tape.

the first time, I had met someone who had taken it farther than I wanted it to go. On *Squeeze Play*, Haim Pekelis had freaked out that I included all the piss and fart jokes. Now . . .

I was in the Troma L.A. office* when James called me.

"James, we're going to have to make some changes in this script."

"All right. I've got a pencil. Go."

"First of all, there's too many things going on. The plot has too many lines, going in all different directions."

"It's a complex plot."

"But it's supposed to be simple. It's the love story of Tromeo and Juliet."

"I was getting kind of bored with the two of them."

"But they're the only likable characters in the movie."

"Right. That's why I was bored, I think."

"I think you ought to cut off some of the excess and leave it to the two of them. The script's too long anyway. It's how many pages now?"

"One hundred twenty-two."

"You should get it down to eighty pages."

"Ow."

"Even better, fifty or sixty pages."

"That's a sitcom. You want me to put Erkel in it too?"

"I'm telling you—these things always end up three times as long as they're supposed to be after I film them. It's two minutes for every page."

"It's supposed to be a minute for every page."

"Not in Tromaville."

"All right."

"Good. Also, do you really think that you need all this pissing?"

---

*We first formed the L.A. office with Marty Sokol, a guy we met through Murikami Wolf while working on *The Toxic Crusader* cartoons. For the past few years, it's been run by David Schultz, a cinephile-surfer who was first hired to play Toxie on TV shows and at conventions. The office is about the size of a Johnny-on-the-spot. Incidentally, while working on *Sgt. Kabukiman*, some of the crew tried to capsize a Johnny-on-the-spot while I was inside urinating. Luckily, the grounding was stable and they gave up, and I escaped with a few sprinkles on my pant leg. The next day I had some swordfish steak, which was delicious.

"*All* this?"

"Four pissing scenes."

"Hmm. I'll cut one out."

"Cut out two."

"Yeah."

"I'll be back in New York on Tuesday. We'll meet then."

"Mm."

I hung up the phone knowing I had broken his heart by all the changes. But he just wasn't a very good writer.

THE REBIRTH OF *TROMEO & JULIET*

A week later James handed me a new draft. Being that I disliked the first draft so much, I was hardly sure that I wanted to read it. To my pleasant surprise, many of the kinks had been worked out. The plot was more linear and consistent. The humor wasn't quite as angry or cynical. And I felt more for the Juliet character; she had become the true protagonist of the story. In many ways, it was now the story of Juliet escaping from the bondage of her baby boomer father as a young person and as a woman. And, along the way, she gets to explode her father's head. For the first time in the three years I'd been working on *Tromeo*, it seemed like we had a starting point.

From there, James and I worked together to improve the script. I was hesitant to lose the Shakespeare dialogue entirely, so we came up with a motif to fit the mood. We had heard of a production of *Romeo & Juliet* in London that performed the play with every character being utterly filthy, except Tr . . . er, Romeo and Juliet, who were fabulously shiny and clean. In a like manner, we would have only certain characters speak in iambic pentameter.

A Quick Lesson in Iambic Pentameter:

Undoubtedly, after reading this book, many of you will be inspired to go out and write action films, horror movies, and works of blatant pornography in strict iambic pentameter. Perhaps in the twenty-first century, spurred on by *Tromeo & Juliet*, the dialogue of all films will be in metered verse. Therefore, we present this quick and easy guide to writing in the Bard's preferred meter. There are two major aspects to iambic pentameter.

1. There are ten syllables per line. This is five metric feet (sets of two).
2. Each metric foot is composed of an unstressed syllable followed by a stressed syllable.

In short, each line is ten syllables with every second syllable being accentuated. Observe (from *Romeo & Juliet*):

$$\quad 1 \qquad 2 \qquad 3 \qquad 4 \qquad 5$$

Whăt's ín | ă náme? | Thăt whích | wĕ cáll | ă róse
Bў án | ў óth | ĕr náme | wŏuld sméll | ăs swéet.

$$\quad 1 \qquad 2 \qquad 3 \qquad 4 \qquad 5$$

Or (from *Tromeo & Juliet*):

$$\quad 1 \qquad 2 \qquad 3 \qquad 4 \qquad 5$$

Ĭ gót | ăn ítch | tŏ fúck | yŏu ín | thĕ áss

In iambic pentameter, there is some leniency involved; for instance, you have the option of leaving the first unstressed syllable off entirely, and occasional lines can be less than five meters.

Every time Tromeo and Juliet are at the peak of their mystical and timeless yearning for one another they speak in true Shakespearean verse. Other times any of the characters are feeling passionate they speak in strict iambic pentameter, although their language is either modern or a mix of modern and verse. In characters who had little lyricism in their natures (such as Sammy Capulet and Vic the oboe instructor/bodyguard), they speak at times without the meter. The same thing went for some of the less important chatting that would occur between the characters.

Between James and me, then, we added some of the most memorable "hooks" in the film. As opposed to having the young people in the film portrayed as your everyday, normal outsiders, we placed them squarely in Manhattan's body-piercing, tattooed culture. We also placed Tromeo smack dab in the center of the Information Highway, with his fondness for CD-ROM sex. The movie was more self-referential than most, with the heads of the Que and Capulet families, Monty and Cap, as ludicrous alter egos of myself and Michael.* As the film's plot dictated, they had originally been partners in an independent

---

*EDITOR'S NOTE: See James Gunn's letter in the last chapter for *his* take on this.

Georgie (Tamara Craig Thomas) and Ness (Debbie Rochon), two of the strongest women in Troma's history, strike a typically defiant pose in this scene from *Tromeo & Juliet*.

film studio, Silky Films. Monty initially made low-budget art films (with scenes from *The First Turn-On** representing these), until Capulet screwed him over, stole the company, and began churning out "the worst motherfucking films in the world" (with close-ups of the subhumanoids' belly-mouths from *Class of Nuke 'Em High Part III: The Good, the Bad, and the Subhumanoid* representing these).

Some of the most successful scenes in the film were written as ping-ponging sessions between Gunn and me. Through the mix of his dark nature and my goofy puns we created some, if nothing else, *unique* scenes. The most memorable sequence in the film, where Tyrone's arm gets ripped off and his head lands on the car of the happy family, was simply an instance of Gunn and my one-upping one another, taking the scene to a further and further level of ludicrousness.

In the end we had Troma's best script. Whether it was too weird

---

*Actually, these scenes were intended to be portrayed by the soft-focus seventies antics in *Sugar Cookies*, but when we set the print up on the upright Moviola to film it, it continually broke. We had to substitute it with scenes from the *The First Turn-On*, which, although it may not work as well, usually gets a pretty good laugh.

to film, I didn't know. James and I had dinner shortly before we started filming.

"It's funny," I said. "You're at the beginning of your career, with nothing to lose, so you're going all the way with this thing, making it as extreme as possible. I feel like I'm at the point of my career when I have everything to lose, so I'm going all the way with it. Somehow, we're at two utterly different points in our lives but in the same exact place."

I looked at James. He nodded.

"This burger's really good," he said. He didn't have much of a personality.

MEAT THE TEAM

Through a fortunate series of occurrences *Tromeo & Juliet* had the best crew we ever had. Early on, we hired two PAs to work on the film. Although one of the PAs left after nine days of the Tromatic pressure,* the other PA, twenty-two-year-old Andrew Weiner, ended up staying on the entire run. In addition to assisting Gunn in rehearsing the actors, he worked as the casting director and unit manager and eventually ended up with the credit of Associate Producer. We also hired Frannie Baldwin as Production Manager, who was tough, tireless, and utterly committed. Brendan Flynt was brought on as Director of Photography. Brendan was unique among DPs I have worked with in that he was able to get fabulous results using about two thirds less equipment. He also introduced us to the pleasures of the Eye-mo crash camera. The Eye-mo† is a small, hardy, extremely portable machine with which you can create fast-moving shots, whipping it around through the air. For a good jolt, you can also slam it directly into things. Also important to the *T & J* crew was Roshelle Berliner, the Production Designer, who was able to create lush, colorful, and unique sets on a non-budget. Finally we had happy-go-lucky Assistant Director Bob Bauer coming

---

*Who had written in a letter to me, "I will do anything that I possibly can to help this movie. I will dedicate my life to it."
†Brendan learned to use this while he was an assistant cameraman on Sam Raimi's classic film *Evil Dead II*.

Over the course of nearly thirty years, Kaufman's "pull my finger" shtick, first seen on the set of *Battle of Love's Return*, has evolved into "pull all my fingers," which he demonstrates on the set of *Tromeo & Juliet*. As seen here, it still keeps the crew in stitches.

over directly from his stint on the movie *Kids*. This crew of young dynamic souls was fond of the script, and they also established intimate friendships amongst themselves. Because of this, *Tromeo & Juliet* has a rare intensity to it.

THE OTHER ROMEO & JULIETS

1936, Directed by George Cukor. The Cukor version is definitely my favorite film adaptation, and one of the inspirations for *Tromeo*. At Troma, we gave video copies to each of the actors for study. I enjoyed the stylized performances of Leslie Howard as a forty-four-year-old Romeo, and especially John Barrymore as a flamboyant and effeminate sixty-year-old Mercutio. From this film, *T & J* stole the opening montage announcing the cast of characters (only we improved it by inserting pieces of gore and a lizard eating a mouse). Willie Wisely also updated the music used in Cukor's dance scene for our own *Tromeo & Juliet* love theme.

1968, Directed by Franco Zeffirelli. Not much has been taken from this version. However, the brief flash of the gorgeous Olivia Hussey's nipples as she gets out of bed with Romeo (the reason video freeze frame was invented) has filled many of my lonely nights.

1983, Martha Coolidge (the film Valley Girl). Gunn claims he was inspired by this ultimate eighties film, which he enjoyed as a kid. "I wanted *Tromeo & Juliet* to be as quintessentially nineties as *Valley Girl* was eighties," he said. "The only better Valley movie is *Valley of Gwangi.*"

1996, Directed by Baz Luhrmann. At the 1995 Cannes Film Festival, Luhrmann told us that he was in prepreproduction on this film. This was just a couple weeks before we began shooting on *Tromeo.* Luhrmann, who claimed to be a Troma fan, said he thought it was great that we were making *Tromeo & Juliet.* He described his movie to us as a "punk version" of Shakespeare. This was extremely disheartening at the time, especially since I considered Luhrmann a talented director after seeing *Strictly Ballroom.*

I put off watching Luhrmann's film until August of 1997, fearing it would be so much better than *T & J* that I would be compelled to blow my brains out. To my great relief, Luhrmann's movie stunk— perfect for my sixteen-year-old daughter and friends who didn't mind Leonardo DiCaprio's spouting off words he didn't understand. Many of our actors had extensive Shakespearean experience, which paid off. It was clear that this wasn't true in Luhrmann's film, except for Jean Luc Picard, who played the priest.

In the end, though, Luhrmann's movie was probably good for us. We got mentioned in a few more articles, and we sold more videos than we would have otherwise. Still, although we finished shooting before Luhrmann even started, some of the media thought we were piggybacking. One publication, the always idiotic *Village Voice* (who I often think have high school students writing their movie reviews*), said that our opening sequence was a "send-up" of Luhrmann's film's opening. The *Voice* reviewer, Justine Elias, then went on to discuss how "skanky" the extras in the movie were and "the angry pustule" on Lemmy's face, and recommended he have it looked at. This was surprising to me since Justine Elias herself is a very fat woman who was wearing way too much black eyeliner at the press screening.

---

*Not including, of course, the great Andrew Sarris, who used to write for the *Voice.*

SPEAKING OF MAGAZINES

I just had the dis-opportunity of flipping through the current issue of *Entertainment Weekly* (June 27, 1997), which has to be one of the most ridiculous issues of all time. The cover story is "The 100 Most Creative People in Entertainment." Some of the people it includes: Winona Ryder, Tom Cruise, Brad Pitt, Jason Priestly, and Noah Wyle. Some of the people it doesn't include: Thomas Pynchon, Ben Kingsley, Peter Bagge, They Might Be Giants, and Lars Von Trier. What a bunch of shit. You suck, *Entertainment Weekly*.*

ANOTHER PIECE OF RUBBER BLEEDING

The cast of *T & J* was also the best we'd yet had. Will Keenan and Jane Jensen exuded vulnerability and passion as the star-crossed lovers, and their performances were unanimously praised. Some of the actors were good friends of Gunn's whom he enlisted in different roles, such as Valentine Miele as Murray Martini, Steve Loniewski as Harry, and his brother Sean as Sammy Capulet. Many of these actors were imported from the classic Goodman Acting Conservatory in Chicago. It's a good thing to keep in mind while producing low-budget films; often it's easier to find great actors willing to work for very little in cities outside of New York and Los Angeles.

The rehearsals were the most in-depth yet, lasting for over a month. By keeping the actors focused more seriously than usual on their roles we were able to elicit performances that had more substance and were funnier because of their relationship to the ludicrous surroundings and situations.

The shooting of the movie was the smoothest I had ever been on. I attribute this to an extremely organized crew, but especially to the hand of God. Tragedies were few and far between.

We were only kicked out of one location, a house in Brooklyn where we shot Juliet's bedroom (although in the film there is one Capulet mansion, it was, in reality, three different locations). The house

---

*EDITOR'S NOTE: Uh, what's going on? Where'd *Tromeo & Juliet* go? Also, Lloyd, *EW* might have to review this book!†

†Oh. Besides this one issue, I always adore *Entertainment Weekly*. Everyone should subscribe.

On the set of *Tromeo & Juliet*—Valentine Miele, Lloyd Kaufman, Sean Gunn and Patrick Conner (l-r). The question here is not what happened to these actors' heads, but where Sean Gunn's other hand is. Only Kaufman knows for sure.

was owned by an old man willing to let us use it for $100 a day. It was important, as we were shooting one of the last scenes there, where Tromeo and Juliet begin to kill Juliet's father with a plethora of girlish items: a curling iron, tampons, a nail file, bobby pins, etc. Unfortunately, three families with children lived in the house. After we started filming, they found the movie set a larger operation than they had anticipated. Although we needed four days, we were told to leave after two. Frannie Baldwin pleaded with the old man, but he refused. Finally, Valentine Miele put on a tight pair of biking shorts and visited the old man at home (the old man was gay). Val used his masculine wiles to get him to change his mind and give us one more day. But that still robbed us of a necessary day of shooting. Roshelle Berliner, the production designer, ingeniously went into the old man's basement and found some extra pink-flowered wallpaper like the wallpaper in Juliet's bedroom. She pasted it to the wall in the Troma office. She stuck a dresser up against it. We shot the rest of the scenes there. No one has ever noticed—and no one ever would if I wasn't telling you now.

Many of the problems had to do with continuity and framing. For some reason, much of the *Tromeo & Juliet* team, including the hardworking, talented editor, Frank Reynolds, considered it funny when there were little cheesy hints of the movie's unreality. Since I never cared much about this either, the film is today replete with such errors. The script supervisor became so disgusted with our apathy that she quit after a couple weeks. We replaced her with a college guy that couldn't give a shit if a person's part in their hair changed from one shot to the next. In the video version today, you can see:

- Juliet playing the guitar on the bed in her room. As she sets the guitar on the ground, a pair of hands come up and take the guitar from her. This was actually a PA who needed to stifle the noise the guitar would make upon hitting the ground, so it wouldn't block her dialogue.

- After Murray slices off Sammy's fingers with a paper cutter, we cut to a close-up of a hand spurting blood and pulling away from the cutter. (Only one of the two sliced fingers actually bled. When Valentine Miele was asked how the special-effect looked, he replied, "It looked like a piece of rubber, and then another piece of rubber bleeding.") If you look at the top of the frame, you can see special-effects artist Louie Zakarian's hand gripping the wooden handle of the rubber hand and dragging it away.

- Numerous shots of actresses, including Rosy, played by Jacqueline Tavarez, and Juliet, wearing skin-colored panties when they're supposed to be totally nude.

- While he's in bed with Juliet, Cappy Capulet holds on to a curling iron; we cut and the iron magically transforms into a blow-dryer.

- A shocking amount of crew reflections; orange cones in the background of stunt scenes; buttons buttoning and unbuttoning from shot to shot; and more.

Most of the other tragedies had to do with physical problems. The actor slated to play Fu Chang, Steve Roberts,* had a heart attack shortly before shooting. Though Gunn wanted me to play Fu Chang, we found another actor, Garon Peterson, the day of shooting. Then there was the "Tromeo Triad of Pain," with Sean Gunn's nose, Stevie Blackehart's lip, and Arthur Jolly's head.† However, the worst on-set occurrence had to do with Jane Jensen and the maggots.

---

*Steve's health improved by the end of the shoot, and he had a cameo as the larva-toting meat packer.
†EDITOR'S NOTE: See chapter 12: Stunts Gone Wrong.

IT WAS A GOOD SHOT

Before I tell you about the maggots, let me tell you some of the things Jane had to put up with during *Tromeo & Juliet*:

1 She was repeatedly beaten, doused in "liquor," and dragged around by her sweaty, underwear-clad father.

2 She was ensconced in an irremovable monster-cow bodysuit for nine hours straight.

3 She had her throat ripped off by the Penis Monster. (This was later cut from the film due to an extremely high quotient of fake-lookingness.)

4 She had, against her protestations, a huge horse penis hung between her legs. And had to pretend to enjoy it.

5 She had "passionate sex" with Tromeo in a glass box with a temperature measured at 104° (it was supposed to be air-conditioned but wasn't due to miscommunications.)

6 She had simulated lesbian sex in a room with six crew members fretting over whether her nipples were lit properly.

7 She masturbated while talking on the phone to 500-pound Joe Fleishaker (me, I'd consider this a plus.)

8 She took a bite of very fatty meat after eight years as a real-life strict vegetarian (also, regrettably, cut from the movie).

And, after all of this, we filmed a dream sequence in which Juliet's belly engorges into pregnancy while Tromeo watches. He is disgusted until he hears the mouth-watering sound of Jiffy-Pop popcorn popping. He tears open Juliet's belly and rapturously digs into the booty of delicious popcorn. Soon after, live rats begin to emerge from her body.*

Now, Jane had no problem with the rats. They were extremely cute—too cute, in fact, to provoke the desired effect. They make you

---

*This is the primary scene that brought on critical comparisons to Buñuel. I would be more likely to compare it to windowpane acid.

want to speak in goo-goo baby talk more than scream in horror. What she didn't like, however, was the last shot of bugs exiting her womb. In reality, they were only mealy worms—the little things that you buy at any pet store to feed your anole or water frog. For some idiotic reason, the crew and I started calling them "maggots." Jane asked me:

"Are you sure we have to have *the maggots* come out of my belly?"

"Yes."

"Really? Aren't the rats enough? Can't we just leave it at that?"

"Sure. If you want to ruin the whole movie."

And then Jane stopped her protestations. Basically, although I knew that Jane was disgusted by the mealy worms, I didn't know *how* disgusted. I thought it was the same feeling as not wanting to have Ultraslime sticking all over you—it was "icky." And I thought her protestations were primarily aesthetic. I thought she believed the movie was going "too far," which I didn't think was valid since what we were trying to do was take *everything* one step too far. In the end, I should have been more aware. This was Jane. She was the most strong-willed, ambitious, and talented actress I've ever worked with. And she wasn't about to complain about minor things. But, while directing a film, you get wrapped up in the technical aspects and forget about the human side sometimes. We went on with the scene as planned.

Brendan was on one camera. I was on the second. After we started filming, James and the prop master, Samara Smith, threw two buckets of maggots on Jane's stomach and then ran out of frame. Just as rehearsed, Jane started to scream.

"Nooo!" she cried. "God, nooo! Nooo!"

She kept going, absolutely wild. Gleefully, I panned the camera from the mealy worms to her face. Boy, I thought, she really seems like she's in pain. This is fantastic!

"NOOOO! PLEASE, NO!" Jane screamed.

What an actress! Amazing! The whole crew was smiling. We were loving it.

Then, suddenly, Jane picked up a pillow and stuffed it over her face.

Wait a second. She's not supposed to do that.

"PLEASE STOP!" she screamed. "CUT! CUT!"

The crew rushed at her from all sides. Efrem, the still photographer,* one of those very rare true and kind souls, arrived first, tearing the fake belly from Jane's skin. James ran toward her and grabbed her in his arms as she sobbed. Samara Smith frantically tried to wipe the mealy worms off her body. And it still took a moment to really strike me.

It was real, I thought. That pain and horror that I was enjoying, that we were all enjoying, it was real.

They finally got Jane clean. They ushered her away from the set. She was still sobbing, stark white. I had never seen even a crack in her strength before, and now here she was, this vulnerable young girl. I didn't know if I should approach her. I didn't know what to say. I was afraid I'd make it worse, and I was ashamed. There's something about that moment that I'll always remember. It was chilling how all of us had been receiving pleasure, even though unknowingly, at the expense of another.

As I waited for her to come back upstairs, I feared that she had cracked somehow, that she'd lost it completely. I envisioned her future: alone in a padded cell with a straightjacket and dark circles around her eyes, a Frances Farmer type of thing; all because of me. I told this to Brendan. He said, as always, I tend to see a situation in the most extreme light possible. Everything's either a horrible tragedy or a tremendous triumph.

"I guess," I said.

Jane was back in an hour and a half. Although completely numb, she was able to film one more short, easy scene, and then go home. I couldn't really sleep that night.

Later, she told me that she had more than a minor fear of "maggots." She was terrified of them. She didn't want to tell us how much, because she didn't want to be a poor sport *and* she didn't know her reaction would be as intense as it was. The animals had gotten all over her body and underneath the stomach contraption. She felt them squirming. She had simply freaked.

Two mornings later, I saw the dailies of the footage. The most horrible irony of it all was that the "maggots" that we poured onto her, from the camera's point of view, looked pretty similar to Chinese stir-

---

*The Nikon-imprint still fresh on his head (again, see Chapter 12).

fry. It could have been anything. In the final cut, we went ahead and used the reaction shots of Jane, screaming, with the tears running down her face. You can see them in the movie today.

AND WHAT ELSE ABOUT *TROMEO & JULIET*?

James, Frank Reynolds, and I edited it for six hard months. The original cut, like most Troma movies, was far too long: almost three hours. We had two marketing screenings: We handed out free invites on NYU's and Columbia's campuses. At the screening, the students filled out questionnaires on how to improve this first cut of the film. It seems that both James and John Avildsen had been right; the audience almost unanimously agreed that using the actual Shakespearean dialogue didn't work.* However, as a whole, the audience was strikingly positive about the film. On a 10-point scale, they rated it on average between 8 and 9 points. This is almost twice as good as the average rating we received on the second best market screening, *Troma's War*.

We did run into trouble marketing the film, however. Because of its extreme nature, we released it Unrated, so some theaters wouldn't take it. Some critics were outraged: A woman from the *London Daily Mail* declared that the film should be burned. Blockbuster Video refused to stock even the R-rated version of the film. And, as of this date, HBO/Cinemax and Showtime are afraid to play the film because of its sex and violence quotient.

BUT

Tromeo & Juliet has played in theaters around the world, breaking house attendance records in Seattle and San Francisco and playing for almost a year in Los Angeles. It has played in more film festivals than any other Troma movie, and won Best Film at the Rome International Festival of Fantasy and Science Fiction and the Audience Award at Raindance in the U.K. The reviews, especially in the States, were astonishingly good, including *The New York Times, The L.A. Times,*

---

*In the movie that you see today, these sections have been cut by about 50% from what they saw in the first market screening.

"EXHILARATING!" NEW YORK TIMES

"HILARIOUS!" L.A. TIMES

"A WINNER!" NEW YORK POST

"SEXY, SILLY, SWEET & SURREAL!" USA TODAY

"TOTALLY OVER-THE-TOP!" SAINT LOUIS POST DISPATCH

"OUTRAGEOUSLY FUNNY!" LONDON DAILY MAIL

A LLOYD KAUFMAN & MICHAEL HERZ PRODUCTION

TROMEO & JULIET

directed by LLOYD KAUFMAN

BODY PIERCING. KINKY SEX. DISMEMBERMENT.
THE THINGS THAT MADE SHAKESPEARE GREAT.

TROMA ENTERTAINMENT

check out the TROMEO & JULIET site at WWW.TROMA.COM

USA Today, and *Entertainment Weekly*. A few brave souls in the underground like Steve Pulchaski of *Fangoria* and *Shock Cinema* and Bill Sinewski of *Bitch Face Plastic Boy* saw it as a groundbreaking film in terms of tone-shift and genre. Often articles mentioned the improved level of acting and, more surprising, the increased production values (*Tromeo & Juliet* was our least expensive production since *The First Turn-On*). Best of all, the fans seemed to love it. The word on the internet groups, who had blasted *Kabukiman* for its meekness, was that it was not only a return to form, but a surpassing of it. Although certainly not the breakthrough into the mainstream that Troma has sought for so long, *Tromeo & Juliet* found its own niche in the communal mindscape of oddballs and rebels.

THE EN–

ONE LAST TIME. THE RENAISSANCE DINER.
SEPTEMBER 1997.

"And that's it?" Barry asked. He sat across from me with the whole shebang, the entire 400 and whatever page manuscript of this book.

"What?"

"The end of the book?" He nibbled a small salad. I had just started on a plate of poached eggs and toast.

"Well, yeah," I said.

"Sort of abrupt, isn't it?"

"Well, you know, *Tromeo & Juliet* was the last Troma movie we made. I mean, we could end it with talking about *Schlock & Schlockability*, or one of the Toxie projects, but those could end up never happening."

"Yeah, but nothing to tie it all together? The chapter's called *'Tromeo & Juliet* and the Future of Troma.' But there's no future of Troma here."

"Yeah, well I didn't know what to—*Tromeo & Juliet*, in a lot of ways, was a striking success. Great reviews. Crowded theaters. Good video sales. But still, we've barely broken even. I don't know what the future of Troma *is*. I don't even know if there *is* a future of Troma."

"Come on, Lloyd. No final words of encouragement for young people out there who want to make films, or who want to defy the establishment like Troma did?"

I thought for a minute.

"No."

"Come on!" Barry said. "What about the kids out there working their asses off making independent films?"

"Listen, I hate these guys that bemoan the loss of sixties values, but the one good thing about the sixties—and even more so the seventies—was that there were people out there like Cassavetes and Warhol and Brakhage—a filmmaking underground that cared about making films with spirit. They were people making films outside the Hollywood mainstream without any goal of getting in. Who do we have like that today? Maybe John Sayles, but that's it. What film was the big independently produced hit of the last few years? That Ed Burns movie, *The Brothers McMullen*. I hear Ed Burns is a nice fellow. Unfortunately, his movie is an interminable fucking bore and everything that's wrong with independent movies. A small group of guys acting macho instead of acting. Sentimentality. Fake happy endings. Lots of scenes in kitchens. Girlfriends who can't act. A writer-producer-director-star who gives himself all of the supposedly witty lines."

"Kind of like you in this book."

"Oh, that's hilarious, Barry. But this isn't funny. *The Brothers McMullen* is quality-wise only slightly better than an episode of *Days of Our Lives*, with less attractive women in looser clothing. Like all the

LET THEM EAT FLESH

Cannibal: The Musical, South Park, and Kaufman's Dry Hump

"Troma were the first people to believe in us, so we're always behind Troma."
—Trey Parker (writer/director/star, Cannibal: The Musical)

"Troma happened because they were there when no one else was.... We did this cannibal movie and everyone thought we were assholes, except Troma."
—Jason McHugh (producer, star, Cannibal: The Musical)

"Troma—just like earmuffs on a cantaloupe."*
—Matt Stone (star, Cannibal! The Musical)

It was way back in 1994 when Lloyd Kaufman first came into contact with the geniuses behind South Park and Orgazmo. As President of Troma, he must review all possible acquisitions for the company.

Kaufman immediately met with the principals of Alferd Packer—Trey Parker, Matt Stone, and Jason McHugh—to discuss distributing the film.† At this meeting, Kaufman found out the young men had been longtime Troma fans, even having parties dedicated to the viewing of Troma classics like The Toxic Avenger while in high school and college. Kaufman decided to help finish the film, fixing its sound problems.‡ The Troma Team, with the approval of Parker and Stone, retitled the film. Thus reborn, Cannibal! The Musical is the story of the only person convicted of cannibalism in U.S. history, told in musical form. The film combines elements of Oklahoma! (Parker's favorite musical), a warped sensibility acquired through long-

---

*Stone actually said, "Troma—yeah, Troma's great,". Kaufman thought the earmuffs thing sounded better.
†At the same time, Kaufman discussed distributing the original Spirit of Christmas, the short animated film on which the South Park series was later based. Kaufman's plans for the film were to retitle it a Very Troma Christmas and change the locale from South Park to Tromaville. It is a testament to the generosity and forbearance of Parker and Stone that they did not kick the shit out of Kaufman, but continue to speak to him today.
‡In a display of his legendary generosity, Kaufman allowed Trey & Pals to do and pay for all the work themselves.

fucking so-called independent films today, it seems to be an audition for mainstream films as opposed to *being* an independent film."

"But the directors of those old Corman films always seemed to be trying out for the mainstream. Dante and Carpenter and Demme, those guys."

"I'm not saying there's anything wrong with wanting to make cotton candy movies. I'm just saying that today *there's not anything else besides that.*"

"There's the Sundance Film Festival."

"Aw! Look, you made me spit out some egg! Sundance is the epitome of modern independent films. They're like the baby pool of glamour, the perfect reflection of their pompous founder Robert Redford, who's the closest thing to a walking piece of beef jerky outside of George

Hamilton. About the only good independent films from the last couple years were *Swingers* and *Daytrippers*, which were both turned down by Sundance. None of the films they choose are too offensive—you can't be too highbrow, you can't be too lowbrow. Almost all of them deal with personal relationships, usually between people in their late twenties. They are all boring. Most of them have Parker Posey in them, an actress who's so excruciatingly aware of her own glib hipness that you feel like she might swirl and give the camera a back-handed high five at any moment. The Sundance organizers have forgotten that, in addition to meaning independently financed, 'independent' also means independence of character and spirit! *They've forgotten that, Barry!*

term exposure to and love of Troma-type movies, and a sense of humor that is uniquely their own. The film was made while its principals were college students in Colorado. Kaufman was sincerely knocked out by their precocity and went on a personal crusade to get the movie into as many hands as possible. He passed hundreds of copies of the tape to people of influence—opinionmakers, critics, agents, studio execs—only to be met by a resounding silence. The idiots in the movie business simply did not "get it." The "gatekeepers"—theater owners, television and video buyers—slammed the door shut on *Cannibal!*. One Showtime film buyer actually subjected Kaufman to a lengthy, detailed explanation of why *Cannibal!* was "unwatchable" and chastised him for distributing such uncommercial fare. When Parker and Stone's *South Park* hit it big three years later, everyone suddenly started to "get it"—videocassettes of *Cannibal!* began flying off the shelves, television was clamoring for it. Due to an enormous spike in public interest, the film will be re-released theatrically. Also, in certain parts of our country, audience members have spontaneously begun to act out and sing along with the movie. The New Cannibal Society is currently launching a merchandising co-venture with *South Park* and Troma called CRAP. "You're already stepping in it!" states the brochure. Hollywood studios are reduced to calling Troma for "screening copies" and the scumbags that work there have tried to get Parker and Stone to take *Cannibal!* back from Troma and give it to them for distribution.

Back in 1994, Trey and Matt had submitted the film to the Sundance Film Festival, paying a $50.00 application fee. They did not get so much as a rejection letter for their $50.00. This did not deter them from attending Sundance and creating a simultaneous alternative festival (with only one film) to showcase *Cannibal!*. This subversive act inspired the creation of an annual alternative festival, Slamdance, which still exists to this day and for which Troma has subsequently become a sponsor. This year, Parker and Stone were invited to Sundance to premiere their new film, *Orgazmo,** and to Slamdance to screen *Cannibal! The Musical*, and they invited Kaufman to accompany them and sleep on the floor of their luxury condo in Park City.

---

*Some say the Sundance selection committee may have been influenced by the recent success of *South Park* or the fact that *Orgazmo* is distributed by the monstrous Seagrams/MCA/Universal/October horror/movie company to choose *Orgazmo*. The Troma Team believes that Sundance recognized the brilliance of *Orgazmo* and selected the film based on its own merits.

> Amid the vice and corruption Hollywood rains on beautiful Park City, the Cannibal boys were a shining example of extraordinary talent combined with grace. In introductory remarks at the packed house premiere of *Orgazmo* (in which Kaufman portrays a "genital doctor"), Parker not only admitted to being associated with Troma, but also introduced Kaufman to the assembled elite. It is clear from Parker behavior at the festival that Troma's time, effort, and idealistic respect for true genius were all well-spent on these good guys.

LIKE EVERYTHING ELSE IN THIS INDUSTRY, IT'S ALL BEEN REDUCED TO A FUCKING ECONOMIC DEFINITION!"

"Lloyd."

"What?!"

"Slow down. There's some spit hanging from the side of your mouth."

I nodded. I wiped it away with a handkerchief. I stuffed another forkful of eggs into my mouth. The eggs were getting cold.

"Now, listen," Barry said. "For the book, that may not be as bad as you think. After all, that's what we're selling this book as. *Troma is the last true independent.* The book is a harangue against the establishment—and even established forms, like grammar and good taste."

"You keep getting funnier, Barry. Why is it you suddenly develop a sense of humor when I feel like blowing my brains out?"

"Lloyd, I don't know how to say it. Throughout the book you've had all this spunk, and now we're left with 'blah blah blah the people on the Internet liked *Tromeo & Juliet.*' The end. Come on! You can do better than that! There should be one last triumphant jab against the mainstream."

"I don't feel any triumph."

"What?"

"I don't feel any triumph. I mean, this is the worst it's ever been. Troma's probably going to die soon. Our distribution channels—the theaters and video stores and TV channels—have been fucked by consolidation. The entire system has been economically restructured to eliminate any chance of our survival." I tapped on the manuscript in front of Barry. "This book, I think, is the death rattle of Troma. Do you want me to end with that?"

"End with—?"

" 'And then the megaconglomerate monsters came and ate Troma and everything else independent and only the asshole fucks lived happily ever after. The End.' How's that ending? Here, give me back the book. I'll rewrite it." I grappled for the book. Barry yanked it back. We tugged it back and forth, knocking Barry's coffee cup and a saltshaker over between us, until finally Barry won the contest of strength. He stuffed it on his lap beneath the table, out of my reach.

"That's not what you said in the speech, Lloyd," he said.

"What speech?"

"The one two chapters ago. The one you supposedly made to me on the phone, where you were talking about the huge corporations, and the people that lived with their hearts and souls. You said, 'In the end, there are more of us than there are of them.' I think you ought to move that speech to the very end of the book. That was triumphant. I mean, sure, it was paranoid-schizophrenic, but I found it kind of moving. I was *moved*, Lloyd. Nothing does that to me. I saw *Field of Dreams*, I'm like, 'Oh, a guy's dead ghost father playing baseball with him. Who cares.' But you moved me. And that would make a great last line: 'Because in the end, there are more of us than there are of them.'"

"But there aren't more of us, Barry. What there are mostly are people that don't give a fuck. Most people *want* McDonald's. They *want* Blockbuster Video. They *want* Tom Cruise and Winona and *Pretty Woman*. Those are the things the American public feels safe with. I mean, I loved *Scream*. But why do you think that was the first big horror movie in years? It's because, in the final analysis, everybody watching knows it's a big joke. They're safe. They're removed from the monsters by one layer of satire."

"*Tromeo & Juliet*'s satire, Lloyd."

"Maybe. But it's not safe. When Sammy Capulet dies and tries to put his brains back in, that's a young man out there who's wailing in pain. It's funny, but it's also disturbing. It's the farthest thing from safe that you can possibly be, because it tricks you into thinking it's safe and then does the opposite. In the seventies, you didn't know who was going to die or live at the end of movies. At the end of *Bullitt*, Steve McQueen is taking a piss. It's sad. The women at the end of *Squeeze Play* lose. That was a time when mainstream movies didn't need to be safe. But at the end of *Con-Air* you can be damn sure that the good Nick Cage guy is gonna live, and that the bad Malkovich is going to die, and nobody's going to be urinating, because these people are action figures without piss-holes. And because audiences know that the hero's going to win, they're happy. And that's why the world doesn't give a fuck whether independent film studios die out or not. So if that's true, and nobody cares, then how can I possibly give people hope, Barry? The only hope I could give them is to tell them to go out there, join the corporate world. Learn how to do things like the other guy. Learn how to make the big man happy to get promoted. Learn how to make films that have been made before, but keep making them easier and easier for an audience to digest. I can tell them to go back and read the first chapter, where I said do everything the opposite of what Troma does. I'll tell them I was half-kidding then, but now I'm completely serious. Use *me*. Use me as an example of what exactly not to do. I'm a dinosaur. The last dodo bird on the beach. I'm a fucking dead man."

"You're in one of your bad moods, I take it," Barry said.

"No, I'm just seeing the truth. You want me to lie. You want me to lie to these kids, to make it safe for them, so in that way you can sell a lot of books. I can see it: 'Lloyd Kaufman's *All I Need to Know about Filmmaking I Learned from the Toxic Avenger* is a resounding bellow of the triumph of the independent human spirit'—*New York Times*."

"A resounding *bellow*?"

"You know what I mean. And it's *bullshit*. Life isn't safe. If you act independently and according to your own conscience, according to what you truly believe, you will fail or you will get killed or you will die by your own hand or you'll cut off your ear. People who fit in are happier than people who don't—that's fact. If you're born unusual, tough shit. You're fucked. Is that what you want me to write, Barry?"

Barry stared at me for a moment.

"No," he said.

He swallowed his last bite of salad. He sipped from his glass of water. I continued to eat, and Dominique's short skirt brushed me as she passed. Barry grabbed the bill. He picked up his backpack. He stood up and began to walk toward the cash register. Then he stopped and turned toward me. He stuttered it out, as if he was only realizing it as he spoke: "But that *isn't* really what you believe, is it?"

I took another bite of my eggs. I looked down at my plate.

"In everything but my heart," I said.

Barry nodded.

"Well, I wish there was some way you could say *that*, Lloyd."

I shook my head.

"I don't think so," I muttered.

He patted my shoulder as he walked toward the cash register. I heard him thank the waitress. He paid the bill.

I took my last bite of eggs. I looked out the large window at the front of the diner. The New York City hoards were passing by. Not *all* of them can like McDonald's, I thought. I pushed aside my plate and stood. I walked back and into the small men's room. I began to urinate, but about halfway through I realized I needed to take a giant shit. I pulled down my pants and sat on the toilet. I tried to think of a way to finish the book. How could I sum up my life to this point? How could anyone? What did the whole mess amount to, all the boobies and Bromo-Seltzer and fake blood and fart jokes—would it have meant more if my movies had been more popular, or had made more money? If people in Hollywood had taken me to lunch more often? Even the things that are meaningful, the critical acclaim for *Tromeo*, the awards and retrospectives, the global recognition, free sex and drugs, what exactly do these things mean? Maybe I was being stupid. Maybe what was necessary was to keep on trying, to act independently and according to your conscience. Maybe it wasn't important whether or not you fail so much as whether or not you acted according to your beliefs.

Maybe that's what I should tell people. My shit was so enormous it hurt my butthole coming out. But then I was finished, and it felt good.*

---

*EDITOR'S NOTE: Well, it's *better* this way. But isn't that how Chaplin's autobiography ended?

Troma Filmography

ADVENTURE OF THE ACTION HUNTERS (1982, Lee Bonner): Not to be confused with *Action of the Adventure Hunters* or *Hunted Adventurers in Action*. In the tradition of *Romancing the Stone*, this is a fantastical, romantic adventure film with plenty of cliff-hangers.

BABY DOLL MURDERS (1992, Paul Leder): John Saxon stars in this tense plot-twister with a shocker ending. A deranged serial killer baffles police with his bizarre stalkings of young women and his signature baby dolls left at the scene of the crime.

BATTLE OF LOVE'S RETURN (1971, Lloyd Kaufman): A whimsical (that means it's boring, folks) story, directed by and starring Troma prez Lloyd Kaufman before he could afford actors. *The New York Times* actually liked it, and other critics of the day compared Kaufman to Woody Allen. So, if you're as staid as *The New York Times*, you might like this one too. Features a cameo by Oliver Stone. Full of alleged comedy. No sex or violence for the peanut gallery. "The best thing about this movie," Stanley Kaufman, Lloyd's father, who also acts in the film, was quoted as saying, "is the part where Lloyd gets killed."

BEST SHOTS (1990, Doug Lodato): Two slackers take their BEST SHOT at getting rich quick with idiot schemes and numbskull misadventures. If The Bowery Boys impregnated Ferris Bueller, this would be the child.

BEWARE, CHILDREN AT PLAY (1995, Mick Cribben): Normal children are frightening enough, but these kids from Tromaville make the movie *Kids* seem like *Child's Play*. If you want dismemberments, if you want gore, if you want parents killing their own children in the ultimate pre-pubescent slaughter-fest (and who doesn't), this one's for you. Make sure you stay for the ending, whatever you do.

BIG GUS, WHAT'S THE FUSS? (We have no idea): There isn't one. This movie sucks and we hope it stays lost forever.

BLADES (1988, Thomas R. Rondinella): Just when you thought it was safe to putt—*Caddyshack* meets *Christine* in this horror-comedy about a monster mower that's really teed off! *Blades* takes a swing at one of the most popular sports today (no, not golf—screwing!).

BLONDES HAVE MORE GUNS (1995, George Merriweather): A titillating slapstick romp which parodies the likes of *Basic Instinct* with razor- . . . er . . . chainsaw-sharp wit. This combination of gratuitous gags, guns, and gams led film critic Joe Bob Briggs to deem director George Merriweather "a genius." That is only one of the many reasons it's not safe to have Joe Bob out on the streets.

BLOOD HOOK (1986, James Mallon): A rock 'n' roll gorefest directed by *MST3K*'s comic genius, James Mallon. A college fishing trip turns deadly in a tourist town stalked by the BLOOD HOOK! Who is the BLOOD HOOK? Watch this film and find out. But be warned: You can't worm your way off of this fishhook of a film.

BLOODSUCKING FREAKS (1975, Joel M. Reed): WARNING: this film, set in a Grand Guignol–type sado-masochistic theater, is only for the demented (even among Troma fans). Probably the most fucked up film in the Troma catalogue. If you're into brainwashing, caged naked teenage girls, dental hijinx, snuff films, sucking brains through straws, and what some say is an utter lack of socially redeeming values, this work of art is for you.

BREAKIN' IN THE USA (1984): A how-to video documentary on the dance craze of the '80s: breakdancing! If you're in for a film as disturbing as BLOOD-SUCKING FREAKS, see this film.

BRIDE OF KILLER NERD (1991, Mark Steven Bosko, Wayne A. Harold): MTV personality and real-life nerd Toby Radloff stars as KILLER NERD, the geekiest guy in high school. Watch the matrimonial mayhem as he weds his female counterpart and these not-so-nice newlyweds kill! kill! kill!—happily ever after.

BUGGED (1996, Ronald K. Armstrong): It's human vs. ferocious man-eating bugs in a battle to the death! A scary and funny first time film from Armstrong. With a great story (*Aliens* meets *Ghostbusters* on a train going to hell) and a talented cast (Priscilla Basque is a fine foxy mama). Check out Troma's first computer-generated effect at the end!

CANNIBAL: THE MUSICAL (1996, Trey Parker): What do you get when you cross six miners lost in the wilds of Colorado, five half-eaten corpses, one survivor, and seven great songs? CANNIBAL: THE MUSICAL. Yup, it's *Oklahoma* meets *Friday the 13th* in a film written, directed by, and starring Trey Parker, the Andrew Lloyd Webber of Horror! This critically acclaimed (honestly) masterpiece has all the singing, dancing, and decapitations you've come to expect from Troma. (Unfortunately, there are no boobies.) Fun Fact! Trey Parker and *Cannibal!* co-star Matt Stone are the creators of Comedy Central's *South Park* and the underground animation classic "The Spirit of Christmas" . . . Pig Fucker!

CAPTURE OF BIGFOOT (1979, Bill Rebane): A band of hunters track down the legendary monster and try to kill it. They would have been better off hunting deer, just so they could have stayed out of this movie. This is the best film ever made about a man in a cheesy fur coat falling down in the snow . . . over and over and over again.

CHILLERS (1988, Daniel Boyd): Critically acclaimed eerie tale of evil and hellish bus rides (and what bus rides aren't?) in the tradition of *Creepshow*. Five lonely travelers swap their private tales of fear and horror.

CHOPPER CHICKS IN ZOMBIETOWN (1989, Dan Hoskins): Cycle sluts cruise a desert town looking for a few good men . . . and find themselves the prey of flesh-hungry zombies! One of Troma's best, funniest films: CHOPPER CHICKS features MTV's Martha Quinn, *Return of The Living Dead*'s Don Calfa, and has an edgy, alternative soundtrack with Alex Chilton, the late, great Camper Van Beethoven, and others. Part of Troma's Strong Woman Series: see also THEY CALL ME MACHO WOMAN; DEADLY DAPHNE'S REVENGE; TOMCAT ANGELS; WAITRESS; and FEMME FONTAINE, KILLER BABE FOR THE CIA. Also a part of Troma's Strong Flesh-Hungry Zombies Series: BEWARE, CHILDREN AT PLAY; CURSE OF THE CAN-NIBAL CONFEDERATES; ZOMBIE ISLAND MASSACRE. Fun Fact! Billy Bob Thornton, recent Oscar winner for *Sling Blade*, plays a hillbilly victimizer of women—a role he did not have to prepare much for.

CLASS OF NUKE 'EM HIGH (1986, Richard W. Haines, Samuel Weil [aka Lloyd Kaufman]): A courageous social statement from Troma about sex, vio-lence, and the power elite's abuse of nuclear power. This Troma classic is set in Tromaville High School where the students are exposed to Readin', Writin', and Radiation! Psychotic punks, stoners, and the honor society alike transform into nuclear mutants, ride their motorcycles through the halls, and trash the school! It's like *The Breakfast Club*, only not as stupid, and really, really drunk. Irrelevant Troma Fact #1: The week NUKE 'EM HIGH premiered at the Cannes Film Festival, the radioactive dust from Chernobyl was blowing over the south of France. Kaufman and Co. have never been the same.

CLASS OF NUKE 'EM HIGH II: SUBHUMANOID MELTDOWN (1991, Eric Louzil): Anarchy and toxic terror rule the campus of Tromaville Tech as students join forces with subhumanoids to battle the conspiracy of government, labor, and corporate slime responsible for the mutant meltdowns, massacres, and the obscene merger of Disney and Cap Cities. Troma-tacular special effects (a squirt bottle full of blood) and a big budget ($102.00) highlight this ambitious (they actually had a script!) sequel to the successful CLASS OF NUKE 'EM HIGH.

THE CLASS OF NUKE 'EM HIGH III: THE GOOD, THE BAD, AND THE SUBHUMANOID (1994, Eric Louzil): Troma star Brick Bronsky (Van Damme's *The Quest*) plays the good, the bad, and the subhumanoid in this demented sequel. It also stars the truly beauteous Troma staple Lisa Gaye (TOXIC 2, TOXIC 3, NUKE 'EM HIGH 2), and the woman with the biggest hair and the best behind in the business, Ms. Lisa Starr. Big breasts! Violence! Mutants! *Tromettes* with mouths on their tummies!

COMBAT SHOCK (1986, Buddy Giovanizzi): Frankie Dunlan thought Vietnam was bad, but it was Disneyland compared to the sleazy nightmare of junkies, prostitutes, and street crime back on the streets of New York! This is a psychological horror film with lots of action. Lloyd Kaufman believes it is a genuine masterpiece, so that tells you something. Huge following in England (COMBAT SHOCK, not Lloyd Kaufman).

CROAKED: FROG MONSTER FROM HELL (1981, Bill Rebane): This film is dedicated to the thousands of frogs who denigrated themselves by appearing in this piece of crap. There are more slimy amphibians in this movie than in the House of Representatives. The worst Troma film since CAPTURE OF BIGFOOT. We love it of course. The only film that tastes like chicken.

CRY UNCLE! (1970, John G. Avildsen): Oscar-winning director John G. Avildsen (*Rocky, The Karate Kid*) presents a hilarious story of murder and blackmail and sex. See an all-star cast including Paul Sorvino (*Goodfellas, A Touch of Class*), and Allen Garfield (*The Cotton Club, Nashville*). If you love horrible acting also check out an appearance by Troma's beloved founder, Lloyd Kaufman. This film is notable for its pathfinding use of necrophilia as a comic vehicle. Had an X rating when it first appeared and it *still* got good reviews in *The New York Times*.

CURSE OF THE CANNIBAL CONFEDERATES (1982, Tony Malanowski): "The South shall rise again . . . and again . . . and again!!" Rebel soldiers come back for revenge as flesh-hungry zombies from an accursed cemetery on a blood-soaked battlefield. Watching this film may be the result of a curse. Lots of exploding heads help to redeem it. Irrelevant fact #2: While I watched this film with a Civil War buff, he noted that it contained *not a single confederate uniform*. Explain that.

THE DARK SIDE OF MIDNIGHT (1984, Wes Olsen): A story of a relentless serial killer, "The Creeper," and super-sleuth Brock Johnson matching wits and weapons in a perilous fight to the finish. Sorry, Troma fans, this film is directed with good taste; there's no graphic sex or violence. Irrelevant fact #3: Last night I played a game of chess with my brother, Patrick. He won. (You wanted irrelevant, you got it! What was that? Irreverent? Oh, sorry.)

DEAD DUDES IN THE HOUSE (1988, J. Riffel): An unwitting tribute to Charles Kaufman's MOTHER'S DAY. A group of hip-hop teens inhabit a house possessed by the spirits of a murdering, maniacal matriarch and her sexy daughter. A fair amount of gruesome, realistic gore and humor.

DEADLY DAPHNE'S REVENGE (1987, Richard Gardener): "Men will be shocked, Women will understand," read the posters for this one. A woman violated and victimized by a hideous crime and a corrupt justice system seeks revenge . . . on her own terms! Horror reminiscent of *I Spit on Your Grave*. Part of Troma's Strong Woman series.

DEATH TO THE PEE-WEE SQUAD (1987, Neal Adams): Legendary comic-book artist Neal Adams directs this tale of children tangling with deadly international spies to protect their father's priceless invention! (What we're trying to say is this film is Wholesome Family Entertainment: see also *Ghost Ship, The Puppetoon Movie*.)

DEF BY TEMPTATION (1990, James Bond III): Samuel L. Jackson (*Pulp Fiction, Jurassic Park*), Kadeem Hardison (*A Different World*), Bill Nunn (*Do The Right Thing, Sister Act*), and Melba Moore star in this critically acclaimed, studio-quality showcase of young black talent. A succubus with a trail of dead men behind her goes head-to-head with a young divinity student who is questioning his faith. *The Los Angeles Times* called this "A potent horror-fantasy," and the *Hollywood Reporter* said it was "Fascinating, intelligent entertainment." Better than anything Spike Lee's ever done.

DEMENTED DEATH FARM MASSACRE (1986, Fred Olen Ray, Donn Davison): Backwoods farmers meet psychotic diamond thieves in this tale of lust, greed, and deadly pitchforks! This tale of the elite meeting the cheap features horror icon John Carradine (*The Astro-Zombies, Billy the Kid versus Dracula, Hillbillies in a Haunted House*, Troma's MONSTER IN THE CLOSET and, oh yeah, something called *Stagecoach*, directed by a guy named Chevrolet, or is that Ford?). This is the Troma Team's pick for the best film by underground auteur Fred Olen Ray (HAUNTING FEAR, WIZARDS OF THE DEMON SWORD).

DIALING FOR DINGBATS (1989, Peter Slodqyk): Troma tackles yet another socially important issue with the addiction of 1-900 party lines. This is the first film about phone sex. Maybe they met over 1 800 83 TROMA. Directed by the man with the hardest-to-pronounce last name of all Troma directors. Produced by Michael Solton.

DREAMS COME TRUE (1984, Mark Kalmanowicz): A young couple meet in their dreams through the power of astral projection and discover that they can go anywhere and do anything together. This one-of-a-kind movie is filled with passion, sensuality, and supernatural special effects. "There's a pretty good sex scene," says Troma president Lloyd Kaufman. "I remember drooling a lot." It stars Michael Sanville (THE FIRST TURN ON).

EAST END HUSTLE (1975, Frank Vitale): Cindy used to be a high-priced call girl; now she's got a gun and is out to get all the people who used to treat her like dirt! After standing up to her pimp and leading a hooker mutiny, Cindy finds herself entangled in a web of danger and blackmail. Another entry in the Troma Strong Woman Series. I wish there was a Troma Series of Hooker Mutiny Films, but there isn't. Yet. Directed by Frank Vitale, who photographed BATTLE OF LOVE'S RETURN (but you can't hold that against a guy forever).

ELECTRA LOVE 2000 (1991, Jay Raskin): This is a futuristic version of Aeschylus' classic Greek Tragedy, *Electra*. Very little sex, but it is excellent art.

ELLIE (1983, Peter Wittman): Shelley Winters (*Big Bad Mamma, Fanny Hill*, and, oh yeah, George Cukor's *A Double Life*) and George Gobel (upper right hand corner—*Hollywood Squares*) star in this murderous romp of revenge and country justice. Penthouse Pet of the Year Sheila Kennedy (THE FIRST TURN-ON) is the young, luscious (very luscious) Ellie who has to take the law into her own hands to battle her greedy and manipulative stepmother. Family values are back . . . beautiful.

EVE'S BEACH FANTASY (1997): This bad girl's got a beach house and she wants to make the most of it. This unbelievable true story follows a girl on her journey from innocence to decadence. It's all for you. She loves you, she wants you, she's looking at you. Starring many people whose names you may not recognize but whose body parts may be familiar to you.

EVIL CLUTCH (1988, Andreas Marfori): Features elegant photography, crisp colors, sensitive performances, and a woman who rips off men's balls. The Clutch, a hideous monster, takes the form of a knockout who uses her seductive powers to wrap the men of a small town around her finger (which hurts bad enough) . . . and then . . . OW!! What do you think, Troma fans? Does it qualify for Troma's Strong Woman series or not?

THE FANATIC (1982, David Winters): Joe Spinell (*Rocky, The Godfather, Maniac*) in his creepiest role since . . . well . . . Okay, he's always been pretty creepy. . . . But how many of those movies can boast that he stalks and kills cute chicks? . . . Well, okay . . . Yeah, but this time he's creepy, and killing cute chicks at the Cannes Film Festival! Bet you wanna see it now, huh? Also features Bond girl Caroline Munro in a sexy shower scene.

FAT GUY GOES NUTZOID!! (1986, John Golden): If you've ever seen a Troma movie, you know we love fat people. This very popular Troma film is the supra-politically incorrect tale of two brothers who befriend an obese, certifiably insane wild man, and accompany him on his misadventures in the big city. Fat Guy's madcap chase from those who would re-institutionalize him results in a suspense-filled rescue attempt by helicopter and winch!

"FEELIN' UP" (1983, David Secter): A non-stop erotic adventure about a community of swinging teenagers who delve into New York City's world of sexual perversion, heavy drugs, and hardcore pornography . . . Other than that it's just like *Bambi*.

FEMME FONTAINE: KILLER BABE FOR THE CIA (1993, Margot Hope): The first Troma film to be written, produced, and directed by a woman! Margot Hope (*Sex Crimes, Virtuosity*) stars with James Hong (*Blade Runner, Wayne's World II*) in this explosive and electrifying tale of psychotic skinheads, karate-chopping gangsters, lesbian femiNazis, and worst of all, sleazy movie producers (and more babes in bikinis than you can shake a g-string at). Definitely part of the Troma Strong Woman series.

FEROCIOUS FEMALE FREEDOM FIGHTERS (1982, Jopi Burnama): Unique (shot in English) Indonesian female wrestling sex film, which Charles Kaufman, Lloyd's brother (see MOTHER'S DAY, WHEN NATURE CALLS), took and made even worse by dubbing in new, humorous dialogue. It's like the Woodman's *What's Up, Tiger Lily*, but instead of pithy verbal exercise this one has fart jokes, children having orgasms, Elvis impersonators, cigarette burns, and incest.

FEROCIOUS FEMALE FREEDOM FIGHTERS PART 2 (1983, Arizal): These fighting females are back to topple the power pyramids of the high-priced Asian sex underworld. This film could not be made worse, so we kept the original soundtrack.

FERTILIZE THE BLASPHEMING BOMBSHELL (Jeff Hathcock): Despite the misleading title, this film concerns a blaspheming bombshell who gets fertilized. Satan falls for a sexy babe from Brooklyn and wants to implant her with his seed (in this way, Satan's just one of the guys). If you like blaspheming bombshells getting cornholed by Beelzebub at midnight while naked hardbodies dance around them in sexual bliss, this film is for you. Featuring Bo Hopkins.

THE FIRST TURN-ON! (1983, Michael Herz and Samuel Weil [aka Lloyd Kaufman]): A sexy romp through summer camp and sexual fantasies as a group of campers and their counselor are trapped together in a cave . . . with nothing but each other to pass the time! "This film was the driving force behind Madonna's popularity," says Michael Herz. "Because she auditioned for a role and we turned her down, she went on to musical success." At least they got Academy Award nominee Vincent D'onofrio and Penthouse Pet of the Year Sheila Kennedy (ELLIE). James Gunn, Tromite and co-screenwriter on TROMEO AND JULIET, says this is his favorite film (mostly because there's a whole lot of sex in it).

FORTRESS OF AMERIKKKA (1989, Eric Louzil): With America under siege by the conspiracy of the beaurocratic, labor, and corporate elite, the only civil right still respected is the right to bear arms and bare asses! Militant mercenaries terrorize the nation and innocent young Americans must rise to the occasion in a bloody fight for their freedom and braless girls in tight tank tops. This features a blonde, who's name I don't know, who a large population of the Troma Team consider to be the best-looking woman in any Troma film . . . yes, there is ample sex and violence.

FROSTBITER: WRATH OF THE WENDIGO (1990, Tom Chaney): Not to be confused with the great American poet Robert Frostbiter or the British talk show host Sir David Frostbiter. This is the FROSTBITER based on the Caliber Press comic book. The cast includes Ron Asheton, former guitarist for Iggy Pop and the Stooges. One of the most horrifying creatures ever committed to celluloid (not Ron, the FROSTBITER!), it destroys those who disturb its resting place . . . when the Frostbiter arrives, Hell has frozen over! Indeed scary.

GHOST SHIP (1993, James Flocker): CAUTION: Be careful when pronouncing this title over the phone: it tends to sound like GOAT SHIT. This leads to problems as GHOST SHIP is a squeaky clean, PG-rated, big-budget film, which came out of Troma's 50th Street Films. Husband: "I showed the kids a great movie today, honey. GOAT SHIT." Wife: "You bastard! I thought you threw those films out when we got married!" Um, anyway, this concerns a lost ship in the desert, a storybook pirate, and a camel named Friday. Stars Jay Robinson. Produced by David Jackson (no relation to Michael).

THE G.I. EXECUTIONER (1984, Joel M. Reed): Imagine a James Bond film if the BLOODSUCKING FREAKS director took a whack at it. Then, again, you don't have to imagine it. Here it is. G.I. EXECUTIONER takes place in Singapore, where they don't allow you to chew bubblegum but they do allow you to trade slaves (at least in this film they do).

GIRLS SCHOOL SCREAMERS (1984, John P. Finegan): A group of sexy sorority girls' getaway in a remote, luxurious mansion turns into a hell weekend as the house unleashes horrors. This one was executive produced by Kaufman and Herz, so you know it has some graphic gore. Not only that, but can a film with scantily clad sorority sisters really be bad? . . . Possibly.

HAUNTING FEAR (1990, three words: Fred. Olen. Ray.): Ray (DEMENTED DEATH FARM MASSACRE and WIZARDS OF THE DEMON SWORD), Troma's favorite non-Kaufman/Herz director, other than Louzil, Giovanizzi, etc., and a great admirer of Ed Wood, is back with a film starring scream queen Brinke Stevens (*Sorority Girls in the Slimeball Bowl-A-Rama*), Karen Black (*Five Easy Pieces*), and Jan-Michael Vincent (*Animal Instincts*). Lloyd Kaufman likes it because it is based on Edgar Allan Poe, but, then again, so is Kaufman.

HOLLYWOOD ZAP! (1986, David Cohen): Director Cohen worked in the Troma editing room for so long it's no wonder he came up with this comedy that involves a demented midget, a sex-starved beach bunny, and a transsexual nun. This film must be credited with it's innovative use of transsexual nuns, long before Whoopi Goldberg in *Sister Act*. It also has . . . Chuck Mitchell! (Porky from *Porky's*).

HORROR OF THE HUNGRY HUMUNGOUS HUNGAN (1991, Randall DiNinni): Jack Palance narrates this story of genetic experiments gone awry. THE HUMUNGOUS HUNGAN is unleashed on a peaceful community and an unsuspecting group of campers. To the Hungan, earth is just an all you can eat buffet (except the $3.49 tip included is more than the budget of this movie).

HOT SUMMER IN BAREFOOT COUNTY (1974, Will Zens): "There are only two commandments in Barefoot County—love they neighbor and do unto others!" An undercover government agent tries to infiltrate a moonshine business and is distracted by a town full of voluptuous country fillies. Bare feet smell, and so does this film. While this movie does not resemble *Deliverance*, the people in it do. Fortunately it contains lots of large, smelly breasts. This film is a must for any fans of Troma's Strong Redneck Series (REDNECK ZOMBIES, PREACHERMAN).

HUNTED TO DEATH (1986, Nikos Tzimas): This is an action film Greek style, or, um, we mean an action film set in Greece.

I MARRIED A VAMPIRE (1983, Jay Raskin): Just like *Interview with the Vampire*, only the vampires are straight, and you don't have to put up with Tom Cruise for what seems like eighteen hours. A teenage girl, violated in every aspect of her life, takes revenge on those who exploited and dishonored her with her vampire lover! Not enough graphic sex or violence, but it's cool!

I WAS A TEENAGE TV TERRORIST (1985, Stanford Singer): Susan Kaufman, art director on SQUEEZE PLAY, MOTHER'S DAY, and WHEN NATURE CALLS, rebels against older brothers Lloyd and Charles by producing a film with good taste and no graphic sex or violence. Two teenagers playing a vengeful bomb-scare prank on a television station assume the role of terrorists that the news reports have given them only to discover that the confrontation is being media-manipulated by the network itself.

KILLER CONDOM (1997, Martin Walz): Remember the last time you got laid? Well, then just imagine that you have ever gotten laid. She made you wear the rubber . . . You complained that it makes you lose all feeling, but you put it on anyway because hey, sex is sex, right? Next thing you knew . . . CHOMP! Mr. Happy was moving through the digestive tract of a rabid rubber . . . Now you can relive that glorious moment with this cool, funny fright flick which boasts beautiful cinematography, splatter effects, drag queen cops and of course the world's first carnivorous condom. Makes Lorena Bobbitt look like a mohel (that's a Jewish guy who performs circumcisions!) Fun Fact! The psychotic prophylactic effects were supervised by the brilliant H. R. Giger, the guy who created the "Alien" and "Species" creatures.

KILLER NERD (1990, Mark Steven Bosko, Wayne A. Harold): And you thought that nerds were already scary! See BRIDE OF KILLER NERD, also by Bosko and Harold. A social satire of middle America made by Ohio filmmakers.

THE LOVE-THRILL MURDERS (1971, Bob Roberts): This great film stars Troy Donahue in this take on the Manson family murders, with teenagers forced to participate in a blood-bath strip-tease orgy. Like *Helter Skelter*, only not so wimpy. Part of the Troma Lloyd Kaufman's Bad Acting Series (BATTLE OF LOVE'S RETURN, CRY UNCLE). Also see *Rocky, Saturday Night Fever, Slow Dancing in the Big City*, and *Final Countdown*, where Kaufman's bad acting goes mainstream.

LUST FOR FREEDOM (1987, Eric Louzil): Great hardbodied, sweaty, writhing women wrestling and insane monkey love are featured in this moist-crotch, braless, hot-women-in-prison picture. A one-woman arsenal of rage and vengeance takes on a town full of corrupt and sadistic perverts who get their kicks by using and abusing innocent female prisoners. She strikes back and turns the tables on those who tortured and exploited her. Part of the Troma Strong Woman series.

MANIAC NURSES FIND ECSTASY (1994, Harry M. Love): At first this may seem like just another erotic horror film, but it is, in fact, a statement on health care in America. It is rumored that Hillary Clinton watched this film before she proposed her health-care plan; that moment was entitled HILLARY CLINTON FINDS ECSTASY. This is the first Troma film made in the birthplace of Franz Liszt (Hungary). And you'll be pretty Hungary for these curvy hot medical professionals. The feminist B-side of that rockin' hit, BLOODSUCKING FREAKS. A sinister sorority of surgically skilled sisters and their captive caged girls perform diabolical dissections and serve up breasts, blood, and a bevy of butchery. Bewitching.

A MIDSUMMER NIGHT'S DREAM (1997, Timothy Hines): Ever wonder what this classic Shakespeare comedy, of love and rivalry, would be like if it was hardcore pornography? Us too . . . Unfortunately this is a very faithful adaptation, and suitable for the whole family. But the porno idea is a good one, huh? Hey, Lloyd, I got an idea!!!

MONSTER IN THE CLOSET (1986, Bob Dahlin): An all-star cast including John Carradine (*The Vampire Hookers, Satan's Cheerleaders, Buried Alive*, and, oh yeah, something called *The Grapes of Wrath*, by a guy named Toyota . . . or was that Ford?), Stella Stevens (*The Nutty Professor*), and Claude Akins (*Rio Bravo*) star in this horror film for the whole family. Every child's worst nightmare, a MONSTER IN THE CLOSET, terrorizes a community by moving from closet to closet, claiming victims until a national emergency erupts! The climax of this film where all the concerned citizens of the United States destroy their closets to protect themselves is not to be missed. This film is hilarious, one of Troma's best (but it is rated PG and contains no sex or violence. We are sincerely sorry).

MOTHER'S DAY (1979, Charles Kaufman): This is a delightful, whimsical social satire featuring maimings, gorgings, electrocutions, and deaths by Draino. This pioneering slasher film, directed by Lloyd's brother, Charles, is a must-see for anyone who's a fan of the gore genre (or anyone who's read Freud). Young girls on a camping trip fall prey to a demented and depraved family. Another film featuring Stanley Kaufman, progenitor of Lloyd and Charles: part of the Troma Strong Stanley Kaufman Acting Series. Another Plus: Lloyd Kaufman makes not a single appearance in his brother's film.

NERDS OF A FEATHER (1991, Gary Graver, Mario Milano): You want nerd movies, huh, jacko!? Troma's got more nerd movies than you can shake a pocket penholder at! This one's an action spy thriller. Mario Milano stars, writes, and codirects.

THE NICK OF TIME (1994, Edward Staroselsky): Eisenstein, Pudovkin, and now . . . Staroselsky! A Soviet seductress gets a rebellious American youth to stroke her perestroika. They work together to recover Czar Nicholas II's stolen pocket watch before it falls into the wrong hands. Very non-Troma (i.e., it's somewhat conventional, stylish, attractive).

NIGHTBEAST (1982, Don Dohler): Just like E. T., only if E. T. ate little Elliot and sucked. Really, really sucked. Not to be confused with late night vegetarian movie, *Night Beet*. Or the famous feminist horror film, *Night Bitch*. Or the famous biographical film about *Hee Haw*'s Buck Owens, *Night Buck*. Or the famous movie about hicks who have spitting contests every midnight, *Night Bile*. Or the—(SHUT THE FUCK UP!!!)

NIGHTMARE WEEKEND (1985, Henry Sala): A tribute to Windows 95, where computer technology is used to control and mutate innocent (well . . .)

college girls into frenzied zombies (Bill Gates wishes . . .). This ahead-of-its-time thriller pits human wits against computer control in the battle against modern technology gone amuck.

A NYMPHOID BARBARIAN IN DINOSAUR HELL (1991, Brett Piper): "The pre-historic and the pre-pubescent, together at last." Whereas Spielberg spent millions of dollars on computer animation to create dinosaurs, we saved millions by raising our own from hatchlings in the smelly, damp basement of Troma Inc. This takes place in a post-nuclear holocaust Tromaville. Deadly, horny dinosaurs (including the Tromasaurus) pursue the last woman alive, who just happens to be a sexy little dirty blond (the dinos got lucky—it could have been Janet Reno). Special effects by Brett Piper and Alex Pirnie.

OCEAN DRIVE WEEKEND (1984, Bryan Jones): Ocean Drive is a strip of cheap motels where teenagers have sex in South Carolina. Sometimes with other people. This is a sixties period piece featuring the groovin' sounds of the Drifters and the Tams (short for Tampons?) and an embarrassing dance called the Shag.

PLAY DEAD (1984, Peter Wittman): Hollywood legend Yvonne DeCarlo (*Satan's Cheerleaders, Blazing Stewardesses*, and, oh yeah, some trash called *The Ten Commandments*) stars as a jilted lover, dead set on murder. Her weapon is Greta, a 200-lb rottweiler who likes the taste of humans more than Alpo. Ms. DeCarlo admired the title of this movie so much she decided to play dead herself a couple years later.

PREACHERMAN (1971, Albert T. Viola): A smooth-talkin', law-breakin' pastor of disaster preaches a gospel of deception to get what he wants! Long, long before scumbags Swaggart and Baker exposed themselves as deceptive freaks of the pulpit, this film starring a dishonest preacher hit the Bible belt. Big boobs! Steaming hot monkey love! In its day, this North Carolina hillbilly fest made more money dollar for dollar in the South than any other film ever. We're not kidding.

PTERODACTYL WOMAN FROM BEVERLY HILLS (1997, Philipe Mora): The movie you've waited your whole lame-ass life for! Beverly D'Angelo plays a sex-starved mom who turns into a flying dino! And if that ain't enough, see Brion James (*Blade Runner, Fifth Element*) play not one, but two roles! One being a Scottish Aborigine and the other, a diaper-wearing witch doctor!

PUPPETOON MOVIE (1986, Arnold Leibovit): Internationally loved characters Gumby and Pokey host this tribute to the genius of puppet animator George Pal. This animated treat is interesting for kids and adults. It showcases the talents of Ray Harryhausen, Willis O'Brien, Louis Armstrong, and Peggy Lee. The work of George Pal is as great as Disney ever was, but due to the conspiracy of the power elite his work has been suppressed. Even PBS refused to air this film because they considered it "politically incorrect" (and now you want to see it, huh, jacko?).

RABID GRANNIES (1988, Emmanuel Kervyn): "They love their grandchildren . . . well done!" Another important Troma social statement: this time on the difficult plight of the elderly. Wee little old ladies unite and grow fangs to take their revenge on society. A truly good film with spectacular special effects and tons of gore that will make you scream and beg for mercy.

REBEL LOVE (1984, Milton Bagby, Jr.): A story of Confederate lust and Yankee passion set against the violence and splendor of the Old South during the Civil War. It's in the tradition of *Gone with the Wind*, except without big ears and it does give a damn. REBEL LOVE is a family film on a large scale. Features the beauteous Jamie Rose (see her surrounded with blood and intestines in CHOPPER CHICKS). For the same story on a lower budget with people being eaten alive, see CURSE OF THE CANNIBAL CONFEDERATES.

RECORDED LIVE (Michael Korican): Imagine if you will, a movie that boasts performances by bands named "Mama Quilla II" and "Hamburger Patti, and the Helpers," and you have Troma's answer to "Evita." Only our movie does not induce vomiting . . . just really bad gas.

REDNECK ZOMBIES (1987, Pericles Lewnes): Director Lewnes did the special effects for such Troma classics as SGT. KABUKIMAN, NYPD and TOXIC AVENGER 2 & 3, so you can be sure the man's been warped by Kaufman and Herz. In this film, some dumb-ass hicks mistake barrels of toxic waste for home-brew moonshine and become even dumber-ass, cannibalistic zombies. Contains more blood and gore than almost any other dish on the Troma Smorgasbord of Love.

ROCKABILLY VAMPIRE (1997, Lee Bennet Sobel): In the wake of the twentieth anniversary of Elvis' "death" we learn that not only is the King not dead, but is in fact a current member of the Undead and is still rocking and rolling (severed heads) right here in Tromaville! Starring TROMEO & JULIET's Steven Blackehart, and Valentine Miele.

ROCKIN' ROADTRIP (1985, William Olsen): A rock and roll fable jam-packed with punks, guns, and jewel thieves. Rock 'n' roll adventurers unite beneath the alternative beat of Love Tractor, Cherry Suicide, and Guadalcanal Diary. The soundtrack kicks.

ROMEO: LOVE MASTER OF THE WILD WOMEN'S DORM (1992, Denis Adam Zervos): By the director who brought you SPACE FREAKS FROM PLANET MUTOID. Romeo finds love and sex with Carol, Debbie, Wendy, and Juliet. He was getting tired of all those showers with men, we guess.

SCORING (1977, Michael de Gaetano): The late Pistol Pete Maravich stars in this film about rivalry between the sexes. Plenty of jiggle and plenty of dribble, not enough fuckle and suckle—if that's what you want (you dirty thing!) tune in to our other sports film, SQUEEZE PLAY.

SCREAM BABY SCREAM (1969, Joseph Adler): This is one of those rare films that looks at first glance as if it stinks, but when you look a little closer you see some interesting things going on (most films, you look at them, they stink, you look at them closer, they stink some more). It concerns an abstract painter who lures luscious damsels into his mansion and then transforms them into hideous creatures through reconstructive cosmetic surgery and genetic implants—some of the most amazing implants, in fact, outside of the CLASS OF NUKE 'EM HIGH series. Talk about cool. Not only that, but it has the most hep jazz score ever. See it, jacko, or forever regret.

SCREAMPLAY (1986, Rufus Butler Seder): The Troma Team believe this is a masterpiece and has therefore voted it into Troma's Unsung Masterpieces Series. Very original and very bloody (though, because the film is in black and white, all the blood is a very dark gray—just like my ex-girlfriend's.) SCREAM-PLAY blurs the boundaries of fiction and reality as a mystery writer's screen-play seems to come to life! Holy chimera! (Dontcha' know what a chimera is? Look it up!) Recommended!

SGT. KABUKIMAN N.Y.P.D. (1993, Lloyd Kaufman, Michael Herz): Kauf-man and Herz directed this ambitious adventure of lethal sushi, heatseeking chopsticks, and projectile parasols! "SGT. KABUKIMAN is the *Citizen Kane* of Troma movies," says Mike Mayo, Video Originals. This is one of the best and the biggest Troma movies of all time. After two years having played in major theaters all over the world, SGT. KABUKIMAN is finally coming to America. Just like with THE TOXIC AVENGER, it took a while to get theaters in America to be open-minded enough to show this film. If you like weird mutated heroes who eat raw fish, stomp people's heads till brains splatter out, and have a thing for chicks with little pillows on their butts, see this movie.

SHADOWS RUN BLACK (1984, Howard Heard): Watch Costner gangly! Watch Costner talentless! Watch Costner be a dork! This is a great film for anyone with a low self-image who wants to see a truly pitiful nerd who later went on to win an Academy Award and pork Sean Young in the back of a limousine (Troma Fans of the Male Persuasion, let's wallow together in com-munal self-pity). This film is based on the famous Los Angeles "Shadow Serial Murders," and Costie is the prime suspect. It's the mega-star's second worst film after *The Bodyguard*.

SILENT BUT DEADLY (Larry Brown): Troma continues it's unflinching ex-aminations of today's important social issues. SILENT BUT DEADLY is an intellectual take on the relevant topic of farting among our elected officials.

Hold your noses as the first black, Jewish President of the Female Persuasion must save America from SILENT BUT DEADLY destruction! Features Michael Anderson, the little midget guy from Twin Peaks. It is the best performance by an itsy bitsy person (see, we're learning to become more and more P.C. here at Troma all the time) since Seamus O'Brien in BLOODSUCKING FREAKS and Norma Pratt in STUCK ON YOU! and TOXIC AVENGER. Part of Troma's Strong Itsy Bitsy Person Series (NERDS OF A FEATHER, SIZZLE BEACH USA).

SIZZLE BEACH USA (1986, Richard Brander): Film historians have found it noteworthy that Kevin Costner started with this film, made for $40,000 and filmed around water, and he ended with *Waterworld*, made for $120 million and filmed in the water. If only the makers of *Waterworld* had consulted Troma fans, they would have been told that *WW* could be a successful Costner film if had as many boobies as this blockbuster. Lots of fun. Next time you're walking on the beach and you think you step on a jellyfish, look again; it might be a silicone implant from one of the SIZZLE BEACH beauties lost during shooting. Whoops!

SPACE FREAKS FROM PLANET MUTOID (1992, Denis Adam Zervos): Mutants and mosh pits intermingle in this rock and roll science fiction fable. From the man who brought you ROMEO: LOVE MASTER OF THE WILD WOMEN'S DORM. Part of Troma's Strong Weird Aliens Series.

SPACE ZOMBIE BINGO (1993, George F. Ormrod): This is one of Lloyd Kaufman's favorite movies. "Totally cheesey," he said. "Definitely hilarious." SPACE ZOMBIE BINGO is a camp send-up of early space invader flicks, featuring space zombettes in flippers and dime-store ray guns. Filmed in Seattle, where flannel shirts and chunky hair are still king.

SQUEEZE PLAY! (1979, Samuel Weil, aka Lloyd Kaufman): Al Corely stars in this saucy, rollicking comedy about a women's softball team. This was the film that broke it open for the Troma Team: it was their first major financial success. Lloyd directed this wild battle of the sexes, where the game between the men and the women heats up the softball field. Lots of good-looking babes, a goodly amount of the old in-out, and even a rocking wet T-shirt contest. The vastly inferior *A League of Their Own* came out fifteen years later. Jennifer Hetrick later went on to the *Law and Order* television show. Don't miss the shock ending!

THE STABILIZER: Made in English in Indonesia. This film contains some all-time great helicopter stunts (though not as good as the one Warner Bros. did with Vic Morrow and the two Vietnamese children in *Twilight Zone: The Movie*). Peter Goldson embarks on a personal vendetta against heroin dealers and the mob.

STAR WORMS II: ATTACK OF THE PLEASURE PODS (1985, Lin Sten): We have found certain correlations between this science fiction film and The Troma Team:

a) In STAR WORMS, pleasure pod implants weaken the will of the Empire. In the Troma Team, certain Tromettes' pleasure pod implants have weakened the wills of Troma Team men.

b) In STAR WORMS, the Empire's denizens succumb to lustful desires, leading the Empire into anarchy. In the Troma Team, the denizens succumb to lustful desires, leading the Empire into anarchy.

c) In STAR WORMS, the Lords of the Evil Empire have, as their sacred source, hedonistic hallucinogenic opiates. In the Troma Team, uh, um . . . no comment. Anyway, this is a low-budget science fiction epic.

STORY OF A JUNKIE (1984, Lech Kowalski): Another film in the Troma's Unsung Masterpieces Series. Mike McGrady from *Newsday* said, "The purity of the horror is fascinating," and Vincent Canby of the *New York Times* said it was "Harrowing." This is the story of a desperate man living in desperate society; it features real drugs and real junkies and it's one of the hardest films to watch without physically recoiling. It takes place in New York's East Village, known as Alphabet City. For those of you that haven't been there, it's a great place to take the wife and kids for vacation next year instead of Disneyland. It's just like "It's a Small World," only with gunshots, crackheads, and three-dollar whores.

STRANGEST DREAMS: INVASION OF THE SPACE PREACHERS (Daniel Boyd): More inbred *Deliverance* types are featured in this amusing film. Made in Virginia (D.C. is only a stone's throw away, where the inhabitants are even more *Deliverance*-y). A science-fiction action comedy. The evil Reverend Lash and his space cohorts attempt to control Earthling minds. Only some Earth nerds and a beautiful alien bounty hunter named Nova can stop these Outer Space Swaggarts.

STUCK ON YOU! (1982, Michael Herz, Samuel Weil [aka Lloyd Kaufman]): A sexy comedy about palimony and the problems couples have faced since we stopped being monkeys. Estranged love birds Bill and Carol travel through the ages and visit such famous lovers as Adam and Eve, Queen Isabella and Columbus, and King Arthur and Lady Guinevere. Although WAITRESS and SQUEEZE PLAY made more money, the Troma Team considers this the best of the Troma-produced sexy comedies. And there's also plenty o' groin-fire for you, jacko.

STUDENT CONFIDENTIAL (1985, Richard Horian): Michael's brother Eric Douglas and Michael's brother Marlon Jackson star in this whacked-out high school drama in the tradition of *Blackboard Jungle*. Ronee Blakely appears in her finest performance since *Nashville*. This thing is truly, truly strange, and some of us around the Troma Studios enjoy it immensely. Written, starring, directed by, and featuring music by Troma's Orson Welles—Richard Horian.

STUFF STEPHANIE IN THE INCINERATOR (1987, Don Nardo, Peter Jones): "Don't throw your love away . . . BURN IT!" is the tag line for this one. This is a good movie with a great title that is somewhat Hitchcockian in tone. A young couple become involved in the sado-masochistic games of the wealthy, and, as they travel deeper, it becomes difficult to establish exactly what is a game and what isn't. WARNING: this film is extremely classy and contains very little graphic sex or violence.

SUGAR COOKIES (1972, Theodore Gershuny): This soft-focus early '70's flick was written by Lloyd Kaufman and associate produced by Oliver Stone. It's Troma's version of *Vertigo*, with two babes instead of Jimmy Stewart and Kim Novak. With Mary Woronov and the absolutely incredible Lynn Lowry. It contains some of the most erotic lesbian grope-fests of any Troma film. And Lynn Lowry's description of her first orgasm is one of the most powerful scenes ever filmed (and I have had quite a few powerful scenes myself just watching it). Stanley Kaufman, Lloyd's father, is also featured. (No, he doesn't play a lesbian. But close: a lawyer.)

SURF NAZIS MUST DIE! (1987, Peter George): One of the most beloved and indeed best Troma films, by Peter George, director of Troma's YOUNG GOODMAN BROWN. It takes place in the near future, where a major earthquake has destroyed the California coastline (don't we New Yorkers wish?). A black kid is killed by the SURF NAZIS, and his big, fat, pistol-packing Mama starts a war along the California beaches, taking revenge on every Nazi gut, throat, face, and crotch she can find. Too much, dude.

TEENAGE CATGIRLS IN HEAT (1993, Scott Perry): When these pussies rub up against your leg, *you* cough up the hairball. This film rocks; it features some of the best gags in Tromadom, as well as some of the best screaming, stuffed cats plummeting through the sky and bouncing off tree limbs. Genuinely original, genuinely funny, and features a man having sex with a cat (although, unfortunately for us, she's in human form at the time . . . This list just keeps getting sicker and sicker, doesn't it?)

THAT'S MY BABY! (1985, Edie Yolles, John Bradshaw): Family Film.

THEY CALL ME MACHO WOMAN! (1989, Patrick G. Donahue): She was born to shop . . . She learned to kill! Sexy blonde Susan Morris (Deborah Sweaney) finds trouble in the woodlands from a bunch of mongo monstrosities who don't care a whit about their environmentally destructive activities. She fights back! She kicks ass! She's got an ax! Part of the Troma Strong Woman Series. If you like women maiming and mutilating men, take your joystick in your hand and enjoy. Also starring Olympic gold medalist Brian Oldfield.

TOMCAT ANGELS (1991, Don Edmunds): Let's see how you do with a Troma mathematical equation. Beautiful women + small costumes + the finest fighting machines in the world =? (Answer: TOMCAT ANGELS! If you got 436, you miscalculated.) Screw *Top Gun*; for real skyway action see this flick, where hardbodied babes defend international airspace against a terrorist army of the perverted power elite.

THE TOXIC AVENGER (1984, Michael Herz, Samuel Weil [aka Lloyd Kaufman]): Originally no movie theater in the world would show this film, but it went on to become a seminal classic in low-budget filmmaking, thrust a new character into the American pop consciousness, garner millions upon millions of dollars in merchandising, spawn two sequels and a cartoon series, and become the most well-known Troma movie of all time. It combined elements of comedy, violence, cartoony superhumans, and adult themes that until then had never before been featured on the same reel of celluloid. Yes, there is an undeniable magic in the story of despised geek Melvin, who is accidentally pushed into a barrel of toxic waste and transformed into the hideously deformed creature of superhuman size and strength, THE TOXIC AVENGER (known affectionately as Toxie), a fearsome creature with a desire to do good and defend the town of Tromaville from corruption and evil. Undeniable magic, and the best scene of a child's head being crushed by a car that you could ever imagine.

THE TOXIC AVENGER PART II (1989, Michael Herz, Lloyd Kaufman): This film is very popular among Oedipally minded young boys: Toxie travels to Tokyo to find his Poppa and to kill him. Troma's figurehead battles Apocalypse, Inc., which plans to take over Tromaville and reinstate the peaceful town as the "Toxic Waste Capital of the World." Toxie's girlfriend is magically transformed from Andree Maranda (the blind girl in the first film) into Phoebe Legere, the beautiful, talented composer and chanteuse. "A shitload of gore," says Lloyd Kaufman. "Ears get pulled off. More heads get crushed. Fists pass through the gray matter like so much cotton candy. It's a movie about the marvels of love." This is the only film where a decapitated man dances a hillbilly jig while his neck is spurting blood. Yee-haw! Grab your partner! Round and round! Fun Fact 2.0.1: Michael Jai White, Spawn in the recent movie *Spawn*, appears in this film as an angry customer at a whitefish stand.

THE TOXIC AVENGER PART III: THE LAST TEMPTATION OF TOXIE (1989, Michael Herz, Lloyd Kaufman): Ol' Beelzebub himself tries to convince Toxie to become a scumsucking yuppie. Will the temptations of the corporate world prove too much for him? Will marriage and upwardly mobile life corrupt America's favorite superhuman creature? In the tradition of Faust, Toxie battles for his very soul! Don't miss Toxie urinating on Satan's face from an amazing distance. There was a kid we knew in grammar school, Dan Sellars, who could do it almost as far. This is a possible future entry in the Strong

Woman Series, with female bodybuilders, Phoebe Legere wrestling Lisa Gaye after Phoebe is tied up and almost gang-banged by a group of bad girls. Also, this film contains Toxie's best, bed-burning ejaculation scene. For you gore-meisters, there's plenty of splattering, spattering, and disemboweling.

TOXIC CRUSADERS (1996): This classic of modern animation, based on the popular series of the same name, brings all the super-mutated heroes of su-perhuman size and strength into the world of cartoons. Join Toxie and his pals as they fight the forces of pollution and corruption in their own backyard of Tromaville. It's fun for kids of all ages.

TOXIC CRUSADERS 2: THE REVENGE OF DR. KILLEMOFF (1997): This movie picks up where the last left off. Like *Empire Strikes Back* except Boba Fett is a good guy and his name is NoZone. If TOXIC CRUSADERS made you laugh and cry, then this one will make you cry and scream. Toxie's got his hands full trying to save Tromaville from greedy industrialists and pleasing his beautiful blind blond girlfriend.

TROMA'S BASEMENT (U.K.): This is the pinnacle of Troma-themed tele-vision programming. These segments were shot as introductions to Troma movies playing on Bravo in the U.K. and feature the loveliest of lovelies, Miss Troma U.K., and two pasty Brit funnymen, Xander Armstrong and Ben Miller. Toxie joins the fun, too. It all adds up to some crazy goings on, like Monty Python pissing up Queen Elizabeth's leg.

TROMA'S WAR (1988, Michael Herz, Samuel Weil [aka Lloyd Kaufman]): This is *the* Troma masterpiece, which never got the recognition it deserved. It is without a doubt part of the Troma's Unsung Masterpiece Series. Beware cheap, chopped up, R-rated, pussyfied imitations—refuse anything but the director's cut. This was Kaufman and Herz's nod to Reagan and Bush trying to make armed conflict glamorous again: Nothing like a good war to make heroes of us all. An elitist terrorist corps, financed by the labor, corporate, and bureaucratic oppressors, starts taking out a group of everyday people. There is a website debate going on whether there are more bullet hits in this film or in *The Wild Bunch* (anyone who cares to count, please write us). No matter who has more, though, *The Wild Bunch* doesn't have a woman whose tits explode after she is shot in the chest, and it doesn't even come close to having as many people who get their ears ripped off their heads as TROMA'S WAR, and *The Wild Bunch* doesn't have a single character named Señor Sida who heads up an AIDS brigade to infiltrate the U.S. while cornholing young Tromettes along the way.

Not only that, but TROMA'S WAR marks the first appearance of the great Joe Fleishaker, the world's largest (and widest) action hero. "I worship Joe," says TROMEO & JULIET screenwriter James Gunn. "In fact, I have an altar set up in my basement to offer him live cattle."

TROMAVILLE CAFE—THE LAUGHS: This television series was developed to show in conjunction with Troma movies on television. In it, the entire wacky citizenry of Tromaville, from Lloyd Kaufman to the Toxic Avenger, from Oliver Stone to Ingmar Bergman, ham it up in support of such films as *CLASS OF NUKE 'EM HIGH* and *CRY UNCLE*. We love to make these and hope that many TV stations around the world will think they are as funny as we do.

TROMEO & JULIET (1996, Lloyd Kaufman): Remember in high school you had to read *Romeo and Juliet*, than regurgitate all that iambic pentameter crap back on some test? Well fear not . . . your kids will never have to go through that torture! Just see Shakespeare the way he was meant to be seen, the Troma way! With body piercing, kinky and/or incestuous sex, and car crashes, Kaufman's instant classic is the greatest Shakespeare adaptation Troma has made in the last couple of years! Backed by a cast of new talents and featuring a kick-ass soundtrack featuring Sublime, Motorhead, and the Ass Ponys, Lloyd shows us how Shakespeare's spirit entered his asshole and came out on film! How many Kenneth Branagh films have ass ponies? Oh yeah? I was talking about the musical group, not Keanu Reeves!

TRUCKER'S WOMAN (1983, Will Zens): Funny, enjoyable film with lots of very long two-shots. Another film made in North Carolina, and another entry in Troma's Strong Redneck series. The trucker's woman isn't really the central character; the central character is some guy whose father was killed by greedy corporate fat boys, who eventually want to kill him, too. He meets Trucker's Woman, a rich chick turned on by his big, throbbing, diesel-pumping rig. Every sex scene ends shortly after the first breast appears, as if the director said, "Cut when you see the nipple!" Even though it was made in '83, it seems like a period piece of, say, '77, and gives off the feeling of the last of the sexploitation pics. Watch TRUCKER'S WOMAN and weep for the end of an era.

VEGAS IN SPACE (1991, Phillip R. Ford): Troma has always supported homos and dykes, and here we present the first science-fiction, cross-dressing musical. This campy comedy with *Flash Gordon*-like special effects has a large cult following. World renowned legendary drag icons, the late Doris Fish and Miss X, star in this glamour odyssey about an all-female pleasure planet in peril. It precedes *Priscilla* and *Judy Newmar* by oh-so-many years, and is more genuine. VEGAS appeared in gay and lesbian festivals around the world, and was a big theatrical success. The homosexual community embraced us and we embraced them back (whenever possible, from behind).

VIDEO DEMONS DO PSYCHOTOWN (1989, Michael A. deGaetano): A gruesome journey through the world of subliminal psychic nightmares as a young girl's mind's eye is recorded on the lens of her video camera. Young film students race against time to gather evidence to solve a crime before they become the next victims. Made by the same man who brought you SCORING, but this one delivers a happy Christmas package of gore.

VIDEO VIXENS (1984, Ronald Sullivan): Features the most humongous breasts outside of Russ Meyers and SIZZLE BEACH, USA. This is a good movie that takes place in the world of network television where you can see all the action without switching the channels. Girls! Girls! Girls! Come on in, jacko, see live, nekkid broads!

VIEWER DISCRETION ADVISED (1996, Tommy Blaze): A comedy (and a funny one at that) in the vein of *Amazon Women on the Moon*. A satire of the American obsession with the idiot box. You may love it, you may hate it, but you certainly won't forget it. Any film that features masochistic hillbillies sawing their own limbs off is cool in my book!

VIRGIN BEASTS (1992, Toby Zoates): The fucking asshole critics pick up on ridiculous films like *The Living End* and *Go Fish* (for the wrong reasons, of course), but miss out when a truly original flick like this comes around. Toby Zoates is a prominent Australian artist and animator, who made this mix of live-action and animation. Grungy survivalist youths meet a death-dealing duo at an erotic post-apocalypse party.

WAITRESS! (1981, Samuel Weil [aka Lloyd Kaufman, aka Squeegee] and Michael Herz): This funny film works on the notion that when you walk into a restaurant, you don't get a waitress—you get an actress, a writer, or a rich, spoiled, monkey-loving babe (cross your fingers and hope for #3). Three young waitresses serve it up with humor and slapstick in an irreverent look at the restaurant business. One of the Troma sexy comedies, in line with SQUEEZE PLAY, STUCK ON YOU, and THE FIRST TURN-ON. See Calvert Deforest (Letterman's Larry Bud Melman) in an earlier incarnation. Two male TV stars also appear, but they were so proud of their Troma connection that they used "special names" just for us.

THE WEDDING PARTY (1966, Brian De Palma, Cynthia Munroe, Wilford Leach): A hilarious black-and-white look at wedding day "cold feet" starring Robert DeNiro in this moving picture directed by Brian De Palma, et al. The *NY Daily News* said, "It's a pleasure to see!" and even Gene Shalit said "This wedding takes the cake!" (Shalit should have been shot for that phrase long before he started refusing to review Troma movies. Hell for Shalit would be screaming eternally in a vat of hot lava. But it would be heaven for us.) De Palma's first film, DeNiro's first film, Jill Clayburgh's first film, and Troma's got it!

WHEN NATURE CALLS (1983, Charles Kaufman): The Troma Team proudly deems Charles Kaufman's (MOTHER'S DAY) WHEN NATURE CALLS a part of Troma's Unsung Masterpieces Series. Willie Mays, Watergate loudmouth and gun eroticizer G. Gordon Liddy, and Morey Amsterdam are among the players in Charles Kaufman's avant-garde montage of raucous comedy. This is a genuinely hilarious movie in the format of a feature film with coming attractions, etc. Another family affair for the Kaufman clan: Susan Kaufman was the art director and father Stanley acted in it. WNC is a take off on the wilderness family; animals from all hemispheres inhabit the same forest. Indeed, many animals were tortured in the making of this film.

WHITE ELEPHANT: THE BATTLE OF THE AFRICAN GHOSTS (1984, Werner Grusch): Peter Firth stars in this excellent film of a clash between cultures. He tries to bring the microchip into an African society that still practices magic, or "juju"—filmed entirely on location in Africa. He never dreamed of the horrifying price he would have to pay to challenge age-old African power. Although we like this film, it could be looked upon as a boring art film, if not for the hot interracial action between Peter Firth and a sweaty, lusting Winnie Mandela lookalike.

WILDROSE (1983, John Hanson): This is a very good movie starring Lisa Eichorn as June Lorich, a female coal miner in a male-dominated world. Lorich must fight against the prejudices of a society beating her emotionally and her husband beating her physically. Set against the brawling background of a Minnesota mining town, WILDROSE is a story of a chick's inner resources. It could use a few mutations or a decapitation scene of some sort, but, besides these drawbacks, it's pretty good. Producer Sandra Schulberg is the founder of the International Feature Project.

WIZARDS OF THE DEMON SWORD (1990, Fred Olen Ray): This is Olen Ray's best moving picture since the artsy-fartsy DEMENTED DEATH FARM MASSACRE. Lyle Waggoner (*The Carol Burnett Show, Wonder Woman*), Michael Berryman, Troma's version of Keanu Reeves (*The Hills Have Eyes*), Russ Tamblyn (*Satan's Sadists, The Female Bunch*, and, oh yeah, some trash my transvestite neighbor watches three or four times every weekend called *West Side Story*), and Dawn Wildsmith (SURF NAZIS MUST DIE!, the former Mrs. Fred Olen Ray—wow, cool!) star in this journey back to the mystical age of wizards, black magic, and some sort of strange dinosaurs (which Troma didn't know were still around in the Middle Ages, but now we have been straightened out on yet another historical fact by the fabulous historian/auteur Fred Olen Ray). This action-adventure combines thrills and satire! Eat your hearts out, Spielberg, Cameron, Harlin, and Verhoeven: Not only is Olen Ray a better filmmaker than the lot of you, he could also KICK YOUR ASSES.

YOUNG GOODMAN BROWN (1995, Peter George): This is a film by the director of SURF NAZIS MUST DIE! It stars John P. Ryan (*Hoffa, Runaway Train, Five Easy Pieces*), Judy Geeson (*To Sir, with Love*), and Mindy Clarke. It's a beautiful, gothic, sensual masterpiece, based on Nathaniel Hawthorne's classic tale of seduction and betrayal. Chancing upon a Black Mass in the woods changes Goodman Brown's life forever; his faith in the inherent goodness of man is shattered and no one is above suspicion, not even his pious and virtuous wife. Intellectual History of Troma Sidenote: In 1968, Lloyd Kaufman produced another film based on Hawthorne—RAPPACCINI, starring Perry King (*Andy Warhol's Bad*). When it was shown at Yale people re-created the fire scene by setting fires to their chairs.

ZOMBIE ISLAND MASSACRE (1983, John N. Carter): See Rita Jenrette's (*Playboy* model and ex-congressman's ex-wife) two best assets, unleashed! Rita is the token "star" in this voodoo fantasy (many Troma films feature one minor celebrity in the way seventies TV shows featured one black person). A mangy gaggle of tourists get caught up in a hellish vacation. Pay close attention to the first ten minutes, where there is lots o' sex, but when the tourists land on the island nary a tit appears for the rest of the film (fortunately, nipples are replaced by blood and intestines). There's a reason this isn't a part of Troma's Strong Zombies series, but I wouldn't want to ruin the shock ending where it ends up being drug dealers and not zombies who are causing the gory deaths. Whoops! I said it! A fun film, since every one of the tourists is completely dislikable, and you get to watch them murdered in horrifying ways . . . one . . . by . . . one . . .

LONG LIVE TROMA.

2-15-18 H2o damage

Made in the USA
Charleston, SC
11 September 2011